LINGUISTICS
AND
COMPUTATION

CSLI
Lecture Notes
No. 52

LINGUISTICS AND COMPUTATION

edited by
**Jennifer Cole, Georgia M. Green &
Jerry L. Morgan**

CSLI *Publications*

CENTER FOR THE STUDY OF
LANGUAGE AND INFORMATION
STANFORD, CALIFORNIA

Library of Congress Cataloging-in-Publication Data

Linguistics and computation / edited by Jennifer Cole, Georgia M. Green, &
Jerry L. Morgan.
   p. cm. – (CSLI lecture notes ; no. 52)
   Includes bibliographical references.
   ISBN 1-881526-82-8 (alk. paper). – ISBN 1-881526-81-X (pbk. : alk.paper).
   1. Computational linguistics – Congresses. I. Cole, Jennifer. II. Green,
Georgia M. III. Morgan, Jerry L. IV. Series.
   P98.L543 1995
   410'.285 – dc20   95-4680
                                CIP

CSLI was founded early in 1983 by researchers from Stanford University, SRI
International, and Xerox PARC to further research and development of integrated
theories of language, information, and computation. CSLI headquarters and CSLI
Publications are located on the campus of Stanford University.

CSLI Lecture Notes report new developments in the study of language, information, and
computation. In addition to lecture notes, the series includes monographs, working
papers, and conference proceedings. Our aim is to make new results, ideas, and
approaches available as quickly as possible.

Contents

Preface

The papers in this volume were presented at a workshop held in June 1991 at the University of Illinois at Urbana-Champaign, in celebration of the twenty-fifth anniversary of the Department of Linguistics. The broad theme of the workshop was *Computational Linguistics and the Foundations of Linguistic Theory,* and its purpose was to provide a forum in which computational linguists, syntacticians, morphologists, and phonologists could come together and discuss important issues of common interest.

The areas of linguistic research represented in this volume are diverse, yet they are united under the notion that the principles of grammatical well-formedness and the principles of language processing are interdependent. Theories of grammar, including at least syntax, morphology, and phonology, are more interesting if they inspire theories of their implementation for language parsing and generation. Moreover, problems in language processing and their solutions can be of serious interest to grammar theorists, to the extent that the computational linguists and the grammar theorists can communicate in a common language, with mutually intelligible formal expressions of linguistic information. Given such interconnections between the computational and theoretical research enterprises, it is essential that developments in the two areas proceed hand-in-hand. The University of Illinois workshop was highly successful in its goal of bringing people together for an exchange of ideas. It is our hope that this volume can extend that same opportunity to a wider audience, and stimulate the ongoing co-operation and collaboration between computational linguists and grammar theorists.

The papers in this volume have been organized (after their submission) into three parts. The papers that deal most directly with the nature of syntactic structure and grammars for syntax are grouped together in Part I; papers in Part II focus on strategies for parsing or generation; and the papers in Part III deal with aspects of phonological structure and grammars for phonology. These divisions are not mutually exclusive, however, and certain papers overlap two or more areas. Thus, in the Syntax and Computation part, Frisch's paper addresses the nature of parsing rules, while in the part on Automated Parsing and Generation, Abney's paper makes proposals regarding the nature of phrase structure. Also, Hirschberg and Sproat's paper in the Part covering Phonology and Computation makes proposals regarding grammatical categories at the level of discourse structure. The fact that many of the papers included here span several areas within linguistic theory underscores the importance of communication between researchers in diverse areas.

Part I on Syntax and Computation begins with a paper grounded in traditional concerns of syntactic theory. In "Formal Devices for Linguistic Generalizations," **Annie Zaenen** and **Ronald M. Kaplan** show how existing mechanisms of LFG (in particular, the principles of functional uncertainty and functional precedence) that were developed for quite different purposes can be exploited to model discontinuous and cross-serial dependencies in Dutch and German. Their analysis preserves the restriction against uninformative non-branching structures which insures that the parsing problem for LFG grammars is decidable. They suggest that it offers a view of the complex relations between constituent order and semantic structure that motivate the domains of traditional syntactic description of Germanic languages.

David E. Johnson and **Lawrence S. Moss** offer a framework for linguistic description that is based on Kasper-Rounds logic, motivated by relational grammar, and informed by the principles of metagraph grammar (formerly) known as arc-pair grammar. They thus provide a rigorous model for multistratal relational analysis that requires that models be projected from the lexicon, and enables the weak generative capacity of languages so defined to be limited to just a subclass of the recursive languages.

Alan Frisch's paper makes a point of emphasizing the distinction between feature structures and their descriptions, by characterizing the nature of a grammar as a system of constraints on feature structures. He shows how this enables a correct and complete parsing rule to use grammar rules that are schematic for a possibly infinite set of CFG rules.

The papers in *Part II* specifically address issues in automated parsing and generation. **Robert C. Berwick** and **Sandiway Fong** offer a valuable historical overview of research on parsing with transformational grammars, covering technical innovations of specific parsers and some of the problems they confront, such as constraining overgeneration or dealing with arbitrary empty strings. They show how modern computational techniques and a constraint-based version of transformational grammar can be combined to build parsers that deal successfully with that inefficiency, describing a modular, parameterized system modelled on the principles and categories of Government and Binding theory.

Steven Abney gives serious consideration to the view that theories of grammar should contribute to theories of linguistic behavior. His focus is phrase structure, and he proposes a chunks-and-dependencies model of phrase structure to reconcile the discrepancy between the sentence parse determined by syntactic theory and the parse represented in prosodic and pausal structures. His model builds clauses through the attachment of chunks, which are fragments of parse trees that also correspond to prosodic constituents. He argues that building chunks before attaching them under S has serious computational advantages, because it allows for parsing with only finite-state techniques. This approach allows for a simple characterization of some well-known parsing strategies concerning the attachment of phrases.

Bidirectional, unification-based parser-generators are efficient when combined with a head-driven control strategy. Problems arise, however, for both Earley-style and left-corner head-driven strategies when the head is an empty category or a type-raised category. **Dale Gerdemann** and **Erhard Hinrichs** show that the problems of completeness and coherence that arise in dealing with heads whose semantics is not sufficiently specified can be solved by distinguishing carefully (echoing concerns of Frisch) between the metalanguage and the object language variables in logical forms.

Tsuneko Nakazawa's contribution explores a means for harnessing the efficiency of LR parsers to the generality of grammars with analyzable (feature-structure) categories. She describes a technique for overcoming the problems that arise in adapting Tomita's extended LR parsing algorithm for grammars with complex feature-value systems. The major innovations include constructing a LR parsing table of minimal size that involves no preliminary instantiation of categories during construction, and a way of organizing the parsing so that desired entries can be identified without search.

The papers in **Part III** address questions that arise in the computation of phonological structures. **John Coleman** presents an overview of computational phonology, as it arises in a variety of research areas, including speech recognition and synthesis, morpho-phonological processing, and laboratory studies of intonation and articulation. He also discusses the implementation of phonological grammar in YorkTalk, the speech synthesis system he has developed with colleagues at the University of York. York-Talk employs a declarative, unification grammar to define richly structured phonological representations, which are then mapped onto corresponding phonetic representations in one step. The YorkTalk algorithms for phonological parsing and phonetic interpretation are described in some detail.

In her paper, **Jennifer Cole** considers the analysis of cyclic phonology within a declarative, constraint-based grammar. She argues that cyclicity does not require derivational grammars, and therefore cyclic grammars are not Turing equivalent, as has been previously argued. She demonstrates that cyclic grammars have a formal expression as constraint-based unification grammars, but only if constraints can be disjunctively ranked.

Julia Hirschberg and **Richard Sproat** examine the problem of how speakers determine what to emphasize and de-emphasize in speech, and propose methods for predicting pitch accent from text analysis. They describe an algorithm for accent location that appeals to syntactic structure and attentional structure–representing the salience of objects in the discourse–and assigns intonational features in the synthesis of unrestricted text. They report on the training and performance of their algorithm, which has been implemented in the Bell Laboratories Text-to-Speech System.

Taken together, the papers included in this volume provide a partial snapshot of the range of issues that are currently addressed by that linguistic research which gives significant or primary consideration to matters of computation. There are some areas of interface between grammar and computation that have not been addressed here at all; most notably absent are papers dealing with morphology or semantics from a computational perspective. It is our hope that work in those areas will also come to the attention of linguists working on syntax, phonology, or automated language processing, to further this very fruitful exchange of ideas.

Acknowledgements

This volume of papers serves as a tribute to the Department of Linguistics at the University of Illinois. The workshop from which it stems was part of the department's twenty-fifth anniversary activities, and we gratefully acknowledge the substantial support of the Department in bringing off that workshop.

Other units of the University of Illinois contributed in important ways to the workshop as well, including the College of Liberal Arts and Sciences, the Cognitive Science/Artificial Intelligence Steering Committee, and the Beckman Institute for Advanced Science and Technology. The Beckman Institute played a special role in the success of the workshop, by providing the workshop venue as well as assisting with planning and logistics. The University of Illinois Research Board provided support in the form of an assistantship to Lynne Murphy for editorial work. The Beckman Institute, through its support of the Cognitive Science group, also provided essential support services for the preparation of these papers for publication. Thanks goes in particular to Linda May of the Cognitive Science group, who devoted time and ingenuity to the LaTeX formatting of papers with diverse requirements.

Finally, we thank the many participants in the workshop for being willing to share their ideas in what turned out to be a truly cooperative effort, and for their patience in waiting to see the current incarnations of their papers appear in print.

Jennifer Cole
Georgia M. Green
Jerry L. Morgan

Urbana, Illinois
April, 1995

Part I

Syntax and Computation

Formal Devices for Linguistic Generalizations: West Germanic Word Order in LFG

Annie Zaenen and Ronald M. Kaplan
Xerox Palo Alto Research Center

1 Introduction

In LFG the phrase structure representation of a sentence is used to divide linguistic strings into a hierarchy of ordered phrasal constituents. It is well known that this kind of representation does not capture all the syntactically significant dependencies that exist in sentences. In this paper we look at some dependencies that cannot be captured in this superficial representation but seem nevertheless to be affected by the order of elements of the string. These dependencies are illustrated by word order constraints in Germanic infinitivals. German infinitivals exhibit a syntactic dependency that is not local in the sense that elements that are syntactically closely dependent on each other are in string positions separated by 'extraneous' material. This case is different from that of the wh-constructions discussed in Kaplan and Zaenen (1989) in that there are no clearly fixed positions for the separated elements of the infinitivals. We show that existing mechanisms, specifically functional uncertainty and functional precedence, that were developed to account for other phenomena can be exploited to model the new data in an insightful way.

2 A case study: Dutch cross serial dependencies

2.1 Basic facts.

Since Evers (1975) several syntactic models have been proposed to account for sentences of the type illustrated in the Dutch example in (1):

(1) ... dat Jan zijn zoon geneeskunde wil laten studeren.
 ... that John his son medicine wants let study.

What is interesting about this sentence pattern is that the verbs and the nominal or prepositional elements that they govern are not adjacent in the surface string or in the phrase structure representation. In Dutch all the dependent elements have to precede all the verbs, but there is no requirement that the verb and its dependents be adjacent either in the string or in the surface tree representation one would naturally assign to such a sentence. In other variants of West-Germanic the verbs and their dependents can be interleaved, as we discuss in Section 4. As an illustration we show in (2) the surface structure proposed in Evers (1975) with the f-structure showing the dependencies that hold in the sentence, assuming some plausible lexical entries consistent with this f-structure. They are given in (3).

(2)

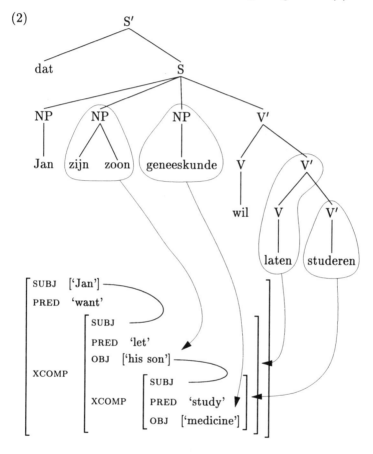

(3) *willen*   ($\uparrow$ PRED) = 'want<($\uparrow$ SUBJ) ($\uparrow$ XCOMP)>'
                  ($\uparrow$ SUBJ) = ($\uparrow$ XCOMP SUBJ)

       laten   ($\uparrow$ PRED) = 'let<($\uparrow$ SUBJ) ($\uparrow$ XCOMP)>($\uparrow$ OBJ)'
                  ($\uparrow$ OBJ) = ($\uparrow$ XCOMP SUBJ)

      studeren   ($\uparrow$ PRED) = 'study<($\uparrow$ SUBJ) ($\uparrow$ OBJ)>'

Of course, if we allowed crossing branches in the c-structure, we could express the dependencies in the c-structure itself, but the c-structures in LFG are assumed to be of the traditional noncrossing type. Given that they are supposed to have a rather direct relation to the phonological representation, it seems reasonable to keep this constraint.

Our problem then is to find a grammar that expresses the correspondences illustrated in (2).

2.2 An early LFG approach

LFG has no movement rules, but discontinuous government dependencies present no problem because of the way the mapping from c-structure to f-structure is defined. As some of the notions we want to use later crucially depend on particular characteristics of this mapping, we summarize here its relevant properties. LFG assumes there is a correspondence function ϕ from c-structure nodes to f-structure units, but this correspondence is not assumed to be one-to-one nor is it required to be onto (Kaplan and Bresnan 1982; Kaplan 1987). Both of these properties are illustrated by the following example of an English gerund construction:

(4)

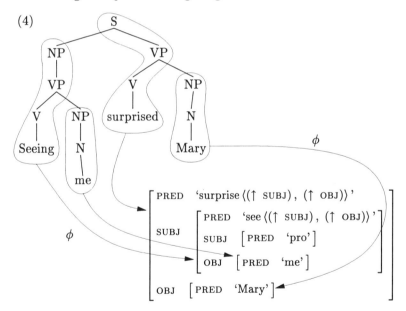

The functional annotations on the English phrase-structure rules would make all the nodes in a circled collection map to the same f-structure unit, demonstrating the many-to-one property of ϕ. There is no node in the c-structure that maps to the pronoun subject of the predicate *see*, so that ϕ is not onto. In English, nodes that map onto the same f-structure tend to stand in simple mother-daughter relations, but this is not the only possible configuration for many-to-one mappings. Bresnan et al. (1982) account for the Dutch discontinuous constituents by mapping two noncontiguous c-structure components into one f-structure. This is specified by the following two simple rules:

$$
(5) \quad \text{a.} \quad \text{VP} \longrightarrow \begin{pmatrix} \text{NP} \\ (\uparrow \text{OBJ}){=}\downarrow \end{pmatrix} \begin{pmatrix} \text{VP} \\ (\uparrow \text{XCOMP}){=}\downarrow \end{pmatrix} (\text{V}')
$$

$$
\text{b.} \quad \text{V}' \longrightarrow \text{V} \begin{pmatrix} \text{V}' \\ (\uparrow \text{XCOMP}){=}\downarrow \end{pmatrix}
$$

and the (simplified) verbal lexical entries given in (3). These rules make use of the standard LFG convention that unannotated categories are assumed to carry the $\uparrow{=}\downarrow$ head-marking schema.

The annotation on the VP preceding the V' in (5a) and the annotation on the V' expanding the V' in (5b) are the same, and hence they both provide information about the shared corresponding f-structure. The main constraint on dependencies of this kind in Dutch is that all the arguments of a higher verb precede those of a lower verb; the arguments of each verb are ordered as in simple clauses. The c-structure rules in (5) insure this ordering because the VP expands to an (optional) NP object followed by an open complement VP (XCOMP). The phrase structure rules thus impose the right ordering: less embedded OBJs always precede more embedded ones. The different parts of the more and more embedded XCOMPs link up in the right way because the XCOMPs are associated with successive expansions on both the VP and V' spines of the tree, as illustrated in (6):

(6)

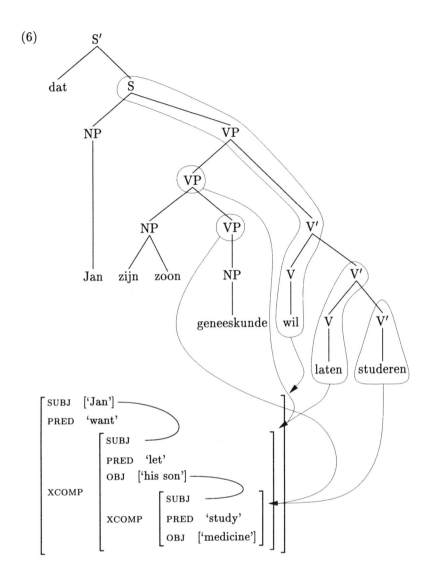

In this approach the context free part of the phrase structure rules encodes the surface linear order and the assumed surface hierarchical order but not the government relations. These are encoded in the functional annotations added to this context free skeleton.

2.3   Inadequacies of this solution

This system gives a correct description of the data considered in Bresnan et al. (1982) and can be extended in a straightforward way to cover further infinitival constructions as shown in Johnson (1986, 1988). However, three drawbacks of this approach have been pointed out, one theoretical, one technical, and one linguistic.

We will not discuss the theoretical problem in great detail. Schuurman (1987) points out that, according to X-bar theory, the VP node should dominate a verb. But, even if one thinks that X-bar principles have some value, it is not clear how they should be adapted to a nontransformational functionally oriented framework like LFG. X-bar theory was mainly developed to allow for the notion head in a representation in which this notion was not native (Lyons 1968). In transformation-based theories the head relation is expressed in deep or underlying tree structures by means of the X-bar schemata (of course, in the surface structure these schemata are only respected by virtue of abstract linking devices such as traces). The head notion itself is functional in nature, however, and LFG provides more explicit and flexible ways of expressing functional relations. For example, LFG identifies the head of a constituent by means of the $\uparrow = \downarrow$ annotation, and it marks the non-head dependents with annotations of the form ($\uparrow$ GF)=$\downarrow$, where GF stands for any governable grammatical function. Still, it may be worthwhile to establish some invariant connections between functions and the phrase structures they correspond to, and Bresnan (1982) offers one proposal along these lines. As a more natural alternative to X-bar theory for characterizing the relation between lexical heads and phrasal categories, we suggest the principle in (7a). This characterizes configurations of the sort illustrated in (7b) in addition to the usual endocentric arrangement in (7c).

(7) a. A maximal (non lexical) category is of type XP if it corresponds to an f-structure that also corresponds to a lexical category of type X.

b.

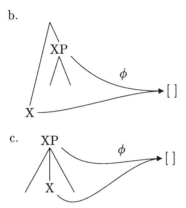

c.

In formal terms, a maximal node n is of category XP if the set of nodes $\phi^{-1}(\phi(n))$ contains a node of category X. This principle for determining category labels justifies the VP label in (6) even though the VP does not dominate the V.

The technical problem was pointed out in Johnson (1986) and in Netter (1988). They observed that the obvious extensions to the Bresnan et al. solution needed to account for a new class of data lead to phrase structure trees that violate the LFG constraint against nonbranching dominance chains (Kaplan and Bresnan 1982). According to this condition on valid c-structures, derivations of the form A →* A, which permit an indefinite number of A nodes dominating another node of the same category, are prohibited. This restriction against nonbranching dominance chains disallows c-structure nodes that provide no information and insures that the parsing problem for LFG grammars is decidable. An example adapted from Johnson (1986) that violates this constraint is given in (8):

(8) ... dat Jan een liedje heeft willen zingen.
    ... that John a song has wanted to sing.

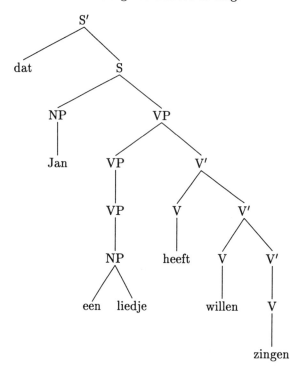

Een liedje is the direct object of the most embedded verb *zingen* and the intermediate VPs are needed to provide the right number of XCOMP levels. In the absence of further difficulties with this approach, we might be tempted to reconsider the value of this formal restriction. But relaxing this condition would not be enough to protect the Bresnan et al. solution from empirical inadequacies.

The linguistic problem is that this analysis does not account for sentences like (9), which are considered perfectly grammatical by most speakers (M. Moortgat, p.c.):

(9) ... dat Jan een liedje schreef en trachtte te verkopen.
    ... that John a song wrote and tried to sell.

Here *een liedje* 'a song' is the OBJ of *schreef* 'wrote' and of *verkopen* 'sell', but these verbs are at different levels of embedding. To be interpreted as the argument of *schreef*, *een liedje* has to be the object, but to be interpreted as an argument of *verkopen*, it has to be the object of the XCOMP. According to the LFG theory of coordination, a coordinate structure is represented formally as a set in f-structure, with the elements of the set being the f-structures corresponding to the individual conjuncts. LFG's function-application primitive is extended in a natural way to apply to sets of f-structures: a set is treated as if it were a function with the properties that are common to all its f-structure elements (see Kaplan and Maxwell 1988b for formal details). As Bresnan, Kaplan, and Peterson (1985) show, this simple extension is sufficient to provide elegant accounts for the wide variety of facts that coordinate reduction rules and across-the-board conventions attempt to handle. Given the rules in (5) and this theory of coordination, *een liedje* will not be properly distributed across the two conjuncts in (9), since it has to have a different function in each. The problem is illustrated by the disjunctive function assignments in diagram (10):

(10)

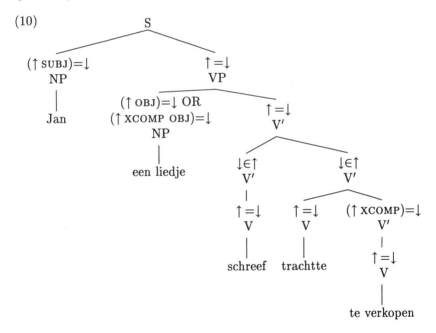

3   A Functional Approach

We now propose a revision that takes care of these problems and then examine some of its other consequences. Some of the elements of this new account can also be found in Johnson (1986) and, for a different set of data, in Netter (1988).

To solve the nonbranching dominance problem, Johnson (1986) proposes to replace the phrase-structure rule (5a) by the one given in (11) (see also Netter 1988):

(11) VP $\longrightarrow$ $\begin{pmatrix} \text{NP} \\ (\uparrow \text{OBJ})=\downarrow \end{pmatrix}$ $\begin{pmatrix} \text{VP} \\ (\uparrow \text{XCOMP}^+)=\downarrow \end{pmatrix}$ (V')

The only difference is in the schema attached to the optional VP. This schema now uses the device of functional uncertainty that was introduced in Kaplan and Zaenen (1989) and developed further in Kaplan and Maxwell (1988a). The f-structure associated with this VP is not asserted to be the XCOMP of the V' at the corresponding level of c-structure embedding. Rather, it is asserted only that it is the value at the end of a chain of one or more XCOMPs, as denoted by the regular expression XCOMP$^+$. This possibility obviates the need for VP expansions in which a VP exhaustively dominates another VP. Predicates and arguments will still be linked up properly because of the completeness and coherence conditions that are independently imposed on f-structure. The right word order is also maintained because the material contained in the VP following an OBJ NP is always at least one level further embedded than the OBJ itself: the annotation is XCOMP$^+$, not XCOMP*. The revised rule associates the correct f-structure for sentence (8) with the more compact tree in (8'):

(8')

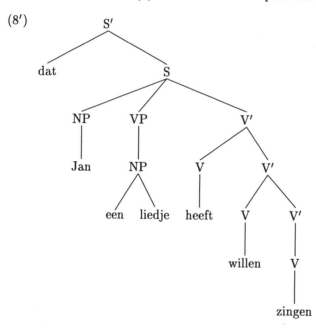

Notice, however, that the rule in (11) does not account for example (9). If the NP is generated as the OBJ of the highest VP under S, then its only function is OBJ, and it cannot be distributed into the second conjunct as an XCOMP OBJ. On the other hand, if it is generated under an embedded VP so that it has the proper function for the second conjunct, it cannot be a simple OBJ for the first conjunct. If we change the annotation on the VP from XCOMP$^+$ to XCOMP*, so that the NP is properly distributed to both conjuncts, then we lose all possibility of imposing the cross-serial ordering constraints by phrase-structure encoding. There are more complicated functional annotations for these rules that will give the desired result in Dutch, but in what follows we explore a different type of solution. This solution exploits functional uncertainty together with functional precedence to assign simpler phrase-structure trees. It accounts for all the data that we have discussed above, including example (9), and has the additional advantage of generalizing in a straightforward way to account for word-order facts in other languages, as is shown in Section 4.

Functional uncertainty was originally developed to characterize wh-movement constructions and to insure their proper interaction with coordination. A second formal device that was introduced into LFG theory after Bresnan et al. (1982) was published is functional precedence. This was applied to anaphoric dependencies by Bresnan (1984) and formally defined in Kaplan (1987). Precedence is a defining relation among the constituents in a c-structure, in the sense that trees with different node-orderings are interpreted as formally different trees. There is no native precedence relation among the parts of an f-structure, but the image of c-structure precedence under the ϕ mapping from c-structure to f-structure naturally induces a relation on f-structure, which we have called f-precedence:

(12) For two f-structure elements f_1 and f_2, f_1 *f-precedes* f_2 if and only if all the nodes that map onto f_1 c-precede all the nodes that map onto f_2:
$$f_1 <_f f_2 \text{ iff for all } n_1 \in \phi^{-1}(f_1) \text{ and for all } n_2 \in \phi^{-1}(f_2), n_1 <_c n_2$$

Even though this relation is defined in terms of conventional c-structure precedence, it has some surprising properties because, as we noted, the mapping from c-structure to f-structure may be neither one-to-one nor onto. For example, if the mapping is many-to-one and f_1 and f_2 correspond to interleaved sets of c-structure nodes, then neither f_1 f-precedes f_2 nor f_2 f-precedes f_1. If the mapping is not onto so that f_1 corresponds to no node at all, then vacuously both f_1 f-precedes f_2 and f_2 f-precedes f_1 for all f_2. This characteristic is exploited in the analysis of null anaphors by Bresnan (1984) and Kameyama (1989) (summarized in Kaplan and Zaenen 1989).

Because of this characteristic, f-precedence is neither transitive nor anti-symmetric and hence is technically not a true ordering relation. Its name is meant to indicate only that it is a functional image of c-precedence, not that it is a precedence relation on f-structure. F-precedence also differs from c-precedence in its linguistic implications: while c-precedence restrictions can only directly order sister constituents, f-precedence constraints can implicitly restrict ordering relations among non-sister nodes by virtue of the common f-structure units they correspond to.

We use the f-precedence relation to provide alternatives to the rules in (5) and (11). We dispense with the VP-dominated subtree altogether and assume a simple succession of NP nodes each of which assigns an OBJ at some indefinite level of XCOMP embedding. Then we add the requirement that the predicate's XCOMP$^+$ OBJ does not precede its immediate OBJ. The revised rules are given in (13):

(13) VP $\longrightarrow$ NP*   V'
$$(\uparrow \text{XCOMP*OBJ})=\downarrow$$

$$V' \longrightarrow V \begin{pmatrix} V' \\ (\uparrow \text{XCOMP})=\downarrow \\ (\uparrow \text{XCOMP}^+ \text{ OBJ}) \not<_f (\uparrow \text{OBJ}) \end{pmatrix}$$

The f-precedence condition is stated negatively because the existential interpretation of a positive relation over uncertainty (namely, that there be *some* string in the uncertainty language for which the relation holds) does not provide the desired effect that the relation must hold for *all* strings chosen from the uncertainty language. The negative statement implicitly transforms the existential into a universal. Moreover, we also assume a non-constructive interpretation of functional uncertainty in which the uncertainty strings range only over paths that are independently instantiated in the f-structure. Under these conventions, the rules above can be easily generalized, for example, by replacing OBJ by a disjunction of OBJ and OBJ2. In this way, the f-precedence constraint on order allows us to propose maximally simple c-structure expansions for Dutch infinitival constructions while still accounting for the ordering dependencies and functional assignments.

A similar flat structure was rejected in Bresnan et al. (1982) for two reasons, one based on word order constraints and the other on the low acceptability of certain coordination constructions. It was thought that the VP node was necessary to account for the fact that the oblique PP arguments of an XCOMP cannot precede an OBJ on a higher level of embedding whereas in a simple clause a PP can precede its OBJ. This argument depends on the assumption that the word order condition can only be stated in c-precedence terms, an assumption which we now reject in favor of the f-precedence relation. The observed pattern of acceptability easily follows when we extend the flat c-structure rules in (13) to include PPs as well.

The unacceptable coordination is exemplified in (14) (example (20) from Bresnan et al.):

(14) ?? ...dat Jan de meisjes een treintje aan Piet en de jongens een pop
...that John the girls a toy train to Pete and the boys a doll

aan Henk zag geven voor Marie.
to Hank saw give for Marie

...'that John saw the boys give a toy train to Pete and the girls give a doll to Hank for Marie.'

This is not considered ungrammatical by all speakers,[1] but even if it were completely out, it would justify the proposed hierarchical c-structure only on the assumption that nothing but a single constituent can be right-node raised in Dutch. This assumption is clearly incorrect since sentences like the following are completely acceptable:

(15) ...dat Annie witte en Marie bruine suiker op haar boterham wil
...that Annie white and Marie brown sugar on her bread wants.
...'that Annie wants brown sugar on her bread and Marie white sugar.'

(16) ...dat drugmisbruik veel bij tennis- en bij voetbalspelers onder
...that drug abuse often in tennis- and in soccer-players under

de dertig voorkomt.
thirty occurs.

...that drug abuse occurs often in tennis players and in soccer players under thirty.

Here the material shared across the conjuncts is not a constituent. While this observation does not explain the contrast noted in Bresnan et al. (1982),

---

[1]Some speakers (W. de Geest, p.c.) consider this sentence to be grammatical as well as the one in (i) which we assume to be a case of right node raising:

(i) ...dat Jan de meisjes een treintje aan Piet en de jongens een pop aan Henk
...that John the girls a toy train to Pete and the boys a doll to Hank

zag geven.
saw give.

...'that John saw the boys give a toy train to Pete and the girls give a doll to Hank.

Other speakers seem to consider both versions to be ungrammatical (Schuurman 1987).

it does undermine their second argument in favor of the hierarchical structure of the NP sequence.

We conclude, then, that the use of f-precedence and functional uncertainty allows a treatment of the Dutch infinitival constructions that avoids the technical and linguistic problems of the Bresnan et al. account. In particular, the NP functional uncertainty in the VP rule (13) interacts with LFG's formal account of constituent coordination (Kaplan and Maxwell 1988b) to provide the appropriate analysis of the Dutch coordination in example (9): the uncertainty on *een liedje* is realized as OBJ in one conjunct and as XCOMP OBJ in the other. It would be surprising, however, if the Dutch facts alone would require f-precedence and functional uncertainty as desirable ingredients in an account of the syntactic properties of infinitival constructions. In what follows we examine some facts of Zurich German that are also naturally handled in these functional terms.

4   Extending the solution to Swiss German

The infinitival constructions of Zurich German are similar to the Dutch ones discussed above in that the verbs generally come in the same order (the least embedded ones precede the more embedded ones). Sentences that are grammatical in Dutch will also be acceptable in Zurich German as the sentence in (17) illustrates:

(17) ... das er sini chind mediziin wil la schtudiere.
       (transcription as given in Cooper 1988)
       ... 'that he wants to let his children study medicine.'

The language allows a broader range of possibilities, however. The verbs have to cluster together in Standard Dutch, whereas NPs and PPs can be interleaved with the verbs in Zurich German, as illustrated in (18):

(18) a. ... das er wil sini chind la mediziin schtudiere.

      b. ... das er sini chind wil la mediziin schtudiere.

      c. ... das er mediziin sini chind wil la schtudiere.

      d. ... das er sini chind wil mediziin la schtudiere.

   But not all orders are allowed:

(19) * ... das er wil la sini chind mediziin schtudiere.

The main constraint on the word order in infinitival constructions in Zurich German seems to be:

(20) All the nominal arguments of a particular verb precede it.

There is some disagreement about whether this is the only syntactic constraint on order. Haegeman and van Riemsdijk (1986) add the requirement that the arguments of a higher verb have to precede those of a lower one. Lötscher (1978) does not imply such a constraint, and Cooper (1988) explicitly rejects it. We will follow Cooper here, although Kaplan and Zaenen (1988) modeled the account given by Haegeman and van Riemsdijk. It seems to us that the disagreement might be less about the data per se than about what counts as marked and unmarked word order, but a further study of the conditions influencing the different orders would be necessary to establish this.

The constraint in (20) also holds in Standard Dutch, as we saw in Section 2, but for Zurich German it cannot be formulated in the same way as was done in Bresnan et al. (1982) for Dutch. This is because in Zurich German the NPs and the Vs whose relative order has to be maintained do not have to be adjacent.

The use of functional uncertainty in conjunction with f-precedence allows us to account for these data again without violating the nonbranching dominance constraint. The appropriate rules are given in (21). The VP rule uses an immediate dominance notation to express the free categorial ordering; this adds nothing to the formal power of LFG (Kaplan 1989). The symbol NGF ranges over the grammatical functions SUBJ, OBJ, ... that are usually associated with nominals.

$$(21)\ \text{VP} \longrightarrow [\quad \begin{array}{cc} \text{NP}^* & , \quad \text{V}'^* \\ (\uparrow \text{XCOMP}^*\text{NGF})=\downarrow & (\uparrow \text{XCOMP})=\downarrow \end{array} \quad]$$

$$\text{V}' \longrightarrow \quad \begin{array}{c} \text{V} \\ \downarrow \not<_f (\uparrow \text{NGF}) \end{array}$$

In this section we have deployed LFG's descriptive devices to account for dependencies and order without relying on nested tree structure configurations to provide the necessary f-structure embeddings.[2] We have illustrated this by developing a flat structure for the NP dependents in infinitival constructions. A moment's reflection will show, however, that we could also use these formal devices to obtain the same f-structures from c-structures

---

[2] We could flatten the structure further. If we include the ordering statements in the lexical entries of the verbs themselves, we can dispense with the V'. Instead of (21), we then get:

$$(\text{i})\ \text{VP} \longrightarrow [\quad \begin{array}{cc} \text{NP}^* & , \quad \text{V}^* \\ (\uparrow \text{XCOMP}^*\text{NGF})=\downarrow & (\uparrow \text{XCOMP})=\downarrow \end{array} \quad]$$

Relevant lexical entries would be the following:

that exhibit more hierarchy, e.g. binary right branching trees. We see then that the availability of richer formal devices to capture linguistic dependencies leaves the c-structure underdetermined. In the conclusion we discuss briefly the general problem of motivating c-structure in LFG.

(ii) *wil*   V   ($\uparrow$ PRED)=$\downarrow$
                        $\downarrow$ = 'want<($\uparrow$ SUBJ)($\uparrow$ XCOMP)>'
                        ($\uparrow$ SUBJ) = ($\uparrow$ XCOMP SUBJ)
                        $\downarrow \not<_f$ ($\uparrow$ NGF)
                        ($\uparrow$ XCOMP) $\not<_f \downarrow$

(iii) *schtudiere* V   ($\uparrow$ PRED)=$\downarrow$
                        $\downarrow$ = 'study<($\uparrow$ SUBJ)($\uparrow$ OBJ)>'
                        $\downarrow \not<_f$ ($\uparrow$ NGF)

(iv) *laa*   V   ($\uparrow$ PRED)=$\downarrow$
                        $\downarrow$ = 'let<($\uparrow$ SUBJ)($\uparrow$ XCOMP)>($\uparrow$ OBJ)'
                        ($\uparrow$ OBJ) = ($\uparrow$ XCOMP SUBJ)
                        $\downarrow \not<_f$ ($\uparrow$ NGF)
                        ($\uparrow$ XCOMP) $\not<_f \downarrow$

The annotations in these entries associate the semantic form predicate of each verb explicitly with its lexical node, so that it can take a position in the f-precedence relation distinct from that of the larger f-structure that it heads. The schema $\downarrow \not<_f$ ($\uparrow$ NGF) specifies that the nominal arguments of every verb must not follow it. For the predicates *laa* and *wil*, the additional schema ($\uparrow$ XCOMP) $\not<_f \downarrow$ indicates that the open complement must come after the verb. The tree representations that these entries and rules allow us to generate are completely flat, as exemplified in (v):

(v)

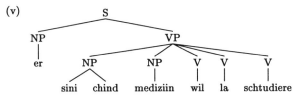

Having proposed a completely flat structure for Zurich German, we could propose a comparable account for Dutch. There are two differences between Dutch and Zurich German: (1) the nominal arguments of higher predicates must precede those of lower ones, and (2) all the NP constituents must precede all the verbs. A lexical entry like *laten* (corresponding to the Zurich German *laa*) will have the additional ordering constraint given in (vi) and the phrase structure grammar will include the c-structure linear-precedence constraint in (vii):

(vi) ($\uparrow$ XCOMP$^+$ NGF) $\not<_f$ ($\uparrow$ NGF)

(vii) NP$<_c$ V

In section 5, we discuss some facts that argue against this flattening of the verbal complex.

5 Other infinitival patterns in Dutch

5.1 Extraposition.

It is well known that the verb-raising patterns discussed above are not the only patterns for verbs taking infinitival complements in West Germanic. Another pattern is so-called extraposition, in which the whole infinitival clause follows the matrix verb. This is illustrated for Dutch in (22):

(22) omdat [Jan Marie verbood [Piet toe te laten [het boek te lezen]]]
because John Marie prohibited Pete to allow the book to read.
'because John prohibited Marie to allow Pete to read the book.'
(relevant internal clause boundaries are indicated by [ ])

Following Schuurman (1991) we hypothesize that extraposed and nonextraposed infinitival complements differ in that extraposed complements are COMPs and nonextraposed ones are XCOMPs. Evidence for the distinction comes from the fact that impersonal passives are possible only with extraposed complements. This is illustrated in the contrasts in (23) and (24). The (a) sentences illustrate that *trachten* 'try' can take both verb-raising and extraposition; the (b) sentences show that the impersonal passive is possible with the extraposed variant but not with the verb-raising variant.

(23) a. omdat Jan heeft getracht Marie te helpen.
because John has tried Marie to help.

    b. omdat er (door iedereen) werd getracht Marie te helpen.
because there (by everybody) was tried Marie to help.

(24) a. omdat Jan Marie heeft trachten te helpen.
because John Marie has tried to help.
'because John has tried to help Marie.'

    b.*omdat er (door iedereen) Marie werd trachten te helpen.
because there (by everybody) Marie has tried to help.

In LFG the subject of an XCOMP is identified with a function of the higher clause by an equation of functional control. According to Bresnan (1982), such an equation can only specify the subject or object of the higher predicate. The rule of impersonal passive formation, however, would produce a control equation that does not satisfy this condition because it identifies the XCOMP SUBJ with an oblique agent function. This accounts for the ungrammaticality of (24b). In the extraposed version the COMP function does not require a functional control equation. Thus, the impersonal passive is permitted, and the appropriate referential dependency is

then established by an identity of semantic structure. In functional control
all the syntactic features of the controller and the controllee are identical.
In a relation of semantic identity, only the referential properties of the two
are identified; the syntactic features are allowed to diverge.[3]

There is another distinction between the extraposition and verb-raising
constructions, as pointed out in den Besten et al. (1988): in verb-raising
constructions the complement of the auxiliary is in the infinitive (24a) while
for extraposition it is a participle (23a). This can be regulated with a simple
feature that we will not spell out here.

We allow for the possibility of extraposed complements by replacing the
Dutch VP rule in (13) with the one in (25):

$$(25)\ \text{VP} \longrightarrow \quad \begin{array}{c} \text{NP*} \\ (\uparrow \text{XCOMP*NGF}){=}\downarrow \end{array} \quad \text{V}' \quad \left(\begin{array}{c} \text{VP} \\ (\uparrow \text{XCOMP*COMP}){=}\downarrow \end{array} \right)$$

The position of the COMP is unambiguously fixed by the phrase structure
rules, so it will always show up in sentence-final position.

5.2   The 'derde constructie'

In some dialects of Dutch, there are sentences that look like a mix of the
two constructions discussed above. This is studied in detail in den Besten
et al. (1988) under the name *de derde constructie*, the third construction.
An example is given in (26):

(26) omdat Jan Marie getracht heeft te helpen.
     because John Marie tried has to help.
     'because John has tried to help Marie.'

As we noted above, verb-raising and extraposition are distinguished by
the fact that the complement of the auxiliary is in the infinitive with verb-
raising and in the participle form with extraposition. Here, however, we see
a sentence that looks like a verb-raising structure but has the complement
of the auxiliary in the participle form. Under our account, it is simple
to model this dialect: the only difference with the standard language is
that now the COMP can also be introduced by functional uncertainty. The
annotated phrase structure rule is given in (27):

$$(27)\ \text{VP} \longrightarrow \quad \begin{array}{c} \text{NP*} \\ (\uparrow \left\{ \begin{array}{c} \text{XCOMP} \\ \text{COMP} \end{array} \right\}^{*} \text{NGF}){=}\downarrow \end{array} \quad \text{V}' \quad \left(\begin{array}{c} \text{VP} \\ (\uparrow \text{COMP}){=}\downarrow \end{array} \right)$$

---

[3]In Icelandic and German (Netter, p.c.) adjuncts that agree with the understood subject show up in the nominative, providing further evidence against a functional control
solution (see Andrews, 1982, for discussion).

We presume that the NP ordering constraints will be similar to those for XCOMP elements. In the absence of any data on this, we leave it as an open question here.

6 Ordering constraints with topicalizations: Relativized f-precedence

In the preceding section we have shown that our account gracefully models some of the differences in the West Germanic infinitival constructions, but there are some interactions that we have ignored. A rather crucial one is the interaction between topicalization and word order in what is traditionally called the middle field (the part of the sentence between the subject and the verb in final position, thus excluding topicalized or extraposed elements).

6.1 Basic facts

In (28) we illustrate the basic topicalization patterns found in Dutch.

(28) a. Het boek heeft Jan zeker gelezen.
         The book has John certainly read.
         'The book John has certainly read.'

      b. Gelezen heeft Jan het boek zeker.
         Read has John the book certainly.
         'John has certainly read the book.'

      c. Het boek gelezen heeft Jan zeker.
         The book read has John certainly.
         'Read the book, John certainly has.'

      d. Jan het boek gegeven heeft Piet zeker.
         John the book given has Pete certainly.
         'Pete has certainly given the book to John.'

      e. Het boek heeft Piet Jan zeker gegeven.
         The book has Pete John certainly given.
         'Pete has certainly given the book to John.'

      f.% Het boek gegeven heeft Piet Jan zeker.
         The book given has Pete John certainly.
         'Pete has certainly given the book to John.'

      g. Het boek heeft Jan de kinderen laten lezen.
         The book has John the children let read.
         'John let the children read this book'.

NP dependents can be topicalized regardless of their level of embedding in an XCOMP. This is illustrated in (a), (c), (e) and (g). Complete XCOMPs can also be topicalized when embedded under auxiliaries or modals, as illustrated in (d). Participles (or infinitives) can also be topicalized as shown in (b). The topicalization of partial XCOMPs is not acceptable in the dialect of the native speaker co-author of this paper, but its equivalent is acceptable in German. We have the impression that speakers vary in their acceptance of several of these patterns and are here describing a rather lax dialect.

6.2   Interactions

The word order constraints that we have discussed above apply properly to arguments and complements when they appear in the middle field, but when we take ordering in topicalized position into account, those constraints are no longer adequate. This is illustrated in (28g), where *het boek* 'the book' precedes *de kinderen* 'the children' although it is a dependent of a lower XCOMP. This topicalized word-order would be generated by the phrase-structure rule (29a),[4] but it would violate the f-precedence condition stated in the rules in (13), generalized here as (29b):

(29) a. S$'$ $\longrightarrow$ XP   S , where

$$XP = \{ \qquad NP \qquad\qquad | \qquad VP \qquad | \dots \}$$
$$(\uparrow \left\{ \begin{matrix} XCOMP \\ COMP \end{matrix} \right\}^* NGF) = \downarrow \qquad (\uparrow XCOMP) = \downarrow$$

---

[4] According to this phrase structure rule COMPs cannot be topicalized in Dutch. In Dutch there are apparent exceptions:

(i) ?? Dit boek te lezen zal ik niet vergeten.
     This book read will I not forget.

     Naar school gaan verzuimt ze nooit.
     To school go she never.

   ?* Naar school gaan tracht ze nooit.
      To school go tries she never.

As in English they only seem to occur with verbs that also take NP objects (cf. examples in (ii)), so an account along the lines of the one given in Kaplan and Zaenen (1989) should be possible.

(ii) Haar plicht verzuimt ze nooit.
      Her duty she never.

    * De taak tracht ze nooit.
      The task tries she never.

Whether this would generalize to German is not clear. Reis (p.c.) gives German *sich verweigern* as a verb that does not take an NP but allows topicalization. We have not investigated the situation in enough detail to propose an account of the COMP topicalization facts.

b. VP $\longrightarrow$ $\quad$ NP* $\quad$ V'
$$(\uparrow \text{XCOMP}^*\text{NGF})=\downarrow$$

$$V' \longrightarrow V \begin{pmatrix} V' \\ (\uparrow \text{XCOMP})=\downarrow \\ (\uparrow \text{XCOMP}^+ \text{NGF}) \not<_f (\uparrow \text{NGF}) \end{pmatrix}$$

Intuitively, it seems that the restrictions on word-order that apply to dependents in their middle-field positions do not operate when those elements appear in topic position. However, the word order constraints imposed by the f-precedence condition in (29b) apply globally across the whole sentence; they are not limited to operate just within the middle field. Given our phrase structure rules, we must be able to restrict our ordering conditions to operate just within the VP domain. In essence, the f-precedence predicate used in (29b), which is not sensitive to domains of constituent structure, must be replaced by a more specific one that takes certain dominance relations into account. This new predicate, f-precedence relative to a category X, defines a relation on f-structure elements according to the c-structure order of only some of the nodes they correspond to. In particular, the c-structure order of two nodes is taken into account only when the lowest node of type X that dominates one is also the lowest node of type X that dominates the other. Formally, we say that two nodes that appear in such a configuration are *X codominated*; the nodes n_1 and n_2 in trees in (30a) and (30b) are VP codominated whereas those nodes in (30c) are not:

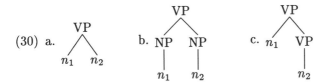

(30) a. [VP with n_1 n_2] $\quad$ b. [VP with NP (n_1) NP (n_2)] $\quad$ c. [VP with n_1 VP (n_2)]

The condition of X codomination enters into a relativized version of f-precedence according to the following definition:

(31) For two f-structure elements f_1 and f_2 and a category X,

f_1 *f-precedes* f_2 *relative to* X iff for all n_1 in $\phi^{-1}(f_1)$ and for all n_2 in $\phi^{-1}(f_2)$, n_1 and n_2 are X co-dominated and $n_1 <_c n_2$.

We write $f_1 <_f^X f_2$ to indicate that f_1 f-precedes f_2 relative to X, and use this predicate in the modified version of the V' rule:

$$(32) \quad V' \longrightarrow V \begin{pmatrix} V' \\ (\uparrow \text{XCOMP})=\downarrow \\ (\uparrow \text{XCOMP}^+ \text{NGF}) \not<_f^{\text{VP}} (\uparrow \text{NGF}) \end{pmatrix}$$

This rule imposes ordering constraints only on the nodes that are codominated by VP (in this case the VP under S), and thus ignores topicalized constituents that are outside of this ordering domain. Note that when a VP itself is topicalized as allowed by (29a), the relativized f-precedence condition must also hold of constituents within that VP.

In section 3 and 4 we proposed a flat structure for the NP dependents of XCOMPs regardless of the level of embedding, but we did not flatten the V$'$ verbal complex. The formal techniques that we have developed could be further exploited to eliminate the intermediate V$'$ constituents. But there are other conditions on what can be topicalized that argue against such a phrase structure simplification. Consider example (33):

(33) ... dat ze het boek heeft willen kopen.
     ... that she the book has wanted to buy.

It is possible to topicalize either of the infinitival complements, as shown in (34), but it is not possible to topicalize the object of a more embedded verb along with a higher verb, leaving the more embedded verb in its middle-field position. This is shown in (35):[5]

(34) Het boek willen kopen heeft ze.
     The book wanted to buy has she.

   ? Het boek kopen heeft ze gewild.
     The book buy has she wanted.

(35)*Het boek willen heeft ze kopen.
     The book wanted has she buy.

If we allow for a completely flat VP in which all the verbs are sisters of each other and daughters of the VP, it would be difficult to state this constraint. If we keep the right branching V$'$ chain as in rule (32), the proper ordering directly emerges. The equation attached to the VP in the topicalization rule (29a) insures that the topicalized material as a whole is part of an XCOMP. The organization of the V$'$ both in topicalized position and in the middle field guarantees that there are no 'holes' in either verbal complex.

7   Conclusion

In this paper we have treated some of the word order variation in infinitival complements in West Germanic. We have shown that our approach allows us to account for the differences and similarities between Dutch and Zurich

---

[5]For a discussion of the participle/infinitive alternation see den Besten et al. (1988).

German in a straightforward way. Within the confines of this paper it is not possible to discuss the corresponding data for all variants of West Germanic, but we think that our approach extends easily to these other dialects. We have also not dealt with certain other issues in full detail: for instance, the constraints on partial VP topicalization are not exactly known and we have probably modeled them incompletely.

At a more fundamental level, our account raises questions about the status of c-structure and of ordering constraints. LFG is different from other frameworks in that it makes a clear division between a level of representation that directly encodes order, the c-structure, and other levels that do not, e.g. the f-structure. This allows us to isolate ordering constraints as either conditions on the c-structure itself or on the interaction between the c-structure and other levels. The study of the constraints in West Germanic show a rather intricate pattern of interactions: on the one hand, ordering constraints have to be sensitive to f-structure information without relying on a c-structure encoding of the f-structure hierarchy; on the other hand, they are sensitive to some basic hierarchical organization of the c-structure that divides the sentence into domains that have traditionally been recognized (e.g. the middle field and the Vorfeld, corresponding here to the topicalization domain) but that are not recognized as major subdivisions of the sentence in the generative tradition. Further study should give us more insight into what motivates these domains.

References

Andrews, III, Avery. 1982. The Representation of Case in Modern Icelandic. In *The Mental Representation of Grammatical Relations*, ed. Joan Bresnan. 427–503. Cambridge, MA: The MIT Press.

den Besten, Hans, Jean Rutten, Tonjes Veenstra and Jacques Veld. 1988. Verb raising, extrapostie en de derde Constructie. Unpublished MS, University of Amsterdam.

Bresnan, Joan. 1982. Control and Complementation. In *The Mental Representation of Grammatical Relations*, ed. Joan Bresnan. 282–390. Cambridge, MA: The MIT Press.

Bresnan, Joan, Ronald M. Kaplan, Stanley Peters, and Annie Zaenen. 1982. Cross-serial Dependencies in Dutch. *Linguistic Inquiry* 13:613–635.

Bresnan, Joan. 1984. Bound anaphora on functional structures. Presented at the annual meeting of the Berkeley Linguistic Society, Berkeley, California.

Bresnan, Joan, Ronald M. Kaplan, and Peter Peterson. 1985. Coordination and the Flow of Information through Phrase Structure. Unpublished MS.

Cooper, Katrin. 1988. Word order in bare infinitival complement constructions in Swiss German. Master's thesis, University of Edinburgh.

Evers, A. 1975. *The transformational cycle in Dutch*. Doctoral dissertation, University of Utrecht.

Haegeman, Liliane, and Henk van Riemsdijk. 1986. Verb Projection Raising, Scope, and the Typology of Rules Affecting Verbs. *Linguistic Inquiry* 17(3):417–466.

Johnson, Mark. 1986. The LFG treatment of discontinuity and the double infinitive construction in Dutch. In *Proceedings of the Fifth West Coast Conference on Formal Linguistics*, ed. Mary Dalrymple, Jeffrey Goldberg, Kristin Hanson, Michael Inman, Chris Piñon, and Stephen Wechsler, 102–118. Stanford University. Stanford Linguistics Association.

Johnson, Mark. 1988. *Attribute-Value Logic and the Theory of Grammar*. CSLI Lecture Notes, No. 16. Stanford University: CSLI/The University of Chicago Press.

Kaplan, Ronald M., and Joan Bresnan. 1982. Lexical-Functional Grammar: A Formal System for Grammatical Representation. In *The Mental Representation of Grammatical Relations*, ed. Joan Bresnan. 173–281. Cambridge, MA: The MIT Press. Reprinted in Part I of this volume.

Kaplan, Ronald M. 1987. Three Seductions of Computational Psycholinguistics. In *Linguistic Theory and Computer Applications*, ed. Peter Whitelock, Harold Somers, Paul Bennett, Rod Johnson, and Mary McGee Wood. 149–188. London: Academic Press. Reprinted in Part V of this volume.

Kaplan, Ronald M., and John T. Maxwell. 1988a. An Algorithm for Functional Uncertainty. In *Proceedings of COLING-88*, 297–302. Budapest. Reprinted in Part II of this volume.

Kaplan, Ronald M., and John T. Maxwell. 1988b. Constituent Coordination in Lexical-Functional Grammar. In *Proceedings of COLING-88*, 303–305. Budapest. Reprinted in Part II of this volume.

Kaplan, Ronald and Annie Zaenen. 1988. Functional Uncertainty and Functional Precedence in Continental West Germanic. In H. Trost (ed.) *4. Österreichische Artifical-Intelligence-Tagung, Proceedings.* Berlin. Springer-Verlag, 114-23.

Kaplan, Ronald M. 1989. The Formal Architecture of Lexical-Functional Grammar. In *Proceedings of ROCLING II*, ed. Chu-Ren Huang and Keh-Jiann Chen, 1–18. Also published in *Journal of Information Science and Engineering 5*, 305-322. Reprinted in Part I of this volume.

Kaplan, Ronald M., and Annie Zaenen. 1989. Long-distance Dependencies, Constituent Structure, and Functional Uncertainty. In *Alternative Conceptions of Phrase Structure*, ed. Mark Baltin and Anthony Kroch. Chicago University Press. Reprinted in Part II of this volume.

Kameyama, Megumi. 1989. Functional Precedence Conditions on Overt and Zero Pronominals. Unpublished MS, MCC, Austin, Texas.

Lötscher, Andreas. 1978. Zur Verbstellung im Zürichdeutschen und in andren Varianten des Deutschen. *Zeitschrift fuer Dialektologie und Linguistik* 45:1–29.

Lyons, John. 1968. *Introduction to theoretical linguistics*. London: Cambridge University Press.

Netter, Klaus. 1988. Non-local dependencies and infinitival constructions in German. In *Natural language parsing and linguistic theories*, ed. Uwe Reyle and Christian Rohrer. Dordrecht: D. Reidel.

Schuurman, Ineke. 1987. A lexical-functional treatment of cross-serial dependencies. Paper presented at The XIVth International Congress of Linguists.

Schuurman, Ineke. 1991. Functional uncertainty and verb-raising dependencies. In *Trends in Germanic Syntax*, ed. W. Kosmeijer W. Abraham and E. Reuland. 223–249. Berlin: Mouton de Gruyter.

Stratified Feature Structures for Multistratal Relational Analyses

David E. Johnson
IBM Research Division
Yorktown Heights, NY

Lawrence S. Moss
Department of Mathematics
Indiana University

Abstract

This paper presents an overview of Stratified Feature Grammar (SFG), a new logic-based linguistic framework motivated by relational grammar and metagraph grammar, as well as by Kasper-Rounds logic. The main innovation in SFG is the generalization of the concept "feature" from an unanalyzable atomic one to a sequence of so-called relational signs (R-signs). The linguistic interpretation of these *stratified* features is that each R-sign denotes a primitive grammatical relation such as subject or direct object in different syntactic "strata". This generalization permits the development of a rigorous feature-structure-based formalism for natural-language grammars based on the view that syntax is "relational" and "multistratal".

In this paper we rigorously define for SFG the basic linguistic concepts *sentence, rule* (or *constraint*), *grammar, grammaticality*, and *language*. We further introduce a concept of *(data) justification*, permitting a distinction between data "presupposed" for a rule to hold and data "asserted" to be justified on the basis of that rule holding. Justification insures that satisfying S-graphs do not have more structure than absolutely necessary and so makes appealing to a notion of "minimal model" otiose. Further, a lexicalized version of SFG is presented that, in essence, requires each "core" datum (each R-sign occurrence, each node-label occurrence and each instance of so-called structure-sharing) of an otherwise well-formed S-graph be justified by some *word* in the sentence. This restriction is the basis for substantially cutting the weak generative capacity of the unrestricted framework from all recursively enumerable languages to a relatively small subclass of the recursive languages.

1 Introduction

1.1 Preview

Stratified Feature Grammar (SFG) is a logic-based linguistic framework motivated by relational grammar (RG) and metagraph grammar (MGG).[1]

---

[1]MGG, originally named Arc Pair Grammar, was first presented in Johnson and Postal (1980). For a brief introduction to MGG, see Chapter 1 of Postal (1986). Other

As the name suggests, SFG provides for "stratification" of syntactic analyses (analogous but not identical to the RG notion of *relational strata*). Formally, SFG represents syntactic structure in terms of a special type of labeled directed graph called a *stratified feature graph* or *S-graph*. S-graph features (labels) are *sequences* of primitive *relational signs (R-signs)*, rather than atomic symbols as in ordinary feature structures. Hence, the use of the term *stratified feature*. The idea underlying this generalization is that a sequence of R-signs represents a "stratification" of the primitive relations one constituent bears to another.

Each R-sign in a sequence of R-signs is interpreted as a primitive grammatical relation, e.g., Subject (1), Direct Object (2), Indirect Object (3), Chômeur(8), Complement (Comp) and Head. For instance, the R-sign sequence 2,1 represents the SFG analog to the RG/MGG concept of "2-to-1 advancement" and hence plays a central role in the SFG description of both passive and unaccusative clauses. The unaccusative case is illustrated in Figure 1.

$$
\begin{bmatrix}
[Cat] & \text{S} \\
[2,1] & \text{glass} \\
[Head] & \text{breaks}
\end{bmatrix}
$$

Figure 1: S-graph of *Glass breaks*.

The key aspect of the unaccusative analysis, in SFG terms, is the stratified feature [2,1]: this indicates that *glass* is initially a direct object, but finally a subject, of the clause. This situation contrasts with that of related sentences such as *John breaks the glass*, where *(the) glass* is both initially and finally the direct object, and *Joe* is both initially and finally the subject. The latter situation is, of course, describable with ordinary (atomic) features, as show in Figure 2.

One central SFG idea is that, except for a special class of *null* R-signs, *initial* R-signs in stratified features denote *predicate-argument* relations, and *final* R-signs *surface* relations. In the unaccusative sentence *Glass breaks*, then, *glass* is the predicate-argument direct object, but the surface subject. In contrast, in the transitive sentence *Joe breaks the glass, (the) glass* is both the predicate-argument direct object and the surface direct

work carried out within the MGG framework includes Aissen (1987), Kubinski (1987) and Postal (1989). For introductions to RG, see Aissen (1991) and Blake (1990). Other volumes containing RG and MGG articles include Dubinsky and Rosen (1987), Dziwirek, Farrell and Mejias-Bikandi (1990), Perlmutter (1983), Perlmutter and Rosen (1984), and Postal and Joseph (1990).

$$
\begin{bmatrix}
[Cat] & \text{S} \\
[1] & \text{Joe} \\
[Head] & \text{breaks} \\
[2] & \text{the glass}
\end{bmatrix}
$$

Figure 2: S-graph of *Joe breaks the glass.*

object of the clause. Stratified features can, and often do, contain more than two R-signs; more details are given in Sections 2.5 and 2.6.

Unlike typical feature structures, S-graphs include a strict partial order on arcs to represent linear precedence.[2] (However, the tabular representation does not show this information.) This strict partial order provides the basis for defining the notions *yield of an S-graph* and, consequently, *SFG language*; see Section 3.4 for details.

Stratified features permit the representation of stratified relational analyses within a feature-structure framework, and they lead to a generalized form of Kasper-Rounds (KR) logic for the description of stratified feature structures. In this way, SFG is *theoretically well-defined*, by which we mean that it provides rigorous definitions of the basic linguistic concepts *sentence*, *rule/constraint*, *grammar*, *grammaticality*, and *language*. Here, SFG goes beyond RG, which has remained informal and incompletely specified in these areas.

1.2 Historical Remarks

The general idea of representing the entire syntactic (relational) structure of a sentence in a *single*, arc-labeled directed graph became a basic part of RG around 1975. This suggestion was first made by Rounds at the 1974 SSRB seminar on Formal Models in Linguistics and independently by Lakoff in 1975 (cf. Lakoff 1977). The RG and MGG graph-theoretic representations of sentence structure are quite close to the more recent concept of feature structure (cf. the discussion on this point in Rounds and Manaster-Ramer 1987). Under the rubric of "multi-attachment", structure-sharing has been used in RG since 1974-75 in the description of the syntax of not only clause-internal constructions involving, e.g., passives, antipassives, and dative advancements, but also the syntax of cross-clause constructions involving, e.g., raising, equi and clause union constructions. (cf. Perlmutter 1983). In 1977, as detailed in Johnson and Postal (1980), MGG expanded

---

[2]The idea of representing linear precedence as a strict partial order on *arcs* was first suggested in Johnson and Postal (1980). In a similar vein, Rounds and Manaster-Ramer (1987) augmented feature structures with two partial orders on *nodes*, one for dominance and one for linear precedence.

the use of structure-sharing, applying it generally to analyses of binding, control and extraction constructions.

Turning to the MGG conception of grammars and grammaticality: Johnson and Postal (1980) argued that grammars should be formalized as axiomatic systems and, correspondingly, sentence (structures) as models of grammars. Thus, SFG follows the early lead of MGG in this regard too. However, the kinds of the logic used in the two frameworks are quite different. MGG regards rules as statements in a full first order logic and adopts the standard model-theoretic semantics provided by that view. In contrast, SFG follows the Kasper-Rounds tradition quite closely, defining a quite limited quantifier-free logic involving, inter alia, label-prefixed formulas and path equations as well as an extension of the typical KR-style semantics.

Over the intervening years, these general ideas – often independently adopted – seem to have gained wide acceptance within the feature-structure community.[3] For instance, although the most recent version of HPSG differs technically in very substantial ways from MGG, HPSG has adopted the MGG view that structure-sharing, rather than movement, is the proper descriptive mechanism for explicating binding, control and extraction constructions (see Pollard and Sag 1987 and Pollard and Sag 1994). As we see it, the above-mentioned items constitute major areas of agreement between those working in the monostratal feature-structure paradigm and those working within the multistratal relational paradigm. Our own work seeks to capitalize further on these areas of agreement.

1.3   Goals

The primary goal of this paper is to present a self-contained overview of SFG. The main exposition consists of three sections, followed by our conclusions. The first, Section 2, provides a very informal overview of various key aspects of SFG and provides some examples of how SFG rules might be used in accounting for English. In Section 3, we develop a formal account of the (unrestricted) SFG framework. Although the basic ideas behind the SFG formalism are relatively simple, many details are needed to work them out properly. These sections are of necessity somewhat formal in nature, but we do attempt to motivate and explain the formal aspects through informal discussion and examples. The formal development of the unrestricted framework concludes with Section 3.5, where we present an SFG grammar for the formal language $\{a^{2^n}\}$. Next, in Section 4, we introduce two linguistically motivated restrictions on the general framework and briefly sketch some formal results on the expressive power of the SFG framework.

---

[3]Moreover, the popularity of structure-sharing seems to be growing outside of the feature-structure community. See, e.g., Huck and Ojeda (1989).

Another goal of our work is to expand as much as possible the above-mentioned areas of agreement between the multistratal relationally-based, and the monostratal unification-based, paradigms. As the reader will no doubt notice, although the sample SFG analyses presented below are, in a real sense, multistratal, they nevertheless exhibit a number of similarities to typical feature-structure analyses found in the literature. This is no accident: The moral to be drawn here is simply that the essential differences between these two paradigms is not nearly as great or clear-cut as might superficially be supposed. That is, there is plenty of room for "cross-fertilization". This might seem surprising to some since it has become commonplace to assume that feature structure-based syntax is necessarily monostratal and "surfacy" (cf. Shieber 1986). In other words, one conclusion that clearly emerges from our work is that the notions "monostratal/surface syntax" and "feature-structure-based" have no necessary connection.

By building on KR logic as a kind of "lingua franca", we provide, for the first time, a common formal basis for comparison of so-called monostratal unification-based, and multistratal relational, approaches to syntax. Besides providing a sound formal basis for developing computationally realizable, multistratal relational grammars, this work will, we hope, act as a catalyst for future discussions of the "monostratality versus multistratality" issue (cf. Ladusaw 1988) as well as other foundational issues underlying unification-based and, more generally, axiomatic approaches to grammar.

2 An Informal Look at SFG

2.1 Stratified Features and S-graphs

In Section 1, we discussed rather briefly the following two aspects of SFG: (i) in order to accommodate multistratal analyses, the notion *feature* has been generalized from an atomic element to a *sequence* of R-signs (*stratified feature*); and (ii) except for a special class of *null* R-signs, *initial* R-signs in stratified features denote *predicate-argument* relations, and *final* R-signs *surface* relations. We begin to elaborate on these ideas by considering Figure 3 which depicts the S-graph for *Joe gave Mary tea*. Here the stratified feature [3,2] indicates that *Mary* is a predicate-argument indirect object, but a surface direct object; and the stratified feature [2,8] indicates that *tea* is a predicate-argument direct object, but a surface chômeur. This configuration of stratified features constitutes the SFG description of so-called Dative Advancement constructions. The initial R-signs determine the predicate-argument relations: in the above example that *Joe* is the giver, *Mary* the recipient and *tea* the given. The final R-signs determine superficial properties such as case and word order: in the above example that *Joe* precedes the verb and that *Mary* and *tea* follow the verb, in that order. The initial R-signs shown in Figure 3 also serve to relate *Joe gave Mary tea* to *Joe gave tea to Mary*, as shown in Figure 4. The right-hand) is used in [3] to indicate that the 3 might not be the last R-sign in the corresponding stratified feature. A more complete analysis would also show the prepositional phrase structure corresponding to *to Mary*, and this would involve extending [3] to [3,0]. The function of the so-called null R-sign 0 in the SFG description of prepositional phrases is explained below.

$$
\begin{bmatrix}
[Cat] & \text{S} \\
[1] & \text{Joe} \\
[Head] & \text{gave} \\
[3, 2] & \text{Mary} \\
[2, 8] & \text{tea}
\end{bmatrix}
$$

Figure 3: S-graph for *Joe gave Mary tea.*

$$
\begin{bmatrix}
[Cat] & \text{S} \\
[1] & \text{Joe} \\
[Head] & \text{gave} \\
[2] & \text{tea} \\
[3) & \text{(to) Mary}
\end{bmatrix}
$$

Figure 4: S-graph for *Joe gave tea to Mary.*

As mentioned previously, stratified features can contain more than two R-signs. For instance, consider a sentence such as *Mary was given tea by Joe.* The standard RG analysis of this type of sentence involves "advancement" of an initial 3 to 2 (via Dative Advancement) and subsequent "advancement" of that 2 to 1 (via Passive). In SFG terms this configuration involves a feature whose initial segment is [3,2,1). The right-hand) indicates that the feature could have more R-signs after the 1. In fact, in the SFG analysis of the English Dative-Passive construction, the complete feature would be [3,2,1,0].

The null R-sign 0, unique to SFG, plays a role in the description of, inter alia, bounded control constructions such as Raising and Equi. Figure 5 illustrates the use of 0 in the description of Raising (*be* is analysed as a Raising verb). The final 0 in [3,2,1,0], occurring in the middle of the figure, indicates that the target node *Mary* bears no surface relation in the phrase headed by *given*. Note that in the clause headed by *was*, *Mary* also heads an arc labeled [0,1]. (The structure-sharing is indicated by the tag $\boxed{\text{i}}$.) The initial 0 in [0,1] indicates that *Mary* bears no predicate-argument relation in the clause headed by *was*, and the final 1 in [0,1] indicates that *Mary* is the surface subject of that clause. The relational analysis of "raising" is thus characterized in SFG in terms of a configuration involving two arcs with the same target node where the feature of the lower arc ends with 0 and the feature of the higher arc starts with 0.

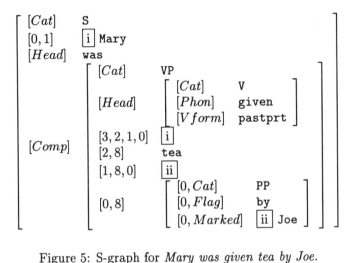

Figure 5: S-graph for *Mary was given tea by Joe.*

The path [*Comp*][*Head*] leads to a substructure showing the approximate internal structure of the past participle *given*. This is a typical feature structure specifying the Cat(egory) to be V(erb), the phonology to be "given" and the Vform (verb form) to be pastprt (past participle). Of more interest is the SFG representation of the internal structure of the prepositional phrase *by Joe*, depicted at the end of the path [*Comp*][0,8]. This structure involves four features: [0,8], [0,Cat], [0, Flag] and [0, Marked]. The 0's in the initial positions indicate that this constituent is not part of the predicate-argument structure. That is, the preposition *by* serves only to "flag" the passive chômeur *Joe*, the "marked" constituent of the prepositional phrase. Observe that *Joe* is also the target of the arc labeled [1,8,0], as indicated by the shared tag ⅱ. The segment [1,8] is part of the "revaluation" characteristic of the passive configuration, i.e., [1,8) represents the "demotion" of the predicate-argument subject to the special status of chômeur; and the final (0] segment is part of the "lowering" structure associated with prepositional phrases *that have no independent meaning*. The relational "core" of Passive is argued in RG/MGG to be universal, i.e., a relational configuration made available by universal grammar and instantiated in many languages. The prepositional flagging of the chômeur with *by*, in contrast, is English-specific, constituting the so-called "side effects" of the rule.[4]

2.2   SFG Rules and Grammaticality

Following Kasper and Rounds, SFG rules have been formalized as statements in a restricted (quantifier-free) logical language (cf. Kasper and Rounds 1986; Kasper and Rounds 1990 and Moshier and Rounds 1986). All SFG syntactic rules are constraints on S-graphs. More specifically, SFG rules hold or fail to hold *at nodes* in S-graphs; that is, S-graph nodes *satisfy* or *fail to satisfy* rules. SFG provides a simple account of *grammaticality*, which, however, involves not just the standard notion of *rule satisfaction*, but also a novel auxiliary concept of *(data) justification*. We defer discussion of the specifics of SFG rules until we introduce the formalism in Section 3.

In the general framework, an S-graph G is grammatical if and only if (i) every node of G satisfies *every* rule and (ii) every core datum of G is justified. The "core data" of an S-graph are the R-sign occurrences, node-label (atom) occurrences and instances of structure-sharing; see Section 3.3 for a complete definition. (Since the SFG description language includes material implication, requirement (i) is not as stringent as it might first appear to be.) The fundamental distinction between justified and non-justified data permits the specification of data "presupposed" for a given rule ϕ to hold, versus data "asserted" to be justified on the basis of ϕ holding. In Section 3.3 we motivate this distinction and in Sections 3.5 and 4 we make use of this concept in crucial ways in determining the expressive power of the framework.

We emphasize that the SFG characterization of multistratal constructions such as Passive and Raising does not inherently involve in any way (information-destroying) derivational operations such as movement or deletion.

2.3   SFG Lexicalism

The unrestricted SFG framework is, from the standpoint of linguistic theory, overly expressive – in fact, as proved in Johnson and Moss (1993), every type 0 (recursively enumerable) language is characterized by some unrestricted SFG grammar. As a step toward remedying this, we impose, in Section 4 a condition requiring that the core data of an S-graph be justified in a formally precise way by some *word* in the sentence. We call this *the (Lexical) Anchoring Principle*. This principle implies that given a sentence

---

[4] *[Comp]* is not part of the standard RG/MGG analysis of, e.g., Raising, which would have [2, 8] instead. Nothing in this paper hinges on these matters of detail.

string σ, the size of an S-graph having σ in its yield is bounded by a linear function of the number of words in σ. (We say "in its yield" because in SFG the yield of an S-graph is generally a set of strings.) The constant is determined by the grammar, independent of σ. This provides the basis for a theorem showing that the corresponding *bounded* SF-languages can be recognized on a non-deterministic Turing machine in $n \log n$ space and polynomial time; hence, they constitute a relatively small subset of the recursive languages. (By "relatively small", we mean informally that there are many classes of recursive languages that are not bounded SFLs.)

The lexicalist orientation of SFG, however, differs from that of, e.g., LFG and HPSG, since "lexical" in SFG does *not* signify the use of lexical rules that are operations on lexical categories. Rather, "lexical" here refers to the assumption that individual words are associated with rules that determine the properties of the phrases those words can occur in (hence, the term *lexical anchoring*). This view can be taken as a generalized notion of "subcategorization". In SFG, lexical rules typically characterize "phrasal skeletons", i.e., structure necessarily co-occurring with a given class of lexical items. For instance, verbs characterize the kind of verb phrases or clauses they occur in, adjectives the kind of adjective phrases they show up in, etc.

The SFG concept of lexical anchoring is analogous to the concept of "lexicalized grammars" as independently developed in the TAG framework (see Schabes and Joshi 1990, Schabes 1990). Another framework that seems to involve an analogous view of lexicalized grammars is McCord's slot grammar (see McCord 1980 and McCord 1992). Slot grammar is a computational framework for natural language processing in which, as we understand it, (i) grammatical relations ("slots") such as subject and object are considered primitive syntactic constructs; (ii) syntactic structure is largely determined by lexical information; and (iii) there is no separate phrase structure component. Slot grammar has not, to our knowledge, been formalized and so it is difficult to compare it with SFG. However, our understanding of slot grammar indicates that it is monostratal and so would require lexical operations of the sort used in LFG and HPSG.

Informally, a lexically anchored rule ϕ is one in which the node satisfying ϕ is labeled with a lexical item w and this node-labeling is a *necessary* condition for ϕ to be satisfied. In this case we often use the informal notation "anchor$(w) := \phi$". Not atypically, lexically anchored rules, e.g., SFG versions of Passive, Dative, Subject-Raising, determine S-graphs that represent partially specified phrases.[5]

---

[5]We caution the reader that the formal condition called the Lexical Anchoring principle in Section 4 is weaker than the linguistically motivated conception discussed above in that the former merely requires that every rule be satisfied by a node labeled with some

2.4   Constituent Structure and Word Order in SFG

SFG, like MGG, does not have a separate grammar of phrase-structure
rules and so contrasts in this regard with, e.g., GPSG (Gazdar et al. 1985);
LFG (Kaplan and Breslan 1982); and Attribute-Value Grammar (Johnson
1988), as standardly conceived. This is also a point of similarity between
SFG and slot grammar (McCord 1992). We note in passing that the version of HPSG as presented in Pollard and Sag (1992, 1994) also does not
have a separate phrase structure *grammar*. However, the HPSG approach
to sentence structure still seems to be constituent structure-based. More
specifically, in HPSG immediate dominance schemata play the role of GB's
X-bar schemata, licensing constituent structures. These schemata function
as "templates" determining acceptable immediate constituent structures.
The constituent structure bias of HPSG is also apparent in the HPSG requirement that each phrase have an attribute DTRS (daughters) whose
value is a feature structure (of type *constituent-structure*) representing the
immediate constituent structure of the phrase.

Unlike HPSG, SFG has no such immediate dominance schemata, nor
do SFG structures directly encode constituent structure. In our view, constituent structure is an epiphenomenon, a derivative of the surface relational
(or functional) structure. Why this is so in SFG will be made clear in Section 3.4, where we present definitions of *yield* and *SFG language*, and in
Sections 3.5 and 4, where we exhibit SF grammars for two formal languages.

One of the main points that will emerge from these sections is that
in SFG, "free (flexible) word order" within constituents is achieved in the
simplest possible manner—by absence of statement. The order placed on
arcs in S-graphs is a strict partial order. Only some pairs of arcs in a
given S-graph G will, in general, need to be ordered in some way to satisfy
a given grammar. Furthermore, in defining the yield of G, we shall, by
general definition, consider all extensions to the linear precedence relation
of G consistent with the word order constraints. In this way, unspecified
orders correspond to having many strings in the yield. [6]

---

lexical item *or other*, that is, the SFG *framework* does not require a specified "linkage"
between particular words and particular rules. Rather, this linkage is up to the grammar
writer. We have set things up this way because the formally defined condition presented
in Section 4 is simpler but sufficient for our formal work, and it is not our intent here to
develop a substantive linguistic theory.

[6] Our general views on the role of linear precedence in natural languages is founded on
the earlier RG position that linear precedence is a "reflex" of unordered, superficial structure and, hence, that movement rules (rules that alter linear precedence relations) do
not exist and that so-called free word-order merely reflects the absence of ordering constraints (cf. e.g., Perlmutter and Postal 1974, Johnson 1979, Johnson and Postal 1980).
Of course, this informal view has a long history in generative grammar (cf. e.g., Sanders
1967, 1970), and a variant on this view has been more recently popularized through the
GPSG notion of ID/LP grammars (cf. Gazdar et al. 1985). The particular treatment of

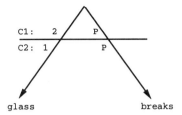

Figure 6: RG Representation for *Glass breaks*

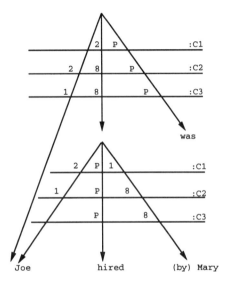

Figure 7: RG Representation for *Joe was hired by Mary*

2.5 A Comparison of RG, MGG, and SFG Representations

To compare the kinds of representations used in SFG, RG and MGG, we depict in Figure 1 above and in Figures 6 and 8 the respective approximate representations of the unaccusative sentence *Glass breaks*. In all three cases, the nominal *glass* is analyzed as bearing two successive grammatical relations to the clause: it is an "initial 2" and a "final 1" (the "unaccusative analysis").

word order offered here differs, as far as we are aware, from these forerunners.

As shown in Figure 1 and discussed earlier, in SFG this stratification is represented by the stratified feature [2, 1]. Notice that the verb *breaks* corresponds to the target node of an arc with an atomic label [*Head*]: In general, stratified features of arcs with the same tail node do *not* have the same number of R-signs. Once again, in SFG the *first* R-signs of stratified features denote initial relations, and the *final* R-signs final relations. Furthermore, except for the class of null R-signs, initial R-signs correspond to predicate-argument relations, and final relations correspond to surface relations.[7] Surface relations determine superficial properties of sentences such as case and word order. In Figure 1, these definitions determine that *glass* is the initial (and predicate-argument) 2, *breaks* the initial (and predicate-argument) Head, *glass* the final (and surface) 1, and *breaks* the final (and surface) Head of the clause.

Next, let us compare the above representation to that found in RG. The RG representation in Figure 6 is given as a "stratal diagram," a pictorial device emphasizing the horizontal stratification typical of RG analyses. In the RG analysis of *Glass breaks*, the entire clause is partitioned horizontally into two strata (indicated by the "coordinates" c1 and c2). In RG, c1 always indicates the initial stratum. The final stratum always corresponds to the highest coordinate (which happens to be c2 in this example). This amounts to a *total horizontal* partitioning of all arcs with a common tail node, and hence indirectly of the constituent heads of those arcs. Thus, the SFG concept of stratification ("vertical stratification") differs from the RG concept ("horizontal stratification").

The nature of RG horizontal stratification is perhaps best understood by a more complicated example. Consider the RG stratal diagram for the clause structure of the passive sentence *Joe was hired by Mary,* shown in Figure 7. (This figure should be compared to the SFG analog in Figure 12). As illustrated, if a clause is multistratal, then arcs not involved in "re-evaluation" typically must "fall through" into the next stratum. This is quite general, but not universal: In the example at hand, in the last stratum of the clause whose predicate is *hired*, the cell associated with the raised nominal *Joe* is empty. Observe also that except for the empty cell, the last stratum in the embedded clause consists of repetitions of the previous

---

[7]A substantive theory developed within SFG would limit the distribution of *null* R-signs to first and last positions in labels. Although space limitations here preclude detailed discussion, we would also assume that a substantive SFG theory would postulate at least two null R-signs: 0 and / (slash). As its name suggests, the R-sign / would be used in the description of (unbounded) extractions, facilitating the incorporation into SFG of an analog to the treatment of extractions originating in GPSG. The interpretation of / with respect to the surface tree and predicate-argument structure is, like any other member of the R-sign class null, the same as that of 0. However, at least some of the laws and rules referencing / would be different from those referencing 0.

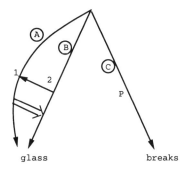

Figure 8: MGG Representation for *Glass breaks*

stratum. This is an informal way of saying that a constituent is missing from the final stratum of the clause. RG has never, to our knowledge, provided a formal characterization of this crucial notion.[8]

To summarize our position on multiple strata: To the extent that stratification is warranted, we contend that it can be modeled in terms of stratified features. This permits the modeling of stratified relational analyses in terms of suitably extended feature structures and a constrained feature-structure logic. Of course, we do not deny that there are some constraints that operate "horizontally" across arcs, e.g., the concept of "initial transitive clause" and "surface transitive clause" are important for an adequate characterization of clause structure. But we do deny that "horizontal constraints" entail horizontal stratification in the RG sense. What horizontal constraints mean internal to SFG is that the SFG description language must provide means for stating constraints that "align" R-signs of arc labels of different arcs in the required ways. For instance, as mentioned above, in SFG "initial" and "final" are definable in terms of *first* and *last* R-signs of labels, respectively.

Next, we compare the SFG type of representation to that characteristic of MGG. The MGG representation in Figure 8 depicts a so-called "meta-

---

[8]Despite the fact that RG evolved into a non-derivational theory around 1974-75, horizontal stratification is reminiscent of transformational practice. Early MGG formalized this aspect of RG in terms of a set of Coordinate Determination Laws, but these involved Sponsor and Erase, the two primitive relations on arcs postulated in MGG, which RG never adopted (cf. Johnson and Postal 1980). Imposing horizontal stratification raised a number of technical problems (cf. the discussion in Johnson and Postal 1980, Chapters 6 and 8.4) and, in retrospect, it appears to be without significant factual motivation. Therefore, current MGG makes no use of coordinates, relying completely on the Sponsor and Erase relations to make whatever distinctions are needed. One consequence of this is that so-called "stratal uniqueness" is only definable on initial and final strata, but there seems to be no reason to maintain "medial stratal uniqueness" anyway.

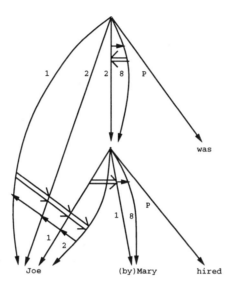

Figure 9: MGG Representation for *Joe was hired by Mary*

graph", the most distinctive aspects of which are the two relations on arcs
called *Sponsor* and *Erase*. The situation "arc A Sponsors arc B" is shown
as "$A \rightarrow B$", the situation "arc A erases arc B" as "$A \Rightarrow B$". The informal
interpretation of "A sponsors B" is that the occurrence of arc B in a metagraph is dependent on the occurrence of arc A, i.e., the existence of arc A is
a necessary condition for the existence of arc B. Predicate-argument structure is definable in terms of the Sponsor relation: The predicate-argument
structure – or, *logical graph*, as it is called in MGG – is the subgraph of all
the *un*sponsored arcs.

The informal interpretation of "A erases B" is that the occurrence of arc
A in a metagraph $\mathcal{M}$ prevents arc B from appearing in the surface graph of
$\mathcal{M}$. The surface graph of a metagraph $\mathcal{M}$ is definable in terms of the Erase
relation: namely, it is defined as that *subgraph* of $\mathcal{M}$ corresponding to all
the *un*erased arcs. That is, being erased is a necessary and sufficient condition to prevent an arc from being part of the surface graph of a sentence. In
the example at hand, it should be clear that the predicate-argument structure corresponds to the arcs labeled B and C. And the surface structure
corresponds to the arcs labeled A and C.

To round out this discussion, we present in Figure 9 the MGG metagraph for the clause structure of *Joe was hired by Mary*. The above definitions of the MGG concepts *logical graph* and *surface graph* pick out the
subgraphs shown in Figures 10 and 11.

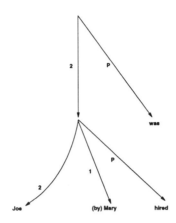

Figure 10: MGG Logical Graph for *Joe was hired by Mary*

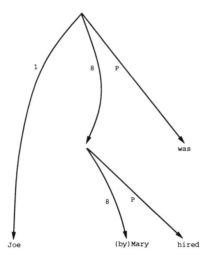

Figure 11: MGG Surface Graph for *Joe was hired by Mary*

It should be apparent from the foregoing discussion that the most distinctive feature of MGG representations are the two binary relations on arcs, Sponsor and Erase. Hopefully, it is also evident how these relations figure in MGG descriptions of constructions involving passive and raising. Now let us see how the purely "local" null R-signs of SFG (which are essentially *properties* of arcs) can do some of the work of MGG's Sponsor and Erase relations.

As touched on earlier, the null R-sign 0 is used on the right ends of labels in *bounded* control constructions. In this role, it indicates that the constituent corresponding to the target node is not part of the surface tree (which determines the yield of the S-graph). As illustrated in various figures above and in Figure 12 below, 0 is also used on the *left* ends of labels in bounded Raising constructions and in cases of "flagging", as occurs in, e.g., prepositional phrases. In this role, it means that the constituent corresponding to the target is not part of the predicate-argument structure. The most direct forerunner of this use of 0 is to be found in the MGG concept *foreign successor*. MGG has no need for 0, since Sponsor and Erase can do the same work, and, in fact, are more powerful descriptive devices. Sponsor and Erase are relations on arcs and hence can hold between arcs unboundedly far apart in a graph. In contrast, the R-sign 0 is strictly local. Also, note that part of the work done by Sponsor and Erase is accomplished in SFG by stratified features. For instance, in the *Glass breaks* example, where SFG has [2, 1], MGG (like RG) has two arcs, viz. a 2-arc that sponsors, and is erased by, a 1-arc.[9]

Consider again Figure 12. To pick out the surface graph, ignore every label that ends in a null R-sign (here, 0). For each remaining arc, ignore every R-sign in its label except the *last*. The resulting surface S-graph (minus word order information) is depicted in Figure 13.

To pick out the predicate-argument structure of Figure 12, ignore every arc whose label starts with a null R-sign (again, here, only 0). For each remaining arc, ignore every R-sign in its label except the *first*. The resulting predicate-argument S-graph is depicted in Figure 14.

2.6   SFG Descriptions of Some English Constructions

In this section, we illustrate SFG's capability to describe some fairly standard relational analyses in a succinct and (we would argue) natural man-

---

[9]Note that although the distribution of null R-signs is limited to the ends of labels, and they are not part of the more familiar repertoire of R-signs, they do represent bonafide relations like any other R-sign. Like any other theoretical constructs, their meanings are indirectly derived from the role they play in the various definitions, principles and rules of the framework and/or theory at hand.

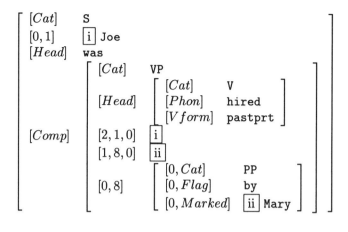

Figure 12: SFG Representation of *Joe was hired by Mary*.

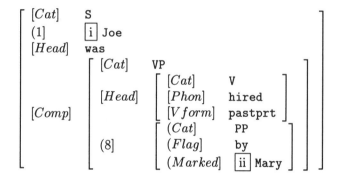

Figure 13: Surface Graph for *Joe was hired by Mary*.

ner. This section will be quite informal, but it should be kept in mind that everything presented here could be stated in the formal SFG description language (SFDL) defined in Section 3.2 For the most part, we present rules in this section in tabular form. This is a weaker format than SFDL since formulas involving negation, material implication, disjunction and linear precedence are not straightforwardly representable. Nevertheless, this format provides a convenient means for presenting many rules and analyses. Moreover, these statements together do not quite constitute a Stratified Feature Grammar. For that, see Section 3.4

First, consider an SFDL formula for *he*, shown below. (The underlining indicates which R-signs and atoms are justified by the rule; here that is all of them.)

$$\begin{bmatrix} [Cat] & \text{S} \\ [Head] & \text{was} \\ & \\ [Comp] & \begin{bmatrix} [Cat] & \text{VP} \\ [Head] & \begin{bmatrix} [Cat] & \text{V} \\ [Phon] & \text{hired} \\ [Vform] & \text{pastprt} \end{bmatrix} \\ (2) & \text{Joe} \\ (1) & \text{Mary} \end{bmatrix} \end{bmatrix}$$

Figure 14: Predicate-Argument Graph for *Joe was hired by Mary.*

<u>he</u> $\wedge$ $[phon]^{-1}[head]^{-1}[cat]$: <u>NP</u> $\wedge$ $[phon]^{-1}[cat]$: <u>Pronoun</u>
$\wedge$ $[phon]^{-1}[agree][person]$: <u>Third</u> $\wedge$ $[phon]^{-1}[agree][number]$: <u>Singular</u>
$\wedge$ $[phon]^{-1}[agree][gender]$: <u>Masc</u> $\wedge$ $[phon]^{-1}[case]$: <u>Nom</u>

The superscript $^{-1}$ indicates that the rule, so to speak, looks *up* an edge from the anchor *he*. We call labels having the superscript $^{-1}$ *inverse labels*. They are necessary for describing structures from the viewpoint of lexical anchors, which are leaf nodes. Notice that *he* anchors, and hence justifies, an NP. This is quite general: words typically justify the phrases they occur in. This provides the motivation for the Lexical Anchoring principle.

The rule for *he* basically says that "starting from a node labeled *he*, there is a path *upward* through $[phon][head]$ and from there *downward* through [cat] to a node labeled NP and there is a path ... ". This rule could, of course, be collapsed into an equivalent shorter statement by factoring out common subformulas using standard equivalences in KR logic. That is, the following rule is an equivalent statement; moreover, it bears a closer correspondence to the tabular form of the rule, shown in Figure 15.

<u>he</u> $\wedge$ $[phon]^{-1}$ ($[head]^{-1}[cat]$: <u>NP</u> $\wedge$ $[cat]$: <u>Pronoun</u> $\wedge$ $[agree]$ ($[person]$: <u>Third</u>
$\wedge$ $[number]$: <u>Singular</u> $\wedge$ $[gender]$: <u>Masc</u>) $\wedge$ $[case]$: <u>Nom</u>)

In the discussion that follows we will typically ignore the inverse paths that, so to speak, take one from the lexical anchor to the "locus of action". These "bridge" paths are, generally speaking, predictable from the category of the anchor and so are of little interest.

Now, we turn to a discussion of the SFG statements for Passive and Dative Advancement. This requires a better understanding of the concept of justification. Roughly, justification permits a kind of conditionalization based on the informal notion of "data presupposed present for a rule to apply" and "data asserted to be present on the basis of the presupposition holding". Now consider how this would work in the case of Passive. The

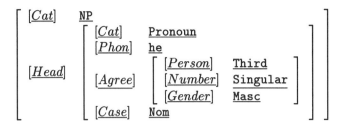

Figure 15: Rule Anchored by *he*

conditional rule of passive as formalized in Section 3.3 below does basically the following: it *asserts the existence* of a unique pair of arcs a1 and a2, where a1 has the sequence (2, 1) in its feature and a2 has the sequence [1, 8) in its feature; and, furthermore, it *justifies* the occurrence of the 1 in the sequence (2, 1) and the 8 in the sequence [1, 8), *on the assumption* that there exist two distinct sister arcs, one having a 2 in its feature and the other a 1 in its feature. That is, Passive does *not* assert the existence of an arc with a 2 in its feature nor the existence of an arc with a 1 in its feature, and furthermore it does *not* justify the 2 in the (2, 1) sequence or the 1 in the [1, 8) sequence. (This round about way of talking is required because of some formal technicalities.) Informally, though, we can think of Passive as justifying the *extension* of a feature from a (2) to a (2,1) and the extension of a feature from a [1) to a [1,8), provided the antecedent conditions of passivization are met, i.e., appropriate 2 and 1 arcs exist. Other rule(s) must assert and justify the existence of the "pre-extension" 2 and 1 required for Passive to apply. We stress that we use underlining in rules to indicate which corresponding data (atoms and R-signs) in S-graphs are justified.

With this background, we present slightly simplified SFDL formulas for Passive and Dative Advancement (for precise details, see Section 3.2):

$$\textbf{Passive} \quad \overset{\text{def}}{=} \quad (2) \wedge (1) \mapsto (2,\underline{1}) \wedge [1,\underline{8}) \; ;$$

$$\textbf{Dative} \quad \overset{\text{def}}{=} \quad (2) \wedge (3) \mapsto (2,\underline{8}) \wedge (3,\underline{2}) \, .$$

These are both extension formulas. The interpretation of Passive is as discussed above; the interpretation of Dative Advancement is similar.

These two formulas can be conventionally abbreviated as:

$$\textbf{Passive} \quad \overset{\text{def}}{=} \quad (2,\underline{1}) \; \& \; [1,\underline{8})$$

$$\textbf{Dative} \quad \overset{\text{def}}{=} \quad (3,\underline{2}) \; \& \; (2,\underline{8}) \, .$$

$$\left[\begin{array}{c} (2,\underline{1}) \\ [1,\underline{8}) \end{array} \right]$$

Figure 16: Passive in Tabular Form

$$\left[\begin{array}{c} (3,\underline{2}) \\ (2,\underline{8}) \end{array} \right]$$

Figure 17: Dative Advancement in Tabular Form

Note that the symbol & is not interpreted as logical conjunction; rather the whole formula receives an interpretation appropriate to extensions, which require a special semantics. We hope that the informal idea is clear.

Now we turn to the corresponding tabular formats for these two rules. These are depicted in Figures 16 and 17. The correspondences to the formal statements should be apparent.

Next we return to the discussion of null-subject control constructions – specifically, so-called Equi and Raising – and expand on our earlier comments. Consider the analysis of the sentence *I want to know*, which is typically taken to involve Equi-type control. In relational terms, Equi is characterized by the identity of an *initial* 1 of a clause C and the *last* 1 of C's infinitival complement. Following the RG and MGG proposals, this dual role is represented by structure-sharing ("multi-attachment" in RG terms, "overlapping arcs" in MGG terms). We also follow the widely accepted proposal that infinitival *to* is a verb (cf. Pullum 1982 for arguments). For us, infinitival *to* is a subject raiser. Informally, what this basically means for the analysis of *I want to know* is that the VP headed by *to* has a null subject that is Equi-controlled by the subject of the clause headed by *want* and that this null subject is itself raised from the VP headed by the verb *know*. This informal description is straightforwardly characterized formally in terms of stratified features, the R-sign 0, and structure-sharing.

Figure 18 depicts the S-graph for *I want to know*. (In order to focus on the salient points, we have omitted the internal structure of the words in this example; we do this selectively on other examples as well.) The node labeled with *I* is syntactically related to three phrases: the matrix clause headed by *want*, the medial VP headed by *to*, and the bottom VP headed by *know*. In the matrix clause *I* is depicted as an initial and final 1; in the medial phrase as a "medial only" 1 (neither initial nor final); and in the bottom clause as an initial but non-final 1. Structure-sharing is indicated by the boxed letter $\boxed{\text{i}}$.

$$
\begin{bmatrix}
[Cat] & \text{S} \\
[1] & \boxed{\text{i}}\ \text{I} \\
[Head] & \text{want} \\
\\
[Comp] & \begin{bmatrix}
[Cat] & \text{VP} \\
[0,1,0] & \boxed{\text{i}} \\
[Head] & \text{to} \\
\\
[Comp] & \begin{bmatrix}
[Cat] & \text{VP} \\
[1,0] & \boxed{\text{i}} \\
[Head] & \text{know}
\end{bmatrix}
\end{bmatrix}
\end{bmatrix}
$$

Figure 18: S-graph for *I want to know*.

$$
\begin{bmatrix}
[1) & \boxed{\text{i}} \\
[Comp] & \begin{bmatrix} (1,\underline{0}] & \boxed{\text{i}} \end{bmatrix}
\end{bmatrix}
$$

Figure 19: Equi in Tabular Format

As shown in Figure 19, beyond the structure-sharing requirement, Equi has the following salient characteristics. The "controller (label)", [1) in the matrix clause, starts with 1, indicating the target is an initial 1, and hence the 1 of the predicate-argument structure of that clause. The open right bracket indicates that the controller might have other (follow-on) R-signs, determined by other rules. The occurrence of 0 on the right in the "controlled label", (1,$\underline{0}$] in the subordinate clause, represents the lack of a final 1 in the infinitive. Although the controlled label requires the penultimate R-sign to be 1, the open left bracket indicates that the controlled label might have other R-signs, whose presence would be dictated by other rules (e.g., by Passive as in *Tom wants to be promoted*). Notice that Equi justifies (only) the 0 in (1,$\underline{0}$].

Figure 20 depicts Raising in tabular format. As in Equi, the dual role of a single constituent is represented by structure-sharing. In contrast to

$$
\begin{bmatrix}
[0,1) & \boxed{\text{i}} \\
[Comp] & \begin{bmatrix} (1,\underline{0}] & \boxed{\text{i}} \end{bmatrix}
\end{bmatrix}
$$

Figure 20: Raising in Tabular Format

Equi, the "controller label", [0, 1), starts with 0, indicating the target plays
no role in the predicate-argument structure of that clause; the 1 in second
position indicates the target is "raised" as a 1; and the open right bracket
indicates that the raised constituent might bear other (follow-on) relations
in that clause not specified by Raising. The presence of 0 on the right in
the "controlled label", (1, 0] in the subordinate clause, represents the lack
of a final 1 in the infinitive, and the open left bracket the possibility that
the target might bear "earlier" relations in that clause. Notice that Raising
justifies the sequence 0,1 in [0, 1) as well as the 0 in (1, 0]. Thus, the data
justified by Equi and Raising differ.

We stress that the only differences in the statement of the two rules
are the difference in the first R-signs of the controller labels and the data
justified (the underlined material). Yet these minor distinctions capture
the relevant differences in these construction types.

Turning to a more complicated example, we present in Figures 21, 22, 23
and 24, the rules anchored by the verbs in *Tom wants to seem to understand.*
(We ignore the structure for the name *Tom*, which is essentially the same
as the structure for pronouns and is of little interest.) We will step through
these rules and explain how they account for all the structure except for
peripheral matters such as verb agreement, which we ignore.

First, consider the rule anchored by *wants (to)*, shown in Figure 21.
Here we see that *wants (to)* requires and *justifies* a clause that takes an
initial 1, indicated by the feature [1] (characteristic of "subject controlled
equi"), a head (anchored by *wants*), and a complement. The complement is
further required to be a VP, more specifically a VP headed by the auxiliary
verb *to*. We stress that none of this latter data is justified by this particular
rule (indicated by the lack of underlining): the rule for *wants (to)* merely
requires the presence of this data; the rule anchored by the verb *to* is
responsible for the justification of this data. Next, as the tag ⌈i⌉ indicates,
the initial 1 is required to be the same constituent as the final 1 of the
complement verb phrase. The fact that this complement 1 does not show
up in the surface graph is capture by the feature (1, 0]. Finally, notice that
the rule requires, but does not justify, the 1 in (1, 0], although it does both
require and justify the 0. This explicates the fact that *wants (to)* controls
a null subject in its complement, i.e., is an "Equi" verb.

Looking at Figure 22, we see that the verb *to* requires and justifies: a
verb phrase, a raised subject – characterized by the feature [0, 1) occurring
in the raising configuration (cf. Figure 20), the feature [*Head*] anchored by
to, a feature [*Comp*], and the 0 in the feature (1, 0] at the end of [*Comp*],
which is part of the raising configuration.

Notice that except for the presence of stratified features to capture the
multistratal relational structure, these characterizations are quite similar

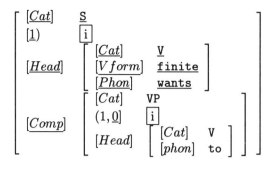

Figure 21: Rule Anchored by *wants (to)*.

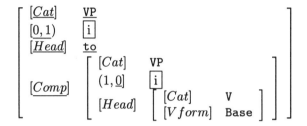

Figure 22: Rule Anchored by Infinitival *to*.

to other feature-structure descriptions commonly encountered in the literature.

Next, Figure 23 depicts the rule anchored by *seem (to)*. This is also a raising configuration and so needs no further explanation (once again, cf. Figure 20). However, we stress the importance of the distinction between open and closed ends of features in these partial descriptions: only open ends permit additional R-signs to be present in a complete description.

Finally, consider the rule anchored by *understand* as depicted in Figure 24. This rule indicates *understand* heads a VP requiring an initial 1. Further, as shown by the open right bracket in [1], there may be other follow-on relations (determined by other rules).

Finally, if we piece all of these separate descriptions together, it is not hard to see that the only fully justified S-graph is as shown in Figure 25. We have left out some details in the above discussion, but hopefully the interested reader can fill them in.

Every core datum of the S-graph displayed in Figure 25 is, with the exception of some minor details which we continue to ignore, justified by one of the rules associated with the words in the sentence. Consider, e.g.,

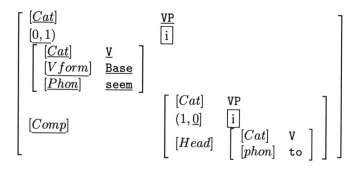

Figure 23: Rule Anchored by *seem (to)*.

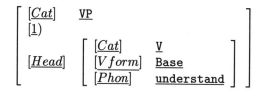

Figure 24: Rule Anchored by *understand*.

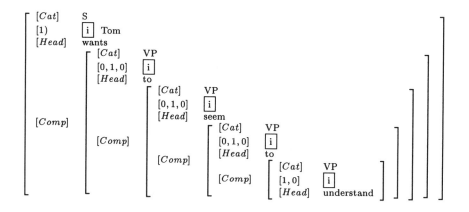

Figure 25: S-graph for *Tom wants to seem to understand*.

[0, 1, 0], which occurs in two places in the middle sector of Figure 25. The data corresponding to [0, 1) in these two occurrences of [0, 1, 0] is justified by Raising and that corresponding to (0] by Equi. Similar remarks apply to [1, 0] at the bottom; the 0 is justified by Raising, and the 1 by the rule anchored by *understand*. All the syntactic information is represented in a clean and compact fashion.

Note that we do not claim that semantic interpretation is completely determined by a sentence's predicate-argument structure. Instead, we assume that the *entire* S-graph is semantically interpreted. This makes information such as linear precedence available to whatever interpretation functions are required for anaphora resolution, quantifier scope determination, etc. Since S-graphs contain all the syntactic structure of a sentence, SFG has no need for "projection functions" like those postulated in LFG to make both surface information and functional structure accessible to semantic interpretation functions (cf. Halvorsen and Kaplan 1988).

3   The Formal Framework

Sections 3.1 and 3.2 define *S-graph* and the syntax and semantics of SFDL, the formal language used to write SFG rules. Most of the innovations in SFDL follow from our generalization of the notion *feature*. Section 2.6 gives a few examples to informally illustrate how SFDL can be used to describe S-graphs. The last section defines and motivates the SFG concept of data justification; this concept appears to have no analog in other feature logics, but could well prove useful in other settings.

3.1   Stratified Features and S-graphs Revisited

The SFG framework uses stratified feature graphs to represent syntactic structure. They are the analog of phrase markers, relational networks, metagraphs, f-structures, and feature structures. S-graphs differ from these primarily in permitting features (arc labels) to be sequences of R-signs. Indeed, features are arbitrarily long sequences drawn from a finite set. Of course, particular theories of grammar and particular grammars of a given class developed within SFG would in various ways restrict the class of admissible features, reflecting substantive linguistic assumptions. From this vantage point, ordinary (monadic) feature structures are simply the limiting case of a range of possibilities. Looked at dynamically, stratified features can be interpreted as providing a record of the relations a given constituent assumes in a phrase in the course of parsing or generation.

To develop a linguistically adequate feature-structure-based formalism for multistratal relational analyses requires more than just a *set* of R-sign sequences. We need a mechanism for stating linguistically motivated generalizations involving R-sign sequences. We provide this by (1) introducing an ordering on stratified features (very roughly, the natural extension ordering) and (2) using stratified features in *the language in which we write grammars*. The semantics of our SFG description language is based on the extension relation among features. SFG also makes use of a primitive notion of *unextendibility*; we shall want to interpret some sequences as extendible, and some as unextendible. At this point, we turn away from motivation to actual definitions.

A **(stratified) feature** (or **label**) is a sequence of R-signs which may be either closed on the left or right or both. We indicate closed sides with square brackets and open sides with parentheses; for example, $(1, 2]$ denotes a label that is open on the left and closed on the right, and $[3, 2, 1, 0]$ denotes a label that is closed on both sides. Labels denoted by expressions of the form $[\cdots]$ are called *(totally) closed*; by expressions of the form $(\cdots)$ *(totally) open*; and the others *partially closed (open)* or *closed (open) on the right (left)*, as appropriate. We use $\mathcal{F}$ to denote the set of features formed over $\mathcal{RS}^*$.

$\mathcal{F}$ is partially ordered by the smallest relation $\sqsubseteq$ which permits *extension* along open sides. For example,

$$(2) \quad \sqsubseteq \quad (0, 2, 1) \quad \sqsubseteq \quad [0, 2, 1) \quad \sqsubseteq \quad [0, 2, 1, 0) \quad \sqsubseteq \quad [0, 2, 1, 0] \, .$$

Another way to describe the partial order on $\mathcal{F}$ is in terms of embeddings. Let l and m be labels. An *embedding* of l into m is an occurrence of l as a substring of m, with the additional conditions that if l is closed on the left (right), then l must be an initial (final) segment of m. For example, there are two embeddings of $(0, 1)$ into $[2, 0, 1, 0, 1]$, and one embedding of $(0, 1]$ into $[2, 0, 1, 0, 1]$. Conversely, we would also say that $[2, 0, 1, 0, 1]$ is an *extension* of $(0, 1]$. The connection is: $l \sqsubseteq m$ iff there is at least one embedding of l into m. Notice that the totally closed labels are the *maximal* elements in the order.

At this point we have moved from sequences to a larger class, preparing the way for later definitions of stratified feature graphs, grammars and the mechanism by which grammars describe graphs. We observe in passing that the general concept of imposing an ordering on *features*, whether stratified or atomic, could prove useful in other frameworks. We now define *S-graph*.

Definition   Given finite sets $\mathcal{RS}$ of R-signs, $\mathcal{A}$ of atoms, and $V \subseteq \mathcal{A}$ of vocabulary items, a **stratified feature graph (S-graph)** is a finite directed graph $\langle \mathcal{N}, \mathcal{E} \rangle$ together with

(i) A total function $\texttt{arc-label} : \mathcal{E} \to \mathcal{F}$ (note that $\mathcal{F}$ is determined by $\mathcal{RS}$);

(ii) A total function node-label : $\mathcal{N} \to Power(\mathcal{A})$. We require that for any node n node-label(n) contains at most one $v \in V$;

(iii) A strict partial order $\prec$ on the arcs. We require that if $e \prec e'$, then e and e' are neighbors.

Note that according to (ii) above, for any node n node-label(n) is a *set*; *interior* (nonleaf) nodes can be node-labeled, and interior nodes can even be node-labeled with lexical items (maximum one lexical item each). Of course, a particular substantive linguistic theory built in SFG might further stipulate that only leaf nodes can be node-labeled with members of V. The looser provision, however, is useful in our formal studies and does not increase the generative capacity of the formalism.

A central concept of our work is *(data) justification*. The motivation behind this concept is familiar from constraint-based grammatical frameworks of all types: Grammars merely constrain a structure, but something must also insure that a structure does not contain "unaccounted-for" data. In SFG, stratified features add an extra dimension to this issue. Something is needed to insure that a structure will not have longer arc labels than a grammar calls for. Typically, constraint-based formalisms appeal to a notion of "minimal model": The smallest models satisfying a set of formulas are taken as the intended models. We propose an alternative. Alongside the standard model-theoretic notion of formula satisfaction, we introduce a distinct notion of data justification indicating which data of an S-graph are justifiably present on the basis of a formula (rule) being satisfied. The syntactic apparatus for determining which data are justified is introduced below. We then require in the definition of grammaticality, i.e., S-graph well-formedness, that beyond satisfying the rules of a grammar, all the "core" data – all node labelings, arc labelings and node identifications – of a well-formed S-graph be justified by some rule. Justification is a powerful concept and plays a key role in a number of our formal constructions described in Section 4. Although the definition of justification given here is tailored to SFG, the general concept may well be of use in other frameworks.

To prepare for the discussion of justification, we introduce the following. First, we enlarge the set of atoms by defining on the basis of $\mathcal{A}$ a set of *underlined* atoms $\underline{\mathcal{A}} = \{\underline{a} : a \in \mathcal{A}\}$ disjoint from $\mathcal{A}$ and then taking the complete set of atoms $\mathcal{CA}$ to be $\mathcal{A} \cup \underline{\mathcal{A}}$. Along with this we assume a function A-strip : $\mathcal{CA} \to \mathcal{A}$ that maps members of $\underline{\mathcal{A}}$ to their non-underlined counterparts in $\mathcal{A}$. Second, we expand the class of R-signs by defining on the basis of $\mathcal{RS}$ a set of *underlined* R-signs $\underline{\mathcal{RS}} = \{\underline{r} : r \in \mathcal{RS}\}$ disjoint from $\mathcal{RS}$. We then form the complete set of R-signs $\mathcal{CRS} = \mathcal{RS} \cup \underline{\mathcal{RS}}$. In a similar fashion, we next enlarge the set of features by defining on the basis of $\mathcal{F}$ a set $\mathcal{BF}$ of *basic* features as the set of strings over $\mathcal{CRS}^*$, which, as before, may be either closed on the left or right or both. Note that $\mathcal{F} \subseteq \mathcal{BF}$ and the set of *underlined* features is then $\mathcal{BF} \backslash \mathcal{F}$. For example, $(2,1)$, $(2,\underline{1})$, $[2,1,0)$ and $(2,\underline{1},\underline{0}]$ are all members of $\mathcal{BF}$.

The next step is to extend $\sqsubseteq$ to include the larger set of labels $\mathcal{BF}$. The resulting extension will only be a preorder; and we will overload our notation by also using $\sqsubseteq$ for this preorder. (Recall a preorder is transitive and reflexive but, unlike a partial order, not antisymmetric.) To help state the definition, we assume a function $\mathtt{Strip} : \mathcal{BF} \to \mathcal{F}$ that maps a label $\underline{l}$ in $\mathcal{BF}$ to its counterpart l in $\mathcal{F}$. Then, the definition is: Given l_1 and l_2 in $\mathcal{BF}$,

$$l_1 \sqsubseteq l_2 \qquad \text{iff} \qquad \mathtt{Strip}(l_1) \sqsubseteq \mathtt{Strip}(l_2).$$

$\mathcal{BF}$ is not partially ordered under $\sqsubseteq$ since, e.g., both $(2,1) \sqsubseteq (2,\underline{1})$ and $(2,\underline{1}) \sqsubseteq (2,1)$ by the above definition, but these are different labels. Here are some examples of the preorder:

$$(2) \quad \sqsubseteq \quad (0,2,\underline{1}) \quad \sqsubseteq \quad [0,\underline{2},\underline{1}) \quad \sqsubseteq \quad [0,2,1,0) \quad \sqsubseteq \quad [0,2,\underline{1},\underline{0}] \ .$$

The idea behind this ordering is that each feature l subsuming a feature f provides a partial description of f. Because f is more defined, we write $l \sqsubseteq f$. The features which are maximal in this ordering are therefore completely defined. The move from a collection of totally defined objects, the primary objects of interest, to a larger class of partially defined objects is familiar from many areas.

Open and closed brackets allow us to say that a given description is or is not complete in a given direction (here we often say a description can or cannot be "extended"). Put differently, the function of closed brackets is to permit reference to the endpoints of closed features. The left-closed bracket [allows reference to the "deepest" (technically, *initial*) R-sign of a closed feature; the right-closed bracket] to the "most surfacy" (technically, *final*) R-sign of a closed feature.

Remarks on Definitions and Terminology

Those readers familiar with RG may have noticed that we have not defined labels like $(1,\ldots,3]$. This would say of an arc that it is a final 3 and an "earlier" 1. A few RG analyses have, in fact, appealed to notions such as "working 1" (defined as "a final term that is a 1 at some stratum"). If "working 1" is required and the above definition is the correct formulation, then the SFG formalism would have to be expanded to allow for such concepts. Also, as the definition of "working 1" illustrates, RG definitions sometimes refer to classes of R-signs, e.g., *term*(1, 2 or 3), *nuclear term*(1 or 2), and *object*(2 or 3). Names of finite classes of R-signs are equivalent to finite disjunctions, and so would not involve expanding the basic expressive power of the SFG formalism. Both kinds of additions would be straight-forward to make, but since they do not bear on any central issues, we have left them out of this presentation.

To avoid any possible confusion, we stress that while we informally use terms such as "earlier", "later", "extension", "extend", "deep", "surface", and sometimes talk about a rule "applying" (for "is satisfied or holds"), SFG is a *nonderivational* framework. Similar disclaimers hold for the in-formal usage of RG terms such as "revaluation", "advance", "demote", etc. We feel that such terminology is suggestive, but would not wish anyone to take this as indicating SFG is in any sense inherently derivational.

3.2 The SFG Description Language

SFDL Syntax and Semantics

The SFG rule writing language, SFDL, is a generalization of a standard version of the KR formalism. Here we assume familiarity with KR-style formalisms. (For readers wishing more background on this, we recommend Kasper and Rounds 1986, Kasper and Rounds 1990, Moshier and Rounds 1986, Rounds and Kasper 1986, Gazdar et al. 1988, and Johnson 1988.)

Syntax of $\mathcal{D}$

Before defining the syntax of $\mathcal{D}$, we must introduce a few more def-initions. First we extend the KR formalism so that labels in formulas can work "backwards" as well as "forwards". That is, we want to de-fine a class of rules that can "look up" arcs from target to source nodes. Without inverse labels we could not state the Lexical Anchoring Principle, since this requires allowing lexical leaf nodes to satisfy formulas other than Boolean combinations of atoms (cf. Section 4). To enable this we define a set $\mathcal{IL} = \{l^{-1} : l \in \mathcal{BF}\}$ of *inverse labels* that is in one-to-one corre-spondence with and disjoint from $\mathcal{BF}$. The union of $\mathcal{BF}$ and $\mathcal{IL}$ forms the complete set $\mathcal{CL}$ of labels.

The class of formulas of $\mathcal{D}$ is then defined on the basis of the complete set of labels $\mathcal{CL}$ and the complete set of atoms $\mathcal{CA}$. $\mathcal{D}$ is the smallest set containing as atomic formulas:

(A) T;

(B) each $\mathbf{a} \in \mathcal{CA}$;

(C) $l_1 l_2 \cdots l_n \doteq m_1 m_2 \cdots m_r$, where $l_1, l_2, \ldots, l_n$ and $m_1, m_2, \ldots, m_r$ are two sequences of labels in $\mathcal{CL}$ (**path equations**);

(D) $f \prec g$, for all labels $f, g \in \mathcal{F}$ (**linear precedence statements**);

and closed under the following formation rules:

(i) if $\phi \in \mathcal{D}$ and $l \in \mathcal{CL}$, then $l : \phi \in \mathcal{D}$ (**label prefixing**);

(ii) if ϕ, $\psi \in \mathcal{D}$, then so are $\phi \wedge \psi$; $\phi \vee \psi$; $\phi \rightarrow \psi$; and $\neg\phi$ (**Boolean operations**)

We often abbreviate $\neg(l : \mathrm{T})$ as $l : \mathrm{F}$; and more generally for $\neg(l_1 : (\cdots(l_k : \mathrm{T})\cdots))$, we write $l_1 : \cdots l_k : \mathrm{F}$. We stress that this convention is not standard, but is quite useful in practice. (KR-style languages often have a primitive atomic formula NIL (or F), which can never be satisfied.) Using the present convention, one can state the condition that a clause is "final intransitive" (has a final 1 but no final 2) as

$$(1] : \mathrm{T} \ \wedge \ (2] : \mathrm{F} \ .$$

An "initially intransitive" clause (has an initial 1 but no initial 2) can be described by

$$[1) : \mathrm{T} \ \wedge \ [2) : \mathrm{F} \ .$$

Semantics of $\mathcal{D}$

Atoms, T and Labeled Formulas   The formulas $\mathbf{a} \in \mathcal{CA}$ and T are interpreted on S-graphs in a standard way:

$$n \models_G \mathrm{T} \qquad \text{always};$$

$$n \models_G \mathbf{a} \qquad \text{iff} \qquad \mathbf{A\text{-}strip(a)} \in \mathbf{node\text{-}label}(n) \ .$$

The semantics for labeled formulas is more subtle, but is still basically a generalization of the standard approach. First, recall the semantics for labeled formulas in standard KR formalisms. One defines a transition function $\delta_0 : \mathcal{N} \times \mathcal{F} \rightarrow \mathcal{N}$ on a graph G, using the functionality of features. Then the definition is:

$$n \models_G l : \phi \qquad \text{iff} \qquad \delta_0(n, l)\!\downarrow \quad \text{and} \quad \delta_0(n, l) \models_G \phi \ .$$

(Note that for a given partial function F and arguments w, $F(w)\!\downarrow$ means that F is defined on w. Also, the notation $F(w) \simeq y$ means $F(w)\!\downarrow$ and $F(w) = y$.)

Now δ_0 is not sufficient for our purposes. The key to the SFG formalism is that labels in rules may only *partially* describe features in S-graphs. Moreover, we need to permit labels containing underlined R-signs and inverse labels to describe S-graph features.

To accommodate the first extension, we generalize δ_0 to a function $\underline{\delta}$: $\mathcal{N} \times \mathcal{BF} \to \mathcal{N}$, where $\mathcal{N}$ is the set of nodes of a given S-graph G, by

$$\underline{\delta}(n, f) \simeq m \quad \text{iff} \quad \text{for some } unique \ g, \ g \sqsupseteq f \text{ and } \delta_0(n, g) \simeq m \ .$$

Then we define $n \models_G l : \phi$ for $l \in \mathcal{BF}$, using $\underline{\delta}$:

For all $l \in \mathcal{BF}, \ n \models_G l : \phi \qquad \text{iff} \qquad \underline{\delta}(n, l){\downarrow} \quad \text{and} \quad \underline{\delta}(n, l) \models_G \phi \ .$

In effect, we have implicitly introduced existential quantification over $\mathcal{F}$ into the definition of the satisfaction predicate. However, we have maintained functionality by the uniqueness requirement in the definition of $\underline{\delta}$.

The next step is to define on the basis of $\mathcal{IL}$ and a given S-graph G, a transition function $\delta^{-1} : \mathcal{N} \times \mathcal{IL} \to \mathcal{N}$ by

$$\delta^{-1}(n, l^{-1}) \simeq m \quad \text{iff} \quad \text{for some } unique \ m', \ \underline{\delta}(m', l) \simeq n \quad \text{and} \quad m' = m.$$

Given δ^{-1}, the semantics for formulas prefixed with inverse labels is:

For all $l \in \mathcal{IL}, \ n \models_G l : \phi \qquad \text{iff} \qquad \delta^{-1}(n, l){\downarrow} \quad \text{and} \quad \delta^{-1}(n, l) \models_G \phi \ .$

To simplify the following presentation, we collapse $\underline{\delta}$ and δ^{-1} into a single function $\delta : \mathcal{N} \times \mathcal{CL} \to \mathcal{N}$ by

$$\delta(n, l) \simeq m \quad \text{iff} \quad \text{either } l \in \mathcal{BF} \text{ and } \underline{\delta}(n, l) \simeq m \text{ or } l \in \mathcal{IL} \text{ and } \delta^{-1}(n, l) \simeq m \ .$$

This permits the following single statement of the semantics of labeled formulas, for all labels in $\mathcal{CL}$:

$$n \models_G l : \phi \qquad \text{iff} \qquad \delta(n, l){\downarrow} \quad \text{and} \quad \delta(n, l) \models_G \phi \ .$$

Equations An equation is an expression of the form $l_1 l_2 \cdots l_n \doteq m_1 m_2 \cdots m_r$. Formally, it is just a pair of sequences of labels in $\mathcal{CL}$. As is standard in feature-based formalisms, we use equations to state structure-sharing conditions.

In giving their semantics, as in KR logics, we first extend δ to a map δ' on $\mathcal{N} \times \mathcal{CL}^*$ by composition in the usual way. So using ϵ for the empty string, we have $\delta'(n, \epsilon) \simeq n$ for all n. Also, if $f \in \mathcal{CL}$ and $w \in \mathcal{CL}^*$, then $\delta'(n, fw) \simeq \delta'(\delta(n, f), w)$. Following the usual convention, we write δ for δ' in the sequel. Now the definition is:

$$n \models_G v \doteq w \quad \text{iff} \quad \delta(n, v) \simeq \delta(n, w) \ .$$

It is important to see that in the case of partially ordered labels, the arc labels may be more informative ($\sqsupseteq$) than the ones listed in the sequences v and w.

Linear Precedence Statements A linear precedence formula is an expression of the form $l_1 \prec l_2$, where l_1, l_2 are in $\mathcal{F}$. Here $\prec$ is a binary relation symbol, denoting a strict partial order $\prec$ on the *arcs* of an S-graph. Recall that the definition of S-graph includes a $\prec$ relation and requires that if (e_1, e_2) are members of $\prec$, then they must be neighbors. As the name implies, linear precedence statements are used in rules determining word order and so play a central role in the definitions of *yield* and *SFG language*. For instance, the formula $[1] \prec [Head]$ says that an arc whose label has a *final 1* precedes any neighboring arc whose label is $[Head]$. Or more informally, "final 1's precede Head's".

To facilitate the discussion, we introduce the following. Let $\mathcal{N}$ and $\mathcal{E}$ be the respective sets of nodes and arcs in a given S-graph. We define a four-place relation $n \overset{l,e}{\to} m$ on $\mathcal{N} \times \mathcal{BF} \times \mathcal{E} \times \mathcal{N}$ by:

$$n \overset{l,e}{\to} m \quad \text{iff} \quad e \text{ is an arc from } n \text{ to } m \text{ such that } l \sqsubseteq \texttt{arc-label}(e) .$$

Now the semantics for $\prec$ is:

$$n \models_G l \prec l' \quad \text{iff} \quad e \prec e', \text{ whenever } e \text{ and } e' \text{ are such that for some } m$$
$$\text{and } m', \, n \overset{l,e}{\to} m \text{ and } n \overset{l',e'}{\to} m' .$$

Although labels in linear precedence formulas are drawn only from $\mathcal{F}$, we have defined the above relation in terms of $\mathcal{BF}$ since this will be needed for the semantics of extension formulas.

Extension Formulas In this section we define a new class of atomic formulas which makes sense only in the context of stratified features. These permit the formal statement of an analog to the informal RG notion "revaluation" and the formal MGG notion "local successor". The full language SFDL is then $\mathcal{D}$ plus the set of extension formulas.

The simplest extension formula has the form:

$$l : \phi \mapsto l' : \phi, \text{where} \quad l, l' \in \mathcal{BF} \text{ and } l \sqsubseteq l'.$$

For example,

$$(2) : \texttt{T} \mapsto (2,\underline{1}) : \texttt{T}$$

is a (unary) extension formula.

The intent here can be expressed roughly as "some arc with a 2 has a unique extension 2,1". (Note that from now on we will freely shorten the phrase "arc with a label with ..." as we have above.) The underlined R-signs in these formulas indicate which corresponding R-signs in features are justified, if the formula is indeed satisfied.

Before turning to the formal semantics of extension formulas, we define the general case. An *extension* formula is any statement of the form:

$$l_1 : \phi_1 \wedge \cdots \wedge l_k : \phi_k \mapsto l_1' : \phi_1' \wedge \cdots \wedge l_k' : \phi_k' \, ,$$

where for $1 \leq i \leq k$, $l_i, l_i' \in \mathcal{BF}$ and $l_i \sqsubseteq l_i'$. The intent of this is most easily grasped through an example:

$$(2) : \mathrm{T} \wedge (1) : \mathrm{T} \mapsto (2, \underline{1}) : \mathrm{T} \wedge (1, \underline{8}) : \mathrm{T}.$$

The above example is essentially the SFG rendering of the traditional RG analysis of Passive. The linguistic interpretation of the above formula is basically "some *pair* of edges with a 2 and a 1 respectively can have unique respective extensions 2,1 and 1,8 ". That is, we want to insure that the atomic formulas $(2) : \mathrm{T}$ and $(1) : \mathrm{T}$ are satisfied only by distinct arcs (the labels themselves do not guarantee this). Thus, extension formulas implicitly quantify over sets of arcs. Quite informally, the above extension formula might be paraphrased as "a 2 and a 1 extend (revaluate) to a 1 and an 8 respectively".

We observe in passing that the general k-ary definition is far stronger than any substantive linguistic theory would require. In fact, RG statements typically seem to require at most binary extensions. This is thus another area in which a linguistic theory could restrict the formalism. It is also important to notice that under the intended interpretation, the conditions on the left do not have to be met uniquely, but the respective extensions on the right do. The motivation behind this can be understood by considering two rules, e.g., Dative and Passive, whose left-hand side conditions partly overlap:

$$\textbf{Passive} \stackrel{\text{def}}{=} (2) : \mathrm{T} \wedge (1) : \mathrm{T} \mapsto (2, \underline{1}) : \mathrm{T} \wedge [1, \underline{8}) : \mathrm{T} \, ;$$

$$\textbf{Dative} \stackrel{\text{def}}{=} (2) : \mathrm{T} \wedge (3) : \mathrm{T} \mapsto (2, \underline{8}) : \mathrm{T} \wedge (3, \underline{2}) : \mathrm{T} \, .$$

Both of these rules have the atomic formula $(2) : T$ on the left; but they differ in their extensions on the right: $(2, \underline{1}) : \mathrm{T}$ (Passive) versus $(2, \underline{8}) : \mathrm{T}$

(Dative). If uniqueness were required on the left, then at most one of these rule could be satisfied at a given node. But of course this is, in general, false, as illustrated by the standard RG analysis of "Dative-Passives" such as *Mary was given tea by Joe*. However, quite crucially, uniqueness can be required on the right. Put differently, if uniqueness were required on the left, then Passive and Dative would have to be combined into one rule. From the standpoint of linguistic theory, this seems undesirable, so we prefer the formulation above.

In order to state the semantics properly, we define a version of the $\underline{\delta}$ function that explicitly references arcs: $\underline{\delta}_e : \mathcal{N} \times \mathcal{BF} \times \mathcal{E} \to \mathcal{N}$, by

$$\underline{\delta}_e(n, l, e) \simeq m \quad \text{iff} \quad n \overset{l,e}{\to} m \text{ and } \underline{\delta}(n, l) \simeq m .$$

(Note that $\underline{\delta}$ on the right of the definition insures that e is unique.) The semantics for extension formulas is:

$$n \models_G l_1 : \phi_1 \wedge \cdots \wedge l_k : \phi_k \mapsto l_1' : \phi_1' \wedge \cdots \wedge l_k' : \phi_k' \quad \text{iff}$$

the following condition holds:

If $e_1, \cdots, e_k$ are distinct arcs such that for $1 \leq i \leq k$, $n \overset{l_i, e_i}{\to} m$ for some m and $m \models_G \phi_i$, then for each i, there exists e_i' such that $\underline{\delta}_e(n, e_i', l_i') \simeq m'$ for some m', and $m' \models_G \phi_i'$.

It is hopefully clear the Boolean conjunction of k unary extension formulas is *not* equivalent to a k-ary extension formula. For instance: the extension formula

$$\mathbf{A} \quad \overset{\text{def}}{=} \quad (2) : \text{T} \wedge (1) : \text{T} \mapsto (2, \underline{1}) : \text{T} \wedge (1, \underline{8}) : \text{T}$$

is not equivalent to

$$\mathbf{B} \quad \overset{\text{def}}{=} \quad ((2) : \text{T} \mapsto (2, \underline{1}) : \text{T}) \wedge ((1) : \text{T} \mapsto (1, \underline{8}) : \text{T}) .$$

The reason is that k-ary conjunction of unary extension formulas does not require the arcs to be distinct. So, a single arc with label $(1, 8, 2, 1)$ could satisfy statement $\mathbf{B}$ but not $\mathbf{A}$.

The syntax of extension formulas is somewhat redundant and awkward insofar as each label l_i on the left necessarily embeds into the respective label l_i' on the right. Therefore, whenever each ϕ_i' on the right is identical to ϕ_i on the left and the additional R-signs on the right are all underlined, we typically abbreviate the formula by writing only the material on the right, replacing "∧" with "&", or if the formula is unary, prefixing the consequent with &. So the rule Passive would be abbreviated as

$$(2, \underline{1}) : \text{T} \ \& \ (1, \underline{8}) : \text{T} \ .$$

The RG unaccusative construction can be characterized by the formula

$$[1] : \text{F} \rightarrow \ \& \ [2, \underline{1}) : \text{T} \ .$$

Observe that this rule is a material implication whose consequent is a *unary* extension formula. The gist of this rule is: "If there is no initial 1, then *assuming there is an initial 2*, there must also be a unique 2,1". More informally, "If there is no initial 1, advance an initial 2 to 1".

Boolean Connectives The semantics of the boolean connectives is as in classical logic. However, this is slightly misleading because in SFG, semantics comes along with an independent feature of *justification*, which we consider in the next subsection. In this sense, for example, $\phi \rightarrow \psi$ is not completely equivalent to $\neg \phi \vee \psi$. Although the semantics of satisfaction are the same, the justification conditions of the two formula types differ.

The semantics of the various SFDL formulas is summarized in Figure 26. Before leaving this subsection we introduce the following locution: For any formula ϕ, if a node n of an S-graph G is such that $n \models_G \phi$, we say that n **anchors** ϕ (in G).

3.3 Justification

There is a crucial issue that arises in the context of SFG (but not in the context of ordinary feature-structure formalisms): R-signs in labels of arcs of well-formed S-graphs must be "linked" in a linguistically motivated way. That is, each pair of adjacent R-signs in a sequence has to be related in a formally specified way via the rules of the grammar. This formal condition corresponds to the usage in RG of terms such as "revaluation" (and sometimes "advancement" or "demotion", depending on whether the second R-sign in a pair is or is not higher on the relational hierarchy $1 > 2 > 3 > Oblique$). A partially corresponding MGG term is "(local) successor". To illustrate, if an arc has the label $[3, 2, 1, 0]$, it is not sufficient for one rule, say Dative (Advancement), to justify the subsequence 3,2 and another, say Raising, to justify the subsequence 1,0. Although these two rules might collectively seem to justify all four R-signs, this is, in view of the linguistic ideas we are explicating, not sufficient. There must also be some rule, say Passive, justifying the subsequence 2,1. That is, the linguistic information implicit in the notion *R-sign sequence* must also be justified.

Informally speaking, we wish to distinguish between data "presupposed" true for a rule ϕ to hold, versus data "asserted" to hold on the basis of ϕ

SFDL Formula	Semantics
$n \models_G \top$	always
$n \models_G a$	iff `A-strip(a)` $\in$ `node-label`(n)
$n \models_G l : \phi$	iff $\delta(n,l)\downarrow$ and $\delta(n,l) \models_G \phi$
$n \models_G v \doteq w$	iff $\delta(n,v) \simeq \delta(n,w)$
$n \models_G\ l_1 : \phi_1 \wedge \cdots \wedge l_k : \phi_k \mapsto$ $l_1' : \phi_1' \wedge \cdots \wedge l_k' : \phi_k'$	iff the following holds: If $e_1, \cdots, e_k$ are distinct arcs such that for $1 \leq i \leq k$, $n \overset{l_i,e_i}{\to} m$ for some m and $m \models_G \phi_i$, then for each i, there exists e_i' such that $\underline{\delta}_e(n, e_i', l_i') \simeq m'$ for some m', and $m' \models_G \phi_i'$.
$n \models_G\ l \prec l'$	iff $e \prec e'$, whenever e and e' are such that for some m and m', $n \overset{l,e}{\to} m$ and $n \overset{l',e'}{\to} m'$
$n \models_G \phi \wedge \psi$	iff $n \models_G \phi$ and $n \models_G \psi$
$n \models_G \phi \vee \psi$	iff $n \models_G \phi$ or $n \models_G \psi$
$n \models_G \phi \to \psi$	iff $n \models_G \phi$ implies $n \models_G \psi$
$n \models_G \neg\phi$	iff $n \not\models_G \phi$

Figure 26: Semantics of SFDL

being satisfied. We call the latter *justified data*. To a first approximation, the R-signs and atoms in an S-graph G justified by an atomic or labeled formula ϕ that is true at some node n of G are those corresponding to whatever R-signs and atoms are underlined in ϕ. This is the functional distinction between underlined R-signs and atoms and their non-underlined counterparts – only members of $\underline{\mathcal{F}}$ and $\underline{\mathcal{A}}$ can justify data. In Figure 27 we present partial descriptions of some English constructions, illustrating the concept of justifying data.

We can use the syntactic mechanism of underlining to solve the hypothetical problem posed above concerning the justification of the label $[3, 2, 1, 0]$. On the assumption that the only rules applicable in this instance are $(3, \underline{2})$ of Dative and $(1, \underline{0})$ of Raising, the justified parts of the label would be as indicated in $[3, \underline{2}, 1, \underline{0}]$. Since 3 and 1 are not justified, for $[3, 2, 1, 0]$ to be totally justified, other rules would have to apply. If the right conditions were met, Passive could justify the 1. The 3 would presumably have to be justified by a rule stating that the clause that $[3, 2, 1, 0]$ occurs in takes an initial 3.

Construction	Formula	Example
Passive	$(2, \underline{1}) : \mathrm{T} \ \& \ [1, \underline{8}] : \mathrm{T}$	*Joe was hired by Mary*
Unaccusative	$[1] : \mathrm{F} \rightarrow \ \& \ [2, \underline{1}) : \mathrm{T}$	*Glass breaks*
Dative	$(3, \underline{2}) : \mathrm{T} \ \& \ (2, \underline{8}) : \mathrm{T}$	*Joe gave Mary tea*
Dative-Passive	$(3, \underline{2}, 1) : \mathrm{T} \ \& \ (2, \underline{8}) : \mathrm{T} \ \& \ [1, \underline{8}] : \mathrm{T}$	*Mary was given tea by Joe*
Raising	$[\underline{0}, 1) \doteq [\overline{Comp}](1, \underline{0}]$	*Tom seems to understand*
Equi	$[1) \doteq [\overline{Comp}](1, \underline{0}]$	*I want to know*

Figure 27: Some Analyses Showing Justified Data

We define **Justification** for the full set of formulas by the recursion in Figure 28. (Note that each conditional line in the definition is to be understood as implicitly having the exclusionary case "otherwise nothing" at the end.) It is important to note that data are justified by a formula ϕ *only* on the assumption that ϕ is satisfied. We further emphasize that (i) only the consequents of extension formulas ($\phi \mapsto \psi$) and conditionals ($\phi \rightarrow \psi$) can justify data and (ii) the consequents of such formulas can only justify data *provided their antecedents hold*. That is, if such a formula holds vacuously at some node, then it justifies no data there. (Incidentally, this is the reason why we take all of the different Boolean connectives as primitives. The different conditions of justification are not interdefinable.) The fact that antecedents of conditionals and extensions cannot justify data also shows that there is no point in having underlined R-signs in their antecedents.

To facilitate our later presentation, we define the **core data** of an S-graph to be the node-labelings (each atom token), arc-labelings (each R-sign occurrence of each feature token), and node identifications (each instance of structure-sharing). (Requiring structure-sharing to be justified means that SFG does not require an "inequality" relation in S-graphs to prevent satisfying graphs from having structure sharing not required by the grammar; cf. Carpenter 1990.)

Given this definition, we can state the basic **justification requirement** for the *unrestricted* framework as: In order that an S-graph G satisfy a grammar $\mathcal{G}$, it is necessary that each core datum of G be justified by some formula (rule) ϕ of $\mathcal{G}$. In the restricted framework, it is further required that ϕ be anchored by some *lexical* node of G, by which we mean a node node-labeled with an element of V.

We must go into detail concerning the justification of node identifications. For example, consider a rule $\left([4] : ([\underline{1}] \doteq [2]) \right) \wedge \left([4] : ([\underline{2}] \doteq [3]) \right)$, and a node n which satisfies it. Then the identification of $\delta(n, [4][1])$ and

True Assertion	Justified Data
$n \models_G \mathbf{T}$	nothing
$n \models_G \mathbf{a}$	provided $\mathbf{a} \in \mathcal{A}$, that A-strip(a) $\in$ node-label(n)
$n \models_G l : \phi$	the R-sign occurrences corresponding to their underlined counterparts in l and whatever $\delta(n,l) \models_G \phi$ justifies
$n \models_G p \doteq q$	whatever $n \models_G p : \mathbf{T}$ and $n \models_G q : \mathbf{T}$ justify, and that $\delta(n,p) = \delta(n,q)$
$n \models_G \phi \mapsto \psi$	provided $n \models_G \phi$, whatever $n \models_G \psi$ justifies
$n \models_G l \prec l'$	nothing
$n \models_G \phi \wedge \psi$	whatever $n \models_G \phi$ and $n \models_G \psi$ justify
$n \models_G \phi \vee \psi$	provided $n \models_G \phi$, whatever $n \models_G \phi$ justifies; and provided $n \models_G \psi$, whatever $n \models_G \psi$ justifies
$n \models_G \phi \rightarrow \psi$	provided $n \models_G \phi$, whatever $n \models_G \psi$ justifies
$n \models_G \neg\phi$	nothing

Figure 28: Justification Definition

$\delta(n, [4][3])$ should be justified even though it is not explicitly stated. Moreover, so is the identification of $\delta(\delta(n, [4]), [1])$ and $\delta(\delta(n, [4]), [3])$. The node identifications of G are justified as follows: Let E be the set of triples (n, p, q) where n is a node of G, and there is some rule of $\mathcal{G}$ which justifies $\delta(n, p) \doteq \delta(n, q)$ according to Figure 28. Let $\bar{E}$ be the closure of E under the laws of KR logic. That is, $\bar{E}$ is the smallest set such that $E \subseteq \bar{E}$ which satisfies the following properties, for all nodes n of G, all paths p, q, and r:

(i) $(n, \epsilon, \epsilon) \in \bar{E}$

(ii) If $(n, p, q) \in \bar{E}$, then $(n, q, p) \in \bar{E}$

(iii) If $(n, p, q) \in \bar{E}$ and $(n, q, r) \in \bar{E}$, then $(n, p, r) \in \bar{E}$

(iv) $(\delta(n, r), p, q) \in \bar{E}$ if and only if $(n, rp, rq) \in \bar{E}$

(v) If $(n, p, q) \in \bar{E}$ and $\delta(n, pr)\!\downarrow$, then $(n, pr, qr) \in \bar{E}$

The conditions above are based on the axiomatization of the validities of KR logic found in Moss (1992). Indeed they correspond to laws of KR logic. They are the natural choice for our definition of justification because they are obtained from a completeness theorem for a logical system having to do with node identifications.

We say that the node identification $\delta(n,p) \simeq \delta(n,q)$ is justified by $\mathcal{G}$ iff $(n,p,q) \in \bar{E}$. We should note that our justification requirement is that all node identifications be justified. If G has directed cycles, then there are infinitely many node identifications so at first glance this condition looks as though it might not be possible to check it effectively. However, it is sufficient to check the finitely many *irreducible* identifications. These are the identifications $\delta(n,p) \doteq \delta(n,q)$ such that there is no pair (p',q') such that either p' or q' is a proper subword of p or q, respectively, and such that $\delta(n,p') \doteq \delta(n,q')$. The set of irreducible identifications of an S-graph may be computed from the graph in polynomial time.

Coupled with the principles of lexical anchoring and boundedness, introduced below, Justification plays a crucial role in putting a bound on the size (number of arcs and nodes plus total length of all features) of a well-formed S-graph having a sentence string σ in its yield by a linear function of the number of words in σ. Thus, Justification, which was originally introduced to solve the problem of R-sign linking, also provides the basis for formulating a computationally realizable version of SFG. That is, given Justification, we have no need to appeal to a separate notion of *minimal model* to pare down the class of satisfying models to the desired ones. Justification plays a crucial role in many of the proofs below.

3.4 SFG Grammars and Languages

SFG Grammars and Grammaticality

We are now ready to state the definitions of *stratified feature grammar* and *grammaticality* (i.e., satisfaction of a grammar by an S-graph). The definition involves a set $\mathcal{NR}$ of null R-signs which underlies the definitions of *yield of an S-graph* and *SFG language*, two related topics addressed in the next section.

Definition Fix finite sets $\mathcal{CA}$ of atoms, $V \subseteq \mathcal{CA}$ of lexical items, $\mathcal{CRS}$ of R-signs, and $\mathcal{NR} \subset \mathcal{CRS}$ of null R-signs. A rule is a formula of SFDL built from $\mathcal{CA}$ and $\mathcal{CRS}$, and let $\mathcal{R}$ be the set of such rules. A **Stratified Feature Grammar** is a finite subset $\mathcal{G} \subseteq \mathcal{R}$. An S-graph G (over V, $\mathcal{A}$ and $\mathcal{RS}$ determined above) **satisfies** $\mathcal{G}$ iff

(i) Each node of G satisfies each rule of $\mathcal{G}$;

(ii) Each core datum of G is justified by some rule of $\mathcal{G}$.

SFG Languages

We next discuss the mechanism whereby an S-graph gives rise to one or more strings of lexical items (members of V). This issue is nontrivial, since there is no necessary requirement that S-graphs have a tree-like structure. We say a pair $(G, \mathcal{NR})$ consisting of an S-graph G together with a set of null R-signs satisfies the **Tree Property** if there is a *root node* n of G such that if the arcs whose labels end in *null* R-signs are deleted from G, then the resulting S-graph is a tree $\mathcal{T}$ rooted at n. Moreover, $\mathcal{T}$ contains every node of G *having a label belonging to* V.

As a special case of this, if $\mathcal{NR} = \emptyset$, then $(G, \mathcal{NR})$ satisfies the Tree Property if and only if G is a tree.

Let $\mathcal{T}$ be a tree. A $\mathcal{T}$-*order* is a strict partial order $\prec$ on the arcs of $\mathcal{T}$ such that if $e \prec e'$, then e and e' are neighbors. Note that a *maximal* $\mathcal{T}$-order linearly orders the sets of neighboring arcs. If $\prec$ is maximal, then we can use it to traverse $\mathcal{T}$ by depth-first search. We write $df(\mathcal{T}, \prec)$ for this depth-first listing of the *lexical* nodes of $\mathcal{T}$. Recall that nothing in the definition of S-graph requires lexical nodes to be leaf nodes; this is carried over in the current definition. Finally, if $\prec$ is any $\mathcal{T}$-order, we define

$$yield(\mathcal{T}, \prec) \quad = \quad \{\sigma : \text{for some maximal} \ll \text{extending} \prec, \sigma = df(\mathcal{T}, \ll)\} \, .$$

Now we define the **yield** of a pair $(G, \mathcal{NR})$ which satisfies the Tree Property: Regard G as a tree by deleting the arcs whose labels end in null R-signs; take the relation $\prec$ on this tree (this is part of the S-graph), and apply the definition above. Notice that the second condition of the Tree Property – that every node of G labeled with a member of V must be in $\mathcal{T}$ – insures that every vocabulary item occurrence will be in each string in G's yield.

The **language** $\mathcal{L}(\mathcal{G})$ determined by $\mathcal{G}$ is the set of strings σ over V such that there is an S-graph (over the sets V, $\mathcal{A}$ and $\mathcal{RS}$ determined by $\mathcal{G}$) which satisfies $\mathcal{G}$ and the Tree property and whose yield includes σ.

It can now be seen that so-called "free word order" within constituents is characterized in SFG in the simplest possible manner – by absence of grammatical statement.

3.5   A Stratified Feature Grammar for $\{a^{2^n - 1} : n \geq 1\}$.

In this section, we present a simple SFG $\mathcal{G}$ whose language is $\{a^{2^n - 1} : n \geq 1\}$. (With minor changes, we could also get a grammar for $\{a^{2^n} : n \in N\}$.) We take the set of atoms to be

$$\{a, b, \textit{first-of-row}, \textit{last-of-row}\},$$

the set of vocabulary items to be $\{a\}$, and the set of R-signs to be $\{1, 2, next\}$, where *next* is a null R-sign. (We write *next* instead of 0 because it is more meaningful in the picture.) Our set of rules is as follows:

$$root \rightarrow \underline{first\text{-}of\text{-}row} \wedge \underline{last\text{-}of\text{-}row} \tag{1}$$

$$\neg last\text{-}of\text{-}row \rightarrow [\underline{next}] : \text{T} \tag{2}$$

$$b \rightarrow \underline{b} \tag{3}$$

$$b \wedge \neg last\text{-}of\text{-}row \rightarrow [next] : b \tag{4}$$

$$b \wedge \neg first\text{-}of\text{-}row \rightarrow [next]^{-1} : b \tag{5}$$

$$\neg b \rightarrow ([\underline{1}] : \text{T}) \wedge ([\underline{2}] : \text{T}) \tag{6}$$

$$first\text{-}of\text{-}row \wedge \neg b \rightarrow [1] : \underline{first\text{-}of\text{-}row} \tag{7}$$

$$last\text{-}of\text{-}row \wedge \neg b \rightarrow [2] : \underline{last\text{-}of\text{-}row} \tag{8}$$

$$[1]^{-1} : \text{T} \rightarrow [next] \doteq [1]^{-1} [2] \tag{9}$$

$$\neg last\text{-}of\text{-}row \wedge [2]^{-1} : \text{T} \rightarrow [next] \doteq [2]^{-1} [next] [1] \tag{10}$$

$$\underline{a} \tag{11}$$

In rule (1), we use *root* as an abbreviation for $(\ )^{-1} : \text{F}$. Then (1) says that if a node is not the target of any arc, then it must be labeled both *first-of-row* and *last-of-row*; moreover, those labels are justified.

Figure 29 contains a picture of a satisfying S-graph whose yield is a^7. We added a name *root* for the root node, and we shall use this in our discussion. We shall call this graph G_2 in the rest of the section. We encourage the reader to check that G_2 satisfies the grammar $\mathcal{G}$ and the Tree Property before reading the discussion below which explains how all of its core features are justified. After reading this, it should be clear that for all $n \geq 1$, there is a satisfying S-graph G_{n-1} whose yield is a^{2^n-1}. G_{n-1} is essentially a binary tree of height $n - 1$, with every node labeled a. We then prove that every S-graph which satisfies the grammar and the Tree Property is isomorphic to G_{n-1} for some $n \geq 1$. The discussion below also contains an explanation of the general ideas underlying the grammar.

It is instructive to check that all of the features of G_2 are justified by the grammar. First, we consider the arc labelings. These are all justified by (2) and (6).

Next, we turn to the node labelings. There are three nodes labeled *first-of-row* and three nodes labeled *last-of-row*, counting the *root*. According to rule (1), the *root* is always labeled *first-of-row* and *last-of-row*. Rule (7) "hands down" *first-of-row* from a *first-of-row* source node that is not labeled with b through a [1]-arc. Mutatis mutandis, rule (8) "hands down" *last-of-row*. That is, the node labelings in G_2 for *first-of-row* and *last-of-row*

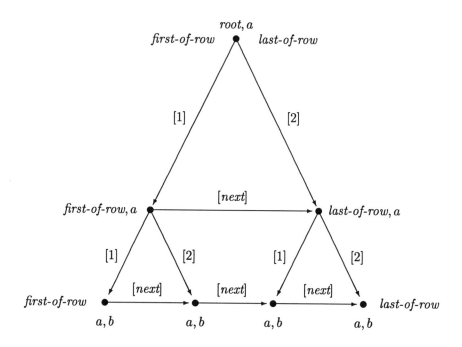

Figure 29: The S-graph for a^7.

are justified by applications of (1), (7), and (8) to nodes in G_2. The node labelings for b are justified by (3). Finally, node labelings for a are justified by (11).

Next we consider the node identifications. G_2 contains three small triangles, each of which has a base labeled [*next*]. These are justified by (9). (We note that the antecedent of (10) contains the condition $\neg$*last-of-row* because otherwise all of the nodes labeled *last-of-row* would have to have [*next*] arcs to satisfy the grammar.) Moreover, G_2 contains a single trapezoid whose parallel faces are labeled [*next*]. This is justified by rule (10) applied to the node labeled with the second b. Now there are other identifications in G_2; for example, the *root* node satisfies

$$[1]\,[\textit{next}]\,[1]\,[\textit{next}] \quad \doteq \quad [2]\,[2]\ .$$

What is the justification for this? Well, the *root* justifiably satisfies $[1][\textit{next}] \doteq [2]$ and $[2] : ([1][\textit{next}] \doteq [2])$. The first of these implies $[1][\textit{next}][1][\textit{next}] \doteq$

$[2][1][next]$, and the second implies $[2][1][next] \doteq [2][2]$. Thus by transitivity, $[1][next][1][next] \doteq [2][2]$ is justified as required.

At this point, we know that G_2 satisfies $\mathcal{G}$. Recall that *next* is a null R-sign. When we delete the $[next]$ edges from G_2, we do get a tree T_2. Further, $\prec$ on T_2 is empty since G_2 comes with no precedence information. However, the depth-first listing of the end nodes of T_2 is $aaaaaaa$ no matter which maximal T_2-order is used. It follows that the yield of G_2 is exactly $\{a^7\}$. Therefore $a^7 \in \mathcal{L}(\mathcal{G})$.

For all $n \geq 1$, there is an S-graph G_{n-1} which satisfies the grammar and whose yield is a^{2^n-1}. To construct G_{n-1}, first take the complete binary tree of height $n-1$, label the appropriate arcs with $[1]$'s and $[2]$'s, and label the appropriate nodes with a, b, *first-of-row*, and *last-of-row*. (For $n = 1$, we just have a single node and no arcs.) Call this labeled tree T_{n-1}. Then G_{n-1} is T_{n-1} with additional arcs (across each row) labeled $[next]$.

Now we claim that every S-graph which satisfies $\mathcal{G}$ and the Tree Property is isomorphic to some G_{n-1}; this proves that $\mathcal{L}(\mathcal{G})$ is $\{a^{2^n-1} : n \geq 1\}$. Let G be such a S-graph, and let T be the tree obtained by deleting the arcs whose labels end in the null R-sign *next*. Let *root* be the root of T. We shall have occasion to speak of the *height* of a node n of T; this is the distance from n to *root*. For example, *root* itself is the unique node of height 0, and its children are exactly the nodes of height 1. We write $height(T)$ for the maximum height of a node of T.

Consider the tree T. The arc labels in T must be $[1]$ and $[2]$. Rule (6) implies that each node not labeled b is the tail of a $[1]$ and a $[2]$ arc; thus the nodes not labeled b are not leaves. By Justification, we have the converse: the nodes which are labeled b may not have children in T since there would be no way to justify the arcs.

Furthermore, the Tree Property implies that there are no distinct paths leading from the *root* to the same node. It follows that T is a *full* binary tree; i.e., that every non-leaf has exactly two children.

The only remaining problem is to insure that all leaves in T are at the same level. Of course, this is the most critical part of the grammar, and the part that uses the SFG apparatus. Up until now, we have not used anything beyond what would be needed to generate a context-free language (cf. Section 4), and the language we seek to generate is of course non-CF.

A fact that we shall need is that for all $k \leq height(T)$, the unique node of height k labeled *first-of-row* is $\delta(root, [1]^k)$, and the unique node of height k labeled *last-of-row* is $\delta(root, [2]^k)$. The proof is an induction on k using (1), (7), and (8) for the existence, and Justification for the uniqueness. The uniqueness part also uses the fact that (7) implies that the $[1]$ child of a given node satisfying *first-of-row* $\wedge \neg b$ is unique; and it uses a similar result for (8). The argument is straightforward, and so we omit the details.

The key fact about T is that the following *Height Accessibility Property* holds: for all nodes m of T, there is some j such that

$$\delta(root, [1]^{height(m)}[next]^j) \simeq m.$$

The proof is by strong induction on the depth first enumeration of T. Take some node m, and assume that for every node m' which precedes m in depth-first order of T, there is some j' such that $\delta(root, [1]^{height(m')}[next]^{j'}) \simeq m'$; we need some j that works for m. If m is the root or any other *first-of-row* node, then we can take $j = 0$. Otherwise, m is not *first-of-row* and has a parent in T. There are two cases at this point. It m is a child via [1], then let $m' = \delta(m, [1]^{-1}[next]^{-1}[2])$. This m' precedes m in the depth-first search of T, so we have some j' as above. Moreover, we claim that m' does not satisfy *last-of-row*. For if it did, then by Justification, $\delta(m', [2]^{-1})$ would also satisfy *last-of-row*. Call this node p. There is a $[next]$ arc from p to $\delta(m, [1]^{-1})$. However, this arc could never be justified, since all justifications of $[next]$ arcs are by (2), and the antecedent of (2) is false at p. This proves that m' does not satisfy *last-of-row*. But then, by (10),

$$\delta(m', [next]) \quad \simeq \quad \delta(m', [2]^{-1}[next][1]) \quad \simeq \quad m,$$

as in the trapezoid at the bottom of Figure 29. Also

$$\delta(root, [1]^{height(m)}[next]^{j'+1}) \quad \simeq \quad \delta(m', [next]) \quad \simeq \quad m .$$

On the other hand, if m is a child via [2], then let $m' = \delta(m, [2]^{-1}[1])$. Again, m' precedes m in the depth-first search of T, so we have some j' as above. This time $\delta(m', [next]) \simeq m$. It follows that $\delta(root, [1]^{height(m)}[next]^{j'+1}) \simeq m$.

This completes the proof of the Height Accessibility Property. Before going on, we should remark that this is the main point in the whole argument where we use the resources of SFG which go beyond context-free grammars. In particular, the reasoning based on geometric repetition (tesselations) seems to be special to SFG.

We are ready to prove that all leaves of T have the same height. Let $n-1$ be the least number such that there is a leaf node m whose height in T is $n-1$. This node m is labeled b since it is a leaf. By Height Accessibility, there is some j such that $\delta(m, ([next]^{-1})^{-j}) \simeq \delta(root, [1]^k)$. So by an induction on j using (5) and the uniqueness fact concerning *first-of-row*, we see that $\delta(root, [1]^k)$ is labeled b also. But then another induction using Height Accessibility, (4), and the uniqueness of *last-of-row*, we see that every node of height n is labeled b and is hence a leaf. The minimality of $n - 1$ shows that all leaves of T have height $n - 1$. This proves that T is a complete binary tree. It follows from this that T must be isomorphic to the underlying tree of the graph G_{n-1} from above. Hence the yield of G is exactly a^{2^n-1}.

This completes the proof that $\mathcal{L}(\mathcal{G}) = \{a^{2^n-1} : n \geq 1\}$.

4 Survey of Formal Results

In this section we provide a survey of the primary results known to date regarding the formal expressive power of SFG. For further details and proofs, the reader is referred to Johnson and Moss (1993).

Unrestricted SFG

Since SFG's and S-graphs are finite, it is clear that every SFG language is recursively enumerable. The converse is also true; that is, we have:

Theorem 1 *Let $\mathcal{L}$ be a Turing acceptable language. Then there is an SFG $\mathcal{G}$ such that $\mathcal{L} = \mathcal{L}(\mathcal{G})$.*

As far as linguistic theory is concerned, therefore, the unrestricted SFG framework is far too expressive. We take a first step toward rectifying this in the next section.

Restricted SFG

Lexical Anchoring and Boundedness Here we consider two linguistically motivated restrictions that reduce the generative capacity of the system to a subset of the recursive languages. First, we institute a strong lexicalism in the SFG framework by adopting a principle of lexical anchoring. This states that the core data of an S-graph G must be justified by some *lexical* node of G, that is by a node n such that `node-label(n)` contains a (unique) vocabulary item.

Given an S-graph G and a rule ϕ, we say that ϕ is **lexically anchored** (in G at n) if there is a lexical node n of G which satisfies ϕ. In stating the definition below, and in the sequel, we shall have occasion to speak of lexically anchored rules. Also, we occasionally use the phrase "lexical justification" to refer to a situation in which data is justified by a lexically anchored rule.

The (Lexical) Anchoring Principle (AP) Let G be an S-graph. In order for G to satisfy a grammar $\mathcal{G}$, each core datum of G must be justified by a lexically anchored rule of $\mathcal{G}$.

Given a grammar $\mathcal{G}$, let $\mathcal{L}_{lex}(\mathcal{G})$ be the language determined by $\mathcal{G}$, assuming the AP. A language of the form $\mathcal{L}_{lex}(\mathcal{G})$ is called a **lexical** SFG language. Our working hypothesis is that natural languages are describable as lexical SFG languages.

Our second proposal to bring the SFG framework closer to linguistic practice is to insure that the arc labels are short. Our point of departure is that all the relational analyses familiar to us use no more than, say, 5 or 6 strata.

Definition A sequence $r = r_1, r_2, \ldots, r_j$ of R-signs is a *cyclic word* for a grammar $\mathcal{G}$ if there are rules $\phi_1, \ldots, \phi_k$, containing labels $l_1, \ldots, l_k$, respectively, and embeddings $\varepsilon_1, \ldots, \varepsilon_k$ of $l_1, \ldots, l_k$ into r such that (a) the images of ε_i and ε_{i+1} overlap for $1 \leq i < k$, and (b) $\phi_1 = \phi_k$. An SFG $\mathcal{G}$ is **bounded** if there are no cyclic words for $\mathcal{G}$. The **language** of a bounded grammar is the language determined by $\mathcal{G}$, *assuming the AP.*

The intuitive idea is that a cyclic word could arise when the labels in rules overlap in such a way that if they justify a label L of length n, $n \geq 1$, then they also justify an extension of L with length greater than n without bound. For instance, the single formula $(\underline{0}, \underline{1}, 0) : \mathrm{T}$ could justify unboundedly long segments of labels of the form $(0, 1, 0, 1, 0, 1, \ldots, 0)$.

We stress that by stipulation, bounded SFG languages are also lexical.

Some Bounded SFG Languages The class of bounded SFG languages is quite robust, and includes, for instance:

(a) Every ϵ-free context-free language.

(b) $\{a^{2^n - 1} : n \geq 1\}$.

(c) $\{a^{n^2} : n \geq 1\}$.

(d) For each m, the set $C_m = \{a_1^n a_2^n \cdots a_m^n : n \geq 1\}$.

(e) For each m, the set $\{w^m : w \in \Sigma^+\}$.

Of these, (b) appears in Section 2.5. The construction there implicitly used only lexical justifications, since all nodes were labeled with the vocabulary item a. That is, all nodes in satisfying S-graphs are lexical, so the Anchoring property is trivial. Further, it is immediate that the grammar presented is bounded, because it uses no labels longer than two R-signs. It follows that this language is a bounded SFG language.

A different construction with the same flavor demonstrates that (c) $\{a^{n^2} : n \in N\}$ is a bounded SFG language. The details may be found in Johnson and Moss (1993). The key point to the demonstration is that even bounded SFG's can characterize rectangular arrays. This aspect of the proof is reminiscent of the earlier construction for $\{a^{2^n - 1} : n \geq 1\}$. involving "triangles". Turning to (d), for a fixed m the "columnar" language C_m is an SFL, the construction of a grammar $\mathcal{G}_m$ for C_m is again based on rectangular arrays. A similar construction involving rectangular arrays is also used with the copy languages of (e). Finally, we turn to a proof of (a).

Theorem 2 *Every ϵ-free context-free language is a bounded SFG language.*

Proof First, recall that every ϵ-free CFL can be generated by a grammar in which the right side of every production contains a terminal symbol. (Greibach Normal Form is lexicalized in a particularly strong sense.) We call such grammars **lexicalized** (an apt term borrowed from Schabes 1990). A very simple example of such a grammar would be

$$
\begin{array}{llll}
S \rightarrow WcX & W \rightarrow aWa & W \rightarrow bWb & W \rightarrow a \\
W \rightarrow b & X \rightarrow ccX & X \rightarrow c &
\end{array}
$$

which generates the language

$$
\mathcal{L} \quad = \quad \{wv \; : \quad w \in \{a,b\}^* \text{ is a palindrome of odd length,}
$$
$$
\text{and } v \in \{c\}^+ \text{ has even length}\} \; .
$$

Rather than give a general proof, we give a complete SFG grammar $\mathcal{G}$ for this context-free grammar.

We take as our set V of vocabulary items the set $\{a,b,c\}$, and as R-signs we take $\{1,2,3\}$. Note that we have no need for null R-signs in this example (or indeed in any CF grammar).

We next specify the rules of the grammar. We shall have a rule which insures that the root of the tree is labeled S: viz., $(\ )^{-1} : F \rightarrow S$. We again conventionally abbreviate $(\ )^{-1} : F$ as *root*; so the needed rule becomes *root* $\rightarrow S$. Further, we take the word order rule $([1] \prec [2]) \wedge ([2] \prec [3])$. Other than these, we shall need one rule for each of the symbols a, b, and c. Before we give the set of such rules, we remark that it is our intention that the rules of the grammar be associated with "primitive" S-graphs as in Figure 30. Indeed, these graphs are all trees. Every parse tree for a string in $\mathcal{L}$ can be expanded to an S-graph composed of these primitives; and if a tree can be decomposed into a union of these primitives, then its yield belongs to $\mathcal{L}$.

Here is the idea for the rule for a (the others are similar): An occurrence of a can arise from the trees for the rules $W \rightarrow aWa$ and $W \rightarrow a$. In either of these, let us call an occurrence of a *primary* if it labels a node that is the target of an arc with feature [1]; otherwise we call an occurrence of a *secondary*. Note that every primary occurrence of a satisfies either the formula $[1]^{-1} : \phi$ or the formula $[1]^{-1} : \psi$, where

$$
\begin{array}{lll}
\phi & = & W \wedge [1] : a \wedge [\underline{2}] : W \wedge [\underline{3}] : \underline{a} \\
\psi & = & \underline{W} \wedge [\underline{1}] : \underline{a}
\end{array}
$$

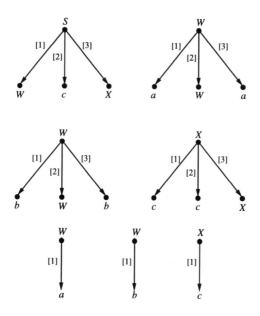

Figure 30: Primitive Trees Associated With $\mathcal{G}$.

It follows that every primary occurrence of a satisfies $[1]^{-1} : (\phi \vee \psi)$. Moreover, every primary occurrence of a satisfying ϕ *justifies* a secondary occurrence of a. Next, notice that ϕ entails ψ. Hence if a primary occurrence of a satisfies ϕ it also satisfies ψ. And it is the latter that justifies the data W and $[1] : a$. This form of the rules insures that each R-sign on an arc and each atom is justified by *exactly one* lexical satisfaction. This is more stringent than our formal definition, and we do things this way merely to point out the possibilities. Somewhat redundant rules are obviously easier to write.

The complete grammar for $\mathcal{L}$ is shown in Figure 31. It is clear that every parse tree of a string $\sigma \in \mathcal{L}$ can be arc-and-node labeled in such a way as to satisfy the grammar and have all arc and node labels justified by a lexical node. Conversely, we can show by induction on the heights of trees that if an S-graph G rooted at S satisfies $\mathcal{G}$ and is fully justified, then G is a valid parse tree for $\mathcal{L}$.

Our approach to proving the general case – that every ϵ-free CFL is a bounded SFL – is quite similar to the special case shown above. The general proof relies on the well-known result of Greibach that every CFG can be put

Data	$Vocabulary = \{a, b, c\}$ $Basic\ R - signs = \{1, 2, 3\}$ $Basic\ atoms = \{S, W, X, a, b, c\}$
Rules	$a \rightarrow \left([1]^{-1} : (\underline{W} \wedge [\underline{1}] : \underline{a})\right.$ $\left. \vee [1]^{-1} : (W \wedge [1] : a \wedge [2] : W \wedge [\underline{3}] : \underline{a})\right)$ $b \rightarrow \left([1]^{-1} : (\underline{W} \wedge [\underline{1}] : \underline{b})\right.$ $\left. \vee [1]^{-1} : (W \wedge [1] : b \wedge [2] : W \wedge [\underline{3}] : \underline{b})\right)$ $c \rightarrow \left([1]^{-1} : (\underline{X} \wedge [\underline{1}] : \underline{c})\right.$ $\vee [1]^{-1} : X \wedge [1] : c \wedge [2] : \underline{c} \wedge [3] : X)$ $\left. \vee [2]^{-1} : (\underline{S} \wedge [\underline{1}] : W \wedge [2] : \underline{c} \wedge [\underline{3}] : X)\right)$ $root \rightarrow S$ $([1] \prec [2]) \wedge ([2] \prec [3])$

Figure 31: Grammar for $\mathcal{L}$

into a normal form in which each rule is of the form $\alpha \rightarrow w\beta$, where w is a terminal node and β is a perhaps empty sequence of variables (nonterminal nodes). The strategy is then quite straightforward: We simply translate the Greibach rules into SFG format and "anchor" the rules appropriately to the vocabulary (terminal alphabet). This procedure, of course, does not, in general, preserve the tree set. ⊣

Upper Bound for Bounded SFG Languages

First we give a few technical results which lead to the upper bound result.

Proposition 3 *Let $\mathcal{L}$ be a lexical SFG language. Then there is a constant k such that for every string $\sigma \in \mathcal{L}$ and every S-graph G whose yield contains σ, the number of arcs of G is at most $k|\sigma|$.*

Proposition 4 *If a cyclic word exists for $\mathcal{G}$, then its length may be bounded by a constant depending on $\mathcal{G}$ alone. Therefore it can be checked in polynomial time whether a grammar $\mathcal{G}$ is bounded. If so, then there is a uniform bound on the length of all arc labels of S-graphs which satisfy $\mathcal{G}$, and there is a also a uniform bound on the total degree of every node*

$\mathcal{L}$ is a **bounded SFG** language if there is some bounded grammar $\mathcal{G}$ such that $\mathcal{L} = \mathcal{L}_{lex}(\mathcal{G})$. (Recall that bounded languages are also lexical.) Propositions 3 and 4 imply that a satisfying S-graph for a sentence σ in a bounded SFG language $\mathcal{L}$ is bounded in total size (number of arcs and nodes + total length of all labels) by a constant times the length of σ. Our claim is that fragments of natural languages may be analyzed as bounded (and hence lexical) SFG languages.

The following is our main upper bound:

Theorem 5 *Every bounded SFG language $\mathcal{G}$ may be recognized by a nondeterministic Turing machine that works in $n \log n$ space and polynomial time.*

Theorem 5 shows that the bounded SFG languages are a relatively small subset of the recursive languages. That is, there are many classes of recursive languages that are not bounded SFL's.

The Recognition Problem for Bounded SFG

This section is concerned with the membership problem for the set

$$\mathcal{SFG} \quad = \quad \{\langle \mathcal{G}, \sigma \rangle : \mathcal{G} \text{ is a } bounded \text{ grammar, and } \sigma \in \mathcal{L}(\mathcal{G})\} \;.$$

This is what Ristad (1986) calls the *universal recognition problem*, and he argues that this is the appropriate object of study rather than individual languages considered without respect to what (type of) grammar generates them (cf. Barton 1985, Barton et al. 1987, and Rounds 1987).

Proposition 4 and Theorem 5 show that $\mathcal{SFG} \in NP$. That is, given a pair $\langle \mathcal{G}, \sigma \rangle$ we first check if $\mathcal{G}$ is bounded, and if so we guess a satisfying S-graph for σ.

Our main result in this section is an NP-hardness result. As a corollary, we observe that $\mathcal{SFG}$ is NP-complete.

Theorem 6 *The recognition problem for $\mathcal{SFG}$ is NP-hard. Specifically, there is a polynomial-time function which takes instances $\langle \{p_1, \ldots, p_r\}, \sigma \rangle$ of 3-SAT into pairs $\langle \mathcal{G}, \sigma \rangle$ such that σ is a satisfiable propositional formula in $\{p_1, \ldots, p_r\}$ iff $\sigma \in \mathcal{L}_{lex}(\mathcal{G})$. Moreover, $\mathcal{G}$ depends only on the set $\{p_1, \ldots, p_r\}$ and not on σ.*

Corollary 7 *The recognition problem for bounded SFG is NP-complete.*

This NP-completeness result is a parallel to similar results obtained by Barton et al. (1987). It supports our contention that the bounded SFG formalism is expressive enough for natural language descriptions. Although we do not take the NP-completeness result negatively, we do, of course, recognize that even the bounded formalism is, as far as linguistic theory is concerned, insufficiently restrictive.

Some Open Problems

We close this section by mentioning some open questions. One open area involves the somewhat controversial notion of "constant growth", which has received some attention since its introduction in Joshi (1983) and early discussion in Berwick (1984) and Berwick and Weinberg (1984); see especially Kac (1987), Manaster-Ramer (1987), Weir (1987), Joshi et al. (1991), and Radzinski (1991). We note that bounded SFG does not have the "constant growth" property. (This follows since $a^{2^n - 1}$ violates this property.) How to embody the "constant growth" property in SFG is an open question.

As the constructions for a^{n^2}, the "columnar" languages and the copying languages discussed above have demonstrated, bounded SFG can generate a number of non-tree-adjoining languages. However, we do not know if the bounded SFG languages contain the ϵ-free tree-adjoining languages. We also do not know whether they contain the language MIX^+, the nonempty strings on $\{a, b, c\}$ with equal numbers of each letter.

We note in passing that the most natural TAG analog to bounded SFG would seem to be a lexicalized version of TAG(ID/LP), in which linear precedence is factored out from local domination in a manner similar to the ID/LP format of GPSG. In this regard, it is interesting to note that according to Joshi et al. (1991), TAG(ID/LP) can generate MIX^+. (This is a consequence of how the yield for a TAG(ID/LP) grammar is determined; see Joshi et al. 1991 for discussion.) On the other hand, TAG(ID/LP) languages still have the constant growth property. Thus, it could well be that there is no simple inclusion relation between bounded SFG and (lexicalized) TAG(ID/LP).

Our last open problem has to do with the upper bound result for bounded SFG. At the present time, all known SFL's are context sensitive. Further, we saw that the bounded languages are recognizable by nondeterministic Turing machines that work in $n \log n$ space and polynominal time. We do not know whether the space bound can be improved to linear space. This would imply that all the stratified feature languages are context sensitive.

5   Conclusion

Our primary goal in developing the SFG formalism has been to lay the
formal groundwork for developing theoretically well-defined and computationally realizable natural language grammars based on the RG/MGG
view of syntax as "multistratal" and "relational". A second goal has been
to build our formalism on a generalization of KR logic, since this would
provide not only a constrained logic but also a common formal basis for
comparison of monostratal unification-based, and multistratal relationally-
based, approaches to grammatical analysis.

To achieve these goals we generalized the concept of a feature from an
unanalyzable atomic attribute to a sequence of R-signs, where each R-sign
in such a sequence denotes a primitive grammatical relation in a "stratum".
Many of the innovations in SFG follow from this generalization. The most
direct one is the idea of imposing a partial order on features. Another,
less direct, example is the SFG concept of *(data) justification*: this was
originally motivated by the linguistic problem of insuring that R-signs in
stratified features be "linked" in a linguistically motivated fashion. The
notion of a *null* R-sign (e.g., 0) is another innovation directly based on
our attempt to model typical RG/MGG analyses and made possible by the
general concept of *stratified feature*.

As mentioned above and discussed in more detail in Johnson and Moss
(1993), the recognition problem for bounded SFG is in NP and thus provides a basis for developing theoretically well-founded and computationally
realizable linguistic theories and specific natural-language grammars based
on the view that syntax is "multistratal" and "relational". This result
contrasts favorably with, on the one hand, RG, which has never been formalized, and MGG, on the other, which has been formalized but whose
recognition problem is undecidable. Since SFG is a feature-structure-based
formalism, it emphasizes the commonalities between multistratal, relational
approaches, and monostratal, unification-based approaches, to syntax. This
should enable those interested in foundational issues to more objectively
compare the two views on syntax.

Acknowledgements

We are indebted to Gerald Gazdar, Warren Plath, Paul Postal and two
anonymous reviewers for helpful comments on this work.

References

Aissen, J. 1987. *Tzotzil Clause Structure*. Dordrecht: Reidel.

Aissen, J. 1991. Relational grammar. In *Linguistic Theory and Grammatical Description*. John Benjamins.

Barton, E. 1985. The computational difficulty of ID/LP parsing. In *Proceedings of the 23rd Annual Meeting of the Association for Computational Linguistics* (pp. 76–81).

Barton, E., R. Berwick and E. Ristad. 1987. *Computational Complexity and Natural Language*. Cambridge: MIT Press.

Berwick, R. 1984. Generative capacity and linguistic theory. *Computational Linguistics* 10.3–4:189–202.

Berwick, R. and A. Weinberg. *The Grammatical Basis of Linguistic Performance*. Cambridge: MIT Press.

Blake, B. J. 1990. *Relational Grammar*. London: Routledge.

Carpenter, B. 1990. Typed feature structures: Inheritance, (in)equalities and extensionality. In *Proceedings of the First International Workshop on Inheritance in Natural Language Processing* (pp. 9–13). The Netherlands: Tilburg

Dziwirek, K., P. Farrell and E.Mejias-Bikandi, (eds.) 1990. *Grammatical Relations: A Cross-Theoretic Perspective*. Stanford Linguistics Association, Stanford University.

Dubinsky, S. and C. Rosen. 1987. *A Bibliography on Relational Grammar Through May 1987, with Selected Titles on Lexical Functional Grammar*. Indiana University Linguistics Club.

Gazdar, G., E. Klein, G. K. Pullum and I. A. Sag. 1985. *Generalized Phrased Structure Grammar*. Cambridge, MA: Harvard University Press.

Gazdar, G., G. K. Pullum, R. Carpenter, E. Klein, T. E. Hukari and R. D. Levine. 1988. Category structures. *Computational Linguistics* 14.1:1–20.

Halvorsen, C. and R. Kaplan. 1988. Projections and semantic description in lexical-functional grammar. In *The International Conference on Fifth Generation Computer Systems* (pp. 1116–1122), Tokyo, Japan.

Huck, G. and A. Ojeda. 1989. *Syntax and Semantics: Discontinuous Constituency*, Vol. 20. Academic Press.

Johnson, D. E. 1979. *Toward a Theory of Relationally-Based Grammar*. New York: Garland.

Johnson, D. E. and L. S. Moss. 1993. Some formal properties of stratified feature grammars. *Annals of Mathematics and Artificial Intelligence* 8:133–173.

Johnson, D. E. and P. M. Postal. 1980. *Arc Pair Grammar.* Princeton University Press.

Johnson, M. 1988. *Attribute-Value Logic and the Theory of Grammar*, Vol. 16. CSLI Lecture Notes, University of Chicago Press.

Joshi A. 1983. Factoring recursion and dependencies: An aspect of tree adjoining grammars (tag) and a comparison of some formal properties of TAGS, GPSGS, PLGS, and LFGS. In *Proceedings of the 21st Annual Meeting of the Association for Computational Linguistics*, 7–15.

Joshi, A., K. Vijay-Shanker and D. Weir. 1991. The convergence of mildly context-sensitive grammar formalisms. In S. Shieber, P. Sells and T. Wasow (eds.), *Foundational Issues in Natural Language Processing* (pp. 31–82). MIT Press.

Kac, M. B. 1987. Surface transitivity, 'respectively' coordination and context-freeness. *Natural Language and Linguistic Theory* 5:441–452.

Kaplan, R. M. and J. Bresnan. 1982. Lexical-functional grammar, a formal system for grammatical representations. In J. Bresnan (ed.), *The Mental Representation of Grammatical Relations* (pp. 183–281). MIT Press.

Kasper, R. and W. C. Rounds. 1986. A logical semantics for feature structures. In *Proceedings of the 24th Annual Meeting of the ACL* (pp. 257–266).

Kasper, R. and W. C. Rounds. 1990. The logic of unification in grammar. *Linguistics and Philosophy* 13:35–58.

Kubinski, W. 1987. *Reflexivization in English and Polish: An Arc Pair Grammar Analysis.* Tuebingen: Niemeyer.

Ladusaw, W. 1988. A proposed distinction between *levels* and *strata.* In *Linguistics in the Morning Calm* 2. Linguistics Society of Korea.

Lakoff, G. 1977. In W. A. Beach et al. (ed.), *Papers from the 13th Regional Meeting* (pp. 236–287). Chicago Linguistics Society.

McCord, M. 1980. Slot grammar. *Computational Linguistics* 6:31–43.

McCord, M. 1992. Slot grammar: A system for simpler construction of practical natural language grammars. In R. Studer (ed.), *Natural Language and Logic: International Scientific Symposium*, Lecture Notes in Computer Science. Berline: Springer-Verlag.

Moss, L. S. 1992. Completeness theorems for logics of feature structures. In Y. N. Moschovakis (ed.), *Proceedings of the MSRI Workshop on Logic from Computer Science* (pp. 387–403. Springer-Verlag.

Moshier, M. D. and W. C. Rounds. 1986. A logic for partially specified data structures. In *Proceedings of the 14th Annual ACM Symposium on Principles of Programming Languages* (pp. 156–167).

Manaster-Ramer, A. 1987. Dutch as a formal language. *Linguistics and Philosophy* 10:221–246.

Perlmutter, D. M. 1983. *Studies in Relational Grammar*, Vol. 1. University of Chicago Press.

Postal, P. M. and B. D. Joseph (eds.) 1990. *Studies in Relational Grammar*, Vol. 3. University of Chicago Press.

Postal, P. M. 1986. *Studies of Passive Clauses*. State University of New York Press.

Postal, P. M. 1989. *Masked Inversion in French*. The University of Chicago Press.

Perlmutter, D. M. and P. M. Postal. 1974. Lectures on relational grammar. LSA Institutes Lectures, Amherst, MA.

Perlmutter, D. M. and C. G. Rosen (eds.) 1984. *Studies in Relational Grammar*, Vol. 2. University of Chicago Press.

Pollard, C. and I. A. Sag. 1987. *Information-based Syntax and Semantics*. CSLI Lecture Notes, University of Chicago Press.

Pollard, C. and I. A. Sag. 1994. *Head-Driven Phrase Structure Grammar*. CSLI Lecture Notes, University of Chicago.

Pullum, G. K. 1982. Syncategorematicity and English infinitival to. *Glossa* 16.2:181–215.

Radzinski, D. 1991. Chinese number-names, tree adjoining languages, and mild context-sensitivity. *Computational Linguistics* 17:277–299.

Ristad, E. S. 1986. Computational complexity of current gpsg theory. In *Proceedings of the 24th Annual Meeting of the ACL* (pp. 30–39).

Rounds, W. C. 1991. The relevance of computational complexity theory to natural language processing. In S. Shieber, P. Sells and T. Wasow (eds.), *Foundational Issues in Natural Language Processing* (pp. 9–30). MIT Press.

Rounds, W. C. and R. Kasper. 1986. A complete logical calculus for record structures representing linguistic information. In *Proceedings of the Symposium on Logic in Computer Science* (pp. 38–48), IEEE.

Rounds, W. C. and A Manaster-Ramer. 1987. A logical version of functional grammar. In *Proceedings of the 25th Annual Meeting of the Association for Computational Linguistics* (pp. 89–96).

Sanders, G. 1967. *Some General Grammatical Processes in English*. Ph.D thesis, Indiana University.

Sanders, G. 1970. Precedence relations in language. *Foundations of Language* 11:361–400.

Schabes, Y. 1990. *Mathematical and Computational Properties of Lexicalized Grammars*. Ph.D thesis, University of Pennsylvania.

Schabes, Y. and A. Joshi. 1990. The relevance of lexicalization to parsing. In *Proceedings of the International Workshop on Parsing Technologies*. Pittsburgh: MIT Press.

Shieber, S. M. 1986. *An Introduction to Unification-Based Approaches to Grammar*, Vol. 4 of CSLI Lecture Notes, University of Chicago Press.

Weir, D. 1987. *From Context-free Grammars to Tree Adjoining Grammars and Beyond*. Ph.D thesis, University of Pennsylvania.

Feature-Based Grammars as Constraint Grammars

Alan M. Frisch[1]
Department of Computer Science
University of Illinois

1 Introduction

This paper clarifies the foundations of feature-based grammars by making three contributions.

1. A grammatical formalism called constraint grammar, which generalizes the basic ideas of feature-based grammars, is introduced. The formalism does not use feature structures directly; rather it uses constraints that describe feature structures.

2. By considering the rules of a constraint grammar to be schematic for a possibly infinite set of rules of a context-free grammar (CFG) we are able to define the language of a constraint grammar without mention of unification or any structure-building operations.

3. We show how a parser can operate directly on the schematic rules of a constraint grammar to build a parse tree that is itself schematic for a possibly infinite set of CFG parse trees. A general parsing rule is defined and proved correct and complete.

The constraint grammar formalism makes a clear distinction between feature structures and their descriptions. Only the latter appear in grammars. The earliest work on feature-based grammars (e.g., Shieber 1986) didn't make this distinction. Most systems at that time were simple enough that one could take the descriptions and structures to be isomorphic. However, as the expressiveness of these formalisms increased, such as with the introduction of disjunction and negation, the failure to make this distinction initially led to some confusion. Today, many researchers make this distinction (e.g., Johnson 1988, Nebel and Smolka 1990, Maxwell III and Kaplan 1991, Smolka 1992, Backofen and Smolka 1992).

However, as more and more researchers have embraced this distinction, they have turned their attention from grammatical systems as whole to one particular aspect: the logic of feature structures. Such research typically

---

[1]Author's current address: Department of Computer Science, University of York, York Y01 5DD, United Kingdom.

focuses on methods for deciding whether there exists a feature structure
that satisfies a given description (Nebel and Smolka 1990, Maxwell III and
Kaplan 1991, Smolka 1992, Backofen and Smolka 1992). This paper turns
the tables, ignoring the issue of satisfiability testing and concentrating on
its role in grammar and parsing.

The driving force behind the results of this paper is the idea that the
rules of constraint grammars are schematic for a possibly infinite set of CFG
rules. Though this is occasionally pointed out, such as in the literature on
Generalized Phrase Structure Grammar, it is rarely taken as seriously as it
is in this paper.[2]

2   Some Terminology

This section gives an incomplete definition of constraint grammars and introduces some useful terminology.

A *constraint grammar* is a six-tuple $\langle \mathcal{F}, \mathcal{V}als, \mathcal{V}ars, \mathcal{W}, \mathcal{R}, \mathcal{S} \rangle$ where:

- $\mathcal{F}$, $\mathcal{V}als$, $\mathcal{V}ars$, and $\mathcal{W}$ are disjoint sets.

- $\mathcal{F}$ is an arbitrary set known as the *features* of the grammar.

- $\mathcal{V}als$ is an arbitrary set known as the *values* of the grammar.

- $\mathcal{V}ars$ is an arbitrary set known as the *variables* of the grammar. These
  are used in grammar rules in a way similar to non-terminals, but their
  scope is local to each rule; a variable in one rule has nothing to do
  with a variable in another rule, even if the variables have the same
  name.

- $\mathcal{W}$ is an arbitrary set known as the *terminals* or *words* of the grammar.

- $\mathcal{R}$ is the set of *rules* of the grammar. The rules are constructed out
  of elements of $\mathcal{F}$, $\mathcal{V}als$, $\mathcal{V}ars$, $\mathcal{W}$, and a fixed set of symbols defined
  later.

- $\mathcal{S}$ is a subset of $\mathcal{R}$ known as the *start rules* of the grammar.

Except for specifying what the rules of constraint grammars are, this is
a complete definition of constraint grammars. The rules for these grammars
are defined in Section 5. That section also defines the language generated
by a constraint grammar.

---

[2]An earlier paper of mine (Frisch 1986) and one by Haas (1989) have also taken this
idea seriously.

Whereas grammars usually use a start symbol to specify what must appear at the root of a parse tree, constraint grammars stipulate that the rule applied at the root of a parse tree must be drawn from a specified set, $\mathcal{S}$. One can easily verify that, for example, a context-free grammar specified with a start symbol can be translated to one with start rules, and vice-versa. The constraint grammar analog to a start symbol is a constrained variable. However, by using start rules instead of a start symbol (constrained variable), the meta-theory of constraint grammars can be presented more cleanly.

The examples of this paper assume that $\mathcal{F}$ contains *cat* (category), *agr* (agreement), *num* (number), and *per* (person), and that $\mathcal{V}als$ contains *s* (sentence), *np* (noun phrase), *vp* (verb phrase), *v* (verb), *sing* (singular), *plural*, *first*, and *third*.

3 Feature Structures

This paper makes a clear distinction between grammatical descriptions that are written in the grammatical formalism and the objects described by those descriptions. The distinction is analogous to that made between a formula in a logical language and the models of that formula. This section defines feature structures, which are the objects described by a constraint grammar. Many papers on feature-based grammars consider feature structures to be part of the grammatical formalism. Because such formalisms need to be able to state that two features have the same value, feature structures must be directed graphs, not merely trees. But here, feature structures are not used in this way, so it suffices to consider them to be trees.

The feature structures of a grammar are constructed from the features, $\mathcal{F}$, and the values, $\mathcal{V}als$, of the grammar. A *feature structure* is a finite tree in which each arc is labeled by a feature, each leaf is labeled by a value, and no node has two emanating arcs with the same label. More precisely, we think of these trees as being made up of paths, where a path is either a value or a pair, $\langle f\ p \rangle$, where f is a feature and p is a path. A path of the form $\langle f_1 \langle f_2 \cdots \langle f_n\ v \rangle \cdots \rangle \rangle$ is often written as $[f_1\ f_2 \cdots f_n\ v]$. A feature structure s is a finite set of paths such that if $[f_1 \cdots f_n\ v]$ and $[f_1 \cdots f_m\ v']$ are members of s then $n = m$ and $v = v'$. This means that a feature structure cannot contain two paths such that the sequence of features in one is a proper prefix of the sequence of features in the other; nor can it contain two paths that are identical except that they terminate with different values. To illustrate this definition, the tree shown in Figure 1(a) is a feature structure. Throughout this paper, feature structures are displayed in array form. In this form, the tree of Figure 1(a) takes the form of the array shown in Figure 1(b). Formally, this feature structure is the set $\{[cat\ v], [arg\ num\ sing], [arg\ per\ third]\}$.

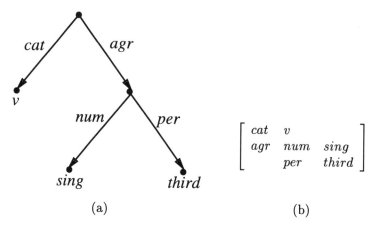

Figure 1: A feature structure displayed as a tree
in (a) and as an array in (b)

If s is a feature structure and f is a feature then the f-subtree of s is $\{p \mid \langle f\ p \rangle \in s\}$. Observe that the empty set is a feature structure, and that the f-subtree of a non-empty feature structure may be empty. For example, the *cat*-subtree of the feature structure in Figure 1 is the feature structure $\{v\}$, the *arg*-subtree is $\{[num\ sing], [per\ third]\}$, and the *num*-subtree is the empty set.

4   Constraints on Feature Structures

Constraint grammars make heavy use of variables ranging over feature structures. Constraints can be placed on a set of variables to limit the values that the variables can take on simultaneously. This section defines the syntax and semantics of these constraints.

To simplify matters a bit, we consider the sets $\mathcal{F}$ and $\mathcal{V}als$ to consist of symbols which can appear in the constraint language. Constraints are made up not only of members of $\mathcal{F}$ and $\mathcal{V}als$ but also of members of a set of variables, $\mathcal{V}ars$. Throughout, f and g denote features, a, b and c denote values, and X, Y, and Z denote variables.

A *term* is either

- a variable (i.e., a member of $\mathcal{V}ars$),

- a value (i.e. a member of $\mathcal{V}als$), or

- an expression of the form $t\ f$, where t is a term and f is a feature (i.e., a member of $\mathcal{F}$).

A *constraint* is an expression of the form:

- $t \doteq t'$, where t and t' are terms,

- $t \uparrow$, where t is a term, or

- $\neg C$, $C \wedge C'$, or $C \vee C'$, where C and C' are constraints.

Here is an example of a constraint that arises later in the paper:

$$X \; cat \doteq v \; \wedge \; X \; agr \; num \doteq sing \; \wedge \; X \; agr \; per \doteq third \tag{1}$$

A semantic account of constraints must tell us whether or not any given assignment of values to the free variables of a constraint satisfy that constraint. Let A be an assignment of feature structures to variables. A can be extended to assign values to terms and constraints as follows:

- $A(a) = \{a\}$, that is, the feature structure consisting of a single node labeled by the value a.

- $A(t \; f) =$ the f-subtree of $A(t)$. Note that this may be the empty set.

- $A(t \doteq t') = TRUE$ if $A(t)$ and $A(t')$ are non-empty and equal; *FALSE* otherwise.

- $A(t \; f \uparrow) = TRUE$ if $A(t \; f)$ is empty, *FALSE* otherwise.

- $A(\neg C) = TRUE$ if $A(C) = FALSE$, *FALSE* otherwise.

- $A(C \wedge C') = TRUE$ if $A(C) = TRUE$ and $A(C') = TRUE$, *FALSE* otherwise.

- $A(C \vee C')$ if $A(C) = TRUE$ or $A(C') = TRUE$, *FALSE* otherwise.

Notice that $A(a \; f)$ is always the empty set.

A constraint C is satisfied by an assignment A if, and only if, $A(C) = TRUE$. A constraint is *satisfiable* if it is satisfied by some assignment and *valid* if it is satisfied by all assignments. The constraint in (1) is satisfied by an assignment that maps X to the feature structure of Figure 1. However, the constraint is not satisfied by any assignment that maps X to a proper subset of that feature structure. Thus, the constraint is satisfiable, but not valid.

The particular constraint language presented here is not crucial to the enterprise of this paper. The language could be expanded with quantifiers or other kinds of constraints, or certain constraints could be removed from the language without affecting the ideas and results of the subsequent sections.

Indeed, by following the lead of Höhfeld and Smolka (1988) and using an abstract notion of a constraint system, the presentation of the remainder of the paper could be made independent of the particular constraint system used. For concreteness we use the constraint system presented here, but the reader should bear in mind that the following sections do not depend on this particular choice.

5 Constraint Grammars

With the notion of constraints and assignments in hand, this section defines the form of the production rules of constraint grammars and the languages that constraint grammars generate.

Recall that a constraint grammar is a six-tuple, $\langle \mathcal{F}, \mathcal{V}als, \mathcal{V}ars, \mathcal{W}, \mathcal{R}, \mathcal{S} \rangle$. We have already been using the first four elements and have seen that they are arbitrary disjoint sets. We now define the form of the rules in $\mathcal{R}$.

Each rule of a constraint grammar is of the form

$$X \longrightarrow Y_1 \; Y_2 \; \cdots \; Y_n \; / \; C$$

where $n > 0$, X is an arbitrary variable, each Y_i is an arbitrary variable or a terminal, C is a constraint containing no free variables other than those that occur in $X \longrightarrow Y_1 \; Y_2 \; \cdots \; Y_n$, and no variable occurs twice in $X \longrightarrow Y_1 \; Y_2 \; \cdots \; Y_n$.[3]

Figure 2 gives a constraint grammar that is similar to the one found in (Shieber 1989). Here, and throughout the paper, start rules are written with the symbol $\xrightarrow{S}$. Observe that without disjunction, it would take three rules to capture the effect of (R7).

In what follows it is useful to extend the domain of every assignment A by stipulating that $A(w) = w$ for every terminal w.

A constraint grammar rule is schematic for a possibly infinite set of context-free grammar rules in which feature structures serve as the non-terminals. Each context-free rule for which a constraint grammar rule is schematic is said to be an instance of the constraint grammar rule. In particular, if an assignment A satisfies the constraint C then

$$A(X) \longrightarrow A(Y_1) \; \cdots \; A(Y_n)$$

is an *instance* of

$$X \longrightarrow Y_1 \; Y_2 \; \cdots \; Y_n \; / \; C.$$

Notice that an instance of a constraint grammar rule is made up of only feature structures and terminals; it contains no variables and no constraints.

---

[3]The effect of duplicate occurrences of a variable in $X \longrightarrow Y_1 \; Y_2 \; \cdots \; Y_n$ can be achieved by conjoining to C an equation between distinct variables.

(R1) $X \xrightarrow{S} Y\ Z$ / $X\ cat \doteq s \wedge Y\ cat \doteq np \wedge Z\ cat \doteq vp \wedge Y\ agr \doteq Z\ agr$

(R2) $X \longrightarrow Y\ Z$ / $X\ cat \doteq vp \wedge Y\ cat \doteq v \wedge Z\ cat \doteq np \wedge X\ agr \doteq Y\ agr$

(R3) $X \longrightarrow$ 'nature'   / $X\ cat \doteq np \wedge X\ agr\ num \doteq sing \wedge X\ agr\ per \doteq third$

(R4) $X \longrightarrow$ 'vacuums'   / $X\ cat \doteq np \wedge X\ agr\ num \doteq plural \wedge X\ agr\ per \doteq third$

(R5) $X \longrightarrow$ 'abhors'   / $X\ cat \doteq v \wedge X\ agr\ num \doteq sing \wedge X\ agr\ per \doteq third$

(R6) $X \longrightarrow$ 'abhorred'   / $X\ cat \doteq v$

(R7) $X \longrightarrow$ 'abhor'   / $X\ cat \doteq v \wedge (X\ agr\ num \doteq plural \vee$
$X\ agr\ per \doteq first \vee$
$X\ agr\ per \doteq second)$

Figure 2: A Feature Constraint Grammar

A string of terminals is in the language of constraint grammar G if, and only if, the string can be derived from the infinite context-free grammar whose rules are the instances of $\mathcal{R}$ and whose start rules are the instances of S. Thus a constraint grammar can be thought of as a finite representation of a grammar that has a possibly infinite set of context free rules and a possibly infinite set of start rules. This possibly infinite CFG is said to be the *ground grammar* of the constraint grammar.

Some of the instances of the rules in the grammar of Figure 2 are shown in Figure 3. As shown by the parse tree in Figure 4, these context-free rules generate *nature abhors vacuums*. Therefore, by definition, the constraint grammar of Figure 2 also generates the string.

Notice that the language of a constraint grammar has been defined without mentioning unification. It is a misnomer to call these "unification grammars." Unification is *not* part of the grammar, it is part of the parser for the grammars.

A variant of a rule is obtained by uniformly renaming variables throughout the rule. Every rule is a variant of itself, obtained by the identity renaming. As a result of the following proposition, observe that the language of a grammar does not change when a rule in the grammar is replaced by one of its variants.

Proposition 1 *An instance of a constraint grammar rule is an instance of every variant of that rule.*

$$(R1') \begin{bmatrix} cat & s \end{bmatrix} \xrightarrow{S} \begin{bmatrix} cat & np \\ agr & num & sing \\ & per & third \end{bmatrix} \begin{bmatrix} cat & vp \\ agr & num & sing \\ & per & third \end{bmatrix}$$

$$(R2') \begin{bmatrix} cat & vp \\ agr & num & sing \\ & per & third \end{bmatrix} \longrightarrow \begin{bmatrix} cat & v \\ agr & num & sing \\ & per & third \end{bmatrix} \begin{bmatrix} cat & np \\ agr & num & plural \\ & per & third \end{bmatrix}$$

$$(R3') \begin{bmatrix} cat & np \\ agr & num & sing \\ & per & third \end{bmatrix} \longrightarrow \text{'nature'}$$

$$(R4') \begin{bmatrix} cat & np \\ agr & num & plural \\ & per & third \end{bmatrix} \longrightarrow \text{'vacuums'}$$

$$(R5') \begin{bmatrix} cat & v \\ agr & num & sing \\ & per & third \end{bmatrix} \longrightarrow \text{'abhors'}$$

Figure 3: Part of a Ground Grammar

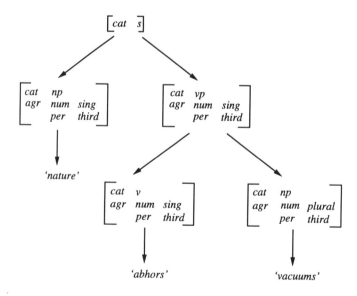

Figure 4: A Parse Tree for the Ground Grammar of Figure 3

6 Parsing

The previous section defined the language of a constraint grammar by considering the constraint grammar to be schematic for a possibly infinite—though enumerable—context free grammar. Though, in principle, one could use this idea directly to enumerate the language of a constraint grammar, this would be a terrible way to parse. This section shows how parsers for constraint grammars can operate directly on the constraint grammar—that is, without generating instances of the rules—by constructing parse trees that are schematic for the parse trees of the ground grammar.

A *parse tree* for a constraint grammar G is an ordered finite tree in which

- every node is labeled by a terminal of G or a variable of G,

- no two nodes are labeled by the same variable,

- every local tree is associated with a constraint of G, and

- every local tree and its associated constraint is a variant of a rule in G.

Figure 5 displays a parse tree for the grammar of Figure 2.

Since we also talk about parse trees for context-free grammars, parse trees for constraint grammars are sometimes referred to as *schematic trees* and parse trees for context-free grammars are sometimes referred to as *ground trees*.

Formally, a ground or schematic tree is taken to be a finite ordered set of paths. (A schematic tree also has an associated set of constraints.) A path in a ground tree is a finite list of feature structures, and a path in a schematic tree is a finite list of variables and terminals.

Because schematic trees are built from variants of the rules of a grammar, the following proposition holds:

Proposition 2 *Every variant of a schematic tree of a constraint grammar G is also a tree of G.*

The *yield* of a ground or schematic parse tree is the string of labels at the leaves of the tree, reading from left to right. A parse tree for a context-free grammar is said to be *initial* if the local tree at the root is a start rule of the grammar. A parse tree for a constraint grammar is said to be *initial* if the local tree at the root and its associated constraint is a variant of a start rule of the grammar. The parse tree of Figure 5 is initial and its yield is *nature abhors vacuums*.

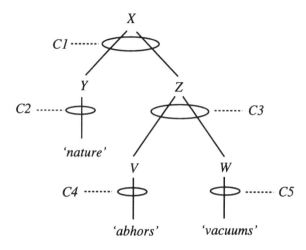

$C1 = X\ cat \doteq s\ \wedge\ Y\ cat \doteq np\ \wedge\ Z\ cat \doteq vp\ \wedge\ Y\ agr \doteq Z\ agr$
$C2 = Y\ cat \doteq np\ \wedge\ Y\ agr\ num \doteq sing\ \wedge\ Y\ agr\ per \doteq third$
$C3 = Z\ cat \doteq vp\ \wedge\ V\ cat \doteq v\ \wedge\ W\ cat \doteq np\ \wedge\ Z\ agr \doteq V\ agr$
$C4 = V\ cat \doteq v\ \wedge\ V\ agr\ num \doteq sing\ \wedge\ V\ agr\ per \doteq third$
$C5 = W\ cat \doteq np\ \wedge\ W\ agr\ num \doteq plural\ \wedge\ W\ agr\ per \doteq third$

Figure 5: A Schematic Parse Tree for the Grammar of Figure 2

The conjunction of all the constraints associated with the local trees of
a schematic tree is known as the *constraint of the tree*. A schematic tree is
admissible if its constraint is satisfiable.

The trivial trees of a CFG or constraint grammar are the depth one
parse trees of that grammar. The trivial trees of a grammar are essentially
the rules of a grammar written as a tree with the left-hand side of the rule
at the root and the right-hand side of the rule at the leaves. A trivial tree
of a constraint grammar is associated with a constraint, which is identical
to the constraint associated with the corresponding rule of the grammar.
A variant of a trivial tree of a constraint grammar is also a trivial tree of
that grammar.

An assignment A can be extended straightforwardly to map schematic
trees to ground trees. Given a schematic tree, a ground tree is obtained
simply by replacing each variable X in the schematic tree with $A(X)$.

A schematic tree T_S whose constraint is C *lifts* a ground tree T_{CF}
if $A(T_S) = T_{CF}$ for some assignment A that satisfies C. Notice that a
schematic tree is inadmissible if, and only if, it lifts no ground trees. Fur-

thermore, notice that the schematic tree of Figure 5 lifts the ground tree of Figure 4.

Theorem 3 (Lifting Theorem) *Let G be a constraint grammar and G' be its ground grammar. Every ground tree for G' is lifted by some admissible schematic tree for G.*

Proof: Let T' be a ground tree for G'. Then by induction on the depth of T' show that T' is an instance of some admissible schematic tree for G.

Base case: depth of T' is zero. This is trivial since no grammar has a tree of depth zero.

Inductive case: (Figure 6 makes the following argument easier to follow.) Assume that every tree of G' that is of depth $n - 1$ or less is an instance of some admissible schematic tree for G. Let T' be a tree of G' of depth n and call the label of its root l'_0. Let $T'_1, \ldots, T'_m$ be the immediate subtrees, from left to right, of T' and call the labels of these subtrees $l'_1, \ldots, l'_m$. Then, for each $1 \leq i \leq m$ either l'_i is a terminal—in which case let A_i be any assignment and T_i be the tree with a single node labeled by l'_i—or, by the inductive hypothesis, there is a tree T_i of G and an assignment A_i that satisfies the constraint associated with T_i such that $A_i(T_i) = T'_i$. Assume, without loss of generality (by Proposition 2), that for every $1 \leq i \leq m$ and $1 \leq j \leq m$ such that $i \neq j$, no node in T_i is labeled by the same variable as a node in T_j. For every $1 \leq i \leq m$, let l_i be the label of the root of T_i. Then there is some rule in G that has $l'_0 \longrightarrow l'_1 \cdots l'_m$ as an instance. Let $l_0 \longrightarrow l_1 \cdots l_m / C$ be a variant of that rule such that l_0 does not occur in any T_i. Then, by Proposition 1, $l'_0 \longrightarrow l'_1 \cdots l'_m$ is an instance of $l_0 \longrightarrow l_1 \cdots l_m / C$, and therefore any assignment that maps each l_i to l'_i satisfies C. Let A be an assignment that maps l_0 to l'_0 and every variable labeling a node in T_i to $A_i(T_i)$, for every $1 \leq i \leq m$. (Such an assignment exists because of the variable disjointness requirements placed on $l_0, T_1, T_2, \ldots, T_m$.) Let T be the tree whose root is labeled by l_0 and whose immediate subtrees, from left to right, are $T_1, \ldots, T_n$. By the way it was constructed, A satisfies C and all the constraints on the immediate subtrees of T; thus A satisfies T. Therefore, T is an admissible tree of G and $A(T) = T'$.

Theorem 4 (Dropping Theorem) *Let G be a constraint grammar and G' be its ground grammar. If T' is a ground tree that is an instance of a schematic tree of G then T' is a ground tree of G'.*

Proof: We show that every local tree in T' is a rule in G'. Consider L', an arbitrary local tree in T'. Let T be a constraint of G that has T' as an instance and L be the local tree in T corresponding local to L' in T'.

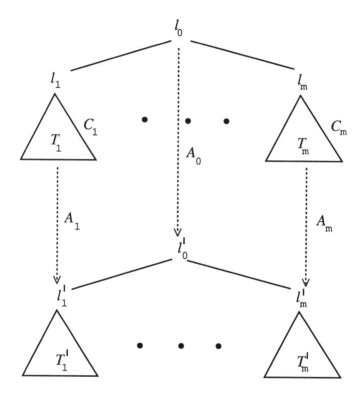

Figure 6: Proof of Lifting Theorem

Then L and its associated constraint is a variant of some rule R in G. By Proposition 1, L' is an instance of R and, therefore, L' is a rule in G'.

For some properties of trees it is the case that if a ground tree has that property then so does every schematic tree that lifts it. Such a property is said to *lift*. For example, the property of having n nodes lifts. Certain properties also *drop*; that is, if a schematic tree has the property then so do all of its ground instances. The property of having n nodes also drops. More interestingly, the property of yielding a particular string of terminals both lifts and drops. So does the property of being initial.

Proposition 5 *Let G be a constraint grammar and G' be its ground grammar. Let T be an admissible parse tree for G and T' be a ground instance of T. Let s be a string of terminals of G (and hence, also of G'). Then, T yields s if, and only if, T' does. Furthermore, T is an initial parse tree of G if, and only if, T' is an initial parse tree of G'.*

Thus we have the following corollary to the Lifting and Dropping Theorems:

Theorem 6 *Let G be a constraint grammar. A string of terminals of G is the yield of an admissible initial parse tree of G if, and only if, the string is in the language of G.*

This theorem tells us that a parser for a constraint grammar can operate by attempting to build an appropriate schematic tree. As we shall see, such a parser can be devised by modifying a CFG parser. The general idea is that since schematic trees are schematic for ground trees, we can view the computations that a constraint grammar parser does to construct a schematic tree as schematic for the computations that a CFG parser does to construct a ground tree. Let us first examine the computations of a CFG parser.

Given a CFG G and a string s, the goal of a parser is to construct an initial ground tree of G whose yield is s. Many algorithms for parsing CFGs can be seen as consisting of a control strategy for applying a single parsing rule:

The CFG Parsing Rule *Let $fs_1, fs_2, \ldots, fs_n$ be feature structures. Given a ground tree $\{[fs_1 \; fs_2 \cdots fs_n]\} \cup T$ and a ground tree T' whose root is labeled by fs_n, derive the ground tree $\{[fs_1 \; fs_2 \cdots fs_{n-1} \; p] \mid p \in T'\} \cup T$. The derived tree is called a* merge *of the first two trees.*

In other words, a merge of a ground tree with a leaf labeled fs_n and a ground tree with a root labeled fs_n is a ground tree produced by merging the leaf labeled fs_n in the first tree with the root of the second tree.

It is not difficult to see that the merge of two ground trees for a CFG is also a ground tree for that grammar. Furthermore, any ground tree for a CFG can be built by a finite number of applications of the CFG parsing rule starting with the trivial trees of the grammar. Thus we have:

Proposition 7 *The closure of the set of trivial parse trees of a context-free grammar G under the CFG parsing rule is precisely the set of parse trees for G.*

Thus, a CFG parsing algorithm that starts with the set of trivial trees of G and repeatedly expands the set by adding a merge of two trees in the set will generate only trees of G . At each point the control strategy must decide what merge to form next. Terms such as "top down," "bottom-up," and "left-to-right" describe properties of such control strategies.

Algorithms for parsing with a constraint grammar can be devised by adapting CFG parsing algorithms to operate on schematic trees instead of

CFG trees. Instead of using the CFG parsing rule, the constraint grammar parsing rule, which is defined below, is used. Adapting the control strategy to constraint grammar may involve some subtlety (e.g., Shieber 1985).

According to Theorem 6 the goal of the parser for a constraint grammar is to construct an initial, admissible schematic tree for G whose yield is the desired string. The parser could utilize any of a range of strategies for ensuring the admissibility of the ultimate tree. At one extreme, the parser could construct a complete tree and then test its admissibility. At the other extreme the parser could check the admissibility of every tree it builds and discard those that are inadmissible. This is justified because every subtree of an admissible schematic tree is admissible; every extension of an inadmissible tree is inadmissible. The cost of testing admissibility is usually cheap compared to the benefits of pruning the search space when an inadmissible schematic tree is discovered. This motivates the following parsing rule:

The Constraint Grammar Parsing Rule *Let $v_1, v_2, \ldots, v_n$ be variables, and let $T_1 = \{[v_1 \ v_2 \cdots v_n]\} \cup T$ and T_2 be admissible schematic trees with constraints C_1 and C_2, respectively. Let T_2' with constraint C_2' be the result of uniformly renaming the variables in T_2 and C_2 so that the root of T_2' is labeled v_n and T_1 and T_2' have no variables except v_n in common. If $C_1 \wedge C_2'$ is satisfiable then from T_1 and T_2 derive the schematic tree $\{[v_1 \ v_2 \cdots v_{n-1} \ p] \mid p \in T_2'\} \cup T$ with constraint $C_1 \wedge C_2'$. The resulting tree is called a* merge *of T_1 and T_2.*

In other words, a merge of a schematic tree with a leaf labeled v_n and an appropriately-renamed schematic tree with a root labeled v_n is a schematic tree produced by merging the leaf labeled v_n in the first tree with the root of the second tree. The constraint of the resulting tree is the conjunction of the constraints of the two original trees. The derivation is permitted only if the resulting tree is admissible.

It is not difficult to see that the merge of two admissible parse trees for a constraint grammar is also an admissible tree for that grammar. Furthermore, any admissible parse tree for a constraint grammar can be built by a finite number of applications of the constraint grammar parsing rule starting with the trivial trees of the grammar. Thus we have:

Proposition 8 *The closure of the set of trivial parse trees of a constraint grammar G under the constraint grammar parsing rule is precisely the set of admissible parse trees for G.*

The principal result of this paper, the correctness and completeness of the constraint grammar parsing rule, is an immediate consequence of Theorem 6 and Proposition 8.

Theorem 9 *A string s of terminals is in the language of the constraint grammar G if, and only if, from the trivial trees of G the constraint grammar parsing rule can build an initial admissible parse tree whose yield is s.*

7 Discussion

The two pieces of work most closely related to this work are the Ph.D. theses of Johnson (1988) and Shieber (1989). Though the formalism presented by Johnson is very similar to constraint grammar, his work focuses much less on parsing and much more on testing the satisfiability of constraints. Shieber's formalism is also very similar to constraint grammar, but when he comes to the topic of parsing he abandons constraints on feature structures, replacing them with feature structures themselves. Thus he loses the idea of building schematic parse trees and he views unification as a structure building operation rather than an operation for testing satisfiability of constraints.

Mendelson (1990) considers the problem of parsing with a feature-based grammar that includes feature co-occurrence restrictions (FCRs). FCRs are viewed as global declarations that place a constraint on every variable in every rule of the grammar. Because the same constraints are placed on every variable, certain optimizations can be made in parsing.

The results presented here could be generalized by abstracting away from the feature-based constraint system. Instead of considering the domain of feature structures and the particular constraint language of this paper, one could present the results in terms of an arbitrary domain and constraint language satisfying certain conditions.[4] All of the results of Section 6 carry over to this more general case. Definite Clause Grammars (Pereira and Warren 1980) are a special case of this generalization in which the domain is the set of ground terms and the constraints are conjunctions of equations between variables and non-ground terms.

Acknowledgements

I thank Jerry Morgan, Erhard Hinrichs and J. Michael Lake for their feedback on this work and Linda May for drawing some of the figures contained in the paper.

References

Backofen, Rolf and Gert Smolka. 1992. A complete and recursive function theory. Research Report RR-92-30, German Research Center for

---

[4]Höhfeld and Smolka (1988) have done this for constraint logic programming.

Artificial Intelligence.

Frisch, Alan M. 1986. Parsing with restricted quantification: An initial demonstration. In A. G. Cohn and J. R. Thomas (eds.), *Artificial Intelligence and its Applications*, pp 5–22. Chichester, UK: Wiley.

Haas, Andrew. 1989. A parsing algorithm for unification grammar. *Computational Linguistics*, 15(4):219–232.

Höhfeld, Markus and Gert Smolka. 1988. Definite relations over constraint languages. LILOG Report 53, IBM Deutschland.

Johnson, Mark. E. 1988. *Attribute-Value Logic and the Theory of Grammar*. Volume 16 of *CSLI Lecture Notes*, Center for the Study of Language and Information, Stanford, CA.

Maxwell III, John T. and Ronald M. Kaplan. 1991. A method for disjunctive constraint satisfaction. In Masaru Tomita (ed.), *Current Issues in Parsing Technology*, pp. 173–190, Kluwer Academic Publishers.

Mendelson, Michael J. 1990. Parsing feature-based grammars with feature co-occurrence restrictions. Master's thesis, Department of Computer Science, University of Illinois at Urbana-Champaign.

Nebel, Bernhard and Gert Smolka. 1990. Representation and reasoning with attributive descriptions. In K. H. Bläsius, U. Hedstück , and C.-R. Rollinger (eds.), *Sorts and Types in Artificial Intelligence*, pp. 112–139. Berlin, Heidelberg: Springer-Verlag.

Pereira, F. C. N. and D. H. D. Warren. 1980. Definite clause grammars for language analysis–A survey of the formalism and a comparison with augmented transition networks. *Artificial Intelligence*, 13:231–278.

Shieber, Stuart M. 1985. Using restriction to extend parsing algorithms for complex-feature-based formalisms. *Proceedings of the 23rd Annual Meeting of the Association for Computational Linguistics*, pp. 145–152.

Shieber, Stuart M. 1986. *An Introduction to Unification-Based Approaches to Grammar*, Volume 4 of *CSLI Lecture Notes*. Center for the Study of Language and Information, Stanford, CA.

Shieber, Stuart M. 1989. Parsing and type inference for natural and computer languages. Technical Report 460, SRI International.

Smolka, Gert. 1992. Feature constraint logics for unification grammars. *Journal of Logic Programming*, 12:51–87.

Part II

Automated Parsing and Generation

A Quarter Century of Computation with Transformational Grammar

Robert C. Berwick and Sandiway Fong

MIT Artificial Intelligence Laboratory

NEC Research Institute, Inc.

1 Introduction: plus ça change...

It seems altogether fitting that a historical celebration of a linguistics department should focus on a bit of history: the history of computation and generative grammar, in particular the history of how computer models of transformationally-based linguistic theories had changed radically, especially recently, to solve computational problems that had haunted them for at least a quarter century. In this article, we would like to show how the promised transparent computational implementations of transformational generative grammar – which made brief appearances in the middle 1960s along with similarly transparent incarnations in psycholinguistic and acquisition models, and then which gave way, in most cases rapidly, to alternative models or "nontransparent" replacements – can now, at long last, be said to have arrived. We can now build efficient parsers for transformational grammar, in its very latest incarnations, and reap all the benefits: transparent coverage of entire linguistic textbooks, top to bottom—one can write Case Assignment or the Empty Category Principle nearly as it appears in a textbook; no special treatment of so-called ungrammatical sentences; easy experimentation and exploration of alternative theory-internal changes; and simple parameter switching to get multiple languages and a better story about language acquisition.

At the same time, we would also like to emphasize the historical continuity of the project—that the transformational generative grammar (TGG) implementations of today face the same problems of overgeneration, constraints, abstraction, arbitrary empty strings, and the like that had to be faced in the 60s. However, we can now at least realize some of the hopes of the earliest researchers of the 60s: we can build a complete, efficient computer implementation, a parser, for the most recent versions of TGG, using an abstract language built on top of PROLOG that remains as close as can be expected to the English (or Italian, or German, ...) one finds in linguistic texts.

The question that naturally arises is: *why* now? Why does TGG parsing work now, and not 25 years ago (the MITRE project (Zwicky et al. 1965),

Friedman (1971), or Petrick (1965) systems)? The answer is two-fold. First, we just know more about linguistic representations, and that constrains the system: the Structure Preservation Hypothesis and constraints on landing sites limit the possibilities for inferring moved elements; deletion is more restricted (though infinite regress in adjunction still comes back to haunt us); X-bar theory limits the possibilities for phrase structures and lexical insertion; there are no ordered rules; and so forth. Second, we know more about computation. We can build efficient structural parsers that build the initial scaffolding (like the covering grammars of the 1960s), via multiple-entry type-inference LR machines. The most important trick in all of this is in using the notion of *language abstraction*: the abstract language stating the linguistic theory is automatically transformed via specially-built (but otherwise standard) compilers, into a form the user never sees, that does the actual work and bridges the gap between the abstract representation and efficient execution. In this regard the system is no different from any other programming language, or indeed from many other computational linguistic formalisms. (It is an open question as to whether we could take our updated technology and show that the older theory could have been implemented this way as well—we see no reason in principle why it could not, but for the improvements in the Structure Preservation Hypothesis, bounding deletion, and the like.)

The end result is that computation and TGG went through a U-shaped roller-coaster ride of transparency or faithfulness to the textual rendering of the theory (like the ups-and-downs of a classic learning curve): the initial ("rose") period of the 60s, when researchers tried to build systems where one actually wrote down structural descriptions, structural changes, the factorization of the rules, etc., ordered them, mimicking *Syntactic Structures* or *Aspects* exactly as one can see from the Petrick or Friedman system examples; followed by the middle ("blue") period of the 70s, when this transparency was cast aside in favor of rule systems that respected the representational descriptions and constraints of TGG (S-structure, etc.), but only relatively indirectly (for instance, the Marcus parser); to the current proposal, which is again deliberately transparent.

The implemented system we outline is ambitious: it attempts to incorporate essentially all of Lasnik and Uriagereka's *A course in GB theory* (Lasnik and Uriagereka 1989, henceforth LU). All of the theory in Chapters 1–4 of LU have been implemented. Chapter 5 of LU, covering alternatives to "classical" Binding Theory such as Aoun's Generalized Binding Theory, have not been implemented. Of the open questions posed in Chapter 6 of LU, we have adopted the prohibition against Case-marking of NP traces, and genitive Case realization to bar illicit NP movement. Certain other changes have been made in the interests of consistency or efficient computation, for instance, the use of erasable features as a substitute for gamma marking; we discuss some of these matters as they arise. (For a full description of the implemented theory, see Fong 1991, and Fong and Berwick 1992.) The parser incorporates a current (parameterized) X-bar theory of ten basic structures and 20 adjunct rules, including a full IP (Inflectional) and CP system, though not VP-internal subjects; general movement principles such as raising and lowering (including V raising/lowering); Full Interpretation (FI) and Functional Determination of empty categories; complete Case, Theta, and Binding conditions, along with LF and quantifier movement (QR); and so forth, totaling 25 modular principles that *interact* to give us the surface sentences that are possible. As far we have been able to determine, this is the most comprehensive parser of its kind, implementing the full range of examples found in a modern generative principles and parameters theory.

As mentioned, with this parser in hand, we can easily reap some of the long-promised rewards of using a well-worked out linguistic theory: without special rules of any kind or any specially-designed movement constraints and so forth, we can in a second or two parse examples as subtle as parasitic gap sentences (*this is the paper that I gave without reading*) as well as fail in exactly the ways that linguists' (and even ordinary people) predict for sentences like *What do you wonder who likes*, assigning exactly the same structures that people seem to. See Figure 1 for a picture of how the implemented system analyzes the parasitic gap sentence; along the righthand side of the screen is a full list of the principles themselves.

Perhaps most importantly, as promised in current approaches, cross-linguistic variation works: using the *same* parsing algorithm and the *same* grammar, but with small parametric variations and a new lexicon, we can parse, for instance, Japanese instead of English, in this case, the Lasnik and Saito (1984) *wh*-questions that illustrate scrambling and a rather subtle distribution of empty elements that are the meat of a modern theory. As an example, consider the Japanese sentence:

(1) *Taro-ga nani-o te-ni ireta koto-o sonnani okotteru no*
     'What are you so angry about the fact that Taro obtained'

Here the subject of the matrix clause (= *you*) has been omitted. *Nani* and *te* ('hand') have been permuted from an assumed canonical indirect object, direct object order—an example of scrambling. The LF for this sentence may be interpreted roughly as, for what x, *pro* is so angry about [the fact that Taro obtained x]. Here, *pro* represents the understood subject of *okotteru* ('be angry'). As we shall see, the implemented system does correctly recover this form (with some subtleties concerning alternative syntactic readings that we return to below). Thus as expected, on this account there is no separate phrase structure grammar for each language

(JapanesePSG or JPSG, GermanPSG, etc.)—just a single UG, plus a handful of switches. Furthermore, again as expected, it did not take long to "implement" the parser for the new language, if indeed one can even call it implementation. Automatic programming is a better name for it.

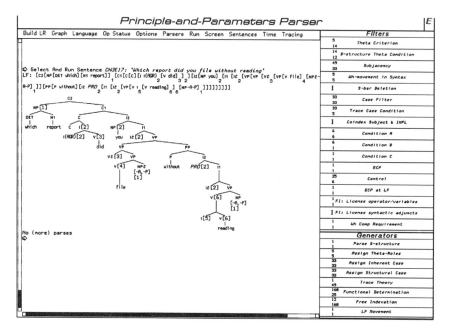

Figure 1: A snapshot of the computer output of the principles and parameters parser analyzing a parasitic gap sentence. The input is the sentence "which report did you file without reading." The output is a logical form tree. Along the righthand side of the screen is a full list of the principles used in the parsing system, that remains invariant from language to language.

Lest no one forget the distinction, this *is* a full-blooded parser. As Figure 1 shows, one supplies a sentence in orthographic form, and the parser returns the proper structural descriptions associated with the sentence: the associated S-structure, LF, and assignment of thematic roles and indices to NPs. Note that this is quite unlike some recent approaches where the computational system acts as a kind of "proof checker" where, given a structural description and LF, the computer will tell one whether or not that particular S-structure, LF, phonetic form triple can be derived from the axioms of the theory via "guided deductions," driven presumably for reasons of computational efficiency because these systems use more powerful theorem provers.

Note that in order to use such systems as parsers, the straightforward approach involves costly analysis-by-synthesis, and indeed timing results for such systems have been so far disappointing (Stabler 1992). We have found such first-order theorem provers and their attendant corner-cutting to be unnecessary. Indeed, their use may introduce a potentially pernicious influence that computer implementation is precisely designed to sidestep, in particular that the linguist knows just what the intended derivation of an example sentence is.[1]

Now of course we all know that linguists are infallible (who could deny it in such surroundings?), but to be sure, the implications of modern linguistic theories can be complex enough that it easy to lose track of what happens if some assumptions change, or even if they do not. In fact, we can document that this is so. For instance, as we shall see, the implemented system – reflecting the linguistic theory exactly – can produce many movement possibilities even in a simple sentence (for example, in the Japanese example above, there turn out to be 106 possibilities for movement and 468 indexings), and it is highly unlikely that a linguist would hit upon them all (present company excepted of course).

As a concrete example, a sentence that is standardly cited as a "Subjacency Violation," *Who does Mary wonder why John hit?* (Example 4:57 in LU) actually admits three structural possibilities that slip by that constraint but are ruled out later down the road by another condition, Condition B (they all involve a base-generated PRO bound to *John*, hence out by Condition B). These possible derivations were evidently never noticed before. Thus, building such a parser can explore unintended avenues of a theory, and so it becomes part of the theory-construction process itself. In general then, the search for *all* possible parses can produce somewhat unexpected results. We note that in such cases the parser is not "wrong" in the sense that it is producing parses that are inconsistent with linguistic theory. (Naturally, the parser falls down where the theory does, but then, so much the worse for the linguistic theory, at least—indeed, as we shall see, this is a benefit of the computer implementation.)

In short, it may well be true that linguistic theory is now deductively rich enough, like mathematics, that it actually *demands* a tireless machine to keep slavish track of all the bookkeeping. We should not be surprised by this. After all, there are now mathematical results, like the 4-color

---

[1] Other systems of this kind have been fragmentary, or else not really parsers at all in the sense of mapping input sentences in their orthographic form to structural descriptions. The best worked-out example that we know of, Stabler's (1992) formalization of Chomsky's (1986) *Barriers* model, has two admitted shortcomings: first, *Barriers* is but a fragment of a principles and parameters syntactic theory; and second, the resulting formalization is not a parser (it can only check structural descriptions for well-formedness, it cannot map sentences to their structural descriptions efficiently enough).

map theorem, proved only by machine. Beyond this however, the parser is complete enough to serve as a kind of linguists' apprentice, if you will—an oft-cited goal from the 1960s, but even more appropriate today. Such a give-and-take partnership is possible only if the system does in fact parse fast enough to make user interaction bearable, and if the system explores all possibilities, rather than letting the user exclude some cases that would actually reveal gaps in the theory.

So, let us give a roadmap then for the remainder of this article. We shall swiftly review the earlier ages that implemented TGG: first, the Dawn Age (classic transformational parsers); followed by the Dark Age (little or no work on parsing and TGG); and then the Middle Ages (the Marcus parser and its relatives), pointing out the relevant difficulties that moved linguists and computation from one age to the next. We conclude with the Renaissance: the computational representation and control of a transparent implementation of a principle and parameters linguistic theory.

2   The Dawn Age

Dawn is marked by rose – the rosy-fingered dawn, or *rotodactylos* as Homer said – and optimism similarly suffused this period of computation and TGG. It was thought that transformational generative grammar could be used directly as a parser for natural languages. Like all dawns however, this early hope faded. Why? Transparent parsers for TGG used the familiar structural description matching/factorization–structural change format along with the usual base context-free structure grammar, thus yielding highly language-particular and surface and construction-oriented rule systems. A standard example would be the "passive" construction in English:

structural	NP	[+V +Aux],		[+V −Aux],		NP
description	1	2		3		4
structural						
change	4	2	Be+en	3	by	1

Note that this rule is in fact particular to English—it explicitly encodes the left-to-right order of English subjects and objects, the morphology of *be*, and so forth. A typical transformational system for even a fragment of a language, say, English, would consist of well over a hundred such rules; for instance, the MITRE system (Zwicky et al. 1965) contained 134 such rules, and Petrick's question answering system (Plath 1976) many more.

We call parsing systems based on such rules *transparent* because they embed rules directly in a parsing device, without additional source-to-source translation. To take another example consider the rule of subject formation from Petrick (1965) that attaches a *wh*-NP to the Auxiliary position, converting for instance *will who eat ice-cream* into *who will eat ice-cream*, while checking that the sentence has not already been turned into a question. Each subtree component is marked with a number (1 through 6, 6= the Sentence; 1= boundary marker #, 2= the Auxiliary tree; 3= NP; 4= any subtree X; and 5= a boundary marker #). The transformation adjoins component 3, the *wh*-NP, to subtree 2, leaving behind nothing:

> RULE SUBJFRMA (subject formation)
> structural
> description: S1 # AUX NP X #
>   1 2 3 4 5
> constraints: or: *not* S1 marked +*Ques*
>   NP is marked +*wh*
> structural
> change: 1 (3 2) 0 4 5

Note that on top of these detailed surface-patterned conditions, transformational rules were marked as obligatory or optional, cyclic or postcyclic, embedding or not, and so forth. These and other systems were intended to be used as full-fledged parsers, linguistic apprentices, and so forth—all the conventional noble goals. However, as is well known, there were many computational problems with such parsing systems—so many problems that the transparent, transformational rule-reversal approach was abandoned in computational linguistics. We summarize some of the familiar difficulties here:

1. Rules were ordered in intricate ways. Further, one could delete items, so a forward transformational rule need not be invertible (if an item is deleted, what do we invert it to?). Thus, in general the mapping backwards from an input string to a structural description would be highly nondeterministic.

2. Since rules operated only on structural descriptions (factorized trees), and we are given a sentence not a tree to parse, any parser must first recover some structure to match against. A common solution to this problem (adopted by MITRE, for example), was to build a phrase structure *covering grammar* for a (superset) of initial structural descriptions, and then attempt to run rules (deterministically) in reverse against these.

3. Arbitrary deletion can loop, or, at best, take at least exponential space. As a simple example, consider any transformation that deletes some element. We cannot literally invert this to say that this element

may be inserted between *any* two positions in a tree. To consider another example, the explicit reconstruction of an empty subject, as in Peters' (1973) example *Their sitting down threatens [empty] to spoil the joke*, where the *empty* position corresponds to *their sitting down*. If we embed this again, as in [*their sitting down promising [empty] to steady the canoe*]$_2$ *threatens [empty$_2$] to spoil the joke*, then the second empty position, when reconstructed, contains the original full subject, with *its* reconstructed subject. If the deep structure of such examples is *explicitly* reconstructed, then the empty subject can be embedded over and over again, which leads to a deep structure that is doubly exponentially larger than the surface structure, and inevitable computational intractability. Of course, there are familiar termination problems with the arbitrary Turing machine computations that can be simulated with unrestricted *Aspects* type systems.

To attempt to overcome these problems the MITRE system used a context-free *surface grammar* with 49 rules and 550 subrules to first recover a set of *presumable surface trees*, and from there use reverse transformations to recover *presumable base trees* (that is, representations of thematic relations, or a combination of what is now D-structure and LF). These were then filtered by a final stage where the presumable base or D-structure tree was driven by forward transformations and then checked against the given sentence. Great effort was expended at developing covering grammars and inverse transformations in the MITRE system. To reduce nondeterminism, the inverse transforms were assumed to be obligatory—that is, the system did not follow the alternative paths of both applying and not applying the inverse. (We shall see that the system we describe overcomes this problem and considers both possibilities.) Even so, practical parsing efficiency was not achieved. The MITRE authors note that even with a much smaller grammar for some simple sentences, *The general that Johnson met in Washington had traveled eight thousand miles*, over 48 presumable surface trees were obtained. Their conclusion was simple. To quote them (Zwicky et al. 1965:325):

> It is clear from even these few numbers that if the procedure is to be practical, it will be necessary to incorporate a highly efficient routine for obtaining surface trees and to work on the rapid elimination of spurious ones.

Strikingly, this efficiency proved very hard to achieve. Perhaps the only widely-publicized example of a TGG system that achieved practical speeds was the method of Petrick (Petrick 1965, Plath 1976), developed at IBM that was actually used in a database question-answering system. This method also used a covering grammar, using powerful augmentations of a context-free grammar to reduce the number of surface trees; however, it remained grounded in transformational models of the 1960s.

3 The Dark Age

After the Dawn Age of the early 1960s we enter Dark Age. Not only were methods based on TGG discredited for parsing, but early transparent approaches to psycholinguistics grounded on TGG lost favor. By the early 1970s it was possible for standard texts to proclaim the demise of TGG. Fodor, Bever, and Garrett (1974:368) have this to say:

> ...there exist no suggestions about how a generative grammar might be concretely employed as a sentence recognizer in a psychologically plausible model.

while a comparable text on language acquisition by Maratsos (1978:246) gave the same message:

> If...transformational grammars represent the essence of the linguistic system captured by the child, the phenomenon of language acquisition seems to be an inexplicable mystery.

As is familiar, to fill this apparent explanatory gap, several more "computationally oriented" approaches were devised, augmented transition network grammars being among the most prominent. Alternative linguistic theories were also proposed, presumably more consonant with processing and acquisition considerations. Transformational approaches, save for efforts like that of Petrick, died out.

Like the Dawn, this Dark Age did not last forever, however. By focusing on at least one of the computational problems with TGG, namely, its computational inefficiency, some insights were soon won about how to emerge from the shadows of the past.

4 The Middle Ages: Transparency Lost and Regained

By the middle 1970s, our understanding of both linguistic and computational theory had advanced to the point where parsers for TGG could again be taken seriously. The key to this advance was *constraint*. On the linguistic side, prompted by empirical and learnability considerations, TGG was constrained in a number of directions. Transformations were made optional; extrinsic rule ordering was eliminated; the Structure Preservation Hypothesis ensured that most derived structures could be base generated (by some context-free grammar) anyway; X-bar theory demonstrated how the lexicon could be used to fix most of the individual phrase structure rules of the base; full copies of empty pronominals were replaced by indexing of empty elements not subject to recursion; and individual rules were shown to be subject to island constraints and other locality conditions, unifying some under a single movement rule—the Extended Standard Theory (EST).

On the computational side, the corresponding constraint was *determinism* as advanced in the Marcus parser (Marcus 1980). Marcus avoided the problems with the MITRE system by eliminating the backwards nondeterminism inherent in the older system: he assumed that local surface cues were enough to fix the inverse application of transformational rules, building an EST-type S-structure. The parser was deterministic in the sense that a single structure was built—hence each operation was deterministic, if one considered the operation of the parsing engine as the operation of an automaton (this was borne out by subsequent analysis by Berwick (1985) and more carefully by Nozohoor-Farshi (1987) in which it was established that the languages recognized by the Marcus-type devices were deterministic context-free languages).

Note how these assumptions remove the problems of the earlier TGG systems: deleted elements are assumed to be recoverable from structural cues; by positing that this is just deterministic context-free parsing a large search space of possible trees to map back to is eliminated. Further, by using explicit phonetically null categories that could not be successively embedded, degenerate examples of the Peters' type were avoided. Of course, the trick in all of this is to show that this is sufficient to cover the entire linguistic theory.

Using the older linguistic terminology, the Marcus parser used a set of structural descriptions and inverse structural changes that were strongly constrained, in the following sense. The structural descriptions, the triggering patterns for structural changes, were constrained to examine only (i) the features of the topmost node in a pushdown stack (say, a VP or NP) and its daughters, along with (ii) the features of perhaps one additional node in this stack, plus (iii) the features three input buffer cells, namely the current input word or phrase of the sentence being analyzed, along with two additional words or phrases. This locality condition on structural descriptions had the effect of enforcing c-command and other locality conditions as required by the EST theory (see Berwick 1985 for details). Put another way, the architectural features of the system constrained structural descriptions, as argued by Marcus (1980). Structural changes were also constrained to be deterministic, as mentioned: they could not remove features or structure, but simply monotonically add to it; further, they also were subject to the same locality restrictions as structural descriptions.

We can now compare an old-style transformational rule, say, passive, with the corresponding structural description–structural change format (if–then rules) in the Marcus parser, and note where the constraints make a difference.

We repeat below the English passive rule as it might be written in an older transformational system:

structural	NP	[+V +Aux],		[+V −Aux],		NP
description	1	2		3		4
structural	4	2	Be+en	3	by	1
change						

Under the constrained formulation, the object NP is base-generated as before (reflecting its underlying thematic role), and then, by the Structure Preservation Hypothesis, can move into an empty Subject position, leaving behind a phonetically null element. The movement does not violate any locality constraints. (The creation of the *by* phrase remains a bit of a mystery on this account.) More importantly from the parsing standpoint, the structure after the movement has occurred can serve as a deterministic triggering surface pattern for a corresponding rule inverse.

This is just what the Marcus parser does. In the Marcus version, this single rule is broken down into three rules, to pick up one piece at a time the left-to-right "proper analysis" of the structure *after* the transformation. The passive rule itself depends on prior marking of the verb as passive, which in turn depends on detecting an auxiliary form of the verb *be* plus a verb with *ed* morphology, as in *Mary was kissed*, roughly as follows (the exact rule formulations have been slightly modified for readability):

Rule 1:
passive-auxiliary:

trigger:	input cell 1	cell 2
	root *be*	verb marked *en*
action:	attach *be* form	
	as passive	
	mark verb as *passive*	

Rule 2:
trigger: verb marked *passive*
action: run Rule 3

Rule 3:
trigger: verb marked *passive*
action: insert NP trace
            as object (link to Subject)

Note that the division into separate rules is required by the way the parser works left to right: the Subject NP must first be parsed as if it were a declarative, and only then is the auxiliary verb and verb with passive morphology picked up. This is the first part of the proper analysis tree factorization (in reverse). (In fact, the whole rule is properly conditioned with features beyond the feature proxy *en* so that only passivizable verbs will be marked as such, this detail being suppressed here.) Next, when the verb such as *kissed* is actually in the first buffer position, the parser creates a VP (not shown here), and then inserts a phonetically null NP, a trace, into the first buffer position. This NP is then parsed just as if it were an ordinary object noun phrase, by the same rule that parses noun phrases. By the determinism hypothesis, it is assumed that there is a unique action for every trigger (where the triggers may be prioritized essentially by specificity).

However, by slicing up the rules in this way the parser does lose some of the modularity of the EST system itself. Not only has one rule been split across three, but the division of the EST theory into an X-bar base (forming D-structure) plus transformations has been partially obscured. In the original Marcus parser, much of the information about phrase structure or X-bar constraints was encoded in a particular sequence of *packet* activations that turned on or off whole rule groups at a time. In our example, the rules to parse specifiers of Inflection phrases (or IP projections in current terminology) are collected into a single group, a *Parse-Subject* packet. Rules can only trigger if the corresponding packet they are in is activated (by some previous rule); this activation sequence corresponds roughly to the Specifier-Head-Complement order of X-bar phrase structure. Similarly, the expansion of INFL itself is guided by a linear sequence of packet activations.

Modularity is obscured (and transparency violated) because there is nothing in the parser's rule-writing framework to guarantee this division into X-bar rules plus transformations. For instance, Rule 3 that actually inserts a trace into the NP object position resides in its own packet, apart from other verb complement rules. Similarly, the division into three separate rules is demanded in part by the exigencies of left-to-right analysis of the input. More generally, one can see that this parser is construction-specific: the rules to handle a sentence that in modern terms is putatively derived from the same constraints, such as *It was believed that the ice-cream was eaten*, requires an entirely different set of four or five completely different rules. In this way, commonalities among syntactic phenomena are obscured rather than illuminated.

Further, ideally the restrictions of movement phenomena generally are motivated in the Marcus parser specifically by determinism and the functional architecture of the parsing machine. This is both a plus and a minus. On the plus side, the locality restrictions on stack and buffer access conspire with determinism to guarantee a linear time parse (this much follows from the formal results about the class of deterministic context-free languages parsable by this device); on the minus side, basic linguistic constraints like c-command and subjacency are thereby implicitly "hidden" from the operation of the rules themselves. Efficiency seems to have been purchased at the price of a loss in theoretical transparency.

Expanding on this last point, and turning to more recent analyses of so-called "passive constructions," we find that passive is not a unitary phenomenon. Passive includes movement of the object; inserting a *be* and altering the main verb's morphology, and adding the *by* phrase. Chomsky noted a decade ago that all of these components can occur on their own. Specifically, the object can be in subject position even without a verb, as in *the destruction of the city* yielding *the city's destruction*); the *by* phrase can appear by itself, as in *the book understandable by everyone*; passive morphology can occur by itself, as in *the melted ice-cream*. Further confirmation comes from examining languages that have different word orders than English, but still exhibit passive-like sentences, say, languages like Japanese, German, or Dutch, where the verb comes at the end, revealing that even the Subject—Verb—Object Passive Rule triggering pattern was illusory: in Dutch we have *Kees zei dat Jan Marie kuste* ('Kees said that Jan Mary kissed') and the corresponding passive form *Kees zei dat Marie door Jan gekust werd* ('Kees said that Mary by Jan kissed was'); (see Kolb and Thiersch 1990:252-253 for these examples).

What the Marcus parser has done, then, is to take presumably deeper underlying principles and "compile" them out via deductive chains, yielding particular surface sequence patterns. Over the past decade, linguistic research in the EST tradition has eliminated language-specific rules in favor of a small set of universal principles plus parametric variation, perhaps restricted to the lexicon; we shall turn to these in the next section. Thus, while the deterministic Marcus parser design achieved a considerable success in terms of efficiency and faithfulness to the input-output representations of linguistic theory within its own era, it does not employ current theoretical vocabulary or mirror precisely the fundamental "atoms" of current *principles and parameters* theory. As a result, cross-linguistic parser construction is difficult. For example, the parser architectural constraint that helps ensure the locality condition known as the Specified Subject Condition actually depends on the specific Subject-Inflection order of items in English. Similarly, the English parser rules rely on the head-first character of phrases: given a preposition, verb, determiner, and so forth, then the parser can easily predict the existence of a prepositional phrase, verb phrase, noun phrase, and so forth. Indeed, this almost makes the parser a *left-corner parser*, using the same strategy for English as Head-Driven Phrase Structure Grammar. Building a parser for a head-final language, such as Japanese or German, entails major surgery; indeed, it is not clear that such a project can be carried out at all.[2]

In short, with the advent of constraints in the TGG theory of the 1970s, determinism and faithful construction of TGG representations TGG proved to be a major step forward out of the Dark Ages for TGG parsing. What remained was to build a system that was efficient and faithful to more recent grammatical theory in both input/output representations *and* operating principles. That is our story for the Renaissance of TGG parsing, described next.

5   The Renaissance: A Principles and Parameters Parser

As is well known, the past decade has seen a shift in transformational generative grammar from homogeneous, language-particular accounts of rules such as passive to a highly modular, non-homogeneous, and parameterized deductive system of universal principles. Following current practice, we shall call such approaches *principles and parameters theories*. On this view, there is no "rule" of passive, but rather a system of (declarative) constraints that interact to yield surface forms in English that may be described as passive. If we think of the principles as axioms, the passive construction emerges as a theorem. But the deductive chain is much longer than in a simple if-then rule system like the Marcus parser, where there is a direct, one-step connection between passive sentences and rules. Let us briefly review this notion here, and then see how to make use of it in a parser.

Assuming some familiarity with the familiar "Y-diagram" of linguistic representations in transformational theory linking phonetic form (the ortho-

---

[2]The only large-scale German Marcus-style parsers that this author knows of, with many hundreds of rules, were constructed for the MIT Athena Foreign Language Instruction Project. This parsing system proved to be extremely unwieldy for both German and Japanese.

graphic input), LF, S-structure, and thematic representation (D-structure), as well as the basic components of this theory, we shall merely note here some of the (universal) principles involved that "force" the derivation of a passive sentence:

(1) X-bar theory: Languages allow just two basic tree shapes or *parameterizations* for their constituent phrases: (i) function–argument order, as in English, where heads begin constituents; or (ii) or the mirror image, argument–function form, as in Japanese or German.

(2) Thematic theory: Every verb must assign a thematic role to its "arguments" that says, roughly, who did what to whom; and every Subject and Object must receive exactly one such role.

(3) Case Theory: Overt or pronounced Subjects or Objects must receive *Case* where by *Case* we mean an abstract version of what one would find in a Latin grammar. The Subject position receives, or is assigned, nominative case from the inflection of a verb; the Object of the verb receives accusative case; the Object of a preposition receives oblique case, and so on.

(4) Movement theory: Any phrase can move anywhere (*move-α*), subject to locality constraints. When it does, it leaves behind a phonetically silent element, a trace, linked to itself.

Given these axioms, then we can derive a passive sentence such as *the ice-cream was eaten* as follows:

X-bar theory sets the basic function-argument order of English
↓
∅ *was eaten the ice-cream*
↓
Eaten is an adjective, and so does not assign Case
↓
Ice-cream must receive Case
↓
Ice-cream (allowably) moves to subject position
where it receives nominative case
↓
Leave behind an empty category, linked to *ice-cream*
(so that *eat* can meet thematic constraints and
make *ice-cream* the thing eaten)
↓
the ice-cream was eaten trace

Just as with the earlier TGG systems, the key question now is how are we to build a parser to invert the derivation and map from sentence to its underlying structural representation (both S-structure and its so-called Logical Form)? Further, how can we do this efficiently? Note that this problem is already different from that of earlier transformational theory, for two important reasons: first, the system is formulated as a system of declarative constraints on representations; second, the constraints themselves are deterministic (given one input tree they produce only one output).

Pursuing this proposal, we can divide principles into one of two classes: *generators* and *filters*. Generators produce or hypothesize possible structures. For example, consider X-bar theory. Given a string of words, say, *eat the ice-cream*, this theory theory would say that *eat* is possibly the beginning of a verb phrase, with *the ice-cream* as its argument. Similarly, movement creates possible structures. Given a valid X-bar structure, move-α can displace various noun phrases like *ice-cream* to create new ones.

Filters weed out possible structures. For example, if the structure *John is proud ice-cream* is input to Case Theory it would be filtered out as a violation (it should be *proud of ice-cream*, where *of* assigns case to *ice-cream*). Our actual system contains 17 filters and eight generators, as shown in Table 1.

Given this generator-filter model, the simplest way to build a parser is as a cascaded sequence of principle modules, with the input sentence piped in at one end and one or more Logical Forms emerging out the other: the sentence must run a gauntlet of constraints. For example, consider the example sentence, *Mary was kissed*. We can imagine passing it first through the X-bar module, producing several output possibilities depending on word and structural ambiguities, as is typical of context-free parsing generally. All the usual techniques for efficient processing, such as lookahead, can be useful here.

Continuing, let us suppose that the hypotheses output from the X-bar component, tree structures, are fed into the next module down the line, say Case Theory. Case Theory now acts as a declarative filter on the output trees, eliminating some of them. Next, Movement expands the possibilities once more, generating all possible structures with displaced phrases; continuing, after several running through several other constraint modules, the final output Logical Form will emerge (if one is possible at all).

Of course, this is still mere conceptual handwaving. We still face the problems of twenty years ago: (1) how can we generate just the right trees to begin with; (2) how can we invert the effects of transformations? In response to these demands, we adopt a more sophisticated parsing approach that *combines* some of the features of analysis-by-synthesis ("generate-and-test") and analysis-by-analysis ("invert from the sentence"), relying on the declarative determinacy of filters (they produce only single outputs) and the

Filters
Theta Criterion
D-structure Theta Condition
Subjacency
Wh-movement in Syntax
S-bar deletion
Case Filter
Trace Case Condition
Agreement of Subject and Inflection
Condition A (anaphors bound in governing category)
Condition B (pronominals free in governing category)
Condition C (referring expressions free)
Empty Category Principle
Control Theory
Empty Category Principle at LF
Full interpretation: license operator-variables
Full interpretation: license syntactic adjuncts
Wh Comp requirement
Generators
Build quasi-S structure
Assign thematic roles
Assign inherent Case
Assign structural Case
Move-α
Functional determination of empty categories
Free indexation
LF movement

Table 1: The principles (filters and generators) used by the principles and parameters parser.

restrictiveness of generators (so-called empty positions are highly restricted in nature).

These are by no means trivial problems. Combining the possibilities of adjunction and empty categories in a simple X-bar theory implies that one can associate with a single lexical token, a verb say, with a countably infinite number of well-formed adjoined VP structures with empty categories at the leaves. To take a concrete example, on common assumptions each terminal element of the following basic clausal structure may be empty, that is, $CP \overset{*}{\Rightarrow} \lambda$:[3]

(2) $[_{CP}$ Spec $[_{C'}$ C $[_{IP}$ NP $[_{I'}$ I $[_{VP}$ $[_{V'}$ V NP]]]]]]

Recursion through CP will then lead immediately to nontermination problems, since we can generate an arbitrarily long string of empty elements.

How do we get around such problems? In brief we use a covering grammar to generate a superset of hypotheses that satisfy X-bar theory and any base-generated empty elements, while incorporating the constraints from the actual sentence elements (thus carrying out analysis-by-analysis of the sentence as well). These candidate structures are then passed through the filters and generators, perhaps in a parallel (interleaved) way.

The reason for starting with X-bar theory is simple. Many, if not most, of the constraints depend on particular structural configurations. For instance, Case is often assigned only under a particular local structural arrangement—the element receiving case is an immediately adjacent sister to a verb or a preposition. These logical dependencies must be respected in any principles and parameters parser design.

The theory components themselves – the principles – are encoded using terms and predicates as close to the linguistic theory as possible; we give examples below. Thus the parser aims to be as transparent as possible, within the constraints of attaining efficient parsability. In fact, both goals seem to be fairly well attained, with average parsing times on the order of a few seconds or less for the several hundred example sentences in the Lasnik and Uriagereka (1989) reference book that we used.

In the sequel, we first describe how the principle-based parser works via a parasitic gap example sentence, while discussing the operation of the covering grammar. We then continue with an illustration of the power

---

[3]The NP may be empty to account for empty categories; by head movement, both V and I may be lexically empty; C may be filled by an empty complementizer; the Specifier of C need not be filled at all. Notational conventions: We adopt a two-level system for all categories except verbs; hence CP=C2, IP=I2; C'=C1, I'=I1; C0= lexical head, etc., in our structures. For VPs we have a 3-level system, to attach indirect and direct objects to V2 and V1, respectively. For readability we sometimes use CP, VP, and so forth instead of C2, V2, and on.

of the system by demonstrating how simple it is to switch to a different language, in this case, Japanese.

6   How the Parser Works

To see how the parser actually works together with the linguistic section we work through the parasitic gap example given in the first section in detail, showing how the 25 principles interact to yield precisely the correct output analysis. As mentioned earlier, the parser produces correct parses in the sense that it succeeds or blocks as described in the LU textbook for each example.

Recall that for this sentence the parser builds an LF with a controlled PRO indexed to *you* as the subject of *reading*, while a pure variable fills the position after *reading* (marked −A(naphoric) −P(ronominal) via the functional determination of empty categories, as adopted here); an NP trace is the object of *file*, coindexed to the parasitic empty category and to *which report*. Note also that head movement has taken place: *do* is raised to Inflection, so as to receive tense, and then the Verb-Inflection complex raised and adjoined to C yielding Subject-Auxiliary inversion. All this detail is captured by the 25 principles shown in Figure 1 and Table 1.

We first give an overview of the computation, and then go back and cover in detail how the parser works (refer back to Figure 1.) Basically, there two main parsing stages: (1) S-structure recovery via a covering grammar; and (2) the application of the remaining filters and generators.

In Stage I a *single* quasi-S-structure is recovered by a special-purpose LR machine, with generic empty categories already placed in the positions of the object of *file*, the subject of *reading*, and the object of *reading*, and with head movement and inversion computed (but *sans* indices for NPs, the identity of the empty categories and so forth). This is done by a full LR(1) parser that uses a 30-rule grammar to generate quasi-S-structures. We use the term "quasi-S-structure" because the phrase structure that is generated does not meet all the constraints on S-structure; in particular, empty categories are inserted in all possible locations without further checking and without their features (as traces, PRO, etc.) being determined. For instance, the first stage LR parser assigns the same structure to *John seems to be happy* and *John wants to be happy*, inserting a *generic* empty category as the subject of the complement CP. Later principles must fix these empty categories as a trace in the first case but not the second. It is this simplification that allows the first stage LR machine to be small and efficient; it does not try to check all principle conditions at once. The LR machine we use has multiple table entries to handle ambiguity in natural languages, including the possibility that an empty category might or might not be inserted in some position.

Free (optional) Movement then fans this single output to 49 candidates, which are whittled down to five by locality and case constraints; Free Indexing expands these back to 36, and then the Theta Criterion, Control, and Condition B cut these back to just a single final LF (we shall see in detail how this is done next).

(3)   *Which report did you file without reading?*

(4)   Stage I (S-structure with underdetermined empty categories):

$[_{C2}$ $[_{NP}$ $[_{Det}$ *which*$][_{N1}$ *report*$]]$ $[_{C1}$ $[_{C}$ $[C]$ $[_{I}$ I(Agr) $[_{V}$ *did*$]]]$ $[_{I2}$ $[_{NP}$ *you*$]$ $[_{I1}$ $[_{I}$ *trace-I* $[_{VP}$ $[_{VP}$ $[_{V}$ *trace-do* $[_{VP}$ $[_{V}$ *file* $[_{NP}$ *NP-ec*$[\pm A \pm P]]]]$ $[_{PP}$ $[_{P}$ *without*$][_{I2}$ $[_{NP}$ *NP-ec*$[\pm A \pm P]][_{I1}$ $[_{I}$ *trace-I* $[_{VP}$ $[V$ I *reading*$]]$ $[_{NP}$ *NP-ec*$[\pm A \pm P]]]]]]]]]]]]]$

(5)   Final LF output:

$[_{CP}$ $[$ NP $[_{Det}$ *which*$]$ $[_{N1}$ *report*$]_{1}]$ $[_{C1}$ $[_{C}$ $[_{C}$ $]$ $[_{I}$ I(Agr) *did*$]]]$ $[_{IP}$ $[_{NP}$ *you*$]_{2}$ $[_{I1}$ $[_{I}$ *trace I–do* $[_{VP}$ $[_{VP}$ $[_{V}$ *trace-do* $[_{VP}$ $[_{V}$ *file*$]]]$ $[_{NP}$ *NP-t*$[-A-P]]_{1}]]$ $[_{PP}$ $[_{P}$ *without*$]$ $[_{I2}$ $[_{NP}$ PRO$_{2}$ $[_{I1}$ $[_{I}$ *trace-I* $[_{VP}$ $[_{V}$ I $[_{V}$ reading$]]$ $[_{NP}$ *NP-*$[-A-P]]]]]]]]]]]$

Between Stage I's Parse S-structure output and the single, final LF output above there is much work done in Stage II. The reader can follow along by noting the numbers at the top and bottom of each principle box in the computer snapshot. Numbers going in denote structures input to a principle module, and numbers out are those that make it through (either generated or filtered).

Briefly, the cascade of the remaining 24 principles runs like this:[4] Full Interpretation of syntactic adjuncts at S-structure and Sbar-deletion do not weed out any structures.

Next, Move-α applies freely, compositionally computing all possible chains and assigning indices, in this example yielding 49 candidates. The actual algorithm is sophisticated, but the central concept is not. The mechanism used here essentially builds all possible chains by computing the set cross-product of possible links between existing empty categories and partial chains as the parser walks a candidate tree structure, extending partial chains or not as the parser compositionally traverses the tree structure it

---

[4]The principles are ordered as shown in the figure, but not the computer snapshot; note that principles may be statically or dynamically reordered, often with significant computational effects. For optimal performance, the operative principle is to delay candidate hypothesis expansion by generating principles like movement as long as possible and apply filtering principles like the Case Filter or Condition B as soon as possible, subject to the logical dependencies of the theory. The connection between principle ordering and "guiding principles" such as Earliness or Least Effort in recent linguistic discussion has not escaped our notice.

has already built, starting with some selected empty category, and keeping track of partial chains built so far as well as remaining free empty NP candidates or a final non-trace NP head for the chain.

This nondeterminism reflects the complete optionality of the underlying linguistic system. All movement is optional. Hence, for each empty category the parser can either decide or not for it to participate in an already existing partial chain, do nothing, be a 1-element trivial chain, or start a new chain, all nondeterministically. Naturally, this process must meet some constraints; for example, no chain can cross more than one bounding node, violating subjacency. In addition, an overt NP optionally heads a chain; an element cannot participate in more than one chain, and all chains must be complete, that is, headed by a non-trace element (hence, an empty Operator can head a chain, for relative clauses).[5]

As a simple example, consider the generic empty NP after *reading*. The parser may freely decide to have this empty NP start a chain, be a trivial 1-element chain, or do nothing at all with it. If it has started a chain (it is the tail), then on composing the subtree in resides in with the subtree of the next highest maximal clause, the VP, we find that there are no additional empty NP candidates in the subtrees below the VP to select, so the VP simply inherits as its (partial) chains the base partial NP trace chain. Compositionally moving one more tree up, to the IP, the parser can now examine the subtrees of IP and take note of the candidate empty NP that is the subject of *reading*. Thus the parser may now freely select to extend its partial chain by using this free candidate or not (if that candidate were already the part of another chain, it would not be on the list of free candidates). Suppose it does. Similarly, a few compositional steps later, the parser may freely select to end the chain with the non-trace head *which report*. Thus the parser can and does output the following (ultimately failed) possibility, where *which report* is linked to both the object of *file* and the subject of *reading*. (Note the coindexing; here, the object of *file* is in effect an intermediate trace, and the object of *reading* is not part of any movement chain.) Note that some (movement) indices are now in place. Of course, we must ensure that this Chain Formation algorithm in complete, so that among all these possibilities we generate at least all the proper chains as well.

(6) $[_{C2}$ $[_{NP}$ $[_{Det}$ *which*$]$ $[_{N1}$ *report*$]]_1$ $[_{C1}$ $[_{C}$ $[_{C}$ $]$ $[_{I}$ (Agr) $[_{V}$ *did*$]]]$ $[_{I2}$ $[_{NP}$ *you*$]_2$ $[_{I1}$ $[_{It}$ $[_{VP}$ $[_{VP}$ $[_{Vt}$ $[_{VP}$ $[_{V}$ *file*$]$ $[_{NP}$ *NP-t*$[$-A-P$]]_1]]$ $[_{PP}$ $[_{P}$ *without*$]$ $[_{I2}$ $[_{NP}$ *NP-t*$[$-A-P$]]_1$ $[_{I1}$ $[_{It}$ $[_{VP}$ $[_{V}$ I $[_{V}$ *reading*$]]$ $[_{NP}$ *NP-*$[$-A-P$]]]]]]]]]]]]]]]]$

---

[5]For reasons of space we must omit here how the parser makes sure it is not building redundant chains as well as checking the *i*-within-*i* condition of circularly referential chains. We have also taken some liberties with the full description of the composition process.

Next, these chain-augmented structures are assigned structural and inherent Case, and run through the Case Filter (in this example, with no effect on eligible candidates). Of these 49 different chain outputs with Case now assigned, all but five will pass through both the Trace Case Condition (traces cannot have Case) and Subjacency, with θ-Roles being assigned in between these two constraints, and *Wh*-movement in Syntax checked (as appropriate for the language).[6] Specifically, the fourth chain output from these two constraints will ultimately prove to be the winning structure (though the system cannot know that yet, of course). This has a single chain linking the object of *file* to *which report*, and leaves the subject and object of *reading* as unspecified empty categories.

Proceeding, Free Indexing greatly expands these five possibilities to 36 by computing all possible indexings between any remaining unindexed NPs. Again, the process works essentially by forming the compositional cross-product of possible indices: if we have three indices i, j, and k, then either they are all unequal; i and j equal, k, unequal, etc.—precisely the problem of partitioning n elements (the NPs) into m sets (the indices). Features of the empty elements are fixed by the theory of Functional Determination, a theoretical choice point that can in fact be altered; the parser would then simply be using a different grammatical theory.

Finally, Control Theory cuts these 36 structures down to ten (ruling out uncontrolled PRO); passing through the Theta-Criterion and Binding Conditions A, B, C, the Empty Category Principle, LF movement, and Full Interpretation at LF, the parser eliminates all but one of the viable candidates, striking out (via Condition B for the most part) cases where PRO is bound in its minimal governing category where it should not be. Out of many hundreds of possible interactions, the single right result emerges, as displayed earlier.

This sketch does not say *how* the Stage I and Stage II processes are carried out in detail. While there is not enough space for a full description here (see Fong and Berwick 1992), we can give at least some of the details about how the quasi-S-structures are computed and how linguistic principles are represented and applied. Let us cover these topics in turn.

6.1   Stage I: Building Phrase Structure

The key idea to build the quasi-S-structures is to take some of the ideas of determinism from earlier systems – namely, using as much of the surface structure cues as possible to deduce the distribution of empty categories – and build that into a bottom-up, shift-reduce LR parser that is small

---

[6]The reader may note that in this example then it might have been fruitful to reorder Subjacency ahead of Case or Theta Role Assignment after the Trace Case Condition, saving some work as suggested earlier since fewer candidates will have survived.

enough to work efficiently, while at the same time producing only a relatively small number of candidate trees. Currently, we do this by building a covering grammar for S-structure, that varies from language to language; each language uses about 30 rules.

Figure 2 shows the major components of this covering grammar. As the figure shows, the covering grammar is formed from two parts: (1) the phrase structure for D-structure, as given by the instantiated X-bar rules for a given language, and certain empty category rules and adjunction rules, introducing empty NPs (*empty was followed John*) and empty elements for Adverbial adjunction ($[_{VP}$ *was followed John*$][_{Adv}$ *why*]; and (2) addition of movement at S-structure, including Argument and Nonargument movement, scrambling (via adjunction), and limited Head movement.

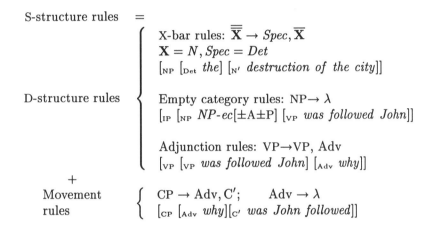

Figure 2: Components of the phrase structure grammar for S-structure are constructed by taking the D-structure grammar and adding adjunction, empty categories, and movement.

In more detail, the X-bar rules are binary branching and use unordered righthand sides. We assume for this parser that subjects are in Spec of IP. Parameters are incorporated by adding constraints on the schemas that are automatically expanded. For example, the rule that reads something like, "XP derives X1 followed by the specifiers of X1 if the parameter specFinal holds such that XP is a maximal projection and X1 immediately projects to XP" can be written as follows, where we leave undefined the obvious auxiliary predicates. A schema compiler turns this form into an actual context-free rule by grounding through the lexicon (the parser compiler lets X range over the requisite lexical categories plus the parameter settings,

valid specifier and complement structures for particular lexical categories
and items based on thematic roles). For instance, for V= *persuade* in
English the system automatically adds the rules,

(7)   VP→ NP CP

To factor in NP movement at S-structure is actually now easy because
empty NPs are already nondeterministically generated by existing covering
grammar rules: all Argument positions (A-positions, subject and object)
and Specifier of COMP already admit empty noun phrases at D-structure.
To cover scrambling (for Japanese), we adopt an adjunction analysis of NPs
at VP and IP, adding a single context-free rule. Other cases of movement,
such as verb lowering and adverbial adjunction, are added in a case-by-case
way.

This completes the outline of how the S-structure covering grammar is
built. The actual phrase structure grammar constructed for S-structure is
language-dependent. For instance, the X-bar schema expansions will be different according to the values of certain parameters such as [±specInitial,
±headInitial], and the lack of *wh*-movement in syntax will bar certain
movements in Japanese. Summarizing the system for the two grammars we
have:

Language	X-bar prototype rules	Empty category rules	Adjunction rules	Others
English	12	5	8	6
Japanese	(same)	4	7	2

Precisely because the resulting grammar is small – one of the properties of principles and parameters theories is to partition constraining work
among different modules – we have only 31 covering grammar rule schemas
for English and 25 for Japanese. We should emphasize this key property
of a modular system: the small grammar size allows us to consider more
powerful computational engines than are ordinarily deployed, in particular,
canonical LR(1) parsing that allows optimal early error detection, a must
for a system that has to dispose of bad candidate structures as quickly as
possible. This is one of the key techniques that was unavailable to TGG
parsers two decades ago. Of course, the LR parser itself must be extended
to handle ambiguity via the use of multiple action entries and backtracking,
but this is now also a standardly available technology. The important point
is that with a small grammar size, we can now achieve a balance between
overgeneration and efficiency: the covering grammar and associated parser
does select few enough candidate S-structures to make the system usable.

6.2 Stage II: Representing and Using Linguistic Principles

Given some (small) set of quasi-S-structures, Stage II of the parser next applies the remaining generators and filters to arrive at zero or more logical forms for the sentence. This is done by encoding the principles almost directly in PROLOG and then applying them to the quasi-S-structures. The exact order in which this is done has obvious implications for processing efficiency. First, principle application obviously must be subject to the *logical* dependencies of the theory, for instance, the Case Filter cannot apply until Case Assignment has been carried out.

The reader will note, however, that the principle ordering as specified does some unnecessary work in that Case Assignment and the Case Filter are applied to 49 structures, when in fact only 33 of these will survive Subjacency. Thus it would save computational work to order Subjacency ahead of the Case operations in this case. Plainly, following standard practice in artificial intelligence search techniques, the operative ordering principle is to delay hypothesis generation (expansion of the search tree) as long as possible, and apply constraints as early as possible. For a given sentence, up to an order of magnitude change in parsing time is possible, given an optimal principle ordering. We have explored this kind of reordering in three ways; see Fong and Berwick 1991 for details.

In one approach, the user may statically reorder the principles. In a second method, the system dynamically selects a tentative optimal ordering for a given sentence based in part on surface sentence cues and a voting scheme potentially based on the previous history of a given ordering's success rate. The implications of this for human sentence processing, namely, a systematic theory of individual processing time variation, has not escaped our attention but goes far beyond the scope of this article. Finally, we have systematically investigated *interleaving* principles, that is, the simultaneous application of two or more principles. For instance, we could enforce simultaneously all X-bar constraints, licensing of syntactic adjuncts, and a condition that traces cannot have Case. While this particular combination improves computation time, in general, contrary to intuition and some published accounts, combining *all* principles does not always improve performance, for more complex reasons that cannot be discussed here but roughly have to do with the computational complexity of each principle vs. the nondeterminism in building a set of S-structures. The current system can in part automatically determine which interleaving possibilities will prove efficacious.

Returning now to our main theme of representing linguistic principles, earlier we stated that a primary objective of this parser is to represent linguistic principles directly and transparently. To be concrete, how is Case Assignment carried out?

In the theory we have implemented, there is both *structural* and *inherent* Case assignment: assignment according to tree configuration and assignment according to the inherent properties of a lexical head item. For example, Structural Case Assignment is standardly done by assignment under government and adjacency (if that holds in a language). To implement this, the parser walks through a candidate structure, and, when it encounters a configuration of Case Assignment, that is, a maximal projection configuration CF with components Assigner (the structural Case assigner), Case (the Assigner assigns this Case) and an NP (the Case receiver), it first checks that (i) the Assigner governs the NP in the configuration; (ii) the NP has the feature *np*; (iii) the Assigner is in fact a Case Assigner, as determined previously; and (iv) the Assigner is adjacent to the NP, if the Case Adjacency parameter holds. If all this is true, then structural case assignment is carried out, by making the NP have the feature Case, and checking that the NP's morphology is compatible with the Case just assigned.

Let us expand on this English statement to see how it is implemented. The actual declarative statements that implement Structural Case Assignment are completely straightforward. First we must state that Structural Case Assignment (sCaseAssign) has been satisfied. This holds whenever, in all tree configurations CF, if CF satisfies the properties of structural case configuration (sCaseConfig), namely, a relation between CF, the Assigner, the Case to be assigned, and an NP, then assignment of Case (assignCase) also holds between the Assigner, Case, and NP:

```
:- sCaseAssign
   in_all_configurations CF where sCaseConfig(CF,Assigner,Case,NP)
        then assignCase(Assigner,Case,NP).
```

Now we must declaratively state the two predicates used above. We can directly translate the English given earlier for the first, sCaseConfig, adding a constraint (not discussed here) that the NP does not have the feature of *indirect Object*. In this statement, cat simply holds when a node has a category, possibly with features as given in lower case, and max holds when that category is maximal. Note that it is precisely here where the "matching" process implicit in interpreting declarative statements comes to the fore: the system "finds" the category C of configuration CF by starting out with C as a variable, without a value given to C, as if we were attempting to find the truth value of a Boolean statement in logic. The interpreted statement returns whatever sequence of assignments to C that makes the relation cat(CF, C) hold; similarly, in turn, once that stream of values is set, those values are tested by the predicate max(C).

```
sCaseConfig(CF,Assigner,Case,NP) :-        % Case assign in config. CF
    cat(CF,C),                             % when CF is a category C
    max(C),                                % and it is maximal
    governs(Assigner,NP,CF),               % and it governs a node NP
    cat(NP,np),                            % and node has feature np
    \+ NP has_feature indirObj,            % and the NP is
                                           % not an indir. obj.
    caseAssigner(Assigner,Case),           % and the Assigner
                                           % is a Case Assigner
    adjacent(Assigner,NP,CF)if caseAdjacency. % and the Assigner is
                                           % adjacent to the NP if the
                                           % caseAdjacency parameter
                                           % is true.
```

Putting aside for the moment exceptional Case marking and the requirement to transmit Case in certain situations, then we can state the second predicate very simply as well:

```
assignCase(Assigner,Case,NP) :-           % Case assignment holds
    NP has_feature case(Case),            % when NP has feature Case
    morphCaseAgreement(NP,Case).          % and that Case agrees
                                          % morphologically with NP,
                                          % if any.
```

We should stress that this declarative way of putting matters does not "make" or "assign" the NP the feature Case. Rather, the system will non-deterministically generate both possibilities where the NP does not have the feature Case, *and* where it does, in an attempt to match against this filter's logical template. Only in this last case will the assignCase predicate be true, as required to pass the filter. In this way, the candidate trees are successively generated and pruned.

7 Linguistic Coverage

To give some idea of the range of examples that the parser can handle, Table 2 gives a partial list of the sentence types from LU that the parser can successfully parse or reject, as appropriate, along with the chapter and example sentence number from LU. About 300 sentence example types can be processed, corresponding to most examples of current interest in linguistic theory, from quantifier raising, to passivization, to exceptional case marking, to superiority effects (*Who will read what*/vs. *What who will read*). As far as we know, this is the most comprehensive system of its kind.

(1:12a)	Someone likes everyone	*Quantifier raising*
(1:15a)	Who that John knows does he like	*Movement & Condition C*
(1:15b)	He likes everyone that John knows	
(1:18)	It is likely that John is here	*Simple Case theory*
(1:19)	*It is likely John to be here	
(1:21)	I am eager for John to be here	*Exceptional Case Marking*
(1:22)	*I am eager John to be here	*(Ecm)*
(1:24a)	I believe John to be here	
(1:24b)	I believe John is here	
(1:25)	*I believe sincerely John to be here	*Case Adjacency*
(1:35a)	I want to be clever	*Optional vs. obligatory*
(1:35b)	*I believe to be clever	*Ecm*
(1:36a)	John was persuaded to leave	*Ordinary passivization*
(1:48)	John was arrested by the police	
(1:36c)	*John was wanted to leave	*Exceptional passivization*
(1:49a)	I believe John to be intelligent	
(1:49b)	*It was believed John to be intelligent	
(1:49c)	John was believed to be intelligent	
(1:52a)	*I am proud John	*Genitive Case realization*
(1:52b)	I am proud of John	
(1:53a)	I wonder who you will see	Wh-*movement*
(1:59c)	*What does Bill wonder who saw	*and Subjacency*
(2:19b)	Their pictures of each other are nice	*Simple Binding theory*
(2:26a)	John likes Mary's pictures of him	
(2:26b)	*John likes Mary's pictures of himself	
(2:45a)	Who does he think Mary likes	*Strong crossover*
(2:88)	*(I am proud of) my belief to be intelligent	*Government of* PRO
(2:91)	The men think that pictures of each other will be on sale	
(2:103)	*The men think that Mary's pictures of each other will be on sale	
(3:17)	Which report did you file without reading	*Parasitic gaps*
(3:18)	*Which book did you file the report without reading	
(3:19)	*Who filed which report without reading	
(3:20)	*The report was filed without reading	✓*Resumptive pronoun*
(3:46)	*The article which I filed it yesterday without reading is (over) here	
(4:3)	*John is crucial to see this	*ECP*
(4:4)	John is certain to see this	
(4:7a)	Who do you think that John saw	*That-trace effect*
(4:7b)	Who do you think John saw	
(4:8a)	*Who do you think that saw Bill	
(4:8b)	Who do you think saw Bill	
(4:18)	*John is believed is intelligent	*Raising and*
(4:20)	*John seems that it is likely to leave	*Super-raising*

(Table 2 continued on next page)

(4:21b)	Who will read what	*Superiority*
(4:21c)	*What will who read	
(4:35a)	Why did you read what	*Compl./Noncompl.*
(4:35b)	*What did you read why	*asymmetries*
(4:45a)	Who believes the claim that Mary read what	*Subjacency and* LF
(4:45b)	*What do you believe the claim that Mary read	
(4:57)	*Who does Mary wonder why John hit	*Ecm and movement*
(4:58)	*Why does Mary wonder who John hit	

Table 2: Some of the examples from LU that are analyzed correctly by the English version of the principles and parameters parser.

8 Parameterizing the parser: Japanese

While the substantial coverage of a set of linguistic examples for English may be impressive, the "proof of the pudding" for the principles and parameters parser is, of course, whether one can easily switch from one language to another by varying just a small number of parameters. In fact this appears to be possible. In this section we show how the parser can easily be reparameterized to handle the *wh*-movement sentences found in *On the nature of proper government* (Lasnik and Saito 1984), listed in Table 3 (sentence numbers in the table refer to the original cited article). In passing, we shall show how the parser may be used in practice, to debug the principles as implemented, and actually "discover" valid linguistic derivations that might otherwise not have been found.

To begin, these Japanese sentences display many familiar typological Japanese–English differences. Let us review these here.

- *SOV Language.*

  As is familiar, Japanese is often classified as a Verb Final or SOV (Subject-Object-Verb) language. Heads such as verbs and adjectives are preceded by their objects and modifiers. However, subjects do normally appear before verbs and objects, as in English. This distinction can be encoded by two binary parameters that specify head/complement and specifier/head order, as is familiar. The X-bar system compiles out schemas with heads last rather than first, as mentioned in the previous section. (To a first approximation, this does not alter the LR machinery in terms of the amount of ambiguity as measured by alternative state changes, but see Fong and Berwick 1992 for additional discussion.) We also assume without further discussion the existence of a VP node in Japanese.

(2)   Watashi-wa Taro-ga nani-o katta ka shitte iru
        (I know what John bought)
        Basic wh-*questions*

(6)   Kimi-wa dare-ni Taro-ga naze kubi-ni natta tte itta no
        (To whom did you say that John was fired why)
        Good in Japanese but not in English

(32)   *Meari-wa Taro-ga nani-o katta ka do ka shiranai
        (Mary does not know whether or not John bought what)
        Semantic parallelism: non-absorption of ka do ka

(37a)   Taro-wa naze kubi-ni natta no
        (Why was John fired)

(37b)   Biru-wa Taro-ga naze kubi-ni natta tte itta no
        (Why did Bill say that John was fired)
        Comp-to-Comp movement at LF

(39a)   Taro-ga nani-o te-ni ireta koto-o sonnani okotteru no
        (What are you so angry about the fact that Taro obtained)
        Complement-noncomplement asymmetries

(39b)   *Taro-ga naze sore-o te-ni ireta koto-o sonnani okotteru no
        (Why are you so angry about the fact that Taro obtained it)

(41a)   Hanoko-ga Taro-ga nani-o te-ni ireta tte itta koto-o sonnani
        okotteru no
        *(What are you so angry about the fact that Hanoko said that
        Taro obtained)*

(41b)   *Hanoko-ga Taro-ga naze sore-o te-ni ireta tte itta koto-o sonnani
        okotteru no
        *(Why are you so angry about the fact that Hanoko said that
        Taro obtained it)*

(60)   Kimi-wa nani-o doko-de katta no
        (Where did you buy what)

(63)   Kimi-wa nani-o sagashiteru no
        (Why are you looking for what)
        *Multiple-*whs *in Comp*

Table 3: *Wh*-movement examples in Japanese from Lasnik & Saito

- *Scrambling.*

  Japanese phrase order is more or less free, apart from the Verb Final constraint. Direct and indirect objects may be interchanged, and appear before the subject in an initial position (which is evidently not a process of topicalization). Typical examples cited by Hoji (1985) of *John gave Mary a book* are these:

  (8) (i) $[_{IP}$ *John-ga* $[_{VP}$ *Mary-ni hon-o ageta*$]]$
       (ii) $[_{IP}$ *hon_i-o* $[_{IP}$ *John-ga* $[_{VP}$ *Mary-ni t_i ageta*$]]]$
       (iii) $[_{IP}$ *Mary_i-ni* $[_{IP}$ *John-ga* $[_{VP}$ t_i *hon-o ageta*$]]]$
       (iv) $[_{IP}$ *John-ga* $[_{VP}$ *hon_i-o* $[_{VP}$ *Mary-ni t_i ageta*$]]]$

  Movement can account for this. Suppose the canonical order is "subject" followed by "indirect object" followed by "direct object," as in (8)-i. The direct object, *hon-o* in this case, is free to move (by *VP-adjunction*) to a position in front of the indirect object *Mary-ni*, as in the fourth example above, or to a sentence-initial position (by *S-adjunction*) as in the second. Similarly, the indirect object may move to a sentence-initial position as in the third example. We take the elements *ga*, *o*, *ni*, etc. to be essentially case-marking, clitic-like particles that do not project to phrases. (We shall see immediately below that in more complex examples the scrambled element can itself be further moved at LF.) In addition, we alter Structural Case Assignment slightly to transmit Case from an A(argument) to a non-Argument position, since a scrambled NP will be adjoined to VP, and would otherwise be unable to receive Case. (This is a temporary move that we have used pending a better account.) [7]

- *Empty subjects.*

  As is also familiar, Subjects and other NPs can be omitted in a "Super Pro Drop" language like Japanese. (In general the conditions that determine which elements can or can not be omitted are largely dependent on discourse considerations, which are not considered here. However, as pointed out earlier, the system can be modified to take "context" into account in a general way, if a theory of context becomes available.) As an example, consider the second sentence below (taken from Makino and Tsutsui 1986).

---

[7] We scramble only from direct object positions here, even though it is straightforward to scramble from indirect object positions. Informally, we have noted that scrambling from the indirect object greatly increases computation time. A tighter set of constraints on scrambling seems called for.

(9) (i)   Taro-wa sono mise-de nani-o kaimashita ka
            (What did Taro buy at the store?)

     (ii)   Pen-o kaimashita
            (He bought a pen)

Standardly, the omitted subject is actually represented in syntax by
a phonologically empty pronoun.[8] Again following conventional practice, we represent the binary option that determines whether this is
available or not as the *pro*-drop parameter. For the initial parses described in this section, we do not extend this ellipsis to non-subject
positions, though again this may be easily changed, simply by saying
that *pro* may occupy other NP positions (though as far as we can
determine informally with a great loss in efficiency).

- *No visible Wh-movement.*

  Following much current work in linguistic theory (Huang 1982), we
  assume that Japanese LF looks like English LF: there is no *wh*-
  movement in syntax, but there is movement at LF. Thus, the option
  of whether to allow *wh*-movement between D- and S-structure is a
  language parameter. As we review below, it is this distinction that
  enables one to explain a variety of facts including why the counterpart
  of a sentence such as (6) in Table 3 (which is well-formed in Japanese)
  is ill-formed in English.

To be sure, this is not in any way meant to be a complete characterization of the differences between these two languages. We defer for now
all the intriguing questions in Japanese of double Subjects, Case marking,
passives, causatives, and so forth. Rather, it is sufficient to demonstrate
what we set out to show: to cover the examples shown in Table 3 with just
a handful of parameter switches. These parameters are shown in Table 4,
with English–Japanese differences starred.[9] This table shows the actual
PROLOG code parametric differences that were entered in order to get the
parser to parse Japanese rather than English—in effect, just four binary
switches to make the system Head final; allow *pro*-drop everywhere; eliminate adjacency for Case marking and thus admit scrambling; and eliminate
wh-movement in syntax for Japanese.

It is remarkable that the same set of principles for English can then re-
combine in different ways to handle the Japanese examples. The important

---

[8]We follow Takezawa (1987) in making this empty category a small *pro*. This option
is evidently not available in English.

[9]Some of these parametric variations lead to implicational universals: for instance,
example (187) in Lasnik and Saito (1984) states that if a language has syntactic *Wh*-
movement then it obeys the *Wh*-Comp requirement at S-structure.

	English and Japanese parameter settings	
	English	Japanese
Spec order	specInitial. specFinal :- \+ specInitial.	specInitial. specFinal :- \+ specInitial.
*Head order	headInitial. headFinal :- \+ headInitial.	headFinal. headInitial :- \+ headFinal.
Agreement	agr(weak).	agr(weak).
Bounding	boundingNode(i2). boundingNode(np).	boundingNode(i2). boundingNode(np).
*Case Adjacency	caseAdjacency.	:- no caseAdjacency.
*Wh in Syntax	whInSyntax.	:-no whInSyntax.
*Pro-Drop	:- no proDrop.	proDrop.

Table 4: The differences between English and Japanese are captured by just a few parameter switches, shown here as actually written in the PROLOG program. Distinct parameter settings for the two languages are marked by asterisks.

point here again is that the system gets (by design) precisely the parses required, and blocks ungrammatical sentences by the same means as well. Figure 3 shows the system in operation for the first five sentences from Table 3, while Figure 4 displays the LFs for the sixth example sentence. Let us review these.

- Wh-*movement at* LF.

    As shown at the top of the snapshot in Figure 3, *nani* has moved at LF to a position that has scope over the embedded sentence (as indicated by the bracketing) leaving behind an (LF) trace LF-*t* to be interpreted as a variable in its original position.

    Because we want our Japanese and English grammars to be as *uniform* as possible and follow a full CP/IP system, the parser moves this item to a Spec of CP position. Additional constituents moved at LF are adjoined to this Spec position. In this example the question particle *ka* fills the Head of the embedded CP (=C2), and *nani* fills Spec of this CP to the left, immediately after the C2 bracket in the figure.

    The key point is why has this (correct) parse been produced with *nani* moved, rather than any others? Remember that the system will nondeterministically try out *all* optional possibilities. So the

```
                          Principle-and-Parameters Parse
Build LR  Graph  Language  Op Status  Options  Parsers  Run  Screen  Sentences  Time  Tracing
⬚⇨ Run Sentences (Examples) e2, E6
e2        Watashi-wa Taro-ga nani-o katta ka shitte iru
LF: [c2[i2[NP watashi]-topic [i1[vp[vp[c2[NP nani]-acc [c1[i2[NP taro]-non [i1[vp LFt [v i(AGR) [v katta] ] ] [i
            1                 2                3           2          3        4 4
t ]][c ka]]][v shitte] ] [vt ][i i(AGR) [v iru] ] ]][c]]]
3       5       6          1 6 1
No (more) parses
e6        Kimi-wa dare-ni Taro-ga naze kubi-ni natta tte itta no
LF: [c2[ADV[NP dare]-dat [ADV naze] ] [c1[i2[NP kimi]-topic [i1[vp LFt [v1[c2 LFt [c1[i2[NP taro]-non [i1[vp
                 1             2 2              1                    2                1              4
LFt [vp[NP kubi]-dat [v i(AGR) [v natta] ]] [it ]][c tte]]][v i(AGR) [v itta] ]]] [it ]][c no]]]
  2      5        4            6 6         4            3       7 7      3
No (more) parses
⇨ Run Sentences (Examples) e32 (keywords) :Statistics (Y or N [default No]) Yes
e32       *Meari-wa Taro-ga nani-o katta ka da ka shiranai
No (more) parses
1 6 Parse S-structure        1 1 Wh-movement in Syntax      5 1 Condition C
6 51 Trace Theory            1 1 Theta Criterion            1 1 ECP
51 49 Subjacency             1 1 D-structure Theta Condition 1 4 LF Movement
49 1 Assign Inherent Case    1 5 Free Indexation            4 3 FI: License operator/variables
1 1 Assign Structural Case   5 5 Functional Determination   3 3 ECP at LF
1 1 Case Filter              5 5 Control                    3 0 Wh Comp Requirement
1 1 Trace Case Condition     5 5 Condition A
1 1 Assign Theta-Roles       5 5 Condition B
⇨ Run Sentences (Examples) e37a, E37b
e37a      Taro-wa naze kubi-ni natta no
LF: [c2[ADV naze] [c1[i2[NP taro]-topic [i1[vp LFt [vp[NP kubi]-dat [v i(AGR) [v natta] ]] [it ]][c no]]]
             1                1                3         2           4 4      2
No (more) parses
e37b      Biru-wa Taro-ga naze kubi-ni natta tte itta no
LF: [c2[ADV naze] [c1[i2[NP biru]-topic [i1[vp[c2 LFt [c1[i2[NP taro]-non [i1[vp LFt [vp[NP kubi]-dat [v i(AGR
             1                1                    2                1              4
) [v natta] ]]] [it ]][c tte]]][v i(AGR) [v itta] ] ] [it ]][c no]]]
  3        5 5      2            6 6      2
No (more) parses
⇨
```

Figure 3: Sample sentences from Lasnik & Saito, as shown in a computer snapshot.

real trick is ruling out the *bad* possibilities, not generating the good one. Among these failed possibilities are candidates where *nani* is not moved at LF, candidates where the incorrect phrase structure is built, and so forth. The good option is where *nani* is moved at LF, leaving behind an LF trace. We can divide our question then into two parts: first, Why is the correct phrase structure built? and second, Why does only the right LF-movement possibility survive the principle gauntlet?

First, as we described earlier, the correct branching phrase structure is built simply because the LR(1) parser has the rules to build it *at least* that way. Although the LR machine may build *more* structures than ultimately required (to be precise, in this case, five others), among them will be just those that obey the branching conditions of the language in question. This is forced by the construction of the covering LR(1) machine given the parameters headFinal and whInSyntax. Note also that the covering grammar will not predict *any* empty categories in this example, simply because they cannot be introduced into the quasi-S-structure at all; they are just not part of the S-structure covering grammar for Japanese (putting to one side inflection-verb Head movement).

Second, the correct movement is forced by the fact that Japanese does not have *wh*-movement in syntax and English does, plus a universal constraint (posited by Lasnik and Saito 1984), the Wh-Comp Requirement, that both English and Japanese must meet: a +*wh* Comp must have a +*wh* head and a −*wh* Comp must not have a +*wh* head. In English, this constraint must be met at both S-structure and LF, while in Japanese, lacking *Wh*-movement in syntax, it holds just at LF. A Comp is +*wh* if marked by its head or, in English, by a Q(uestion)-operator, if the specifier is +*wh*. We must modify this constraint slightly in our X-bar system, since the parser has both a Spec and Head position: since the *wh* element is moved into Spec, the revised constraint says that a +*wh* Comp must have a +*wh* Spec, and a +*wh* Head, if there is one.

In the current Japanese example, the embedded CP is marked +*wh* by its head *ka*, as indicated in the lexicon. *Nani* must move because by assumption *wh* elements are operators and to be licensed, an operator must bind something, either an S-structure or LF-trace. Only the second option is possible in Japanese. So the movement must occur or else the operator won't be licensed. The movement is licensed because it passes the Wh-Comp Requirement, as modified above. Thus, structures where *nani* is not moved do not meet this restriction: if the Spec of CP is left empty, the Wh-Comp Requirement is unmet. In fact, two of three final candidates are blocked in just this way, leaving the single correct parse shown. Of course, the LF trace left behind must also meet the Empty Category Principle at LF, and it does: it is lexically governed as a complement of the verb *katta*, 'buy,' as may be seen in Figure 3. So all is well.

- *Multiple wh-elements at* LF.

  Consider example (6) in Figure 3. There are two *wh*-elements: (1) *dare* ('who') the indirect object of *itta* ('said' as in "said something to somebody"), and (2) *naze* ('why'). As the second parse in Figure 3 shows, both elements will move at LF to a sentence-initial position, with *naze* moving Comp-to-Comp; this is the LF given by Lasnik and Saito (1984). The usual ambiguity arises. We can gloss the sentence meaning as a double question: "for which x, x a person, *and* for what reason y, you said y (a reason such that [taro was fired]) to x."

  Why does this sentences pass in Japanese but not in English? Again the reason is the lack of *wh*-movement at S-structure in Japanese coupled with the Wh-Comp Requirement. Assuming the particle *no* marks the Comp as +*wh*, then for CP to receive a +*wh* Spec, both *dare* and *naze* must move, as in the previous example, and the candidates where these elements do not move are ruled out.

All other options explored by the parser are ruled out. If the intermediate trace is not present, or if *dare* as an NP moves into Spec *first* and *naze* is then adjoined to it, then the base trace is not properly governed, with CP or NP as barriers, respectively. The (declaratively stated) Empty Category Principle blocks these possibilities. Thus only the winning output structure shown can run the entire constraint gauntlet.

Note that the corresponding English sentence would be ruled out: example 4:35b in the previous section is similar (*what did you read why*). Because English has movement at S-structure, the LR machine (*not* a later operation) will put *what* in Spec of CP, and place an empty category after *read*. *Why* must move as an operator as before, but the LF trace of *why* cannot be properly governed because it is adjoined to the NP *what*; this NP acts as a barrier for proper government, ruling out the possibility of antecedent government. The LF trace cannot be lexically governed either by *read* since it is not a complement. In this way, the parser captures a basic difference between English and Japanese in the same way, while maintaining a single Empty Category Principle.

- *Nonadsorption/semantic parallelism and the Wh-Comp requirement.*

  Sentence example (32) in the table illustrates another Japanese grammatical effect. Evidently the question element *ka do ka* ('whether or not') and the *wh* phrase *nani* ('what') cannot both appear in the same (lower) Comp at LF. The relevant condition is one of "semantic parallelism," which we have implemented by a feature unification check. We simply add the feature *yn* in the lexicon to items such as *ka* or *ka do ka*, but not to *nani*, and require this feature to be compatible with the element in Spec. The example output in Figure 3 shows that in fact three candidates are produced by the parser but none of them meet the Wh-Comp Requirement, so the sentence is blocked.

- *Comp to Comp movement at LF.*

  Like example sentence (6), example sentence (37b) ('Why did Bill say that John was fired', literally, 'fired'='cut off at the neck') shows how *naze* can move at LF out of its position adjoined to the verb *natta*, first to the lower Spec of CP, and then to the Spec of the matrix CP, leaving behind an intermediate trace governing the original trace of *naze*.

- *Complement & noncomplement asymmetries; Scrambling and unexpected parses; Trace deletion.*

Finally, consider example (39a) (and the corresponding illicit 39b) from Figure 3, repeated here, where a complement *wh* but not a noncomplement *wh* can be extracted from a complex NP:

(10) (i) Taro-ga nani-o te-ni ireta koto-o sonnani okotteru no
(What are you so angry about the fact that Taro obtained)

(ii) * Taro-ga naze sore-o te-ni ireta koto-o sonnani okotteru no
*(*Why are you so angry about the fact that Taro obtained)*

This example illustrates several Japanese typological differences with English. The subject of the matrix clause 'you' has been omitted. *Nani* and *te* ('hand') have been scrambled, with the direct object marked *-o* now appearing in front of the indirect object *te*. Our relaxation of the Case Adjacency parameter and the rule that allows adjunction of NP to VP, plus transmission of Case to the scrambled NP will let this analysis through. The LF for this sentence might be glossed something like this:

(11) for what x, *pro* is so angry about the fact that Taro obtained x

In this example *pro* denotes the understood subject of *okotteru* ('be angry'). Note the LFs actually returned by the system in Figure 4. As one can see, the system does correctly recover this form, as the last LF in the snapshot. However, it also recovers three *additional* LFs:

(12) for what x, Taro is so angry about the fact that *pro* obtained x

The parser has also admitted the LF where the embedded subject *Taro* is interchanged with the matrix subject *pro*.

Before we address where the additional ambiguity comes from, we should account for the expected derivation itself. *Nani* ('what') undergoes both S-structure and LF movement. At S-structure, the direct object "scrambles" by VP-adjunction, leaving the trace NP_1. At LF, *nani* undergoes *wh*-movement into the specifier position of CP. This would leave an illicit intermediate trace in the adjoined VP, as indicated here:

```
                    Principle-and-Parameters Parse
Build LR  Graph  Language  Op Status  Options  Parsers  Run  Screen  Sentences  Time  Tracing
⇨ Run Sentences (Examples) e39a
e39a      Taro-ga nani-o te-ni ireta koto-o sonnani okotteru no
LF: [c2[NP nani]-acc [c1[I2[NP taro]-nom [I1[VP[VP[NP[C2[I2 pro [I1[VP[] [VP[NP te]-dat [V1[NPt-A-P] [V I(AGR)
                  1              2                         3        1                4                 1          3
[V ireta] ] ]]] [It ]][c]][N koto]]-acc [V[ADV sonnani][V okotte] ] ] [Vt ][I I(AGR) [V iru] ] ]][c no]]]
         5 5        3               3                            6 6          7    I I       2     7 2
LF: [c2[NP nani]-acc [c1[I2[NP taro]-nom [I1[VP[VP[NP[C2[I2 pro [I1[VP[] [VP[NP te]-dat [V1[NPt-A-P] [V I(AGR)
                  1              2                         2        1                4                 1          2
[V ireta] ] ]]] [It ]][c]][N koto]]-acc [V[ADV sonnani][V okotte] ] ] [Vt ][I I(AGR) [V iru] ] ]][c no]]]
         4 4        2               5                            6 6          7    I I       2     7 2
LF: [c2[NP nani]-acc [c1[I2[NP taro]-nom [I1[VP[VP[NP[C2[I2 pro [I1[VP[] [VP[NP te]-dat [V1[NPt-A-P] [V I(AGR)
                  1              2                         2        1                4                 1          3
[V ireta] ] ]]] [It ]][c]][N koto]]-acc [V[ADV sonnani][V okotte] ] ] [Vt ][I I(AGR) [V iru] ] ]][c no]]]
         5 5        3               6                            7 7          8    I I       2     8 2
LF: [c2[NP nani]-acc [c1[I2 pro [I1[VP[VP[NP[C2[I2[NP taro]-nom [I1[VP[] [VP[NP te]-dat [V1[NPt-A-P] [V I(AGR)
                  1                        1                          1                4                 1          3
[V ireta] ] ]]] [It ]][c]][N koto]]-acc [V[ADV sonnani][V okotte] ] ] [Vt ][I I(AGR) [V iru] ] ]][c no]]]
         5 5        3               6                            7 7          8    I I       2     8 2
No (more) parses
⇨
```

Figure 4: Japanese examples illustrating ambiguous logical forms and scrambling.

(13) $[_{CP} [_{NP} nani]$-acc$_1$ ... $[_{I1} [_{VP} [_{VP} [_{NP} [_{CP} [_{IP} pro [_{I1} [_{VP} NP$-$t_1$ ...

This structure should be ruled out: the intermediate LF trace is barred by the Empty Category Principle because it is in a non-argument position, and it is neither lexically governed as the complement of a verb nor antecedent governed by *nani* (too many barriers intervene, with two CPs and an NP, at least, blocking antecedent government). This is just what we discovered when the parser was first run on this example sentence.

To repair this example, observe that this is precisely the situation where a trace deletion approach would work. We therefore implemented something along these lines, permitting LF trace deletion in just this configuration. Thus we find the form as actually shown in the top line of every LF in Figure 4, with the LF trace being subsequently deleted, as indicated by [VP [ ]$_1$]. This element is thus no longer subject to the Empty Category Principle, and the structure passes. In effect, we have optional deletion of LF traces only.

Turning now to the ambiguity the parser discovered, the basic prediction seems to be correct. The sentence happens to be ambiguous with respect to the two basic interpretations.[10]

---

[10]This was pointed out by Pesetsky, and confirmed by Saito. However, presumably the use of *wa* rather than *ga* and intonational pauses could be exploited by a computer (or a person) as a surface cue to rule out more general ambiguity in this example and others like it. See Fong and Berwick (1991) for a discussion of how to integrate sentence surface cues into the principle-based system.

For completeness, here are the three variants that correspond to the first three LFs reported by the parser. S. Miyagawa (p.c.) informs us that the last two, given proper context, are in fact possible.

1. *pro* is coreferent with *koto* ('fact'):

   for what x, Taro is so angry about the fact that the fact obtained x

   This interpretation can be eliminated by imposing selectional restrictions on the possible "agents" of *okotteru* (let us say that they must be animate).
2. *pro* is coreferent with *taro*:

   for what x, Taro is so angry about the fact that Taro obtained x
3. *pro* is free in the sentence:

   for what x, Taro is so angry about the fact that (someone else) obtained x

To summarize, using a very simple and automatic parameterization, exactly as suggested by theory, we can accommodate a range of Japanese constructions that differ markedly from English. Without any rule reprogramming or changes in the principles or parsing algorithm we can obtain a parser for Japanese that works as the English system did (in particular, there are no difficulties with Head final constructions). This is the promise of the principles and parameters theory, now met by a concrete implementation.

9 Conclusions

Coming full circle then, just as it seems altogether fitting that a historical celebration of a linguistics department should be in part historical, it seems particularly fitting that just in time for this celebration we have been able to develop a full, efficient parser for TGG. The barriers have at last come down: it took a quarter-century of research into constraints on TGG—in particular, restrictions on movement and empty categories along with a modular, declarative design—and a quarter-century of research on computation—in particular, LR parsing and its integration with an efficient system for non-deterministic, declarative computation (here, PROLOG). What lies in store a quarter-century ahead remains hidden. No doubt our current views will look as curious to us then as the MITRE system does now. However, if we are on the right track, then the same lessons of constraint and efficiency that guided work in the 60s until the current day will continue to apply in full force into the foreseeable future—more than enough of an historical moral with which to conclude.

References

Berwick, Robert C. 1985. *The acquisition of syntactic knowledge.* Cambridge, MA: MIT Press.

Chomsky, Noam. 1986. *Barriers.* Cambridge, MA: MIT Press.

Fodor, Jerrold, Thomas Bever, and Merrill Garrett. 1974. *The psychology of language.* New York: McGraw-Hill.

Fong, Sandiway. 1991. *Computational properties of principle-based grammatical theories.* Ph.D. dissertation, Department of Electrical Engineering and Computer Science, Massachusetts Institute of Technology.

Fong, Sandiway and Robert C. Berwick. 1991. The computational implementation of principle-based parsers. In M. Tomita (ed.), *Current issues in parsing technologies,* pp. 9–24. Norwell, MA: Kluwer.

Fong, Sandiway and Robert C. Berwick. 1992. *Cartesian computation.* Cambridge, MA: MIT Press.

Friedman, Joyce. 1971. *A computer model of transformational grammar.* New York: American Elsevier.

Hoji, H. 1985. *Logical form constraints and configurational structures in Japanese.* Ph.D. dissertation, Department of Linguistics, University of Washington, Seattle.

Huang, James. 1982. *Logical relations in Chinese and the theory of grammar.* Ph.D. dissertation, Department of Linguistics and Philosophy, Massachusetts Institute of Technology.

Kolb, Hans and Craig Thiersch. 1990. Levels and empty categories in a Principles and Parameters approach to parsing. In H. Haider and K. Netter (eds.), *Representation and derivation in the theory of grammar.* Dordrecht: Kluwer.

Lasnik, Howard and Mamoro Saito. 1984. On the nature of proper government. *Linguistic Inquiry* 15:2.235–289.

Lasnik, Howard and Juan Uriagereka. 1989. *A course in GB syntax.* Cambridge, MA: MIT Press.

Makino, S. and M. Tsutsui. 1986. *A dictionary of basic Japanese grammar.* Tokyo: The Japan Times.

Maratsos, Michael P. 1978. New models in linguistics and language acquisition. In M. Halle, J. Bresnan, and G. Miller (eds.), *Linguistic theory and psychological reality,* pp. 247–263. Cambridge, MA: MIT Press.

Marcus, Mitchell P. 1980. *A theory of syntactic recognition for natural language.* Cambridge, MA: MIT Press.

Nozohoor-Farshi, R. 1987. Context-freeness of the language accepted by Marcus' parser. In *Proceedings of the 25th Annual Meeting of the Association for Computational Linguistics,* pp. 117–122.

Peters, P. Stanley. 1973. On restricting deletion transformations. In M. Gross, M. Halle, and M. Schutzenberger (eds.), *The formal analysis of natural language,* pp. 372–384. The Hague: Mouton.

Petrick, Stanley Roy. 1965. *A recognition procedure for transformational grammars.* Ph.D. dissertation, Department of Foreign Languages, Massachusetts Institute of Technology, Cambridge, MA.

Plath, Warren J. 1976. Request: A natural language question-answering system. *IBM Journal of Research and Development* 20:4.326–335.

Stabler, Edward P., Jr. 1992. *The logical approach to syntax.* Cambridge, MA: MIT Press.

Takezawa, T. 1987. *A configurational approach to case marking in Japanese.* Ph.D. dissertation, Department of Linguistics, University of Washington, Seattle.

Zwicky, Arnold, Joyce Friedman, Barbara Hall, and Donald Walker. 1965. The Mitre syntactic analysis procedure for transformational grammars. In *AFIPS Fall Joint Computer Conference,* pp. 317–326. Washington, DC: Spartan Books.

Chunks and Dependencies:
Bringing Processing Evidence
to Bear on Syntax

Steven Abney
Bellcore

1   Introduction

At least some psycholinguists exploring how sentences are structured in
linguistic behavior have concluded that the "performance structures" that
emerge from experimental data differ from the syntactic structures hypothesized by linguists. For example, one measure of structure is the location
and relative prominence of pauses when subjects read sentences aloud. Experiments have indicated that the syntactic prominence of boundaries is
only a moderately good predictor of the prominence of pauses at those
boundaries (Grosjean, Grosjean, and Lane 1979). Other experiments have
looked at parsing by linguistically-naive subjects: when asked to group
words together (Martin 1970) or to subdivide sentences at their natural
joints (Grosjean, Grosjean, and Lane 1979). Yet another set of experiments
examined the probability of errors in performance, the highest probability
of error representing the most significant boundaries. Levelt (1970) investigated comprehension of spoken sentences mixed with noise, and Dommergues and Grosjean (1981) looked at errors in recall of sentences heard
previously. In all these studies, significant divergences were noted between
standard syntactic structures and the structures derived from experimental
data. Indeed, Grosjean, Grosjean and Lane (1979) observe that structures
obtained from pausing data and structures obtained from parsing data cor-
relate better with each other ($r = 0.92$) than either do with linguistic
structures ($r = 0.76$ for pausing, $r = 0.82$ for parsing).

Phonologists studying prosody have also remarked on the mismatch
between prosodic structures and phrase structure. Chomsky's (1965) example is frequently cited: *this is the cat that chased the rat that ate the
cheese.*[1] More systematic investigations into prosodic structure also conclude that prosodic structure differs from syntactic structure. Selkirk (1978,
1980, 1981) argues for a hierarchy of prosodic units, including *phonological phrase, intonational phrase*, and *utterance*. (See Figure 1.) They do

---

[1]Though it is actually a rather curious example. Chomsky presents it as an example
where syntactic boundaries and prosodic boundaries diverge: he assumes that major
prosodic breaks ought to fall at the left brackets of noun phrases, rather than the left
brackets of sentences. However, that seems an odd assumption, and Chomsky does not
explain why he makes it.

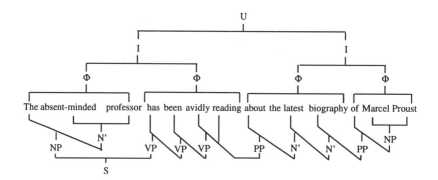

Figure 1: Selkirk's prosodic structure

not correspond to syntactic phrases. The most significant difference is that Selkirk's prosodic structures are not recursive. One consequence is that the sizes of prosodic units do not vary as much as the sizes of syntactic phrases. Phonological phrases (ϕ-phrases) comprise a few words, intonational phrases a few ϕ-phrases, and utterances a few intonational phrases. By contrast, because English is so heavily right-branching, the length of syntactic phrases depends less on their category than on how early they appear in the sentence.

Significantly, performance structures and prosodic structures appear to differ from phrase structure in similar ways. Gee and Grosjean (1983), for example, present a model of performance structures based on Selkirk's phonological phrases. They argue that the ϕ-phrase model predicts performance structures better than their earlier models based on syntactic structure. In turn, Bachenko and Fitzpatrick (1990) use a modification of Gee and Grosjean's model to predict intonation for speech synthesis.

If psycholinguistic and prosodic evidence agree on common structures for sentences—on common data structures for sentence processing, in effect—but those structures differ from standard linguistic structures, then we face serious issues about the relationship of linguistic theory to language processing. If syntactic theory is not a model of the data structures of sentence processing, then what is it a model of?

In this paper, I consider how we might modify standard approaches to phrase structure in order to account for the behavioral and prosodic evidence alluded to above. Fortunately, I believe the required modifications are modest. I argue that we need only distinguish two types of syntactic relation previously considered homogenous, thereby permitting the definition of units I call *chunks*, which correspond much more closely to the units of prosodic structures and performance structures than do standard phrases.

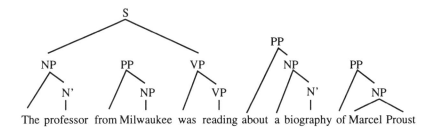

Figure 2: Chunks

At the same time, I hope that this work will be of interest for its methodology. For the most part, information flow between theoretical linguistics and the study of language processing has been one-way. Psycholinguists have often designed experiments to probe questions raised in theoretical linguistics, but rarely have the resulting data had any effect on linguistic theory. The one exception that occurs to me is the lexicalization of grammatical function changing operations in LFG, which was motivated at least in part by psycholinguists' disconfirmation of the so-called Derivational Theory of Complexity (Bresnan and Kaplan 1982). I offer this paper as another exception to the rule, and, if nothing else, I hope that it encourages other linguists to think seriously about syntactic structures as partial models of linguistic behavior.

2   Chunks and Dependencies

I would like to approach chunks via some very practical considerations. It is generally accepted that prepositional phrase attachment cannot be adequately resolved without a good deal of semantic information. Consequently, the most explosive source of ambiguity in parsing, especially if we do not use semantic information, is the attachment of prepositional phrases and similar elements, including conjuncts and modifiers (cf. Church and Patil 1982). Since the semantic information necessary to resolve PP attachment in unrestricted text is not easily available, it makes sense to leave prepositional phrases unattached.[2] Figure 2 illustrates the resulting structure, using a slightly modified example from Selkirk (1978).

We can define *chunks* as the parse tree fragments that are left intact after we have unattached problematic elements. It is difficult to define precisely which elements are "problematic." They include not only modifiers and

---

[2]For example, Don Hindle's parser Fidditch (Hindle 1983) "punts" nodes (leaves them unattached) when it cannot decide where they belong. Punted nodes occur very frequently.

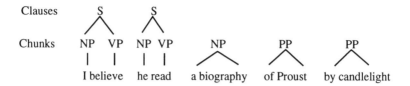

Figure 3: Strata

conjuncts, but some arguments as well (in fact, the ambiguity is often between attachment as a modifier and attachment as an argument). The smallest natural class that includes the important cases appears to be *post-head sisters*, including arguments, modifiers, and conjuncts.

When we unattach post-head sisters, S nodes become distinguished as the only nodes containing "floating" fragments. As noted by Emonds (1976) and Williams (1982), there is a prohibition in English against complements within pre-head elements, in every category except S. For example, **the proud of his son man* is bad because the pre-head element *proud* appears with a complement, *of his son*. S is obviously an exception, inasmuch as it is perfectly grammatical for prehead elements within S (for example, the subject) to contain complements.

Thus a consequence of the Emonds/Williams constraint is that each clause consists of a sequence of chunks, with no nesting of chunks within chunks. Another constraint, the well-known prohibition against center-embedding, prevents multiple nesting of clauses. Unbounded clausal embedding occurs only at the beginning or end of matrix clauses, never in the middle. A single clause may be embedded at an interior position, but only one. Hence if we unattach clauses, an utterance consists of a sequence of simplex clauses, with no nesting of clauses within clauses (ignoring singly-center-embedded clauses for the moment). The resulting picture is remarkably similar to Selkirk's prosodic structures: utterances are sequences of simplex clauses, clauses are sequences of chunks, and chunks are sequences of words (see Figure 3). Singly center embedded clauses complicate the picture somewhat, in that we must introduce a layer between clauses and chunks for them, but we still have a small, fixed number of layers, each with a distinctive character.

Chunks are justified not only as a practical expedient in the face of shortcomings of current lexical resources. First of all, the Emonds/Williams constraint – which to now has been an unexplained, and rather odd, descriptive generalization – follows as a direct consequence of stratal phrase structure. Examples like (1) are ill-formed because they involve proper nesting of the chunk *to be an American* within the chunk *a proud man*.

The intended phrase structure cannot even be represented without adding another stratum.[3]

(1)   *a proud to be an American man

Further, there are possible computational advantages to building chunks before doing attachment, even when the semantic information for disambiguating attachments is available. If ambiguities in the placement of chunk boundaries can be reliably resolved without factoring in attachment issues (as I believe they can), then we can deal with the two questions separately, simplifying the parsing task considerably.

An additional benefit of the stratal representation is that we can use computationally cheap finite-state techniques to build it. We can use a finite-state recognizer to build each stratum from the previous one: one recognizer builds chunks from words, another one builds clauses from chunks, and another collects the clauses into an utterance. Ejerhed (1988) pursues just such an approach. She also explores stochastic techniques for building clauses from chunks.

Further, there are certain parsing preferences in English that are characteristic of finite-state recognition by stratum. In finite-state recognition, ambiguities arise concerning when a pattern has been matched; the usual rule is to choose the longest match. A similar parsing preference appears to be operative in English. Consider (2) and (3).

(2)   John sold old folks homes
(3)   the emergency crews really hate is family violence

In the preferred reading of (2), John is a seller of old folks homes; in the dispreferred reading, he sold homes to old folks. A plausible account is that the parser chooses the longest match when seeking a chunk starting with *old*—the longest match is *old folks homes*, not *old folks*. Similarly, (3) involves competition between the chunks *the emergency* and *the emergency crews*. Plausibly, the preference for the longer chunk leads to the garden path effect in this sentence.

Such constructed examples do not tell us very much about whether English possesses a general longest-match preference. To address the general

---

[3]The interpretability of such examples may seem problematic if the intended phrase structure cannot even be represented. However, we may assume either that the stratal discipline may be relaxed, at the cost of easy parsability, or that an ill-formed phrase structure is used to get an interpretation, for example, in (a) where the first NP lacks a head, and the second is construed as appositive to the first.

(a)   [NP a proud] [PP of his son] [NP man]

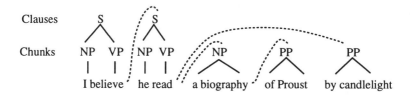

Figure 4: Dependencies

question, I constructed two stochastic parsers. One simply used lexical frequency information for part-of-speech assignment to compute probabilities of phrases, and the other used a stochastic analog of the longest-match rule, based on the same frequency information. The longest-match model performed significantly better on natural text, both in the number of sentences incorrectly parsed, and in the degree to which it considered the correct parses to be most probable. This result, though hardly definitive, suggests that there is a tendency in English to choose longest chunk candidates, which implies in turn that a chunk stratum indeed exists.

Now whatever the advantages of stratal phrase structure, essential information has clearly been lost by "unattaching" chunks. Fortunately, we can re-introduce the deleted information, without losing the phrase boundaries we require to account for processing facts, by including the severed attachments as a relation *distinct from* immediate constituency. Since post-head sisters are canonically licensed by θ-role assignment, it is natural to reintroduce the severed attachments as relations between post-head sisters and their *governors*, rather than their immediate dominators. Such a move would lead us to what is essentially a mixed immediate-constituency/dependency structure, in which dependency relations contribute to semantic interpretation and syntactic constraints involving binding and movement, but immediate-constituency boundaries are reflected in prosodic and various behavioral measures. (See Figure 4.)

3   Accounting for the Experimental Data

3.1   A Model

In the remainder of the paper, I would like to consider whether the stratal model also accords with the psycholinguistic and prosodic evidence that is difficult for standard phrase structure analyses. In particular, I would like to consider whether the phrasal boundaries in the stratal model correspond to boundaries in the empirical data. In the psycholinguistic data that I discuss below, the experimental measures assign real numbers to each boundary between two adjacent words, representing the strength or prominence of that boundary. To gauge how well the theoretical boundaries correspond to the empirical boundaries, we must assign strengths to theoretical boundaries. I adopt the following general rules assigning strength to theoretical boundaries:

a. Chunk boundaries are strong
b. Clause boundaries are stronger than chunk boundaries
c. Dependencies between adjacent chunks can weaken the boundary between them

As they stand, these are more guiding principles than rules. I try to make them more explicit, beginning with (c).

I propose two types of weakening. "Phonological" weakening occurs between two adjacent phrases if: (1) one of them consists of a single function word, and (2) they are syntactically related in one of the following ways:

verb – object	have seen – it
verb – particle	give – up
wh-pronoun – aux	who – does
aux – subject	does – the president
subject – verb	he – left

It would be nice to be able to give a syntactic definition of *dependency* that covers exactly these relations, but I will be content to list them for the time being.

The second type of weakening, syntactic weakening, is occasioned when the adjacent phrases participate in one of the following syntactic relations:

subject – verb
verb – any dependent
noun – of-NP
noun – restrictive relative

I would like to emphasize that either type of weakening occurs only between *adjacent* phrases. For example, if a PP chunk intervenes between subject and verb chunks, there is no weakening.

(4) [the professor] – [was reading]   weak
(5) [the professor] [from Milwaukee] – [was reading]   not weak

The only exception is that two phrases separated only by a phonologically weak phrase are considered adjacent. For example, in (6), the boundary

between *up* and *his car* is weakened because *his car* is dependent on, and
"adjacent enough" to, the verb *fix*.

(6)   [fix] [up] – [his car]   weak

Next we must quantify boundary strength. For convenience, I assign the
following values to boundaries, though all that really matters is the relative
values. (The first column gives the symbol I use to annotate boundaries.)

||	3	Clause
|	2	Chunk, weak relative clause
;	1	Syntactically weak boundary
,	0	Phonologically weak boundary
	0	No phrase boundary
–	2	Break: interjections, false starts

Distinguishing weak relative clause boundaries from other weak clause boundaries (such as complement clauses) seems to give a better fit to the data.
Also, for completeness' sake, I have included a type of boundary I did not
previously mention: in the prosodic data, syntactic discontinuities like interjections and false starts are common, so I have included a special phrase
boundary for them.

Finally, we require a measure of the correspondence between theoretical
and empirical boundaries. As mentioned, I am only concerned with the
relative strength of theoretical boundaries. Thus I consider the theoretical
assignments to be borne out by the data if, for every substring *s* of a
sentence, the boundary that has the highest theoretical strength in *s* also
has the highest empirical value. Define the *domain* of a boundary *b* to be
the longest substring in which it is the (unique) theoretical maximum. Then
we require that each boundary be an empirical maximum in its domain.

These definitions are perhaps more meaningful with an example. Consider the sentence *children who attend regularly appreciate lessons greatly*,
shown in (7).

(7)   children | who , attend ; regularly || appreciate ; lessons | greatly

The boundaries on either side of the relative clause are clause boundaries;
every other boundary is a chunk boundary. The clause boundary between
children and *who* is weakened because it involves a head noun and restrictive
relative that are adjacent. The chunk boundary between *who* and *attend*
is phonologically weak because *who* is a pronoun. The chunk boundaries
after *attend* and *appreciate* are syntactically weak because they involve a

verb and its dependent. The remaining boundaries are not weakened. The domains are as in (8).

(8)

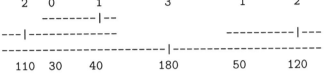

```
children who attend regularly appreciate lessons greatly
      2    0      1        3          1       2
           --------|--
      ---|-------------            ----------|---
      -----------------------|----------------------
    110   30     40          180        50      120
```

The top line shows theoretical strengths. The bars show domains of boundaries. The bottom line gives the data from one of the psycholinguistic experiments to be discussed below. In this example, theoretical and empirical relative strengths correspond exactly. For example, the domain of the first boundary includes the second and third boundaries, and the empirical strength of the first boundary (110) is greater than that of the second and third boundaries (30 and 40, respectively). Again, the fourth boundary subsumes all others in its domain, and its empirical strength (180) is also maximal in the sentence. The remaining boundaries likewise have maximal empirical values within their domains (the second and fifth boundaries trivially so, inasmuch as they are the sole boundaries in their respective domains).

3.2 Performance Structures

We can consider now how well theoretical boundary strengths correspond to empirical strengths. There are a number of relevant psycholinguistic experiments, as discussed in the introduction. Unfortunately, they report mostly summary statistics, with very little data on single sentences. I have been able to glean data on two sentences from Martin (1970), one sentence from the parsing experiment of Grosjean, Grosjean, and Lane (1979), and fourteen sentences from the pausing experiment of Grosjean, Grosjean, and Lane (also discussed in Gee and Grosjean 1983).

Martin (1970) reports on a naive-parsing experiment, in which subjects were asked to divide sentences into any number of disjoint groups of words, each group containing any number of words. Data was reported on two sentence types. The data was not broken down by sentence, though the sentences in a type were syntactically identical, differing only in lexical items. I present the data on the entire type as if it were data for a single sentence. The measure of boundary strength was based on how often words were grouped together, across subjects and sentences within a type. The derivation of the numbers is not difficult, but somewhat involved, so I

refer the reader to the original paper for the details.[4] These are the results
obtained for the two types, as shown in (9) and (10).

(9)

```
Parents ; were assisting ; the advanced teenage pupils
        2      0           2      0       0        0
--------|-----------
              -------------|-----------------------------
    135    25           176    60      52       27
```

(10)

```
Children | who , attend ; regularly || appreciate ; lessons | greatly
         2     0        1          3              1         2
                -------------|-----
---------|--------------------                  -----------------|--------
------------------------------------------|--------------------------------
    110    30           40          180              50         120
```

For these two examples, the theoretical strengths correspond exactly to the
empirical strengths.

Grosjean, Grosjean, and Lane (1979) report on two experiments. In one
experiment, they asked subjects to bisect sentences at the most natural
break, then bisect the fragments likewise until they were left with single
words. In this way, each subject produced a binary parse tree for each
sentence. For an individual parse, the strength assigned to a boundary was
the size of (that is, number of nonterminal nodes in) the smallest subtree
that includes both words adjacent to the boundary. The final value for
boundary strength was obtained by averaging across subjects the values
for individual parses.

Grosjean, Grosjean, and Lane only give parsing data for one sentence,
noting that the remaining data was highly correlated with the pausing data,
which they give in full. This was the parsing example:

---

[4] Readers who do refer to Martin (1970) should note that I have used his "maximum
method," and I have converted his similarities into distances by subtracting each value
from the maximum value (255, for Frame A; 220, for Frame B).

(11)

```
our disappointed woman ; lost ; her optimism || since , the
prospects ; were , too limited

our   dis  wom  1st  her  opt  snc  the  prs  wer  too  lim
 0     0    1    1    0    3    0    0    1    0    0
-------------|-  -|-------        ------------|-------------
-------------------------------|---------------------------
 1.5   1.2  5.5  2.0  1.0  9.1  2.2  1.0  4.0  1.8  1.0
```

Again, the correspondence between theory and data is exact.

The pausing experiment was conducted by having subjects read 14 sentences at five different reading rates. The strength of a boundary was taken to be the mean pause duration at that boundary, across all reading rates and all subjects. (The values are normalized so that the sum for each sentence is 100.) Of the 14 sentences, 11 show the predicted relative strengths. Each of the remaining three sentences has one *inversion*, that is, a domain in which the theoretical maximum is not the empirical maximum. (In the 14 sentences, there are 55 non-trivial domains, that is, opportunities for inversions.) All three inversions occur at the ends of sentences, when the final noun phrase contains a multisyllabic modifier. The pauses around the modifier are longer than predicted. Plausibly, there is a single sentence-final lengthening effect, not captured in our model, that accounts for all three discrepancies.

Here are a few examples, including one of the inversions (marked by an asterisk):

(12)

```
When , the new lawyer ; called , up ; Reynolds || the plan ;
was discussed ; thoroughly

 0  0  0  1  0  1  3  0  1  0  1
-------------------|-------------
         ----|-         ----|-
----------|---         ----|----
 5  0  2 20  3  5 30  3 10  1 21
```

(13)

closing ; his client's book || the young expert ; wondered ;
about this extraordinary story

```
1   0   0   3   0   0   1   1   0   0   0
----------|----------------------
-|------        -------|  |----------
                       *
6   5   6  26   2   4  15   8   9  11   8
```

(14)

John ; asked ; the strange young man | to be quick | on the
task

```
1   1   0   0   0   2   0   0   2   0   0
----------------|-------
   -|---------        -------|------
10  17   3   8   5  25   5   3  19   5   0
```

I include the complete set of sentences as Appendix A.

3.3 Prosody

The data on prosody were kindly provided by Julia Hirschberg of AT&T
Bell Laboratories. It consists of 127 spoken sentences from DARPA's ATIS
task. Julia Hirschberg hand-marked three degrees of prosodic boundary:
strong (%%), weak (%), and no boundary.

Even a casual glance at the data reveals that there is at least one prominent effect not included in my model: the data is rife with what appear
to be hesitation pauses, as opposed to the prosodic boundaries that occur
even in perfectly fluent speech. For example:

(15)   the morning % of %% april % twenty fifth

My approach to this problem has been to define which boundaries I consider
to be hesitation pauses, and which I consider my model to be responsible for.
Boundaries that appear immediately following a preposition, conjunction,
or infinitival *to*, I consider to be hesitation pauses, as well as boundaries
among the pre-modifiers of N, as in (16)-(18).

(16)   on april % twenty fifth %
(17)   what % does % f y % q %% h k % stand for %
(18)   flight % four fifty nine

All other boundaries I treat as genuine prosodic boundaries.

Here are a few sentences from the data set. I have mapped strong boundaries to 2, weak boundaries to 1, and no boundary to 0. Hesitation pauses I have deleted (mapped to 0).

(19)

```
yes -- i , would like ; some information / on the flights /
on april twenty second -- evening flights / from dallas /
to denver / leaving ; around five p m

 2 0 0 1 0 2 0 0 2 0 0 0 2 0 2 0 2 0 2 1 0 0 0
    ----|--                                |------
|--------      ----|------    --|--    --|--------
 --------|----    ------|--    --|--
 2 0 0 0 0 2 0 0 1 0 0 0 2 0 2 0 2 0 2 0 0 0 0
```

(20)

```
what type ; of ground transportation / is available /
from airport / in denver / to boulder / at three p m /
on the twenty third

 0 1 0 0 2 0 2 0 2 0 2 0 2 0 0 0 2 0 0 0
 --|----    --|--    --|--    ------|------
 --------|--    --|--    --|------
 0 0 0 0 0 0 2 0 0 0 2 0 2 0 0 0 1 0 0 0
```

(21)

```
show , me ; the nonstop flights / on american airlines /
from denver / to san francisco / leaving ; after one p m /
on april twenty third

 0 1 0 0 2 0 0 2 0 2 0 0 2 1 0 0 0 2 0 0 0
 --|----    ----|--          |------
 --------|----    --|----    --------|------
                  ----|--------
 0 0 0 0 2 0 0 2 0 2 0 0 2 2 0 0 0 2 0 0 0
```

There are no inversions in this sample – that is, there are no cases in which a boundary is empirically *weaker* than some other boundary in its domain – but there are some cases in which a boundary is empirically *no stronger* than some other boundary in its domain. We can distinguish two types of cases: *deletions*, in which a theoretical boundary is ignored (empirical value 0), and *conflations*, in which boundaries of differing theoretical strength are assigned the same empirical value. Given that in this data set we have fewer empirical distinctions than theoretical distinctions, conflations are unavoidable in certain situations, though they do occur even where they are avoidable. We could introduce more empirical distinctions by collecting data from more speakers and considering the probability of producing strong or weak boundaries. I expect that we would eliminate both deletions and conflations if we did so, though I do not have the data to verify it.

In the complete data set, there are 12 inversions (out of 127 sentences, containing 363 non-trivial domains). There are also eight cases where an empirical boundary does not correspond to a theoretical boundary. Such cases do not (necessarily) constitute inversions, but given that there are so few empirical distinctions, it seems they should be considered discrepancies. Of the 20 inversions and unpredicted boundaries, seven appear to be attributable to effects not included in the model, six appear to be noise in the data, and it is unclear how to categorize the remaining three cases.

Examples (22)-(24) show the types of cases I considered noise in the data:

(22)   do all fares %% include a meal % on this flight
(23)   how do i make % reservations __ on this flight
(24)   the m eighty aircraft %% flying % out of
         san %% francisco __ to atlanta

For example, I feel it would be more natural to speak (22) with a stronger break after *meal* than after *fares*, and that is what the model also predicts.

Examples that I classified as probable model error are shown in (25) and (26).

(25)   explain % base b %% and q
(26)   give me information __ on all classes %% of united airlines flights

For example, in (26), the model weakens the boundary before an *of* complement to N, but not before an *on* complement. That is probably not the correct distinction.

4 Conclusion

To summarize, I have tried to motivate a chunks-and-dependencies model of phrase structure, by appealing to a much wider range of evidence than is usually considered in discussions of phrase structure. The model corresponds well to performance structure data, it corresponds well to prosodic data, it has computational advantages as a data structure for parsing, it gives an account of longest-match parsing preferences, and it gives a natural account for the hitherto inexplicable Emonds/Williams constraint.

I hope also that this work provides an illustration of how processing evidence can be brought to bear on syntactic questions. I have tried to take seriously the idea that linguistic theory (specifically, phrase structure) provides at least a partial model of linguistic behavior. To do that, one must make some concrete assumptions about the behavior in question, assumptions that may have little to do with syntax. But I believe it is unavoidable. In particular, we cannot avoid it by appealing to introspection. Despite all the rhetoric about "psychological reality," introspection does not provide a secret window onto the structures and processes constituting the human language faculty. Introspection itself is a collection of linguistic behaviors – paraphrasing, making grammaticality judgments, et cetera – that are still poorly understood. To see the structures of linguistic interest through them, we must understand how they distort our view of those structures, much as we must be able to undo the effects of hesitation pauses to see the prosodic structures of linguistic interest.

A   The Pausing Data from Grosjean, Grosjean, and Lane

The following are the fourteen sentences from Grosjean, Grosjean, and Lane 1979. Note that the data is actually pieced together from Grosjean, Grosjean, and Lane 1979 and Gee and Grosjean 1983. They sometimes disagree about the precise values, though fortunately they always agree on relative values.

Inversions are marked by asterisks.

```
1. the expert || who , couldn't see ; what , to criticize ||
   sat , back | in despair

   0  3  0  0  1  0  0  3  0  2  0
      ----------------|---------
   ---|---------------
        -------|------      ----|---
   3 14  2  4 11  7  3 41  5  7  3   (GGL)
   3 19  3  5  9  7  4 29  5 14  2   (G&G)
```

```
2. since , she , was indecisive | that day || her friend ;
   asked , her ; to wait

    0  0  0  2  0  3  0  1  0  1  0
       ----------------|---------------
                           ----|---
    ----------|---      ----|---
    7  1  8 18  1 44  2 10  4  4  1   (GGL)
   11  2 13 13  2 34  2 12  2  9  6   (G&G)
```

```
3. after the cold winter ; of that year | most people ; were ,
   totally fed-up

   0  0  0  1  0  0  2  0  1  0  0
      --------------------|------------
   ----------|------      ----|------
   7  1  5 12  1  5 38  5  9  5 12   (GGL)
   5  5  5 14  3  5 32  5 10  5 11   (G&G)
                   *
```

4. our disappointed woman ; lost ; her optimism || since ,
   the prospects ; were , too limited.

```
0   0   1   1   0   3   0   0   1   0   0
---------------|---------------
------- | - | ---    ------- | ------
5   6  24   8   4  28   5   1  15   3   1    (both)
```

5. When , the new lawyer ; called , up ; Reynolds || the plan
   ; was discussed ; thoroughly

```
0   0   0   1   0   1   3   0   1   0   1
-------------------|-------------
            ---- | -            ---- | -
---------- | ---            ---- | ----
5   0   2  20   3   5  30   3  10   1  21    (G&G)
```

6. closing ; his client's book || the young expert ; wondered ;
   about this extraordinary story

```
1   0   0   3   0   0   1   1   0   0   0
---------- | ----------------------
- | ------       ------- |   | ----------
                    *
6   5   6  26   2   4  15   8   9  11   8    (both)
```

7. John ; asked ; the strange young man | to be quick | on the
   task

```
1   1   0   0   0   2   0   0   2   0   0
---------------- | -------
    - | ---------       ------- | ------
10  17   3   8   5  25   5   3  19   5   0    (both)
```

8. By making ; his plan ; known || he , brought , out ;
   the objections ; of everyone

```
0   1   0   1   3   0   0   1   0   1   0
------------ | ------------------
        ---- | -               --- | ---
--- | ---            ------- | ---
0  11   2   5  38   0   4  19   2  16   3    (both)
```

9. In addition ; to his files | the lawyer ; brought ;
   the office's best adding-machine

```
0   1   0   0   2   0   1   1   0   0   0
-------------|--------------------
----|-------     ----|  |----------
2  10   3   3  33   1   8  17   0  10  13
```

10. That , a solution ; couldn't be found || seemed ,
    quite clear | to them

```
0   0   1   0   0   3   0   0   2   0
----------------|-------------
-------|-------     -------|----
5   5  15   7   3  30   9   6  17   3
```

11. the agent ; consulted ; the agency's book || in which |
    they , offered ; numerous tours

```
0   1   1   0   0   3   0   2   0   1   0
---------------|---------------
                ----|---------
---|  |------          ----|---
1  18  11   2   5  25   2  13   3  10  10   (both)
```

12. That , the matter ; was dealt , with | so fast || was ,
    a shock | to him

```
0   0   1   0   0   2   0   3   0   0   2   0
----------------------|-------------
----------------|----
-------|-------        -------|----
7   2  13   2   2  18   5  28   5   3  13   2   (G&G)
```

13. Not quite all ; of the recent files | were examined |
    that day

```
0   0   1   0   0   0   2   0   2   0
--------------------|---
--------|----------     ----|----
11  10  17   4   3   9  23   7  10   6
```

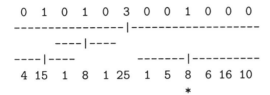

```
14. She , discussed ; the pros ; and cons || to get , over ;
    her surprisingly apprehensive feelings

    0  1  0  1  0  3  0  0  1  0  0  0
    ----------------|--------------------
        ----|----
    ----|----           -------|----------
    4 15  1  8  1 25  1  5  8   6 16 10
                       *
```

References

Bachenko, J. and E. Fitzpatrick. 1990. A computational grammar of discourse-neutral prosodic phrasing in English. *Computational Linguistics* 16:3.155–170.

Bresnan, Joan and Ronald M. Kaplan. 1982. Introduction: Grammars as mental representations of language. In Joan Bresnan (ed.), *The mental representation of grammatical relations*. Cambridge, MA: MIT Press.

Chomsky, Noam. 1965. *Aspects of the theory of syntax*. Cambridge, MA: MIT Press.

Church, Kenneth and Ramesh Patil. 1982. Coping with syntactic ambiguity or how to put the block in the box on the table. *American Journal of Computational Linguistics* 8:3–4.139–149.

Dommergues, Jean-Yves and François Grosjean. 1981. Performance structures in the recall of sentences. *Memory and Cognition* 9:5.478–486.

Ejerhed, Eva. 1988. Finding clauses in unrestricted text by finitary and stochastic methods. In *Proceedings of the Second Conference on Applied Natural Language Processing*, pp. 219–227. Association for Computational Linguistics.

Emonds, Joseph E. 1976. *A transformational approach to English syntax*. New York: Academic Press.

Gee, James Paul and François Grosjean. 1983. Performance structures: A psycholinguistic and linguistic appraisal. *Cognitive Psychology* 15:411–458.

Grosjean, F., L. Grosjean, and H. Lane. 1979. The patterns of silence: Performance structures in sentence production. *Cognitive Psychology* 11:58–81.

Hindle, Donald. 1983. *User manual for Fidditch.* Naval Research Laboratory Technical Memorandum #7590–142.

Levelt, W. J. M. 1970. Hierarchial chunking in sentence processing. *Perception and Psychophysics* 8:2.99–103.

Martin, Edwin. 1970. Toward an analysis of subjective phrase structure. *Psychological Bulletin* 74:3.153–166.

Selkirk, Elisabeth O. 1978. On prosodic structure and its relation to syntactic structure. In T. Fretheim (ed.), *Nordic prosody II.* Trondheim: Tapir.

Selkirk, Elisabeth O. 1980. Prosodic domains in phonology: Sanskrit revisited. In M. Aronoff and M-L. Kean (eds.), *Juncture.* Saratoga, CA: Anma Libri.

Selkirk, Elisabeth O. 1981. On the nature of phonological representations. In T. Myers, J. Laver, J. Anderson (eds.), *The cognitive representation of speech.* Amsterdam: North-Holland Publishing Company.

Williams, Edwin. 1982. Another argument that passive is transformational. *Linguistic Inquiry* 13:160–163.

Some Open Problems in Head-driven Generation[1]

Dale Gerdemann and Erhard Hinrichs

Seminar für Sprachwissenschaft
Universität Tübingen

1 Introduction

In recent years, a great deal of effort has gone into developing natural language systems that are reversible between parsing and generation (Shieber 1988, Shieber et al. 1990, Gerdemann 1991). A number of advantages of having such a grammar are discussed in Appelt (1987). The primary advantage is that having a single knowledge source ensures consistency between the two modes of processing. The grammar writer can write a single grammar, which will account for both the sentences which can be parsed and the sentences which can be generated. This differs significantly from the older Augmented Transition Network (ATN) approach of Woods (1970) and Bates (1978), in which a completely different ATN would have to be written for each mode of processing.

The idea of having a declaratively represented grammar which is neutral between parsing and generation originated in the Functional Unification Grammar framework of Kay (1979). The fact that unification is both associative and commutative allows processing in any order with the same results. Thus, in principle, there is no problem with using such grammars bidirectionally. The major issue, however, is the question of control strategy. Simple parsers such as the Prolog-based interpreter for definite clause grammar may be run in reverse, but the result is hopelessly slow and in some cases may not terminate.

The most promising control strategy explored in previous studies has been the idea of *head-driven* generation. The basic idea of this approach is that heads should be generated first using top-down information and then the bottom-up information from the heads' subcategorization list should be used to generate its dependents. Although this is a natural idea, there are nevertheless problems with the approach when the head is an empty category or otherwise noncanonical (such as a type-raised NP).

---

[1] Research reported in this paper was supported by Sonderforschungsbereich SFB 340 sponsored by the Deutsche Forschungsgemeinschaft. The views and conclusions contained herein are those of the authors and should not be interpreted as representing official policies.

2   Head-Driven Algorithms

In principle, it is likely that any parsing algorithm could be adapted to run in reverse for generation. In practice however, two algorithms, Earley's algorithm (Earley 1970) and the left corner algorithm originally due to Rosenkrantz and Lewis (1970), have been most widely used. The reason for the preference of these algorithms is clearly that both allow a mixture of bottom-up and top-down information flow. This mixture is crucial in generation since the top-down semantic information from the goal category must be integrated with the bottom up subcategorization information from the lexicon. Top-down algorithms suffer additionally from what may be called *head recursion*, i.e., the generation analog of left recursion in parsing. Shieber et al. (1990) show that top-down algorithms will fail for rules such as VP → VP X, even when these algorithms are extended with goal freezing as proposed in Dymetman and Isabelle (1988).

Although both Earley's algorithm and the left-corner algorithm allow for a top-down/bottom-up mixture, they do so in rather different ways. Earley's algorithm is essentially a bottom-up algorithm in that the nodes of a parse tree are constructed in postorder (i.e., all daughters before the mother). Nevertheless, the top-down information from the prediction step is used to guide this bottom-up construction. The left-corner algorithm, on the other hand, is more truly a mixture of top down and bottom up in that the nodes of the parse tree are constructed in an inorder (i.e., left daughter, then the mother, then the remaining daughters[2]). Thus the left-corner parser can be described as bottom up for the left most daughter in each subtree and top down for the remaining daughters.

When these algorithms are adapted for head-driven generation, however, the tree traversals become rather different in that heads are constructed first, rather than left most daughters. Nevertheless, the basic top-down/bottom-up information flow remain the same. These two algorithms differ also, however, in other respects as we can see by exploring each of them in more detail.

2.1   Adaptations of Earley's Algorithm

Earley's algorithm provides a mixed regime, in which the bottom-up *completion* and *scanning* steps are guided by the top-down *prediction* step. The algorithm, then, is basically bottom up, since the parse tree is constructed by the completion and scanning steps. The easiest way to understand Ear-

---

[2]The *inorder* and *postorder* tree traversals are defined more precisely in Illingworth (1990).

ley's algorithm is in terms of chart parsing.[3] Suppose, for example, that we want to parse the sentence *The duck dreams.* with the following grammar:

S   → NP VP   V   → duck|dreams
NP → Det N   N   → duck|dreams
VP → V   Det → the

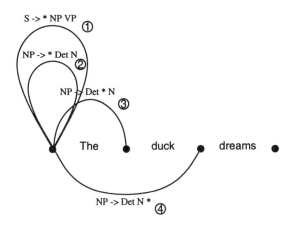

Figure 1: The Chart After Two Predictions and Two Scans.

The parser begins by predicting S → * NP VP since the left hand side of this rule matches the start symbol (step 1 in fig. 1). The "dot" in this rule indicates how much of the right hand side has already been recognized, i.e., none. Then, in step 2, the predictor applies to predict NP → Det N, since NP matches the category to the right of the dot in the previous prediction. At this stage, the scanner may apply twice (steps 3 & 4) first to scan *the* and then to scan *duck.*[4] Note here that although *duck* is ambiguous between N and V, the top-down prediction only allows it to be parsed as a V.

---

[3]Chart parsing was introduced by Kaplan (1973) and Kay (1973). Introductory treatments are provided in Pereira and Shieber (1987), Gazdar and Mellish (1989) and Ross (1989). The discussion of Earley's algorithm here will be necessarily brief. For details of the algorithm, the reader is referred to Earley (1970). For a logical reconstruction of this parsing algorithm, see Pereira and Warren (1983). For augmentation of Earley's algorithm with feature structures, see Shieber (1985).

[4]To follow Earley (1970), the predictor would have to first predict every rule of the form N → *terminal* and then scanning would be performed just for the prediction N → duck. The scanner assumed here avoids this inefficiency by scanning preterminals instead of terminals.

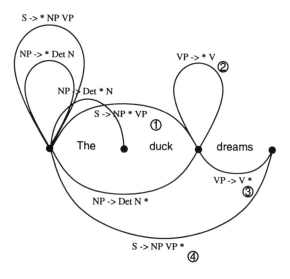

Figure 2: The Finished Chart.

The remaining steps of the parser are then shown in fig. 2. First, since the inactive edge,[5] NP → Det N * was added in the previous step,[6] the completer may apply to complete part of the S → NP VP rule. The dot is moved to the right of the NP to indicate that this category has been recognized. Then since VP is to the right of the dot, the VP → V rule is predicted. This results in the scan of *dreams* in the third step. Notice again that even though *dreams* is ambiguous, the top-down prediction allows it only to be recognized as a V. Finally, since both the NP and the VP have been recognized, the completer recognizes the full sentence.[7]

Now how can this parser be turned into a generator? First, the generator will, of course, need to start with an uninstantiated string and the scanner will need to work in reverse to instantiate this string. In parsing, it makes sense to go from left to right since then the input string can guide the parser. On the other hand, in generation, going from left to right provides

---

[5]*Inactive/active edges* are referred to as *final/nonfinal states* in Earley (1970) and as *nonconditional/conditional items* in Shieber (1988).

[6]We follow Ross (1989) here in putting active states on the top and inactive states on the bottom.

[7]A parser can be obtained from this recognizer either by building up a tree structure with each scan/completion step or by incorporating features and building up the tree structure as a complex valued feature as described in Pereira and Shieber (1987). The latter approach is more general since it allows a semantic analysis of the sentence to be built up in the same manner as the syntactic structure.

no guidance. It makes more sense to follow the strategy of generating heads first and then complements.[8] The other main difference is that for the generator the start category will need to be much more fully specified. It is pointless to generate just an S. One normally wants to generate a sentence with a particular semantic reading (represented as a feature structure) or perhaps a semantic reading with some additional syntactic properties. To be able to specify such a complex start category, we must assume that Earley's algorithm is augmented to allow feature structures as described in Shieber (1985).

2.1.1 Shieber's Approach

Earley's algorithm was first adapted for generation by Shieber (1988). Shieber's approach is based on Pereira and Warren's (1983) idea of *Earley deduction*. In this approach, each edge is represented as a state $[i, N \leftarrow V_m \ldots V_n, j]$. This state represents an edge from i to j with categories $V_m \ldots V_n$ yet to be found. The categories "to the left of the dot" are ignored. This representation for states differs from Earley (1970) primarily in the index j. In Earley's algorithm, this right index corresponds to the notion of a *state set*. A Shieber state with right index j thus corresponds to an Earley state in the jth state set. We will return to the notion of state sets in the next section, where these sets are manipulated to provide an alternative control structure for generation.

Given this representation of states, the rule of prediction is as shown in (1) and the rule of completion is as shown in (2).

$$(1) \quad \frac{[i, A \leftarrow BC_1 \ldots C_m, j] \quad B' \rightarrow D_1 \ldots Dn \quad \theta = mgu(B \upharpoonright \Phi, B')}{[j, B' \rightarrow D_1\theta \ldots D_n\theta, j]}$$

$$(2) \quad \frac{[i, A \leftarrow BC_1 \ldots C_m, j] \quad [j, B', k] \quad \theta = mgu(B, B')}{[i, A\theta \rightarrow C_1\theta \ldots C_m\theta, k]}$$

The rule of prediction in (1) says that if we have an edge from i to j, with category B to the right of the dot, and if we have a rule whose left hand side unifies with B, then we can infer the instance of this rule with

---

[8]This head-driven approach has also been applied to parsing by Kay (1989) and van Noord (1991). For parsing, however, this approach is more controversial. In particular, given an input string, it is difficult to guess which element of the string might be the head. In Kay's approach, a chart parser is used in order to save partial results in case some structure is built up from the wrong element. A head-driven parser can, however, make errors which don't lead to useful partial results. For example, in parsing the sentence *The duck swims*, the parser might guess that *duck* is the head, since *duck* is also a verb.

variable substitution θ as an edge from j to j.[9] The variable substitution θ requires restriction as expressed by $B \upharpoonright \Phi$ in order to ensure that prediction terminates (see Shieber (1985), Gerdemann (1989)). The basic problem is that without restriction, an infinite sequence of predictions might be made, where new predictions are not subsumed by previous predictions. Restriction solves this problem by specifying finite bounds on feature values. $B \upharpoonright \Phi$ expresses the category B restricted to just the information specified by the paths in the restrictor Φ. Since restriction involves eliminating information which could be used for top-down prediction, its use in generation is problematic. We will return to this problem in Section 2.1.2.

The completion rule in (2) says that if there is an edge from i to j with B to the right of the dot and if there is an inactive edge B'[10] from j to k, then we may infer a new edge from i to k with the dot moved to the right of B and with the variable substitution θ. Since the lexical items in the input string are encoded as inactive edges, this rule of completion also covers Earley's scanning step.

With the parsing steps expressed as logical inferences, it then becomes possible to explore parsing and generation simply as different theorem proving strategies, which differ in the heuristics they use to infer new items. To parse then *Sonny left*, the parser would start with the items $[0, sonny, 1]$ and $[1, left, 2]$ for the string and the item $[0, S \leftarrow NP\ VP, 0]$ assuming this is the only rule, whose left hand side unifies with the start category. The goal criterion for this case, is to infer an item from 0 to 2 which is subsumed by the start category. This goal can be achieved, however, in different ways. Shieber shows both a breadth-first strategy, which he refers to as Earley style parsing, and a depth-first strategy, which he refers to as shift-reduce style parser. Both parsers are bottom up, however, since the bottom up nature of Earley's algorithm is inherent in the rules of prediction and completion.

Shieber then argues that a generation system could be developed using the same basic architecture but with a different set of heuristics. The initial prediction and the success criterion in such a system would remain the same as in a parser, but it is not clear what to do with the lexicon, since we don't know ahead of time which lexical items will be used or where they will occur. As a first approximation, Shieber claims that, in principle, one could insert each lexical item at each position. He rejects the idea, however, since it would obviously be inefficient.[11] Moreover, he argues that

---

[9]The rule is stated in terms of term unification and variable substitution. The same idea applies for graph unification, though it is somewhat more difficult to express.

[10]This is equivalent to $B' \rightarrow$. I.e., since elements to the left of the dot are ignored, a final item has an empty right hand side.

[11]In fact, since we don't know in advance how long the generated sentence will be, this

string position indexing is problematic in general for generation, since it may cause a phrase to be redundantly generated at two or more different string positions. For example, a rule allowing adverbs to come optionally before or after a VP, would force the VP to be generated at two string positions depending on where the adverb is placed.

Instead of this approach, Shieber proposes that each lexical item should be inserted at just the single position where $i=j=0$. The same inference rules in (1) and (2) can still be used, but the effect of string position indexing is essentially eliminated. Shieber then erroneously suggests that removing string indexing will cause the algorithm to become non-goal directed in the sense that "many phrases might be built that could not contribute in any way to a sentence with the appropriate meaning." Shieber then goes on to propose a semantic filter to eliminate this supposed problem.[12] In fact however, even with string position indexing eliminated, no phrases can be completed which are not unifiable with some prediction. More precisely, the feature structure of the mother must be unified with the category to the right of the dot in some prediction. The algorithm, in fact, becomes more or less goal directed depending only upon how much information is eliminated by the restrictor in the prediction step.[13]

Thus, it appears that Shieber's algorithm will work, even without the extra semantic filtering that he proposes. The primary disadvantage is that eliminating the state sets may eliminate possible control strategies, such as the strategy proposed in the next section. In general, if multiple strings could be generated from a single goal semantics, it would be reasonable to generate shorter strings before longer strings. It is hard to see how a regime that completely eliminates string indexing could follow this strategy. A second disadvantage is that the generation algorithm no longer corresponds to the parsing as deduction model that Shieber argues for in the case of parsing. The problem is that the lexical items with indices $i=j=0$ corre-

---

approach involves inserting each lexical item into an infinite number of positions, so the problem is more than just inefficiency.

[12]The semantic filter suggested requires the principle of *semantic monotonicity*, which holds if for each grammatical phrase with semantics *Sem* the semantics of each subphrase is subsumed by some portion, i.e. sub-DAG, of *Sem*. When this condition holds, then any lexical items whose semantics is not subsumed by some portion of the goal semantics can be eliminated before the generation process begins. This of course places a rather strong condition on the grammar. But since Shieber has not convincingly shown that the condition is necessary, we will not consider it further here.

[13]The question of choosing an appropriate restrictor for generation is a complex issue, which Shieber does not discuss. In general, however, the choice of restrictor is even more important in generation than in parsing. In Gerdemann (1991), it is argued that no information corresponding to the semantic translation of a phrase should be eliminated by restriction. It is also argued that it may be advantageous for the restrictor to eliminate other semantic features, such as those corresponding to selectional restrictions, since such features may lead to local ambiguities.

spond to no reasonable premises, i.e., we don't want premises saying that all of the lexical items correspond to the empty string. Moreover, the lexical premises used will not indicate the word order of the string that is generated, so some other extra-logical mechanism is needed for this purpose. More reasonably, lexical items should have variable indices so that they may be inserted at any position. One could have an indexing scheme where $j = i + 1$ (assuming lexical items correspond to single words). Then the precise values for i and j would be determined only when the lexical item is used by the completion inference.

2.1.2   Our Approach

The approach presented in Gerdemann (1991) is more conservative than Shieber's approach in that the state sets as in Earley (1970) are preserved. However, when the predictor would make a prediction which is subsumed by a prediction in a previous state set, a readjustment is made to the chart so that this new prediction will not be necessary. In order to detect cases where duplicate predictions would be made, a record is kept of each restricted category RC that has been used to make predictions.[14] The list of these records is kept in the global restricted category list GRC. Each record in the GRC is of the form $[RC, F, C]$, where F is the number of the state set in which RC was used to make some predictions and C is a list of the completions that have been found so far. In addition to this GRC, states are also modified to include a back pointer BP, which indicates with which restricted category the state was originally predicted.[15] Thus, each state is of the form $[BP, F, A \rightarrow B_1 \ldots B_m]$. For the sake of comparison, the state is written in a similar form to Shieber's *items*. Shieber's left index corresponds to F, and the right index corresponds to the state set number in which this state occurs.

In addition to these chart readjustments, Earley's algorithm also needs to be modified to achieve head-driven generation. For the sake of simplicity, we assume that this is implemented by reordering the right hand sides of all rules so that the head comes first.[16] Thus the order of right hand side categories represents order of processing and not word order. The actual word order can be given by an HPSG-style **phon** attribute as in Gerdemann

---

[14]We use the term *restricted category* here in order to be neutral between restricted terms or restricted DAGS for term unification or DAG unification, respectively.

[15]In Gerdemann (1989, 1991), these back pointers were added originally to optimize the completion step. In completion the back pointer of the final state must match the forward pointer of the non-final state. The special back pointer r is also used to mark the initial prediction for the termination condition. In this paper, however, we will ignore this additional complication.

[16]The algorithm could, of course, be modified to do this reordering on line.

(1991).[17] Given these additions, the prediction and completion steps are then as follows:[18]

Prediction Given a state $S = [BP, i, A \leftarrow BC_1 \ldots C_m]$ in state set j, let $RC = B \restriction \Phi$. Then:

1. If there exists a $[RC', F, C] \in GRC$ such that $RC' \sqsubseteq RC$, then:
   - Remove S from state set j;
   - Add S to state set F;
   - For each $B' \in C$ such that $\theta = mgu(B, RC)$, add $[BP, i, A \leftarrow C_1\theta \ldots C_m\theta]$ to state set j.

2. Otherwise:
   - Add $[RC, j, [\,]]$ to GRC;
   - For each rule $B' \to D_1 \ldots D_n$ such that $\theta = mgu(B', B)$, add $[RC, j, B' \leftarrow D_1\theta \ldots D_n\theta]$ to state set j.

Scanning Given a state $S = [BP, i, A \leftarrow BC_1 \ldots C_m]$ in state set j and lexical item B' such that $\theta = mgu(B', B)$, add $[BP, i, A \leftarrow C_1\theta \ldots C_n\theta]$ to state set $j + 1$.[19]

Completion Given a final state $[BP, j, B']$ in state set k. Then:

- For $[BP, F, C] \in GRC$,[20] add B' to C;
- For each $[BP', i, A \leftarrow BC_1 \ldots C_m] \in$ *state set* j such that $\theta = mgu(B', B)$, add $[BP', i, A\theta \leftarrow C_1\theta \ldots C_m\theta]$ to state set k.

Compared to Shieber's Earley deduction approach, this algorithm is certainly more procedural. The readjustments to the chart are really nonmonotonic inferences from the perspective of Earley deduction. A readjustment corresponds to retracting a premise with right index j and then reasserting this same premise with right index $j - N$ (for some number N). By including the state sets from the original Earley's algorithm, it becomes possible to do these readjustments in a fairly natural way. The disadvantage

---

[17] Following the practice of definite clause grammars, this attribute should have a difference list value. Thus, ignoring other features, the standard sentence rule could be written **s(phon(P0,P))** $\to$ **np(phon(P0,P1)) vp(phon(P1,P))**.

[18] Unlike Gerdemann (1991), the algorithm here uses term unification. No different claims are being made. The difference is only to simplify the presentation and, for the sake of comparison, to make it more similar to Shieber's presentation of Earley deduction.

[19] This rule of scanning assumes that all lexical items consist of single words. A generalization to allow for compounds and traces is given in Gerdemann (1991).

[20] There must be such a member of GRC since new back pointers are only created by the predictor, and whenever the predictor creates a new back pointer, it adds an entry to GRC.

of using a chart, however, is that it takes up considerable space and access times may be slow. The use of the chart is made somewhat more efficient by applying the subsumption test to restricted categories in the first case of the prediction rule (Gerdemann 1989, 1991). In the case of generation, however, these restricted categories will be rather large since they must at least contain the semantic information from the full (unrestricted) category. At least for some grammars, then, it may be advantageous to consider a back-tracking style generator as presented in the next section.

2.2   Adaptations of Left-corner Parsing

The basic idea of left-corner parsing is quite simple. One could think of the left-corner parser as having two basic operations: *matching* (as in a top-down parser) and *reduction* (similar to shift-reduce parsing). Reduction in left-corner parsing differs from reduction in shift-reduce parsing in that reduction in left-corner parsing is made before the full right hand side of a rule is found. In fact, reductions are made as soon as the first element on the right hand side of a rule (i.e. the *left corner* of the rule) is found. This overanxious reduction will only be justified if the list of categories in the rest of the right hand side of the rule can serve as top-down goals to parse some prefix of the remaining input. Once this "justification" has been performed, the left hand side of the rule becomes the new left corner of the input[21] and then further reductions and matches are tried in order to satisfy the remaining goals.

In order to make this idea more concrete, consider the Prolog program in fig. 3 for a rather simple left-corner parser.[22] The first clause is the termination condition: given no more goals, then none of the input can be parsed. The second clause is the matching procedure.[23] Notice here that rather than a single goal, there will always be a list of remaining goals. Each goal may be either terminal or nonterminal. The third clause is the reduction procedure. The first recursive call of **parse** justifies the "overanxious reduction" by parsing the rest of the right hand side for the reduction, and then **parse** is again called recursively to parse the goals with a new left corner.

----

[21] The term *left corner* is standardly used in this ambiguous way to mean either the left most element of the right hand side of a rule or the left most element in the input string. In reduction, the left most element in the first sense must match the left most element in the second sense.

[22] This parser is given for simple context free grammars. It is quite trivial, however, to add term unification to the rules.

[23] Shieber et al. (1990) argue that this matching step should really use correct unification with the occurs check. Without the occurs check, it is possible that difference lists used for gap-threading would become circular.

```
parse(Cat,String):-
  parse([Cat],String,[]).

parse([],String,String).                        % terminate
parse([Goal|Goals],[Goal|String0],String):-     % match
  parse(Goals,String0,String).
parse([Goal|Goals],[LC|String0],String):-       % reduce
  rule(LHS,[LC|RestRHS]),
  parse(RestRHS,String0,String1),
  parse([Goal|Goals],[LHS|String1],String).

rule(s,[np,vp]). rule(n,[boy]). % format of rules
```

Figure 3: The Left-Corner Parser

This style of parsing provides a mix of top-down and bottom-up information flow, which makes it attractive to be adapted for generation. The reduction step is clearly bottom up (as in shift-reduce parsing) but each time a reduction is performed, a new set of top-down goals is obtained, which need to be satisfied before any higher reduction can be performed.

Shieber et al. (1990) in their head-corner adaptation of the left corner algorithm (henceforth referred to as the head-corner algorithm) rely on the fact that unification grammars frequently employ *chain rules*, i.e., rules in which the translation of the mother is reentrant with the translation of one of the daughters. For any constituent whose root node is licensed by a chain rule, the daughter whose translation is reentrant with that of the mother can be referred to as the *semantic head*. Assuming that *semantic head* is a transitive relation, the lowest semantic head is referred to as the *pivot*.[24] The pivot itself does not have a semantic head, since otherwise it would not be lowest. Typically, pivots will be lexical items. But it is also possible that the pivot will be an unheaded phrase such as an idiom or possibly a conjunction.[25] The pivot in the head-corner algorithm plays the same role as the left corner in the standard left-corner algorithm.

---

[24]This is essentially the definition of pivot given by Shieber et al. It may be useful, however, to have a slightly more general notion of pivot. In the left-corner parser, when a left corner is reduced it is replaced by a new left corner. Similarly, it makes sense to say that when a pivot is reduced, it is replaced by a new higher pivot, even though this new pivot is no longer the lowest semantic head.

[25]Conjunctions are not unheaded in all linguistic analyses, but they are unheaded in Gazdar et al. (1985) in the sense that there is not one unique head.

In fig. 4 we give a simplified version of the head-corner generator, which is intended to show the similarity to the left-corner parser in fig. 3. This generator differs from the parser in two main respects. First, phonology must be handled differently since the string is not simply built up from left to right. For simplicity, we assume that phonology is given in lexical entries and rules as the value of an attribute **phon** as in footnote 17. Thus, a result of generating Cat will be that the **phon** attribute of Cat will be instantiated.

```
generate(Cat):-
   generate([Cat],[]).

generate([],[]). % terminate
generate([Pivot|Goals],[Pivot]):- % match
   generate(Goals,[]).
generate([Goal|Goals],[]):- % reduce1
   applicable_non_chain_rule(Goal,Pivot,RHS),
   generate(RHS,[]),
   generate([Goal|Goals],[Pivot]).
generate([Goal|Goals],[Pivot]):-     % reduce2
   applicable_chain_rule(Pivot,LHS,Goal,RHS),
   generate(RHS,[]),
   generate([Goal|Goals],[LHS]).
```

Figure 4: The Head-Corner Generator

The second difference corresponds to the difference between choosing a left corner and choosing a pivot. Choosing a left corner is easy since the left corner is simply the left most element on the input string.[26] Choosing a pivot, however, requires the special procedure **applicable_non_chain_rule** to select a pivot and the procedure **applicable_chain_rule** to reduce a pivot to a higher pivot.[27] The first of these procedures selects a pivot, which will be a non-chain rule for which the semantic features are unified with the goal semantic features. The second procedure selects a chain rule and unifies the current pivot with the semantic head of the rule. The left hand side of this chain rule then becomes the new pivot. Both of the procedures incorporate linking (Matsumoto et al. 1983, Pereira and Shieber 1987) so

---

[26]The term *input string* is perhaps misleading since the algorithm in fig. 3 allows non-terminals to be pushed onto this list after a reduction is made.

[27]These procedures are defined in Shieber et al. (1990).

that a pivot will only be used if it can be connected to the current goal by a series of chain rules.

One potential problem for this generator is that for certain types of grammars it may not terminate. The problem arises in the recursive call **generate(RHS,[])** in the third and fourth clauses. If, for example, the top level goal is to generate an S and an embedded S occurs as a member of **RHS**, then, unless the features on the embedded S are significantly different from the features on the top level goal S, the generator will go into a loop. The left-corner parser has no trouble with such recursion since (assuming off line parsibility[28]) each loop will involve consuming some of the input. The Earley generator, as well, would have no problem with such cases, since the algorithm is primarily bottom up and the subsumption test in the predictor rules out making duplicate top-down predictions. It is not clear, however, whether or not this is a practical problem. It is likely that for reasonable grammars, the features on goal and embedded categories will be different enough so that it will not go into a loop.

A more serious problem for both the Earley generator and the head-corner generator is that they both make assumptions about headedness that may not be valid for all grammars. Both generators will be significantly slower when some of the rules are non-headed. Moreover, non-canonical heads, such as empty heads and type-raised heads, are problems for both algorithms as described in the next section.

3 Problematic Constructions for Head-Driven Generation

Ideally, a reversible approach to parsing and generation should allow precisely the same grammars for both directions of processing. In practice, however, generation systems have placed restrictions on the grammar that are not required for parsing (Russell et al. 1990). The primary restriction imposed by generation systems is the chain-rule restriction of Shieber et al. (1990), requiring that phrases should generally have semantic heads. Beyond just having heads, however, these algorithms impose restrictions on the types of heads involved. Empty heads (Section 3.1), for example, are problematic since typically they inherit their subcategorization lists from elsewhere. A similar problem is posed by type-raised functors in Categorial

---

[28]The idea of off line parsibility (Kaplan and Bresnan 1982) is that a grammar should not contain chains of rules allowing a non-terminal N to derive just N. Obviously, if such chains exist then (assuming that the features on the top N are the same as the features on the bottom N are the same) the parser could loop forever. This idea is extended to PATR syle grammars (without a context free backbone) in Shieber (1989).

Unification Grammar (Section 3.2).[29] If these functors count as heads, the generation process will not be sufficiently constrained, since these functors clearly do not contain the proper subcategorization information to guide the generation process. Other deviations from head-complement types of structure, such as specifier-head or head-adjunct, may cause problems for such generators as well, though the problems for these constructions have been studied less thoroughly.

3.1   Empty Heads

As pointed out previously (Shieber et al. 1990, Russell et al. 1990), the position of verbal elements in main clauses of modern German provides an interesting challenge to the family of head-driven generation algorithms that we presented in Section 2. We will briefly review some basic facts about German word order in different clause types, before we can comment on the issues that the syntactic distribution of verbal elements raises for head-driven generation.

Sentences in modern German exhibit systematic differences with respect to the placement of the finite verb. Subordinate clauses, as the *daß*-clauses in (3), obey SOV order, with the finite verb occurring in sentence final position, regardless of whether it is an auxiliary such as *wird* in (3a) or a main verb such as *kaufte* in (3b).

(3)   a. *Fritz glaubt,   daß   Peter das Buch kaufen wird.*
         Fritz believes that Peter the book buy   will.
         'Fritz believes that Peter will buy the book.'

      b. *Fritz glaubt,   daß   Peter das Buch kaufte.*
         Fritz believes that Peter the book bought
         'Fritz believes that Peter bought the book.'

If the main clause is a yes/no question, as in (4), the finite verb occurs in sentence-initial position. In the case of constituent questions, as in (5), or assertion clauses, as in (6), the finite verb appears in second position, following a single topicalized constituent. Again, this generalization holds for main verbs and auxiliaries alike, as (4)–(6) show.

(4)   a. *Wird Peter das Buch kaufen?*
         Will Peter the book buy
         'Will Peter buy the book?'

---

[29]By this term we intend to refer to various unification-based extensions to categorial grammar (Uszkoreit 1986, Bouma 1987) and including what has also been called Unification Categorial Grammar (Zeevat 1988).

    b. *Kaufte Peter das Buch?*
       BoughtPeter the book
       'Did Peter buy the book?'

(5) a. *Welches Buch wird Peter kaufen?*
       Which   book will Peter buy
       'Which book will Peter buy?'

    b. *Welches Buch kaufte   Peter?*
       Which   book bought Peter
       'Which book did Peter buy?'

(6) a. *Peter wird das Buch kaufen.*
       Peter will the book buy
       'Peter will buy the book.'

    b. *Peter kaufte   das Buch.*
       Peter bought the book
       'Peter bought the book.'

In assertion main clauses, the sentence-initial topicalized constituent is not limited to the subject of the sentence. Rather direct objects, as in (7a), or non-finite verbal constituents, as in (7b), can appear in sentence-initial position as well.

(7) a. *Das Buch wird Peter kaufen.*

    b. *Kaufen wird Peter das Buch.*

In fact, a descriptive generalization about assertion main clauses that virtually any syntactician will agree on, is that any major syntactic constituent can appear sentence-initially, as long as the topicalized material constitutes a **single** constituent.

It is generally agreed upon in the GB literature (cf. Haider and Prinzhorn 1986, von Stechow and Sternefeld 1988) and its precursors (cf. Thiersch 1978) that the word order in subordinate clauses is the basic word order, with the word order in main clauses being derived transformationally via move-alpha. There is no general agreement as to the structural position that the finite verb moves to at S-structure (INFL and COMP being the two chief options), nor as to the factors that in such analyses condition the obligatory fronting of finite verbs in main clauses (see Haider (1986) for an review of the issues involved).

One way to flesh out such a movement analysis of verb-second position is to posit a mapping between D-structure and S-structure as shown in (8).

The d-structure would map into the corresponding s-structure by two applications of move-alpha: movement of the N″ into the head position of C″ and of the finite verb into the head position I″.

(8)

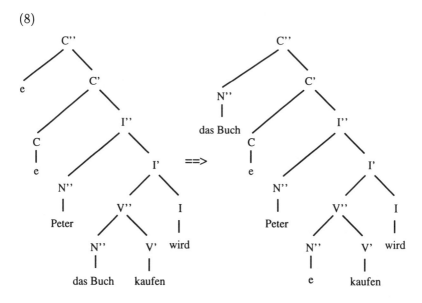

Monostratal analyses of German main clauses, on the other hand, have challenged the view that verb-initial or verb-second position of the finite verb in German is due to syntactic movement. Uszkoreit (1985) in the framework of GPSG and Pollard (1990) in the framework of Head-Driven Phrase Structure Grammar have proposed analyses in which the finite verb is generated as a sister of S, regardless of clause type. The position of the finite verb in a particular clause type is accounted for by linear precedence rules which impose constraints on the linear order of (sister) constituents. According to Pollard's analysis, an assertion main clause such as *Das Buch wird Peter kaufen* is assigned the structure in (9).

The placement of the finite verb in Pollard's analysis is conditioned by a linear precedence rule which requires that a constituent carrying the feature specification [+INV] precede its sister constituents. If finite verbs in subordinate clauses are marked by the feature specification [-INV] and a linear precedence rule is added which requires that a constituent carrying the feature specification [-INV] has to follow its sister constituents, then the correct word order for subordinate clauses can be effected as well.

(9)

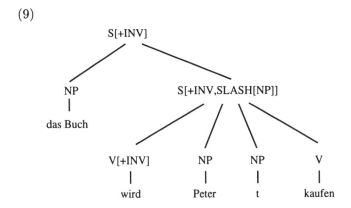

While monostratal and GB-style analyses differ considerably in their treatment of the verb-second phenomenon, both types of syntactic approaches show remarkable similarity in the treatment of sentence-initial topicalized constituents in assertion main clauses and constituent questions. Regardless of syntactic framework, it is generally agreed upon that topicalization involves a syntactic dependency between the fronted constituent and a syntactic position marked by a trace. The main difference between monostratal analyses à la GPSG or HPSG and GB-style multistratal analyses involves the mechanism that accounts for this dependency: a slash mechanism or a transformational account via move-alpha, respectively. It goes beyond the scope of this paper to enter into a full discussion of the verb-second or the topicalization phenomenon, two of the central topics of German syntax. However, see Hinrichs and Nakazawa (1989a, 1989b) for additional discussion.

For a head-driven strategy, the displacement of verbal constituents via topicalization or via verb-fronting—if a movement analysis is assumed— can cause serious problems. Assuming that the verbal trace is the lexical head of the sentence, then the first lexical item that the generator will try to generate is this verb in final position. Since the verb turns out to be gapped, only a trace is generated at this point. However, it is imperative for efficient generation that the generator find the full lexical entry for the verb at this point in order to know what complements to generate.

Notice that this problem is going to arise for monostratal and multistratal analyses alike when the strategy of head-driven generation is applied to sentences in which a verbal constituent is topicalized. This is due to the fact that both types of analyses presuppose that there is a syntactic dependency between such a fronted constituent and a trace within the VP. In addition, the same type of problem arises in the case of sentences whose finite verb is in second position, if verb-second placement is treated via a trace-mechanism.

From the perspective of computational linguistics, it is highly desirable to develop truly general algorithms for natural language generation that can accommodate a variety of well-motivated analyses of the same syntactic or semantic phenomenon. Since the problems for head-driven generation are particularly pervasive for those analyses that treat topicalization and verb-second phenomenon via a trace mechanism, we will concentrate on such GB-style analyses in the remainder of this section. In order to clarify this problem further, it will be useful to consider a specific grammar. Since virtually all head-driven generation algorithms presuppose unification-based grammar formalisms for the encoding of grammatical information, we will attempt to recast a movement style analysis of topicalization and verb-second in German in such a unification-based framework. The resulting analysis is mono-stratal. In fact, the grammar we present here is encoded in a simplified version of HPSG, though the same problem can easily be illustrated within other linguistic frameworks.

We will begin considering the lexical entry for a verbal trace in this grammar. This entry is shown in (10), whereas the lexical entry for the non-null verb *gibt* is show in (11).

$$
(10)\quad
\begin{bmatrix}
\text{head:} & [1]\begin{bmatrix}\text{maj:} & \text{vp}\end{bmatrix} \\[2pt]
\text{bind:} & \begin{bmatrix}\text{v2-slash:} & \begin{bmatrix}\text{head:} & [1] \\ \text{subcat:} & [2]\end{bmatrix} \\ \text{top-slash:} & \text{none}\end{bmatrix} \\[2pt]
\text{subcat:} & [2]
\end{bmatrix}
$$

$$
(11)\quad
\begin{bmatrix}
\text{head:} & \begin{bmatrix}\text{maj:} & \text{vp} \\ \text{sem:} & \text{give}([1],[2],[3])\end{bmatrix} \\[2pt]
\text{bind:} & \begin{bmatrix}\text{v2-slash:} & \text{none} \\ \text{top-slash:} & \text{none}\end{bmatrix} \\[2pt]
\text{subcat:} & \langle\begin{bmatrix}\text{cat:} & \text{np} \\ \text{sem:} & [3]\end{bmatrix},\begin{bmatrix}\text{cat:} & \text{np} \\ \text{sem:} & [2]\end{bmatrix},\begin{bmatrix}\text{cat:} & \text{np} \\ \text{sem:} & [1]\end{bmatrix}\rangle
\end{bmatrix}
$$

In these lexical entries, the **v2-slash** attribute may take as its value the verbal category that appears in second position and the **top-slash** attribute may take as its value a category to be topicalized. The **none** value for these attributes is simply an arbitrary atomic value, which indicates that a complex value is not allowed. The primary difference between these two lexical entries is that whereas *gibt* has a fully instantiated subcategorization list, the trace simply indicates that its **subcat** value is the same as the

subcat value in the category value of the **v2-slash** attribute. The idea that this lexical entry for trace represents, is that traces do not have inherent properties such as subcategorization, but rather inherit these values from elsewhere. Although the lexical entry in (10) is cast in the framework of HPSG, any other linguistic theory that allows traces would also need a way of expressing the fact that traces have inherited properties.[30]

The grammar should allow categories to be cancelled off of the subcategorization list in either of two ways. The rule in (12) allows a VP to combine with a category that it is subcategorizing for and the rule in (13) allows a category to be moved from the subcategorization list to **top-slash**.[31]

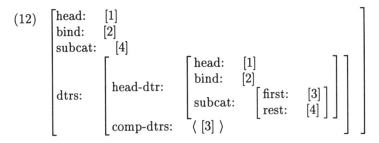

(12)
$$
\begin{bmatrix}
\text{head:} & [1] \\
\text{bind:} & [2] \\
\text{subcat:} & [4] \\
\text{dtrs:} & \begin{bmatrix}
\text{head-dtr:} & \begin{bmatrix}
\text{head:} & [1] \\
\text{bind:} & [2] \\
\text{subcat:} & \begin{bmatrix} \text{first:} & [3] \\ \text{rest:} & [4] \end{bmatrix}
\end{bmatrix} \\
\text{comp-dtrs:} & \langle\, [3]\, \rangle
\end{bmatrix}
\end{bmatrix}
$$

(13)
$$
\begin{bmatrix}
\text{head:} & [1] \\
\text{bind:} & \begin{bmatrix} \text{v2-slash:} & [2] \\ \text{top-slash:} & [3] \end{bmatrix} \\
\text{subcat:} & [4] \\
\text{dtrs:} & \begin{bmatrix}
\text{head-dtr:} & \begin{bmatrix}
\text{head:} & [1] \\
\text{bind:} & \begin{bmatrix} \text{v2-slash:} & [2] \\ \text{top-slash:} & \text{none} \end{bmatrix} \\
\text{subcat:} & \begin{bmatrix} \text{first:} & [3] \\ \text{rest:} & [4] \end{bmatrix}
\end{bmatrix}
\end{bmatrix}
\end{bmatrix}
$$

Finally, the sentence rule is shown in (14). For simplicity, we have assumed flat structure at the top even though most linguistic analyses assume a binary branching structure.

---

[30] One alternative approach which avoids the use traces altogether is suggested by current research in extended categorial grammar (Steedman 1985; Moortgat 1988, 1990). These researchers account for unbounded dependencies by including non-Lambek versions of functional composition and type raising (Steedman) or by adding discontinuous type constructors (Moortgat). While we believe that this line of research is a very promising one to pursue, very little work has been done so far on applying these formalisms to the problem of natural language generation (however, see van der Linden and Minnen 1990).

[31] The Head Feature and Binding Inheritance principles are, in effect, incorporated into these rules. Since there are so few rules in HPSG, it makes little computational sense to try to extract out general principles applying across all rules.

(14)
$$
\begin{bmatrix}
\text{head:} & [1] \\
\text{dtrs:} &
\begin{bmatrix}
\text{head-dtr:} &
\begin{bmatrix}
\text{head:} & [1] \\
\text{bind:} &
\begin{bmatrix}
\text{v2-slash:} & [2]\ complex\,[] \\
\text{top-slash:} & [3]\ complex\,[]
\end{bmatrix} \\
\text{subcat:} & \text{none}
\end{bmatrix} \\
\text{comp-dtrs:} & \langle\ [2],\ [3]\ \rangle
\end{bmatrix}
\end{bmatrix}
$$

The most important thing to notice about this rule is that the head daughter is designated to have complex values for both of its **slash** attributes. As a sentence is generated, these values will percolate downward. The rule in (13) will allow the value for **top-slash** to become **none**, though the complex value for **v2-slash** will percolate all the way down to the lexical head. Thus, given the start DAG [head|sem|give(hans,marie,book)], when the generator gets to the point of generating a lexical item, this start DAG will have become instantiated to the DAG in (15).

(15)
$$
\begin{bmatrix}
\text{head:} &
\begin{bmatrix}
\text{maj} & \text{vp} \\
\text{sem:} & \text{give(hans,marie,book)}
\end{bmatrix} \\
\text{bind:} &
\begin{bmatrix}
\text{v2-slash:} & complex\,[] \\
\text{top-slash:} & \text{none}
\end{bmatrix}
\end{bmatrix}
$$

The goal DAG at this point, of course, contains all of the needed semantics but still it will not unify with the lexical entry for *gibt* since the complex value for **v2-slash** will not unify with the atomic value **none** in the lexical entry for *gibt*. So at this point it is still not possible to generate this lexical item with its subcategorization list.

This complex value for **v2-slash** will, however, unify with the complex value for **v2-slash** in the lexical entry for the trace in (10). Thus, only the trace can be generated as the lexical head. Once the lexical head is generated, the subcategorization list of this head needs to be used to build the rest of the phrase bottom-up. But the subcategorization list of the trace in (10) is completely uninstantiated, so the generator will, at this point, have no constraints at all that can be used to build the rest of the phrase. The semantics of the phrase is available, as shown in (15), but it is not known how this semantics corresponds to a subcategorization list.

One strategy to avoid this problem was proposed by Shieber et al. (1990). These authors propose that rules such as (14), which introduce gap filler constructions, should be given some kind of mark or flag by the grammar writer. Then when the generator encounters such a flagged rule, the head-driven strategy can be temporarily abandoned in order to generate the filler first. In the grammar given here, the head features of the trace (including the semantic value) are identical to the head features of the verb in second position. Thus, the goal semantics could be used to immediately generate the second position verb before generating the head daughter. If this is done, then when the trace is generated as the lexical head of the head daughter, it will have an instantiated subcategorization list.

A general problem with this idea is that it reduces the modularity between the grammar and the processor. In this case, the grammar writer needs to be aware of processing concerns in order to properly annotate the rules.

A more specific problem with this approach is that it will fail when the same rule sometimes results in the displacement of a head and sometimes results in the displacement of a non-head. Topicalization appears to be an example of such a rule. In (16), a lexical non-head *Das Buch* is topicalized, while in (17) the lexical head *lesen* is topicalized.[32]

(16) Das Buch lesen wird Peter.

(17) Lesen wird Peter das Buch.

Given the existence of rules of this sort, it will not be possible for the grammar writer to determine once and for all whether or not the topic constituent needs to be generated first. Whether or not the topic needs to be generated first depends on how the topic is instantiated in a particular application of the rule.

Another strategy for dealing with dependencies is suggested in Gerdemann (1991). The strategy suggested there was to treat all dependencies as being strictly phonological. Given the existence of a **phon** attribute as in HPSG, it would be possible for the phonology of a constituent to pass up a tree, say as the value of a **slash** type of attribute. Then it would be possible for a phrase to "actually" occur in a lower part of a tree, while its phonology occurs somewhere higher in the tree. In this analysis, a phonological dependency could be introduced by a rule such as that in (18).

$$
(18) \quad
\begin{bmatrix}
\text{phon:} & \langle\,\rangle \\
\text{head:} & [1] \\
\text{bind:} & \begin{bmatrix} \text{phon-slash:} & [2] \end{bmatrix} \\
\text{dtrs:} & \begin{bmatrix} \text{head-dtr:} & \begin{bmatrix} \text{phon:} & [2] \\ \text{head:} & [1] \\ \text{bind:} & \text{none} \end{bmatrix} \end{bmatrix}
\end{bmatrix}
$$

This approach, then, would allow for certain mismatches between syntax and phonology. The idea is reminiscent of Hendrix's (1987) idea of having

---

[32] *Lesen* is the head here in the sense that it contains the relevant subcategorization list (Hinrichs & Nakazawa 1989b).

different algebras apply in the syntax and semantics to account for quantifier scopings that don't match surface word order. More generally, the idea is similar to the idea of having multiple levels of representation in Government Binding Theory or Lexical Functional Grammar. It would be interesting to compare these various approaches to see how they relate.

One problem with this approach, though, is that with such phonological dependencies, it may no longer be possible to parse in a strictly left-to-right fashion. Thus it may turn out that the optimal grammar for generation is no longer optimal for parsing. There appears to be two possible solutions to this problem. One idea would be to develop new parsing algorithms which could deal with such dependencies. Or a second idea would be to use a grammar compiler to produce separate grammars for parsing and generation.

At this point, we do not know which of the above solutions will ultimately be preferable. We conjecture that the problems involved in efficient generation can only be fully understood if the range of data is significantly expanded. Although we have concentrated here on the problem of verb second constructions in German, it may ultimately turn out that other phenomena are even more problematic. In this regard, cases of VP ellipsis (Sag 1976), empty head nouns (Nerbonne et al. 1989) or the possibility of empty prepositions in phrases such as *next Tuesday* (Larson 1985, McCawley 1988) constitute related phenomena that will require close attention.

3.2   Type Raising in Categorial Unification Grammar

The problem of empty heads can be thought of as a special case of the general problem of applying the head-driven strategy to lexical heads whose semantics is not sufficiently specified. One limiting case is, of course, a lexical entry whose semantics is specified only in terms of a reentrancy. It may often be the case that empty phonology correlates with empty semantics as in the case of a trace, but this need not be the case. In versions of categorial unification grammar, for example, the lexical entries for type-raised NPs may have unspecied semantics, though the phonology is certainly not null. In Gerdemann and Hinrichs (1990), we give an example of such a grammar. In this simple grammar, there is just the one function application rule in (19), which conforms to the chain rule condition, and yet, given type-raised lexical entries for proper nouns, the generator may go into an unconstrained search.

(19)
$$
\begin{bmatrix}
\text{x0:} & [1]\,[\text{trans:} & [2]] \\
\text{x1:} & \begin{bmatrix}
\text{cat:} & \begin{bmatrix}\text{result:} & [1] \\ \text{arg:} & [3]\end{bmatrix} \\
\text{trans:} & [2]
\end{bmatrix} \\
\text{x2:} & [3]
\end{bmatrix}
$$

(i.e. X/Y Y → X)

The PATR-style rule in (19) clearly corresponds to the function application rule of categorial grammar, though there are two main differences. Most importantly, we satisfy the chain-rule condition by having the translation of the mother reentrant with the translation of the functor. The other difference is that forward and backward application are collapsed into one rule. This collapse is possible since phonology is handled by means of a **phon** attribute which takes difference list values. This allows functors to specify either left or right concatenation of phonologies.[33]

As is shown in Gerdemann and Hinrichs (1990) and Gerdemann (1991), the function application rule (19) may lead to unconstrained generation (i.e. generate and test) when proper nouns are given type-raised lexical entries as they would be in Montague (1973). The problem is, essentially, that when a proper noun is given a type-raised entry, its translation will have to be reentrant with the translation of the functor it combines with. This is the reentrancy marked with number 2 in the lexical entry for a proper name like *Tom* (20).

(20)
$$
\begin{bmatrix}
\text{cat:} & \begin{bmatrix}
\text{result:} & [1] \\
\text{arg:} & \begin{bmatrix}
\text{cat:} & \begin{bmatrix}
\text{result:} & [1] \\
\text{arg:} & \begin{bmatrix}\text{cat:} & \text{np} \\ \text{trans:} & \text{tom}\end{bmatrix}
\end{bmatrix} \\
\text{trans:} & [2]
\end{bmatrix}
\end{bmatrix} \\
\text{trans:} & [2]
\end{bmatrix}
$$

To understand this type-raised entry, suppose that this higher functor combines with the first order functor *smiles* whose lexical entry is given in (21).

(21)
$$
\begin{bmatrix}
\text{cat:} & \begin{bmatrix}
\text{result:} & [\text{cat:} \quad \text{s}] \\
\text{arg:} & \begin{bmatrix}\text{cat:} & \text{np} \\ \text{trans:} & [1]\end{bmatrix}
\end{bmatrix} \\
\text{trans:} & \begin{bmatrix}\text{pred:} & \text{smiles} \\ \text{arg1:} & [1]\end{bmatrix}
\end{bmatrix}
$$

---

[33]For details, see Gerdemann and Hinrichs (1990) and Gerdemann (1991).

The entry for *smiles* specifies a function from **np** to **s**. The translation for this functor is (translated into a term) **smiles(X)**, where the value of **X** comes from the argument that *smiles* combines with. When *tom* combines with *smiles*, the resulting translation cannot be just the translation of *smiles*, but rather the translation that *smiles* would have if it were to combine with a non-type raised lexical entry for *tom*. The path ⟨cat arg cat arg trans⟩ in the lexical entry for *tom* "feeds" this non-type raised semantics for *tom* into ⟨cat arg trans⟩ path of *smiles*. Thus the translation of *tom* after it has combined with *smiles* is just the translation of *smiles* with this argument position instantiated.

To generate the sentence *tom smiles*, the generator would begin by unifying the goal semantics with the translation for **x0** in (19). The result of this unification is shown in (22).

$$(22) \quad \begin{bmatrix} x0: & [1]\begin{bmatrix} trans: & [2]\begin{bmatrix} pred: & smile \\ arg1: & tom \end{bmatrix} \end{bmatrix} \\ x1: & \begin{bmatrix} cat: & \begin{bmatrix} result: & [1] \\ arg: & [3] \end{bmatrix} \\ trans: & [2] \end{bmatrix} \\ x2: & [3] \end{bmatrix}$$

Now the generator must find the lexical entries for *tom* and *smiles*. Since the resulting parse tree will be only of depth 1, there is essentially no difference between top-down, bottom-up or head/left-corner generation. In any case, the first thing the generator must find is the head (i.e., the functor). Clearly the lexical entry for *tom* will unify with the **x1** path in (22), but so would the lexical entry for any other proper noun in the lexicon. Suppose, for example, that the **x1** path unified with the lexical entry for *harry*. Then the instantiated rule would appear as in (23).

$$(23) \quad \begin{bmatrix} x0: & [1]\begin{bmatrix} trans: & [2]\begin{bmatrix} pred: & smile \\ arg1: & tom \end{bmatrix} \end{bmatrix} \\ x1: & \begin{bmatrix} cat: & \begin{bmatrix} result: & [1] \\ arg: & [3] \end{bmatrix} \\ trans: & [2] \end{bmatrix} \\ x2: & [3]\begin{bmatrix} cat: & \begin{bmatrix} result: & [1] \\ arg: & \begin{bmatrix} cat: & np \\ trans: & harry \end{bmatrix} \end{bmatrix} \\ trans: & [2] \end{bmatrix} \end{bmatrix}$$

The unification with *harry* succeeds, but then the **x2** path will no longer be able to unify *smiles* (21). So what a head-driven generator will need to do is to try unifying every possible proper noun with the **x1** position and then weed out those cases where this causes failure to generate anything for the **x2** position. Clearly, this is a case of generate and test.

As seen then from this example, type-raised NPs provide another case where unspecified semantics may lead a head-driven generator into uncontrolled search. As noted in Gerdemann and Hinrichs (1990), the problem does not arise with higher type NPs in general, but rather only with proper NPs which are type raised following Montague's strategy of generalizing to the worst case. It seems then, that the generator imposes the constraint on the grammar writer that NPs should be assigned minimal types and then only raised when necessary.[34] Interestingly, the principles of *minimal type assignment* and *type raising only as needed* have been argued for on entirely independent semantic grounds by Partee and Rooth (1983). This seems to be one of the interesting cases where constraints imposed by generation systems correspond to the constraints which are linguistically motivated.

The question of how *type raising only as needed* can be incorporated into the grammar, however, is a tricky issue. In Gerdemann and Hinrichs (1990), we advocate an approach based on *supercombinators* as discussed in Wittenburg (1987) and Wall and Wittenburg (1989). The basic idea of this approach is to combine two (or possibly more) rules into one encompassing rule. Thus, for example, if type raising is only needed in the context of coordination, then type raising could be built into the coordination rule. This, then, forces type raising only where it is needed.

Calder et al. (1989) provide an alternative approach to generation of type-raised NPs in the context of Unification Categorial Grammar.[35] Calder et al. use essentially the same head-corner algorithm as in Shieber et al. (1990). However, since all proper names have type-raised lexical entries, a special case needs to be added to the algorithm to handle this case. In their approach, when a type-raised NP combines with a VP (i.e., s/np), the normal functor driven routine is reversed so that the VP is generated first. Since the VP requires a non-type raised NP argument, this argument is first

---

[34]Type raising would be necessary, e.g., if an untyped NP were to coordinate with a higher type quantifier NP.

[35]Unification Categorial Grammar (UCG) is a unification version of categorial grammar that encodes directionality in types by means of an **order** attribute taking values **pre** and **post**. Thus, simplifying somewhat, **A:pre** is a simple type which precedes its functor and **A/(B:post)** is a functor taking a following argument **B**. This encoding of types becomes highly problematic, however, in the case of type raising. This is so since type raising in their approach reverses direction of combination; e.g., an NP marked **pre** becomes a functor looking for an argument which is also marked **pre**. In effect, Calder et al. allow only harmonic type-raising to the exclusion of the disharmonic type raising standardly used in categorial grammar. Since Calder et al. incorporate type raising into their generation algorithm, this is a problem not only for their grammar, but also for their algorithm.

raised and then the generation procedure is recursively called to generate this type-raised argument.[36] There are two main problems with this approach. First, as we argue in Section 3.1, the general strategy of marking specific rules as exceptional for the generator does not always work, since at least some rules may require exceptional treatment only in special cases. Second, Calder et al.'s approach is fixed specifically for a grammar in which all proper NPs are given type-raised lexical entries. But, as shown by Partee and Rooth (1983), there are strong semantic arguments against such a treatment. Since Calder et al.'s approach lacks modularity between the processor and the grammar, it would be difficult to modify it for a different grammar which would conform to Partee and Rooth's principles of *minimal type assignment* and *type raising only as needed*.

The Gerdemann and Hinrichs (1990) approach and the Calder et al. (1989) approach provide examples of two general approaches to the problem of applying the head-driven strategy to heads whose semantics is not sufficiently specified. In the Gerdemann and Hinrichs approach, restrictions are placed on the form of the grammar, whereas in the Calder et al. approach, the algorithm is extended to handle special cases. It is still an open question which of these two approaches is better, since at present, neither is fully adequate. If restrictions on grammar are to be accepted, then one would like a general mechanism to enforce these mechanisms. For example, one might want a compiler to automatically create the supercombinators required in Gerdemann and Hinrichs (1990). On the other hand, if extensions are made to the generator, then one would like these extensions to generalize to a variety of cases rather than ad hoc extensions for each special case.

4   Completeness and Coherence

A further problem for unification-based generation systems is that they normally only generate phrases whose semantics is unifiable with the goal semantics. The semantics of the generated string may be either more or less specific than the goal semantics. Wedekind (1988) has dubbed this the *completeness* and *coherence* problem for generation. If the goal semantics always subsumes the semantics of the generated string then, the generator is complete. And if the semantics of the generated string always subsumes the goal semantics, then the generator is coherent.

A coherent generator may be thought of as one that does not overgenerate. For example, if the semantic representation for *John eats* is **eat(john,X)**, the incoherent generator may instantiate variable **X** and gen-

---

[36]In fact, for complex reasons, this recursive call to **generate** causes their algorithm, as presented in the appendix, to go into an infinite loop.

erate *John eats peanuts.* A complete generator, on the other hand, may be thought of as a generator that does not undergenerate. For example, if the goal semantics is **eat(john,peanuts)**, then the incomplete generator may simply generate the string *John eats.* As seen from these examples, completeness and coherence become practical problems most when the semantics representations follow the common practice of using the Prolog (metalanguage) variables for (object language) variables in the semantic representation. This use of Prolog variables causes a problem since the incoherent generator may simply instantiate the variable **X** in **eat(john,X)** to **peanuts** in order to generate the string *John eats peanuts.* Similarly, if the lexical entry for intransitive *eat* is of the form **lex(subcat([sem(X)]),** **eat(X,Y))**, then the incomplete generator may simply instantiate the variable **Y** in this lexical entry to **peanuts** in order to generate *John eats* from the goal semantics **eat(john,peanuts)**.

The naive way to solve the completeness/coherence problem is to follow the strategy of generate and test. This, however, will be very inefficient since many strings may be generated only to be weeded out by the completeness and coherence tests. Shieber et al. (1990) suggest a better way to handle the coherence problem. They suggest that this problem could be solved if variables in the goal logical form were not represented by Prolog variables but rather by constants.[37] Thus if the goal semantics for *John eats* is **eat(john,var23)**, there is no possibility that the constant **var23** could be instantiated to *peanuts* to generate *John eats peanuts.*

For completeness, however, Shieber et al. can only suggest a generate and test type of strategy. What they fail to notice is that the completeness problem could also be solved in an entirely analogous manner if Prolog variables in lexical entries were instantiated to constants. Thus, if the lexical entry for intransitive *eat* were **lex(subcat([sem(X)]),eat(X,var19))** then it would not be possible for the semantics of this entry to unify with the goal semantics **eat(john,peanuts)**. Unfortunately, it would also not be possible to generate an intransitive sentence with the goal semantics **eat(john,var23)** since the two variables will not unify. So it seems that the practice of numbering variables allows one to solve either completeness or coherence but not both at the same time.

In Gerdemann (1991) an alternative is proposed within the framework of graph unification. In the term unification approach, each different variable must be given a different unique constant name. In the graph unification approach, however, all variables could be represented by the same constant, say **var**. Then the distinction between same and different variables can be recaptured by using reentrancies. Instead of having two instances of the

---

[37]They suggest using Prolog procedure **numbervars** may be used for the purpose of turning Prolog variables into constants.

same variable type, it is possible in graph unification for the two variables to be represented by exactly the same variable token.[38]

This approach of using atomic values for variables in logical form goes in the direction of making completeness and coherence the grammar writer's responsibility. This is even more the case for the problem of adjuncts. One might imagine that the logical form for *John eats* subsumes the logical form for *John eats quickly*. This will be the case, for example, if the logical forms are [**pred: eat, arg1: john**] and [**pred: eat, arg1: john mod: quickly**] respectively. Again, it would have to be the grammars writer's responsibility to ensure that logical forms do not subsume each other in this manner. In this case, however, there is a good alternative. Instead of having the **mod** attribute take an atomic value, it would be more reasonable to say that **mod** takes as its value a list of modifiers.[39] Then the first logical form should really contain the **mod** attribute with an empty list as a value. Since the empty list will not unify with a non-empty list, the completeness/coherence problems are again solved. Thus the completeness/coherence problems can be avoided, but the burden is really placed on the grammar writer.

Another approach to this problem might be to consider why completeness and coherence do not create problems for the parser. In principle, of course, these problems could arise for a parser. A parser that further instantiated the input string would be "incoherent". Whereas a parser that returned a parse after only consuming part of the input string would be "incomplete". It's clear that these problems do not arise because parsers are designed to go from left to right through the input string and terminate precisely at the end of the input list. It would be interesting to consider whether a generator could traverse an input logical form in a similar deterministic manner. If the logical form is represented as a graph, it would not be hard to fix some traversal order. It would be more problematic, however, to develop a generation control routine which would generate in the order of this fixed traversal. Moreover, given that reentrancies may enter into the logical form, it would be difficult to stop the logical form from being further instantiated during the traversal. In short, it is much easier to traverse through a simple input list than it is to traverse through a complex logical form graph.

---

[38]For this type/token distinction in feature structures, see Shieber (1986). Although the feature structure logic of Kaspar and Rounds (1986) makes no type/token distinction for atomic values, this is by no means a necessary assumption. In HPSG (Pollard and Sag 1987), for example, the type/token distinction is made for atomic types, which correspond to atomic values in untyped approaches.

[39]Another alternative would be for *quickly* to be interpreted as a higher predicate.

5 Conclusion

Unification based grammars are inherently neutral with respect to processing direction. So, at least from a logical perspective, there is no problem with using these grammars for generation. The practical problem arises, however, when it is required that the generator function with reasonable efficiency. As we have argued in this paper, this requires that the generator be able to use both top-down and bottom-up information. This desideratum can be met either by using a left/head-corner type of routine or by using a bottom-up approach such as Earley's algorithm, which includes top-down filtering. Since subcategorization information in lexically-driven linguistic theories is encoded in the lexical head of a phrase, algorithms for generation need to adopt a head-driven strategy. Both left-corner and Earley-style generation algorithms can be modified in this manner. However, as we have shown in Section 3.1, the efficiency of head-driven strategies is jeopardized when they encounter heads whose semantics is not sufficiently specified, as is the case with traces, certain type-raised NPs and semantically vacuous head constituents such as case-marking prepositions. At this point, it remains unclear whether such cases are best handled by suspending the head-driven strategy under certain circumstances or by imposing constraints on the grammar. Furthermore, as discussed in Section 4, generation algorithms for unification grammars, regardless of whether they adopt a head-driven strategy or not, are subject to the problems completeness and coherence, in the sense of Wedekind (1988). That is, these algorithms may generate strings which encode somewhat more or somewhat less information than is contained in the goal semantics. We have shown that both of these problems can be solved by eliminating the confusion between metalanguage and object language variables in logical forms.

References

Appelt, D. E. 1987. Bidirectional grammars and the design of natural language generation systems. In *Theoretical Issues in Natural Language Processing-3*, 185–191.

Bates, M. 1978. The Theory and Practice of Augmented Transition Network. In *Natural Language Communication with Computers* 151–259. Berlin: Springer.

Bouma, G. 1987. A Unification-based analysis of unbounded dependencies in categorial grammar. In *Proceedings of the Sixth Amsterdam Colloquium*, ed. J. Groenendijk, M. Stokhof, and F. Veltman.

Calder, J., M. Reape and H. Zeevat. 1989. An Algorithm for Generation in Unification Categorial Grammar. In *Proceedings of the Fourth Conference of the European ACL*, 233–240.

Dymetman, M. and P. Isabelle. 1988. Reversible logic grammars for machine translation. In *Proceedings of the Second International Conference on Theoretical and Methodological Issues in Machine Translation of Natural Languages*. Pittsburgh, PA, Carnegie-Mellon University.

Earley, J. 1970. An Efficient Context-free Parsing Algorithm. *Communications of the ACM* 13(2):94–102. Also in Grosz et al. 1986.

Gazdar, G., E. Klein, G. Pullum and I. Sag. 1985. *Generalized Phrase Structure Grammar*. Cambridge, MA: Harvard University Press.

Gazdar, G. and C. Mellish. 1989. *Natural Language Processing in Prolog/Lisp/Pop 11*. Addison-Wesley. These are different books, one for each language.

Gerdemann, D. 1989. Using Restriction to Optimize Parsing. In *Proceedings of International Workshop on Parsing Technologies*, 8–17.

Gerdemann, D. 1991. *Parsing and Generation of Unification Grammars*. PhD thesis, University of Illinois. Published as Beckman Institute Cognitive Science Technical Report CS-91-06.

Gerdemann, D. and E. W. Hinrichs. 1990. Functor-Driven Natural Language Generation with Categorial-Unification Grammar. In *COLING-90, vol 2*, ed. H. Karlgren, 145–150.

Grosz, B., K. S. Jones and B. L. Webber (ed.). 1986. *Readings in Natural Language Processing*. Los Altos, CA: Morgan Kaufmann.

Haider, H. 1986. V-Second in German. In *Verb Second Phenomena in Germanic Languages*, Vol. 21, 49–86. Dordrecht: Foris.

Haider, H. and M. Prinzhorn (ed.). 1986. *Verb Second Phenomena in Germanic Languages*, Vol. 21 of Publications in Languages Sciences. Dordrecht: Foris.

Hendrix, H. 1987. Type change in Semantics: The scope of quantification and coordination. In Ewan Klein and Johan van benthem (eds.), *Categories, Polymorphism and Unification*, 95–120. Edinburgh/Amsterdam: CCS/ILLI.

Hinrichs, E. and T. Nakazawa. 1989a. Flipped Out in AUX in German. In *Papers from the 25th Regional Meeting of the Chicago Linguistic Society*, 193–202.

Hinrichs, E. and T. Nakazawa. 1989b. Subcategorization and VP Structure. Talk presented at the *Third Symposium on Germanic Linguistics*, (published as "Aspects of German VP Structure." SFS-Report-01, Seminar für sprachwissenschaft, Eberhard-Karls-Universität, Tübingen, Germany, 1993).

Illingworth, V. (ed.). 1990. *Dictionary of Computing*. Oxford University Press. Third Edition.

Kaplan, R. 1973. A General Syntactic Processor. In *Natural Language Processing*, ed. R. Rustin, 193–241. New York: Algorithmics Press.

Kaplan, R. and J. Bresnan. 1982. Lexical-functional grammar: A formal system for grammatical representation. In *The Mental Representation of Grammatical Relations*, ed. J. Bresnan, 171–281. Cambridge, MA: MIT Press.

Kaspar, R. and W. Rounds. 1986. A Logical Semantics for Feature Structures. In *ACL Proceedings, 24th Annual Meeting*, 257–271.

Kay, M. 1973. The MIND System. In *Natural Language Processing*, ed. R. Rustin, 155–188. New York: Algorithmics Press.

Kay, M. 1979. Functional Grammar. In *Proceedings of the Fifth Annual Meeting of the Berkeley Linguistics Society*, 17–19.

Kay, M. 1989. Head-Driven Parsing. In *Proceedings of International Workshop on Parsing Technologies*, 52–62.

Larson, R. 1985. Bare-NP Adverbs. *Linguistic Inquiry* 16:595–621.

Matsumoto, Y., H. Hirakawa, H. Miyoshi and H. Yasukawa. 1983. BUP: A Bottom-Up Parser Embedded in Prolog. *New Generation Computing* 1(2):145–158.

McCawley, J. 1988. Adverbial NPs: Bare or clad in see-through garb? *Language* 64:583–590.

Montague, R. 1973. The Proper Treatment of Quantification in Ordinary English. In *Approaches to Natural Language*. Dordrecht: Reidel.

Moortgat, M. 1988. *Categorial Investigations: Logical and Linguistic Aspects of the Lambek Calculus*. Dordrecht: Foris Publications.

Moortgat, M. 1990. Discontinuous type constructors. Workshop Categorial Grammar and Linear Logic, Leuven.

Nerbonne, J., M. Iida and W. Ladusaw. 1989. Running on Empty. In *Proceedings of the Eighth West Coast Conference on Formal Linguistics*, ed. E. J. Fee and K. Hunt, 276–288.

Partee, B. and M. Rooth. 1983. Generalized Conjunction and Type Ambiguity. In *Meaning, Use and Interpretation of Language*, ed. R. Bauerle, C. Schwarze and A. von Stechow, 361–383. Walter de Gruyter.

Pereira, F. and D. Warren. 1983. Parsing as Deduction. In *ACL Proceedings, 21st Annual Meeting*, 137–144.

Pereira, F. and S. Shieber. 1987. *Prolog and Natural Language Analysis.* CSLI Lecture Notes No. 10. Chicago: Chicago University Press.

Pollard, C. 1990. On Head Non-Movement. In *Proceedings of the Tilburg Conference on Discontinuous Constituents*.

Pollard, C. and I. Sag. 1987. *An Information-Based Approach to Syntax and Semantics: Volume 1 Fundamentals.* CSLI Lecture Notes No. 13. Chicago: Chicago University Press.

Rosenkrantz, D. and P. Lewis. 1970. Deterministic left corner parser. In *IEEE Conference Record of the 11th Annual Symposium on Switching and Automata Theory*, 139–152.

Ross, P. 1989. *Advanced Prolog.* Reading MA: Addison-Wesley.

Russell, G., S. Warwick and J. Carroll. 1990. Asymmetry in Parsing and Generation with Unification Grammars: Case Studies from ELU. In *ACL Proceedings, 28th Annual Meeting*, 205–211.

Sag, I. 1976. *Deletion and Logical Form.* PhD thesis, MIT.

Shieber, S. 1985. Using Restriction to Extend Parsing Algorithms for Complex-Feature-Based Formalisms. In *ACL Proceedings, 23rd Annual Meeting*, 145–152.

Shieber, S. 1986. *An Introduction to Unification-Based Approaches to Grammar.* CSLI Lecture Notes No. 4. Chicago: Chicago University Press.

Shieber, S. 1988. A Uniform Architecture for Parsing and Generation. In *COLING-88*, 614–619.

Shieber, S. 1989. *Parsing and Type Inference for Natural and Computer Languages.* PhD thesis, Stanford University. Published as SRI International Technical Note 460.

Shieber, S., G. van Noord, R. C. Moore and F. Pereira. 1990. Semantic-Head-Driven-Generation. *Computational Linguistics* 16:30–42.

Steedman, M. 1985. Dependency and coordination in the grammar of Dutch and English. *Language* 61:523–568.

Thiersch, C. 1978. *Topics in German Syntax.* PhD thesis, MIT.

Uszkoreit, H. 1985. *Word Order and Constituent Structure.* CSLI Lecture Notes No. 8. Chicago: Chicago University Press.

Uszkoreit, H. 1986. Categorial Unification Grammar. In *COLING-86*, 187-194.

van der Linden, E.-J. and G. Minnen. 1990. Algorithms for Generation in Lambek Theorem Proving. In *Proceedings of the 28th Annual Meeting of the Association for Computational Linguistics*, 220–226. Pittsburgh.

van Noord, G. 1991. Head Corner Parsing for Discontinuous Constituency. In *Proceedings of the 29th Annual Meeting of the Association for Computational Linguistics*, 114–121.

von Stechow, A. and W. Sternefeld. 1988. *Bausteine Syntaktischen Wissens.* Opladen: Westdeutscher Verlag.

Wall, R. and K. Wittenburg. 1989. Predictive Normal Forms for Composition in Categorial Grammars. In *Proceedings of International Workshop on Parsing Technologies*, 152–161.

Wedekind, J. 1988. Generation as Structure Driven Derivations. In *COLING-88*, 732–737.

Wittenburg, K. 1987. Predictive Combinators: A Method for Efficient Parsing of Combinatory Categorial Grammars. In *Proceedings of the 25th Annual Meeting of the Association for Computational Linguistics*, 73–80.

Woods, W. A. 1970. Transition network grammars for natural language analysis. *Communications of the ACM* 13:591–596.

Zeevat, H. 1988. Combining categorial grammar and unification. In *Natural language parsing and linguistic theories*, ed. U. Reyle and C. Rohrer. Dordrecht: Reidel.

Construction of LR Parsing Tables for Grammars Using Feature-Based Syntactic Categories

Tsuneko Nakazawa
NTT Laboratories

1 Introduction

The LR method is known to be a very efficient parsing algorithm that involves no searching or backtracking. However, recent formalisms for syntactic analyses of natural language (e.g., Lexical Functional Grammar in Bresnan 1982, Generalized Phrase Structure Grammar in Gazdar et al. 1985, and Head-driven Phrase Structure Grammar in Pollard and Sag 1987) make maximal use of complex feature-value systems rather than atomic categories that are presupposed in the LR method. This paper is an attempt to incorporate feature-based syntactic categories into Tomita's extended LR parsing algorithm (Tomita 1986), an LR parsing algorithm modified for natural language.

A straightforward adaptation of feature-based categories into the algorithm makes it necessary to instantiate categories during preprocessing of a grammar, that is, during construction of an LR parsing table. A logical alternative is to drive a parser with grammar rules stated in terms of atomic categories, the so-called context-free skeleton, while using feature specifications as a filter on parse trees either during or after parsing. The alternative may be a plausible computational approach to a grammar formalism such as LFG in which the feature description called functional annotation is a separate component of grammar from atomic phrase structure rules. However, in other formalisms in which grammar rules are stated in terms of feature-based categories, the features which convey category information such as NP and VP have the same status as those of any other features and the values of those features may be unspecified in feature description. Thus, the alternative approach imposes an otherwise undesirable requirement on grammar rules that category information be fully specified.

The incorporation of feature-based categories without the context-free skeleton gives rise to at least two major problems. First, the LR parsing table construction algorithms which instantiate categories do not in general terminate. Such algorithms instantiate categories while making top-down predictions and a partially instantiated category may predict itself during the next cycle of prediction-making, possibly with more features instantiated. The second problem is that the parser is forced to search through instantiated categories for desired table entries during parsing. This is due to the fact that the categories partially instantiated during construction of the LR parsing table may not be identical to those that arise during parsing since the former is the result of top-down instantiation while the latter results from bottom-up instantiation.

The major innovations of the proposed algorithm include the construction of a minimal sized LR parsing table that does not involve any preliminary instantiation of categories during construction of the table. Furthermore, the algorithm organizes parsing tables in such a way that the parser can, without a search, identify desirable table entries during parsing.

Some details of the LR parsing algorithm are assumed from Aho and Ullman (1987) and Aho and Johnson (1974), and more formal definitions and notations of a feature-based grammar formalism can be found in Pollard and Sag (1987) and Shieber (1986).

2 The LR Parsing Algorithm

The LR parser is an efficient shift-reduce parser with optional lookahead. Parse trees for input sentences are built bottom-up, while predictions are made top-down prior to parsing. The parsing table, which consists of an ACTION and GOTO tables, is constructed during grammar preprocessing and deterministically guides the parser at each step during parsing. The ACTION table determines the next action, either a shift action or a reduce action, that the parser should take next. The GOTO table determines the state the parser should be in upon the completion of each action so specified.

Figure 1 shows a parsing table for a toy grammar with three rules.[1] The table combines ACTION table entries (shown to the left of '/') and GOTO table entries (shown to the right of '/'). Henceforth, entries of the parsing table are referred to as the values of functions, ACTION and GOTO. The ACTION function takes the current state and the lexical category of the next input word to return the next action, while the GOTO function takes the current state and the topmost category of the stack to return the next state.

Figure 2(i) depicts the stack of the LR parser at the point the parser has processed the first two words of the input 'the dog saw the cat $', as indicated by ']' after 'the dog' in the input sentence. The symbol '$' indicates the end of input. The topmost state of the stack is called current

---

[1] In all examples throughout the paper, table entries are calculated with the lookahead of length 1, that is, LR(1) items. Although the lookahead is not discussed in the following for the sake of simplicity, the proposed algorithm is valid regardless of the size of the lookahead.

	V	Det	N	$	VP	NP	S
I_0		sh/3				/2	/1
I_1				acc/			
I_2	sh/5				/4		
I_3			sh/6				
I_4				re(1)/			
I_5		sh/8				/7	
I_6	re(3)/						
I_7				re(2)/			
I_8			sh/9				
I_9				re(3)/			

(1) S → NP VP
(2) VP → V NP
(3) NP → Det N

Figure 1: A Parsing Table with Atomic Categories

state, and the current state is state I_2 in Figure 2(i). States of the LR parser are sets of rules with a dot at some position in the right hand side (rhs). These dotted rules are called items.[2] Intuitively, the dot indicates how much of the rhs the parser has found. The current state I_2 in Figure 2(i), for example, includes two items, <S→NP.VP> and <VP→.V NP>, reflecting the discovery of the NP 'the dog'.

At this point, the parser consults the ACTION table for the next action. The ACTION function takes the current state I_2 and the lexical category V of the next input word 'saw', and directs the parser to shift the next word and to push it onto the stack: i.e., ACTION(I_2, V)=sh. Then, GOTO(I_2, V)=5 determines that the new current state is I_5 from the previous current state I_2 and the category V of 'saw' which has just been pushed. The resultant stack is shown in Figure 2(ii). The new current state I_5 contains two items, <VP→V.NP> and <NP→.Det N>. The dot positions in the items indicate that a V has been found, and that the next input may be an NP or a Det.

The subsequent two shift actions push two more words 'the' and 'cat' as shown in Figure 2(iii). At this point, ACTION(I_9, $)=re(3) calls for a reduce action by using rule (3), i.e., NP→Det N. Accordingly, the parser pops 'N(cat)' and 'Det(the)' off the stack along with the states 'I_9' and 'I_8', and pushes the parse tree 'NP(Det(the)N(cat))' admitted by rule (3).

---

[2]Items usually contain lookahead strings as well as dotted rules.

The GOTO function takes the state I_5, the topmost state after I_9 and I_8 are popped, and NP, the category of the constituent just discovered, and determines the next current state I_7, GOTO(I_5, NP)=7, as shown in Figure 2(iv). The state I_7 contains the item $<V \rightarrow V\ NP.>$, in which the dot position reflects the discovery of an NP.

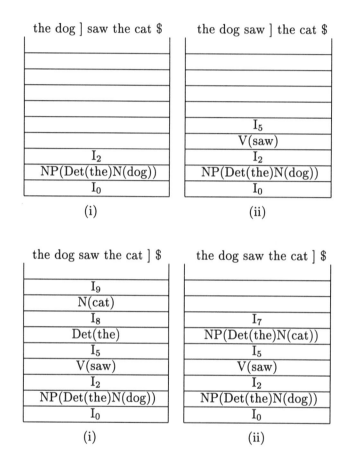

Figure 2: Stack of the LR parser for Atomic Categories

The parser now encounters the end-of-input symbol '$'. The next two reduce actions directed by the sequence of table entries, ACTION(I_7, $)=re(2), GOTO($I_2$, VP)=4, and ACTION($I_4$, $)=re(1), leave the stack with the very first state I_0 and the parse tree 'S(NP(Det(the)N(dog))VP(V (saw)NP(Det(the)N(cat))))'. Finally, GOTO(I_0, S)=1 pushes the new current state I_1, and ACTION(I_1, \$)=acc declares that the input has been accepted.

As should be clear from the above example, the parsing table drives the parser at each step of parsing. The current state, or set of items, encodes the part of the rhs of rules that have been found, and predicts what the next input may be. When the entire rhs is found, a reduce action pops them off the stack, and pushes the left hand side (lhs) of the rule. Note that the subsequent actions of the parser is independent of (partial) parse trees constructed during reduce actions, and only the lhs category, or the root of the parse trees, needs be pushed if only a recognizer, rather than a parser, is necessary. For example, it is irrelevant to the subsequent actions of the parser if the reduce action re(3) following Figure 2(iii) pushes only the lhs of rule (3) 'NP' instead of the entire local tree 'NP(Det(the)N(cat))'.

3 Construction of Parsing Tables for Atomic Categories

The parsing table used in the above example can be constructed prior to parsing, using the procedures given in Figure 3 (adapted from Aho and Ullman (1987)). C_0 and C_1 represent single categories, and w, x, and y represent a sequence of zero or more categories. The procedure CLOSURE computes all items in each state I, and the procedure NEXT-S calculates the next state for each current state I and category C_1.

The CLOSURE procedure makes all predictions $C_1 \rightarrow$.y from the category C_1 that appears right after the dot. This is similar to the Predictor Step of Earley's algorithm (Earley 1970) except that in Earley's algorithm, predictions are made during parsing. Since there is no state at the beginning of the table construction, the initial state I_0 is defined to contain a theoretical item <acc→.S> in every grammar. With the grammar in Figure 1, CLOSURE({<acc→.S>}) returns the closure I_0={<acc→.S>, <S→.NP VP>, <NP→.Det N>}, which includes all predictions that can be made from S.

The NEXT-S procedure computes the next state J by advancing the dot over C_1 for every item in I in which C_1 immediately follows the dot. In the above example grammar, the procedure takes I_0={<acc→.S>, <S→.NP VP>, <NP→.Det N>} and NP, advances the dot over NP in the second item, <S→NP.VP>, and returns CLOSURE({<S→NP.VP>})={<S→NP. VP>, <VP→.V NP>} as the new state I_2. Except for the initial state I_0, which is defined to include <acc→.S>, the state numbers are arbitrary. As demonstrated in the previous section, I_2 is the next state of the parser when the parser in the current state I_0 finds an NP 'the dog'.

```
procedure CLOSURE(I);
begin

    repeat
    for each item <C₀ →w.C₁x> in I, and each rule C₁→y such
    that <C₁ →.y> is not in I do

        add <C₁ →.y>to I;
    until no more items can be added to I;
    return I

end;
```

```
procedure NEXT-S(I,C₁); for each category C₁ in grammar
begin

    let J be the set of items <C₀ →wC₁.x> such that <C₀ →w.C₁x>
    is in I;
    return CLOSURE(J)

end;
```

Figure 3: CLOSURE/NEXT-S Procedures for Atomic Categories

4   Construction of Parsing Tables for Feature-Based Categories: A Preliminary Version

Figure 4 is an example of a rule using feature-based categories.[3] The tags $\boxed{1}$, $\boxed{2}$, ... indicate value-sharing, following the notation in Pollard and Sag (1987) and Shieber (1986), and roughly correspond to variables of logic unification with a scope of a single rule: if one occurrence of a particular tag is instantiated as a result of unification, so are other occurrences of the same tag within the rule. In the rule in Figure 4, for example, if one of the values $\boxed{3}$ of the FIN(ite) feature is instantiated as '+' in either the lhs category or the first category on the rhs, the value in the other category must also be instantiated as '+'.

Informally, the rule expands a projection of V to a verbal head and an NP complement. The value of the SUBCAT feature is a list of complements which are required by the verbal head, but have not been found. The SUBCAT values are instantiated as in Figure 5, which shows the constituent

---

[3]NP is taken to be a lexical category and is an abbreviation of some appropriate feature structure. No linguistic claim is made by its lexical status, and the exact internal structure is irrelevant in the following discussion.

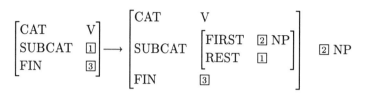

Figure 4: VP expansion rule

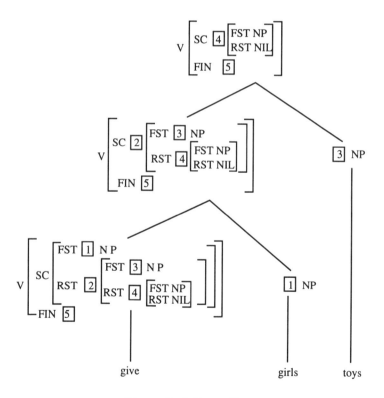

Figure 5: A Parse Tree

structure assigned to 'give girls toys'.[4] Both binary local trees in Figure 5 are admitted by the same rule in Figure 4.

In each binary local tree, the SUBCAT value of the verbal head contains one more complement NPs than the mother's SUBCAT value due to the tags $\boxed{1}$ and $\boxed{2}$ in the rule. The singleton list of NP as the SUBCAT value at the root of the parse tree indicates that 'give girls toys' is a VP since it is a verbal projection which still lacks the subject NP. The total number of NP complements in a sentence is determined by the lexical category of the head verb 'give' given in Figure 6, where the SUBCAT value is a list of three NPs.

$$
V \begin{bmatrix} \text{SC} & \begin{bmatrix} \text{FST} & \text{NP} \\ \text{RST} & \begin{bmatrix} \text{FST} & \text{NP} \\ \text{RST} & \begin{bmatrix} \text{FST} & \text{NP} \\ \text{RST} & \text{NIL} \end{bmatrix} \end{bmatrix} \end{bmatrix} \end{bmatrix}
$$

Figure 6: Lexical Category for 'give'

In grammars that use feature-based categories, categories in rules and lexical entries are taken to be underspecified. They are further instantiated through the unification operation during parsing as constituent structures are built. In the local tree for 'give girls' in the constituent structure in Figure 5, for example, the preterminal category for 'give' is the result of unification between the lexical category for 'give' in Figure 6 and the first category on the rhs of the rule in Figure 4. Since the first category on the rhs shares the tags with the lhs category, this unification also results in the instantiation of the mother of the local tree through the tags.

In order to incorporate the instantiation of underspecified categories through unification, the CLOSURE and NEXT-S procedures in Figure 3 can be modified as in Figure 7, where $\wedge$ is the unification operator.

The preliminary CLOSURE procedure makes a prediction $C_2 \to .y$ from C_1, not only when C_2 is identical to C_1, but also when C_2 is unifiable with C_1. The lhs C_2 is actually unified with C_1, $<C_1 \wedge C_2 \to .y'>$, before the item is added to the state I. This approach is essentially top-down propagation of instantiated features and well documented by Shieber (1985) in the context of Earley's algorithm. Note that y is also instantiated to y' as a result of the unification $C_1 \wedge C_2$ if C_2 shares tags with some members of y.

---

[4]The values for the CAT feature are placed outside the feature structures, and SUB-CAT, FIRST and REST are abbreviated as SC, FST and RST respectively.

procedure CLOSURE(I);
begin

> **repeat**
> for each item $<C_0 \to w.C_1x>$ in I, and each rule $C_2 \to y$ such
> that C_2 is unifiable with C_1 and $<C_1 \wedge C_2 \to .y'>$ is not in I **do**
>
>> add $<C_1 \wedge C_2 \to .y' >$ to I;
>
> **until** no more items can be added to I;
> **return** I

end;

procedure NEXT-S(I,C_2); for each category C_2 that appears to the
right of the dot in items in I
begin

> let J be the set of items $<C_0 \to wC_1.x>$ such that $<C_0 \to w.C_1x>$
> is in I and C_1 is unifiable with C_2;
> **return** CLOSURE(J)

end;

Figure 7: Preliminary CLOSURE/NEXT-S Procedures

In calculating a next state J of the parser when the parser discovered
a category C_2, the preliminary NEXT-S procedure advances the dot over
the category C_1 which is unifiable with C_2. If C_1 is identical to C_2, C_1 is
trivially unifiable with C_2. The procedure is repeated for different current
states I and categories C_2. Unlike the NEXT-S procedure for atomic categories, however, it cannot be repeated for every category C_2 in a grammar
since there are, in general, an infinite number of possible categories. Instead, the procedure can be repeated for each category C_2 that immediately
follows the dot in each I.

These preliminary procedures for feature-based categories have at least
two undesirable consequences. First, the preliminary CLOSURE procedure
does not in general terminate. Second, parsing tables constructed through
the preliminary NEXT-S procedure do not allow the parser to uniquely
identify desirable entries during parsing. Consequently, the parser is forced
to search through a parsing table for applicable entries.

In order to illustrate the preliminary procedures and their problems, a
new toy grammar is given in Figure 8. Intuitively, the first rule states that

a sentence consists of a subject NP and a finite VP. The second rule is for question sentences which consist of a finite AUX, a subject NP, and a nonfinite VP. The last rule is the same as the VP expansion rule given in Figure 4.

$$(1)\ \begin{bmatrix} \text{CAT S} \\ \text{FIN +} \end{bmatrix} \rightarrow \boxed{1}\text{NP}\ \begin{bmatrix} \text{CAT V} \\ \text{SC}\ \begin{bmatrix} \text{FST}\ \boxed{1} \\ \text{RST NIL} \end{bmatrix} \\ \text{FIN +} \end{bmatrix}$$

$$(2)\ \begin{bmatrix} \text{CAT S} \\ \text{FIN +} \end{bmatrix} \rightarrow \begin{bmatrix} \text{CAT AUX} \\ \text{SC}\ \begin{bmatrix} \text{FST}\ \boxed{2} \\ \text{RST}\ \boxed{3} \end{bmatrix} \\ \text{FIN +} \end{bmatrix}\ \boxed{2}\text{NP}\ \boxed{3}\ \begin{bmatrix} \text{CAT V} \\ \text{SC}\ \begin{bmatrix} \text{FST}\ \boxed{2} \\ \text{RST NIL} \end{bmatrix} \\ \text{FIN}\ - \end{bmatrix}$$

$$(3)\ \begin{bmatrix} \text{CAT V} \\ \text{SC}\ \boxed{1} \\ \text{FIN}\ \boxed{3} \end{bmatrix} \rightarrow \begin{bmatrix} \text{CAT V} \\ \text{SC}\ \begin{bmatrix} \text{FST}\ \boxed{2} \\ \text{RST}\ \boxed{1} \end{bmatrix} \\ \text{FIN}\ \boxed{3} \end{bmatrix}\ \boxed{2}\text{NP}$$

Figure 8: A Toy Grammar using Feature-Based Categories

Suppose that a state contains the first rule with the dot after the NP on the rhs. The preliminary CLOSURE procedure then predicts new items in Figure 9 among others. Since the lhs of rule (3) is unifiable with the category following the dot, i.e., V[SC [FST NP][RST NIL]][FIN +], the procedure adds to the state the first item (i) which is a partial instantiation of rule (3). In item (i), in turn, the category following the dot is unifiable with the lhs of rule (3), and another instantiation (ii) of rule (3) is added again to the state. Clearly, the procedure never halts.

As demonstrated in Figure 9, the preliminary CLOSURE procedure will add an infinite number of different instantiations of the same rule to the state. Each execution of the repeat-loop adds a new item from which a new prediction is made during the next execution. That is, instantiation of rules introduces the nontermination problem of left-recursive rules to the procedure, as well as to the Predictor Step of Earley's algorithm.

$$(i) < V \begin{bmatrix} SC \boxed{1} \begin{bmatrix} FST\ NP \\ RST\ NIL \end{bmatrix} \\ FIN \boxed{3} + \end{bmatrix} \rightarrow .V \begin{bmatrix} SC \begin{bmatrix} FST\ \boxed{2}NP \\ RST\ \boxed{1} \begin{bmatrix} FST\ NP \\ RST\ NIL \end{bmatrix} \end{bmatrix} \\ FIN\ \boxed{3} + \end{bmatrix} \boxed{2}NP >$$

$$(ii) < V \begin{bmatrix} SC \boxed{1} \begin{bmatrix} FST\ NP \\ RST\ \begin{bmatrix} FST\ NP \\ RST\ NIL \end{bmatrix} \end{bmatrix} \\ FIN\ \boxed{3} + \end{bmatrix} \rightarrow .V \begin{bmatrix} SC \begin{bmatrix} FST\ \boxed{2}NP \\ RST\ \boxed{1} \begin{bmatrix} FST\ NP \\ RST\ \begin{bmatrix} FST\ NP \\ RST\ NIL \end{bmatrix} \end{bmatrix} \end{bmatrix} \\ FIN\ \boxed{3} + \end{bmatrix} \boxed{2}NP >$$

$$(iii) < V \begin{bmatrix} SC \boxed{1} \begin{bmatrix} FST\ NP \\ RST \begin{bmatrix} FST\ NP \\ RST \begin{bmatrix} FST\ NP \\ RST\ NIL \end{bmatrix} \end{bmatrix} \end{bmatrix} \\ FIN\ \boxed{3} + \end{bmatrix} \rightarrow .V \begin{bmatrix} SC \begin{bmatrix} FST\ \boxed{2}\ NP \\ RST\ \boxed{1} \begin{bmatrix} FST\ NP \\ RST \begin{bmatrix} FST\ NP \\ RST \begin{bmatrix} FST\ NP \\ RST\ NIL \end{bmatrix} \end{bmatrix} \end{bmatrix} \end{bmatrix} \\ FIN\ \boxed{3} + \end{bmatrix} \boxed{2}NP >$$

Figure 9: Items Created from Rule (3) in Figure 8

To overcome this problem, Shieber (1985) proposes 'restrictor', a depth specification of feature paths beyond which instantiation is prohibited. When an instantiated feature path in a predicted item exceeds the limit imposed by the restrictor, further instantiation of the feature path in new items is truncated. The Predictor Step eventually halts when it starts creating a new item whose feature specification within the depth allowed by the restrictor is identical to, or subsumed by, a previous item.

The notion of the restrictor can be applied to the preliminary CLOSURE procedure in a straightforward way. If the restrictor in Figure 10 is imposed on feature instantiation by the procedure, for example, the value of the feature path [SC [RST [RST]]] is truncated in the rhs of the item (ii) in Figure 9 since it involves a longer path than allowed by the restrictor. The next item predicted from the truncated category is also truncated and no more new items are created. Hence the procedure halts.

Although the restrictor guarantees the termination of the preliminary CLOSURE procedure, the incorporation of feature-based categories into grammars poses another problem unique to the LR parser. That is, the exact category pushed at the top of the stack after a reduce action may not be included in the domain of the GOTO function.

Given a grammar, the preliminary CLOSURE procedure instantiates categories in rules while making predictions as demonstrated above. The preliminary NEXT-S procedure then computes the next state for each state and instantiated category pair, which involves making more predictions.

$$\begin{bmatrix} \text{CAT} \\ \text{SC} \begin{bmatrix} \text{FST} \\ \text{RST} \begin{bmatrix} \text{FST} \\ \text{RST} \end{bmatrix} \end{bmatrix} \\ \text{FIN} \end{bmatrix}$$

Figure 10: A Restrictor

The states and instantiated categories thus created constitute the domain of the GOTO function which the parser consults during parsing. After each reduce action during parsing, the GOTO function takes the current state and the category at the top of the stack and returns the next state, as demonstrated in Section 2. Unlike the case of atomic categories, however, the category at the top of the stack may not be identical to any of the categories in the domain of the GOTO function. This discrepancy results from the fact that the categories in the stack arise through bottom-up instantiation during parsing, while the categories in the domain of the GOTO function arise through top-down instantiation during prediction making.

Consequently, the parser is required to search through the domain for a category unifiable with the category at the top of the stack after every reduce action in order to determine the next state. The search operation, unnecessary in the original LR parsing algorithm, imposes considerable computational burden on the parser. Furthermore, the search must be conducted through the entire domain of the GOTO function because there may be more than one unifiable category.

In order to illustrate the problem, the parsing table in Figure 11 is constructed by the preliminary procedures, with the restrictor in Figure 10, for the grammar in Figure 8.[5] The categories in the table are numbered for the reference purposes only. The category (7) is the category which immediately follows the dot in Figure 9(i), and the category (8) is the result of truncating the category after the dot in Figure 9(ii). These categories are consequently used as input to compute the next states I_5 and I_6 by the preliminary NEXT-S procedure. The categories (10) and (11) are also instantiations of the first category on the rhs of rule (3) which is predicted from V[SC[FST NP][RST NIL]][FIN -] in rule (2).

---

[5]The values of FST and RST are abbreviated using the more usual list notation '{ }'. The dots '...' in the lists indicate the unspecified value of the RST feature, i.e., the lists are open-ended. Also, only three lexical categories are included in the table for simplicity: NP, AUX[FIN +] and the ditransitive verb in Figure 6.

	(1) NP	(2) AUX[FIN +]	(3) V[SC {NP,NP,NP}]	(4) $	(5) S[FIN +]	(6) V[SC {NP}][FIN +]	(7) V[SC {NP,NP}][FIN +]	(8) V[SC {NP,NP,...}][FIN +]	(9) V[SC {NP}][FIN -]	(10) V[SC {NP,NP}][FIN -]	(11) V[SC {NP,NP,...}][FIN -]
I_0	sh/2	sh/3			/1						
I_1				acc/							
I_2			sh/6			/4	/5	/6			
I_3	sh/7										
I_4				re(1)/							
I_5	sh/8										
I_6	sh/9										
I_7			sh/12						/10	/11	/12
I_8				re(3)/							
I_9	re(3)/										
I_{10}				re(2)/							
I_{11}	sh/13										
I_{12}	sh/14										
I_{13}				re(3)/							
I_{14}	re(3)/										

Figure 11: Parsing Table Created by the Preliminary Procedures for the Grammar in Figure 8

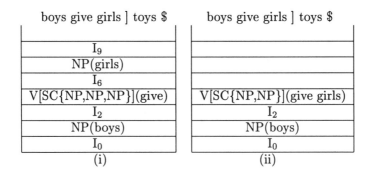

Figure 12: Stack of the LR parser for Feature-Based Categories

Figure 12(i) shows a stack with the input sentence 'boys give girls toys $' at the point the first three words 'boys give girls' have been pushed. At this point, the ACTION function applies to the current state I_9 and the lexical category NP of the next input word, and calls for a reduce action by rule (3): ACTION(I_9, NP)=re(3).

The stack after the reduction is given in Figure 12(ii).[6] Now the parser is in current state I_2, and the next state needs to be determined. The domain of the GOTO function, however, does not include the category V[SC{NP,NP}] of the reduced constituent. Instead, four categories (7), (8), (10), and (11) in the domain are unifiable with the category V[SC{NP,NP}].

The preliminary procedures are sound in the sense that at least one of the unifiable categories eventually leads the parser to the correct parse as long as input sentences are grammatical and the rest of the categories eventually to a dead end. In the above example, the search paths with categories (8) and (9) reach the same correct parse, while the search with the categories (10) and (11) fails. In general, the parser needs not only to search through the domain of the GOTO function for all unifiable categories, but also to pursue all the possibilities nondeterministically to find the correct parse.

5   Construction of Parsing Tables for Feature-Based Categories: the Final Version

The final version of CLOSURE/NEXT-S procedures given in Figure 13 circumvents the described problems. While the final CLOSURE procedure makes top-down predictions in the same way as before, the new item

---

[6]Only the root category of the reduced constituent is shown in the stack.

procedure CLOSURE(I);
begin

    repeat
    for each item $<C_0 \rightarrow w.C_1x>$ in I, and each rule $C_2 \rightarrow y$ such
    that C_2 is unifiable with C_1 and $<C_2 \rightarrow .y>$ is not in I **do**

        add $<C_2 \rightarrow .y>$ to I;
    until no more items can be added to I;
    return I

end;

procedure NEXT-S(I,C_2); for each category C_2 on the lhs of rules
begin
    let J be the set of items $<C_0 \rightarrow wC_1.x>$ such that $<C_0 \rightarrow$
    $w.C_1x>$ is in I and C_1 is unifiable with C_2;

    return CLOSURE(J)
end;

Figure 13: Final CLOSURE/NEXT-S Procedures

$<C_2 \rightarrow .y>$ is added without instantiation. The final NEXT-S procedure constructs next states with the lhs category of each rule as input, rather than the categories to the right of the dot.

Since only uninstantiated rules in a grammar are added as items by the final CLOSURE procedure, each rule can be added to the state I as a new item at most once and therefore the procedure is guaranteed to halt. No restrictor is necessary as is the case of the LR parsing algorithm with atomic categories.

The final NEXT-S procedure computes next states for each pair of a current state I and the lhs category C_2 of a rule. Consequently, the domain of the GOTO function consists of lhs categories without instantiation. When a reduce action is completed during parsing, the parser can determine the next state by applying the GOTO function to the lhs category of the rule just used in the reduce action. No search for unifiable categories is involved during parsing, while the lhs category is instantiated in the stack as the result of the reduce action as before.

Figure 14 gives the parsing table constructed by the final procedures for the grammar in Figure 8 for comparison.

	NP	AUX[FIN +]	V[SC {NP,NP,NP}]	$	S[FIN +]	V
I₀	sh/2	sh/3			/1	
I₁				acc/		
I₂			sh/4			/4
I₃	sh/5					
I₄	sh/6			re(1)/		
I₅			sh/7			/7
I₆	re(3)/			re(3)/		
I₇	sh/6			re(2)/		

Figure 14: Parsing Table Created by the Final Procedures for the Grammar in Figure 8

Figure 15(i) shows the stack with the same input sentence as Figure 12, 'boys give girls toys', where the three words 'boys give girls' have been pushed as before in Figure 12(i). ACTION(I_6, NP)=re(3) then directs the parser to reduce 'give girls' by rule (3) as in Figure 15(ii). At this point, the next state can be identified as I_4 from the current state I_2 and the lhs category V of rule (3) without any search operation, that is GOTO(I_2, V)=4, while the category of the constituent reduced by rule (3) is further instantiated to V[SC {NP,NP}] in the stack.

Note that the size of parsing tables produced by the final procedures is usually smaller than the table produced by the preliminary procedures for the same grammar. This is because the preliminary CLOSURE procedure creates one or more instantiated categories out of a single category, each of which the preliminary NEXT-S procedure applies to, creating separate parsing table entries. Although a smaller parsing table does not necessarily imply less parsing time since there are entry retrieval algorithms that do not depend on table size, it does mean fewer operations to construct such tables during preprocessing.

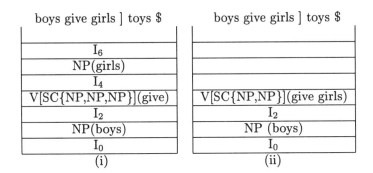

Figure 15: Stack of the LR Parser for Feature-based Categories

6 Further Comparisons and the Conclusions

The blank entries in ACTION tables are called error entries and when returned as the value of the ACTION function, they indicate that the input sentence is ungrammatical. With grammars using atomic categories, ungrammatical input sentences are always detected by the error entry as soon as enough input words are pushed. With grammars using feature-based categories, on the other hand, ungrammaticality is detected by the failure of reduce action as well as error entries.

In parsing with atomic categories, reduce actions never fail. In other words, ACTION tables are constructed in such a way to direct the parser to reduce the constituents that appear on the rhs of a rule only when those constituents are actually stored at the top of the stack. Thus, the parser only needs to pop the correct number of constituents off the stack. With feature-based categories, it is not guaranteed that constituents in the stack are actually reducible by the rule selected by the ACTION function. Those constituents are already partially instantiated in a bottom-up manner and if they are no longer unifiable with the categories on the rhs of the rule, the reduce action must fail, indicating that the input sentence is ungrammatical.

The following example illustrates the error discovery through unification failure during a reduce action. In addition to the lexical category of the verb 'give' in Figure 6, which is indeterminate in finiteness, the lexical category of 'gave' is assumed to be included in the lexicon and labeled as V[SC {NP, NP, NP}][FIN +]. With the same grammar as before (Figure 8), the parsing table is constructed by the final CLOSURE/NEXT-S procedures as shown in Figure 16. With the ungrammatical input 'do boys gave girls

	NP	AUX[FIN +]	V[SC {NP,NP,NP}]	V[SC {NP,NP,NP}][FIN +]	$	S[FIN +]	V
I_0	sh/2	sh/3				/1	
I_1					acc/		
I_2			sh/4	sh/4			/4
I_3	sh/5						
I_4	sh/6				re(1)/		
I_5			sh/7	sh/8			/7
I_6	re(3)/				re(3)/		
I_7	sh/6				re(2)/		
I_8	sh/6						

Figure 16: Parsing Table for the Grammar in Figure 8 Created by the Final Procedures

toys \$', the stack in Figure 17 describes the state after 'gave girls toys' is reduced by rule (3).

The ACTION function applies to the current state I_7 and the next input '\$', and calls for a reduce action by rule (2): ACTION(I_7, \$)=re(2). The parser pops three categories off the stack and tries to unify them with those that appear on the rhs of rule (2). While the first and second categories on the rhs of rule (2), AUX[SC {NP, V[SC {NP}][FIN -]}][FIN +] and NP, are unifiable with AUX[FIN +] and NP stored in the stack, the third category in the rule V[SC {NP}][FIN -] is not unifiable with V[SC {NP}][FIN +] in the stack. Hence, the reduce action fails and the parser declares the input to be ungrammatical.

Note that the failure of unification during a reduce action may not occur until the parser pushes more input words than are strictly necessary to detect an error. The error in the above example can actually be concluded as soon as the first three words 'do boys gave' are pushed since no sentences do boys gave girls toys] $

I_7
V[SC{NP}][FIN +](gave girls toys)
I_5
NP(boys)
I_3
AUX[FIN +](do)
I_0

Figure 17: Stack of the LR parser for Feature-based Categories

starting with those three words are admitted by the grammar. Although parsing tables constructed for feature-based categories do detect all errors eventually, they cannot be constructed in such a way to detect all errors in terms of the error entry returned by the ACTION function right after enough input words are pushed. Construction of such ACTION tables would require complete instantiation of categories during preprocessing, which is generally not possible. Consequently, it is unavoidable to unify the constituents popped off the stack and the rhs of the rule every time a reduce action is called for during parsing.

Since categories cannot be completely instantiated in every possible way during preprocessing, and it is not possible to eliminate instantiation through unifications during parsing anyway, then what motivates the partial instantiation of rules during preprocessing as is done by the preliminary CLOSURE procedure? It can sometimes prevent wrong items from being predicted and consequently prevent too permissive shift actions from entering into an ACTION table. As a result, errors may be detected by an error entry at an earlier stage of parsing, if parsing tables are constructed by the preliminary CLOSURE/NEXT-S procedures.

In the above example, after the first two input words 'do boys' are pushed, the parsing table in Figure 16 directs the parser to push another input word 'gave', i.e. ACTION(I_5, V[SC {NP,NP,NP}][FIN +])=sh, leaving the error undetected until a later stage. Contrary to the parsing table in Figure 16, which is constructed by the final procedures, the parsing table constructed by the preliminary procedures will return an error entry upon encountering the third input word 'gave', indicating that V[SC {NP,NP,NP}][FIN +] is not a possible category of the next input word.

Given the grammar in Figure 8 and the input 'do boys gave girls toys $', the preliminary CLOSURE/NEXT-S procedures outperform the final version. All grammars that solicit this performance difference in error detection have one property in common. That is, in those grammars, some feature specifications in rules which assign upper structures of a parse tree prohibit particular feature instantiations in lower structures. In the case of the above example, the feature specification [FIN -] in the S expansion rule (2) prohibits the main verb of the sentence from being [FIN +]. If the grammar is modified so as not to specify the FIN value in the S expansion rules (1) and (2), for example, then the parsing tables created by the preliminary CLOSURE/NEXT-S procedures do not detect errors any earlier, but rather create a larger parsing table through which an otherwise unmotivated search must be conducted for unifiable categories to find GOTO table entries after every reduce action.

The final output of the parser, whether constructed by the preliminary or the final procedures, is identical and correct. The choice between the two approaches depends upon particular grammars and is an empirical decision. In general, however, a clear tendency among grammars written in recent linguistic theories is that rules tend to be more general and permissive and lexical specifications more specific and restrictive. That is, information that regulates possible configurations of parse trees for particular input sentences comes from the bottom of trees, and not from the top, making top-down instantiation useless.

With the recent linguistic trend of lexicon-oriented grammars, partial instantiation of categories while making predictions top-down gives little to gain for added costs. Given that run-time instantiation of rules is unavoidable to build constituents and to detect errors, the advantages of eliminating an intermediate instantiation step is evident.

References

Aho, Alfred V. and Jeffrey D. Ullman. 1987. *Principles of Compiler Design*. Reading, Massachusetts: Addison-Wesley Publishing Company.

Aho, Alfred V. and Steven C. Johnson. 1974. LR Parsing. *Computing Surveys* Vol. 6, 2:99–124.

Bresnan, Joan (ed.). 1982. *The Mental Representation of Grammatical Relations*. Cambridge, Massachusetts and London: the MIT Press.

Earley, Jay. 1970. An Efficient Context-Free Parsing Algorithm. *Communications of the ACM* 14, 453–460.

Gazdar, Gerald, Ewan Klein, Geoffrey Pullum and Ivan Sag. 1985. *Generalized Phrase Structure Grammar*. Boston, MA: Harvard University Press.

Pollard, Carl and Ivan A. Sag. 1987. *Information-Based Syntax and Semantics* Vol. 1. CSLI Lecture Notes 13. Stanford: CSLI.

Shieber, Stuart. 1985. Using Restriction to Extend Parsing Algorithms for Complex-Feature-Based Formalisms. *23rd ACL Proceedings*, 145–152

Shieber, Stuart. 1986. *An Introduction to Unification-Based Approaches to Grammar*. CSLI Lecture Notes 4. Stanford: CSLI.

Tomita, Masaru. 1986. *Efficient Parsing for Natural Language: A Fast Algorithm for Practical Systems*. Boston: Kluwer Academic Publishers.

Part III

Phonology and Computation

Phonology and Computational Linguistics — a Personal Overview

John Coleman
Oxford University Phonetics Laboratory

1 Introduction

This paper is in two parts, either of which can probably be read independently. In the second half, I summarize some of my own research in implementing a phonological theory for the purposes of speech generation. But since phonology is usually a neglected area of computational linguistics, in the first half I attempt to briefly review the great variety of research areas in which phonological theory and computation are brought together. I originally envisaged that this would be a fairly short section. It turned out that a great deal more work falls under the rubric of "computational phonology" than I had expected to find. This overview is, therefore, necessarily personal and selective. If there is important work that I have neglected, it is due solely to my ignorance.

2.1 Computational Phonology in Speech Technology Applications I: Speech Recognition

The SPE theory of phonology (Chomsky and Halle 1968) has been the dominant paradigm for computational implementations of phonological theory. Although phonologists usually conceive of phonological rules as mapping *from* lexical representation *to* surface representations, SPE theory is in principle amenable to implementation in both speech synthesis and recognition, the latter application being the inverse of the usual "generative" view. However, as Church (1983:28), Bear (1990) and Coleman (1990), among others, have observed, inversion of a set of SPE rules is rarely simple, and is not always possible. Consequently, early attempts to employ SPE rules in the phonological component of a speech recognition system were usually based upon precompilation of all possible surface phonetic variations, into an "allophonic dictionary." Woods and Zue (1976) proposed to employ SPE-type rewriting rules in such a fashion. Alternatively, Cohen and Mercer (1975) proposed a method for mapping phonemic dictionary representations into graphs which encode alternative possible pronunciations, on the basis of SPE-type rules.

One of the problems besetting recognition of phonemes in the speech signal is the allophonic variation of phonemes in different environments.

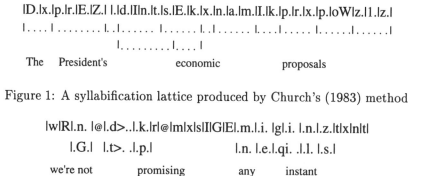

Figure 1: A syllabification lattice produced by Church's (1983) method

Figure 2: A lattice of ranked allophone hypotheses (Church 1983:162)

For example, the phoneme /t/ in English is fairly strongly aspirated word-initially, less strongly aspirated word-finally, pretty much unaspirated after /s/, and may be an unaspirated, voiced tap intervocalically in North American dialects. Such variability was often regarded as phonetic "noise" which made speech recognition harder by requiring segments in different environments to be phonemically normalized (e.g., Klatt 1977:1346, 1980:548-9).

Church (1983) argued that rather than being a hindrance, the allophonic variation observed in particular phonological environments could actually be used to assist in phonological parsing in speech recognition. By concentrating on accurate recognition of allophones, rather than attempting to recognize the phonemes directly in the speech signal, Church showed that a fairly simple parser, employing a context-free phrase-structure grammar of word and syllable structure could be used to derive a lexical representation (such as Fig. 1) from a parse-tree of the allophonic input.

By a minor extension to this method, the parser may be made probabilistic, in order to determine the *most likely* phonemic analysis, based on an input lattice of allophone hypotheses, in which several candidate allophones proposed by the acoustic processing software might be considered at each sequential position, along with an associated measure or ranking of the relative likelihood of each candidate allophone (Fig. 2).

The input to Church's parser was nevertheless a segmental string: a string of candidate allophones produced by the signal-analysis part of the speech recognition system. Although his idea of parsing allophone strings using standard context-free parsing techniques was novel, the phonological theory of phonemes and allophones underlying that method was already rather out-of-date.

Randolph (1989) proposed an improvement on Church's parser whereby asynchronously organized *acoustic autosegments*, rather than segments, were taken as the input to the speech parser. In his words (Randolph 1989:60):

> The assumption that underlies the organization of distinctive features at the surface phonemic level is that feature values align into columns, and the resulting feature columns are assigned to terminal positions of the syllable's hierarchical structure. If, however, acoustic properties are associated with features, one then may observe that such an alignment is not always to be found at the acoustic level.

Like the speech synthesis system developed by Coleman and Local (Local 1992, Coleman 1992a), described below, Randolph's model employed two distinct kinds of nontransformational constraints: context-free phrase structure rules, for defining syllable structure, and finite-state *realization rules* for associating acoustic autosegments with phonological features.

Church's parser is by no means the only implementation of new phonological concepts in speech recognition research. But it was one of the few applications to use theoretically sophisticated phonological concepts for a practical purpose, a development which was both innovative and influential.

2.2 Morphology and Phonology in NLP Systems

As well as in speech-based applications such as speech recognition, phonological theory finds applications, to a limited degree, in Natural Language Processing systems such as sentence parsers, text generation, and database enquiry. As Klein's (1987) manifesto for declarative phonology judiciously points out:

> it is difficult to do syntax without doing some morphology; and it is difficult to do morphology without doing some phonology. For example, non-concatenative morphology is hard to talk about without some way of representing phonological structure ....

In the NLP domain there have been two main approaches to morphology and phonology: "two-level phonology" (2LP) and sign-based phonology.

2.2.1 Two-level Phonology

Two-level phonology derives its name from the fact that unlike SPE phonology, with its many intermediate levels of derivation, two levels alone are claimed to be sufficient. These two levels are the morphophonemic and surface (either phonemic or allophonic). The relationship between them is held to be the composition of a number of simple, finite-state relations. One of the principal originators, Koskenniemi (1983), built a 2LP system for the preprocessing of Finnish. The 'surface' level was in fact orthographic, rather than phonemic (Finnish orthography is often claimed to be almost phonemic). The 'lexical' level was a morphophonemic level which abstracted over vowel harmony and consonant gradation, and encoded morphological boundaries. The function of this 2LP was simply to mediate between orthography and lexical entries in an NLP system: there was no need for the phonological sophistication of Autosegmental, Metrical, or Lexical phonology in order to achieve this task. Nevertheless, by an interesting extension of 2LP to a multi-level system, Kay (1987) demonstrated that the challenging phonological problems of Arabic nonconcatenative phonology were also amenable to a finite-state analysis. Touretzky et al. (1990a,b) are currently perhaps the principal practitioners of this approach in phonology, as opposed to morphology.

2.2.2 Sign-based Phonology

A number of researchers have recently attempted to extend nontransformational grammar formalisms, such as Generalized Phrase Structure Grammar (GPSG), Categorial Grammar (CG) and Head-Driven Phrase Structure Grammar (HPSG), to the phonological domain. The motivation for such research is twofold: firstly, to eliminate the use of transformational grammars from phonology as well as syntax, and secondly to provide nontransformational grammar formalisms with a complementary nontransformational phonology. The earliest work in this direction is Bach and Wheeler's (1981) "Montague Phonology," based on a kind of categorial grammar. Central to this work is the idea that phonetics is to phonology what semantics is to syntax, or content to form. For example, in Montague Grammar and theories it has shaped, such as GPSG, the semantic interpretation of constituent may be expressed side-by-side with the syntactic category of that constituent, as Figure 3 (from Sag 1982:453) illustrates.

Semantic interpretations may be represented in a formal language such as Intensional Logic, which is entirely separate from the formal language of phrase-structure grammar by which the syntactic representations are defined. In phonological theory, by analogy, the phonetic interpretation of a phonological representation can be regarded as an entirely separate object from the phonological representation itself. Thus there is no question of "converting" the phonological representation "into" a surface phonetic representation in the manner of transformational phonology.

Wheeler's work laid foundations for phonological research based on GPSG at the University of York (see below), and the University of Ed-

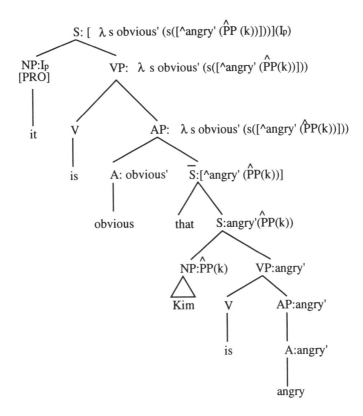

Figure 3: Side-by-side semantic interpretation of syntactic structure.

inburgh (Broe 1988, Klein 1987, Klein and Calder 1987). In both these groups, the more recent proposals introduced in HPSG (Pollard and Sag 1987) have influenced nontransformational phonology. The resulting mélange of representation-oriented, nontransformational analytical techniques is well illustrated in Bird (1990), Bird and Blackburn (1991), and Scobbie (1991).

An independent outgrowth of the GPSG syntactic theory is the DATR morphological system (Evans and Gazdar (eds.), 1989, 1990, Evans and Gazdar 1989a,b). DATR is based on PATR-II, a general purpose parsing and translation system developed at SRI (Shieber et al. 1983, Shieber 1985, 1986). The PATR-II formalism provides for the definition of monostratal, phrase-structure based grammars augmented by structural constraints expressed using unification equations. DATR extends PATR-II by the addition of *default inheritance* as the principal feature propagation mechanism.

The relevance of DATR to phonology is that a number of researchers have employed the DATR formalism to phonological effect. Gibbon and Reinhart (1991) describe a DATR phonology of German words, with specific attention to umlaut. In a further extension to DATR, the MOLLUSC language, Cahill (1990) provides morphophonological descriptions of subregularities in word-formation in English and German.

2.3 Partial Implementations of Partial Phonological Theories

While 2LP and sign-based approaches to phonology involve some novel departures from orthodox generative phonological theory, a number of researchers have attempted 'straight' implementations of (aspects of) orthodox theories. (Most of these areas of theoretical phonology are nevertheless also addressed in sign-based phonology.)

2.3.1 Autosegmental Phonology

I have already mentioned Kay's (1987) demonstration that by extending 2-level phonology to n-level phonology, finite-state transducers are adequate to model the nonconcatenative distribution of consonants and vowels in Arabic. Kay's demonstration is based on McCarthy's (1979) Autosegmental analysis of Arabic. The natural (though as yet untried) lesson of Kay's demonstration is that Autosegmental analyses involving any number of separate phonological tiers may be implemented using n-tape finite-state transducers.

2.3.2 Lexical Phonology

There have been numerous attempts to implement SPE-type transformational phonologies, many of which are unpublished proprietary research associated with commercial speech recognition and synthesis systems. A few references to such work were given above. In addition, an important contemporary successor of the SPE framework, Lexical Phonology, has been implemented computationally by Sheila Williams at Sheffield University. Williams (1990) has reported implementing both principal versions of Lexical Phonology, Halle and Mohanan (1985) and Booij and Rubach (1984). In this system, an ordered set of transformational rules is used to map morphophonemic lexical representations into allophonic surface representations, via many intermediate forms, as in SPE theory. But the rules are grouped into "blocks," each of which is limited to particular morphological processes.

Church (1985) has proposed a nontransformational, context-free model for the organization of morphemes into sublexical "levels." The grammar which he proposes:

$$\text{word} \rightarrow \text{level3 (regular-inflection)}^*$$

$$\text{level3} \rightarrow \text{(level3-prefix)}^* \text{ level2 (level3-suffix)}^*$$

$$\text{level2} \rightarrow \text{(level2-prefix)}^* \text{ level1 (level2-suffix)}^*$$

$$\text{level1} \rightarrow \text{(level1-prefix)}^* \text{ syll (level1-suffix)}^*$$

imposes structure on the arrangement of morphemes within words according to the phrase-structure tree in Figure 4. This structure, as several morphologists have noted previously, enforces the affix-ordering generalization that in words containing both Latinate and Germanic affixes, all of the Latinate affixes occur inside all of the Germanic affixes (see Selkirk 1984:75–82).

As well as encoding the ordering of affixes, Selkirk's and Church's structural accounts of lexical domains also provide the domains within which phonological rules are constrained to operate in Lexical Phonology, though in Church's system this potential use of lexical domains was not exploited for other than stress placement. Sproat and Brunson (1987) combined a structure-based implementation of lexical phonology similar to Church's with a structural characterization of vowel-harmony domains in Warlpiri. The analysis trees which their grammar of Warlpiri defined, and which their parser computed, encoded both lexical constituency and vowel-harmony domains.

2.3.3 Metrical Phonology

Ideas from Metrical Phonology have been readily incorporated into a number of speech synthesis systems. The work described in Pierrehumbert and Beckman (1988), and Bachenko and Fitzpatrick (1990) are notable examples, but other less well-known systems, such as Pros3 (Dirksen and Quené 19991), DIXI (Oliveira et al. 1991), Youd and Fallside (1987), exemplify the adoption of concepts drawn from Metrical Phonology in computationally implemented systems. An offshoot of Metrical Phonology, Nespor and Vogel's (1986) Prosodic Phonology, also shows an influence in some of these systems (see also "Intonation Models," below).

Two systems in particular stand out as theory-driven attempts to implement Metrical Phonology computationally. The first, Dresher and Kaye's YOUPIE system (Dresher and Kaye 1990, Dresher 1991), is an algorithm which "learns" the metrical phonology of a set of input strings by parameter-setting. The input to the system consists of phonemic strings (representing words), containing integers which denote the stress-levels. By analysis of the patterns of stress-levels in the input strings, the system sets 11 binary parameters of metrical structure. These parameters, and the examples of

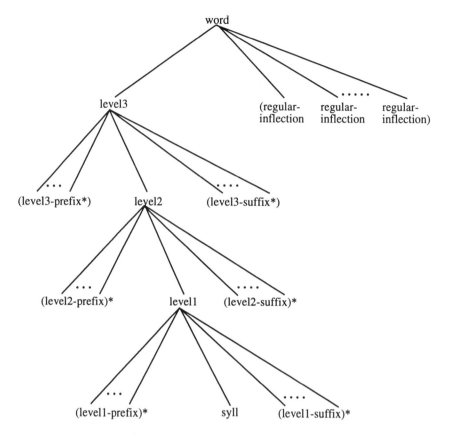

Figure 4: Church's (1985) view of word structure

stress-systems that Dresher and Kaye cite in support of their model, are closely based on the work of Halle and Vergnaud (1987).

The YorkTalk speech synthesis system (Coleman 1992a), described further below, incorporates a detailed, context-free grammar of metrical structure in order to determine lexical stress and syllabification, as well as the metrical part of the nonsegmental phonological structures from which speech synthesis parameters are computed.

2.4 Laboratory Phonology

2.4.1 Intonation Models

Synthesis-by-rule systems of various kinds designed during the 1960s and 1970s had of necessity to model intonation in some way or other. The systems developed during this time leaned more towards the practical problems of producing reasonably acceptable synthetic intonation (particularly fundamental frequency and segmental durations) from highly impoverished input—impoverished because many of the linguistic and paralinguistic factors which may affect intonation are not deterministically derivable from textual input. Pierrehumbert (1981) marks a major departure from purely engineering concerns towards a more linguistically oriented approach to intonation modelling. Pierrehumbert's system, which was influenced by Liberman's (1975) phonological analysis of English intonation, takes as its input strings such as the following:

> {325 260 195 165}(0.4) SIL 8 ih 4 n 3* n 4 ow 7
> v 9 eh 10(1.0) m 8 b 4 er 13%(0.3) SIL 34
> *dh 2 ax 2* r 5 iy 7(0.6) jh 10 en 8 z 10*
> w 3 eh 7(0.8) dh 4 er 8* w 6 ax 5 z 7*
> ax 4 n 9 yu 16(0.8) zh 6 ax 5 1 4 iy 9*
> d 8 r 5 ai 24(1.0)%

This is an ARPABET phonemic transcription SIL ih n n ow v eh m b er SIL dh ax r iy jh en z w eh dh er w ax z ax n yu zh ax l iy d r ai ("in November the region's weather was unusually dry"), together with durational and pitch scaling numbers. Word boundaries are indicated by asterisks. Minor phrase boundaries are marked by the percent sign, introducing a degree of prosodic structure to the string. A similar example for Japanese synthesis is given in Pierrehumbert and Beckman (1988:207).

Pierrehumbert's system is not greatly different from other speech synthesis systems of the same period, such as the nascent MITalk-79 system (Allen et al. 1987), but it is noteworthy for explicitly attempting to be a phonologically motivated, computationally implemented model of intonation, rather than a practical text-to-speech system. Her work was profoundly influential on subsequent research in this area, such as that of Horne (1987, 1988) and Ladd (1987). In addition, it marked the commencement of an area of experimental phonetic work specifically related to phonological questions, including computational modelling, for which Pierrehumbert coined the term "Laboratory Phonology" (see Kingston and Beckman 1990).

2.4.2 Articulation Models

Many mathematical models of various aspects of articulatory dynamics have been studied and implemented by phoneticians and speech researchers (e.g., Stevens et al. 1966, Coker 1976). In general, these have been primarily phonetic studies of little direct phonological interest. Articulatory synthesis models, like acoustic synthesis models, have tended to be little more than systems for numerically interpolating between the values of parameters entered in a look-up table for each allophone in succession. Most of the early work was concerned with the nature of such interpolation, and its relation to the kinetics of the vocal tract.

More recently, Browman and Goldstein (1986, 1990, 1992) have attempted to elevate a particular theory of articulatory kinetics into a non-segmental phonological theory. In this theory, Articulatory Phonology, the phonological units are held to be the independently coordinated basic "gestures" of the various articulators, such as lips-closing-and-opening (or narrowing-and-widening) gesture β^1, tongue-tip-closing-and-opening gesture τ, velic-opening gesture $+\mu$, velic-closing gesture $-\mu$, etc. Each such gesture is, phonetically, a particular instantiation of a generalized damped sinusoidal motion. The phonology-to-phonetics mapping determines the precise values of the coefficients of this generalized motion: its amplitude (difference between maximum and minimum tract aperture), angular frequency (rapidity of the gesture), and phase (coordination with respect to other gestures that make up the utterance).

It is somewhat debatable whether Browman and Goldstein's model merits the adjective "phonological," since the conception of phonology implied in their model only reflects phonetic generalizations, and does not include any of the non-phonetic, arbitrary, abstract, or even counter-phonetic phenomena that distinguish phonology from phonetics. I have in mind such phenomena as phonotactic constraints, the Great Vowel Shift, trisyllabic shortening, -*ic* shortening, divergent categorial partitions of the acoustic space in different dialects, stress retraction, and so on. It seems to me that Browman and Goldstein will be able to incorporate such phenomena into the scope of their model by grafting on the decidedly non-articulatory, purely symbolic techniques of more orthodox phonological theories. Nevertheless, this model is adding to the development of better phonetic models of articulatory dynamics and control, a contribution that will undoubtedly be of much value, not least of all in demarcating phonology and phonetics.

2.5   Computational Phonology in Speech Technology Applications II: Speech Synthesis

The idea of "synthesis-by-rule" predates the SPE model of phonology. The first sets of synthesis rules were codified techniques for controlling the parameters of analogue synthesizers such as the Pattern Playback synthesizer at Haskins Laboratories, and the PAT synthesizer at Edinburgh University.

---

[1] Not to be confused with the I.P.A. category [β]. Browman and Goldstein's β gesture does not express any particular *degree* of labial closure.

These "rules" defined the formant shapes and excitation functions associated with each phoneme or allophone, and the method of interpolation between each segment and its neighbours. According to Mattingly (1968:40), the first computational implementation of this kind of "synthesis-by-rule" was performed by Kelly and Gerstman (1961). In similar systems of the same period, such as Holmes, Mattingly and Shearme (1964), phonological rules of the post-SPE kind were largely absent: the rules were almost exclusively phonetic.

Within ten years, the SPE theory had blossomed, and computers increased in utility to the point at which Carlson and Granström (1974) were able to develop a general-purpose rule compiler, enabling both SPE-type rules and the older kind of segmental interpretation and interpolation rules to be implemented. This is the "standard" approach to synthesis-by-rule, exemplified also by the work of Hertz (1982) and Allen et al. (1987). Systems of this kind abound, as a glance through the contents pages of speech technology conference proceedings will show. Yet although SPE phonology has now been effectively superseded by a combination of Lexical, Metrical and Autosegmental theory, synthesis-by-rule has been slow to take advantage of these developments. There are, of course, exceptions. Hertz's Delta system (Hertz 1990) implements certain aspects of Autosegmental theory, while the YorkTalk system, to be described in the remainder of this paper, implements many aspects of Metrical and Lexical theory.

3.1 YorkTalk

For the last few years, in collaboration with other phonologists and phoneticians at the University of York, I have been developing a phonological theory and a "synthesis-by-rule" program which does not employ such string-to-string transformations (Coleman and Local 1992, Local 1992, Coleman forthcoming, 1992a).

An underlying hypothesis of this (and related) research is that there is a trade-off between the richness of the rule component and the richness of the representations (Anderson 1985). According to this hypothesis, the reason why transformational phonology needs to use transformations is because its data-structure, strings, is not sufficiently richly structured. Consequently, it ought to be possible to considerably simplify or even completely eliminate the transformational rule component by using more structured data-structures than just well-ordered sequences of feature-vectors. For instance if we use graphs such as Figure 5 to represent phonological objects, then instead of copying or movement, we can implement phonological harmony and agreement phenomena using the *structure-sharing* technique (Karttunen and Kay 1985, Pereira 1985), as for the distribution of the feature *chk* and the ambisyllabic C in Figure 5.

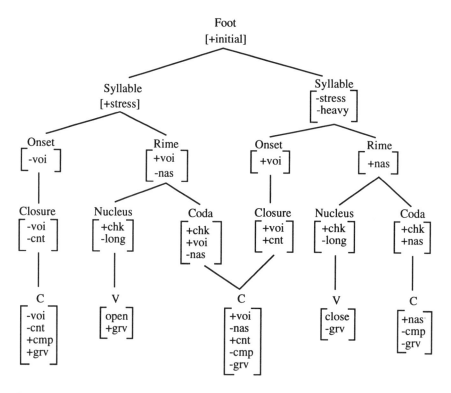

Figure 5: Part of a nonsegmental phonological representation of the word *cousin*

The fact that phonological representations such as Figure 5 and phonetic representations such as the parametric control matrices for speech synthesizers are very different kinds of objects (see Ladefoged 1977) is less problematic for the interpretive, declarative approach than for the derivational, rewriting approach. In the declarative model, the function which assigns a phonetic interpretation to a phonological representation cannot be applied more than once over, because the objects in its domain—expressions in the language of phonological descriptions—are not of the same *type* as the objects in its codomain—expressions in the language of parametric phonetic descriptions. This has two important consequences. The first is that the mapping is *arbitrary*; there is no "free ride" in relating phonetics to phonology. (This is true of parametric interpretation in most speech synthesizers, of course.) The second is that the phonetic interpretation mapping is *highly constrained*; it is a homomorphism between parts of phonological representations and parts of parametric phonetic representations, so it must "get

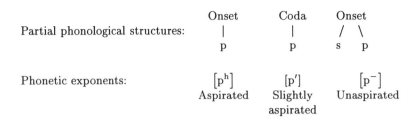

Figure 6: Declarative characterization of allophony

it right" in one step. There is no possibility of applying subsequent rules to fix up "intermediate" phonetic representations that are not surface-true. (Some examples of phonetic interpretation statements are presented below.) The mapping underdetermines the phonetic descriptions somewhat, to the extent that nonsignificant variability is permissible. These properties of the phonetic interpretation mapping are crucial to my claim that the York "synthesis-by-rule" program does not employ rewriting rules, for rewriting rules map phonological representations onto phonological representations, and may be composed with each other in series to form derivational cascades in which the order of rule-application is critical. Interpretation rules of the sort I have described above cannot be cascaded in this way, and they may be applied in any order or in parallel.

Employing richer data-structures than strings allows many if not all rewriting rules to be abandoned, to the extent that the standard phonological rewrite-rule mechanism can be eliminated, along with the problems it brings. Consider how the phonological processes discussed above can be given a declarative (or *configurational*) analysis. (In the examples I shall use alphabetic symbols to abbreviate phonological structures and to represent parts of parametric representations in the usual fashion. Note that this is purely expository, however. No alphabetic symbols appear in the phonological or phonetic representations in our theory or the synthesis system, other than normalized spelling in the input, and no intrinsic relationship between phonological and phonetic objects abbreviated by the same alphabetic symbol is intended.)

Allophony can be regarded as the different interpretation of the same element in different structural contexts, rather than as involving several slightly different phonological objects instantiating each phoneme (see Figure 6).

Assimilation can also be modelled non-destructively by unification (see Figure 7). See Local (1992) for a more complete description.

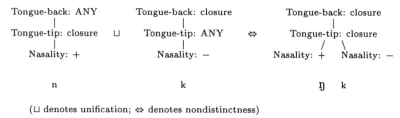

(⊔ denotes unification; ⇔ denotes nondistinctness)

Figure 7: A declarative view of assimilation

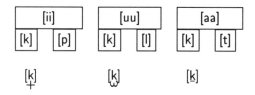

Figure 8: Declarative (coproduction) model of coarticulation

Coarticulation is simple to model if parametric phonetic representations may be "glued together" in parallel, rather than simply concatenated. Consonants may then be coproduced with vowels, rather than simply concatenated to them (Öhman 1966, Perkell 1969, Gay 1977, Mattingly 1981, Fowler 1983). This analysis is implemented in the temporal interpretation of phonological objects in the mapping from phonological to phonetic representations. The temporal arrangement of the coarticulated objects can be portrayed using representations of overlapping events (Griffen 1985, Bird and Klein 1990), as in Figure 8.

It is now common to analyze *epenthesis*, not as the insertion of a segment into a string, but as a manifestation of minor variations in the temporal coordination of independent parameters (Jespersen 1933:54, Anderson 1976, Mohanan 1986:162-164, Browman and Goldstein 1986) (see Figure 9). It has been demonstrated (Fourakis 1980, Kelly and Local 1989:135-139, 150-153) that epenthetic elements are not phonetically identical to similar nonepenthetic elements. The transformational analysis, however, holds that the phonetic implementation of a segment is dependent on its features, not its derivational history (a view which might be caricatured by the phrase "a [t] is a [t] is a [t]"), and thus incorrectly predicts that an epenthetic [t] should be phonetically identical to any other [t]. Where epenthesis is lexicalized, for example in the word *bramble*, it is not necessary to introduce an epenthetic phonological segment /b/ into the phonological representation, or to import the temporal-coordination analysis into the phonology. It is sufficient to determine the phonetic interpretation function for just these words with lexicalized epenthesis, so that the usual underdeterminacy of phonetic interpretation is, in these cases, more specific.

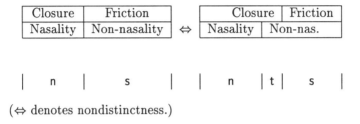

(⇔ denotes nondistinctness.)

Figure 9: Declarative characterization of epenthesis

Elision is the phonetic counterpart of epenthesis (see Figure 10), and is thus in some sense "the same" phenomenon. Taking the "unelided" form as more primitive than the "elided" form, as is done in transformational analyses, is both unnecessary and meaningless in the declarative, interpretive account.

Closure	Non-closure		Closure	Non-closure
Nasality	Non-nasality	⇔	Nasality	Non-nasality

| | n | | d | | w | | | | n | | w | |

(⇔ denotes nondistinctness.)

Figure 10: Declarative characterization of elision

Metathesis is another instance of the same phenomenon, that is, different temporal alignment of an invariant set of phonetic exponents (see Figure 11).

Epenthesis, elision and metathesis may all be regarded as instances of the more general phenomenon of non-significant variability in *phasing* (the temporal coordination of parallel events), arising from the underdeterminacy of the phonetic interpretation mapping.

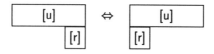

($\Leftrightarrow$ denotes nondistinctness.)

Figure 11: Declarative characterization of metathesis

As well as these relatively low-level phonological phenomena, work in Metrical Phonology (Church 1985) and Dependency Phonology (Anderson and Jones 1974) has shown how stress assignment, a classic success transformational phonological analysis, can be given a declarative analysis. Inkelas (1989) gives an essentially declarative account of the interactions between morphological and prosodic structure in Lexical Phonology, and Coleman (forthcoming) gives a declarative account of the phonological transformations presented in Halle and Mohanan's (1985) analysis of the Lexical Phonology of English.

The reanalyses of various phonological and phonetic phenomena presented above are, as the copious references should make clear, not particularly original. Similar analyses are proposed in other approaches to nonlinear phonology. It is important not to "jump out of the frying-pan into the fire," however, and introduce new formal devices such as *autosegmental transformations* which might undermine the computational benefits of using hierarchically-structured phonological representations. For this reason, we employ a mildly context-sensitive type of grammar, which goes beyond context-freeness in only two respects. Firstly, a phonological unit may be in two constituents at once, so a degree of overlap between syllable onsets, nuclei and codas is permitted. For example, in the analysis of between-word assimilation such as *ra/ŋ/ quickly*, the place-of-articulation of the coda of the first syllable [ŋ] is inherited from the place-of-articulation of the first consonant in the onset of the following syllable [k], although the other features of the [ŋ] must still form a coda, since short vowels such as [a] may not occur in open syllables. (See Local 1992.) The second cause of mild context-sensitivity is that two sister categories in a phrase-structure rule may dominate *the same* substring, rather than consecutive substrings. (This is equivalent to adding intersection to a context-free grammar. Since context-free languages are not closed under intersection, this operation makes our formalism non-context-free, although still strictly monotonic. See Chomsky 1963:380-381.) For example, Greco-Latinate words in English have separate, non-congruent morphological and metrical structures. The morphological structure of the word *photographic*, for instance, is *photograph-ic*, whereas its division into metrical feet is *photo-graphic*. A nearly-context-free analysis of the structure of such words is possible if context-free-type rules such as $\begin{array}{c}\text{Word}\\ \text{[+Latinate]}\end{array} \rightarrow \begin{array}{c}\text{Stress}\\ \text{[+Latinate]}\end{array} \cap \begin{array}{c}\text{Morphology}\\ \text{[+Latinate]}\end{array}$ are permitted. This type of rule is employed in an analysis of morphological structure and phonological vowel harmony in Warlpiri by Sproat and Brunson (1987:69). (According to Ted Briscoe, personal communication, a strictly context-free analysis of such bracketing mismatches may be possible using categorial grammars. A variant of this proposal is presented in Inkelas 1989. Alternatively, we might employ a word-grammar which is context-free but 2-ways ambiguous, assigning a metrical structure with one parse and a morphological structure with the other.)

3.2 Overview of Phoneme-to-parameter Conversion in YorkTalk

The nontransformational theory of phonology sketched above has been employed in the development of a nontransformational, nonsegmental text-to-speech system, YorkTalk. The YorkTalk system has two main components: a *phonotactic parser*, which constructs headed phonological structures from strings in normalized spelling (the input to the system), and a *phonetic interpreter*, which determines parametric phonetic descriptions from the phonological structures. The parametric phonetic descriptions are suitable for high-quality synthesis of natural-sounding speech by the Klatt formant synthesis software (Klatt 1980, Allen et al. 1987). The YorkTalk system is implemented in Poplog Prolog and runs in several times real time on a MicroVAX 3400 or a VAXstation 2000. The system currently assumes a "spelling normalization" front-end, which is similar to a standard grapheme-phoneme algorithm, except that the linguistic plausibility of the normalized spelling is of no consequence, since the phonological representations used by the system are generated from the normalized spelling by a phonological parser. This parser could be tailored to the analysis of any context-free set of strings, so in future it is hoped that the parser might generate phonological structures directly from orthographic input.

The system is at present deliberately limited to the generation of single words. In our phonological theory, however, even single words and syllables are richly structured objects. Nevertheless, they are not qualitatively different from larger units such as phrases or sentences, so we concentrated on perfecting the quality and naturalness of smaller units such as words and parts of words before moving on to work on larger units.

Although YorkTalk is a declarative system, it is possible to give a procedural description of its run-time operation. First of all, an input string

Phrase-structure constraints　　　　　　　　　　　　　　Examples and notes

$$\underset{[+\text{inflected}]}{\text{Word}} \;\to\; \underset{[-\text{inflected}]}{\text{Word}} \;\text{Inflection}$$

cat-s, underdetermine-s

$$\underset{[-\text{inflected}]}{\text{Word}} \;\to\; \underset{[-\text{inflected}]}{\text{Word}} \;\underset{[-\text{inflected}]}{\text{Word}}$$

black-bird

$$\underset{[-\text{Latinate}]}{\text{Word}} \;\to\; \underset{[-\text{Latinate}]}{\text{Prefix}^*} \;\underset{[-\text{inflected}]}{\text{Word}} \;\underset{[-\text{Latinate}]}{\text{Suffix}^*}$$

over-disorder-ly

$$\underset{[+\text{Latinate}]}{\text{Word}} \;\to\; \underset{[+\text{Latinate}]}{\text{Stress}} \;\cap\; \underset{[+\text{Latinate}]}{\text{Morphology}}$$

photo-graphic ∩
photograph-ic

$$\underset{[+\text{Latinate}]}{\text{Stress}} \;\to\; \left(\underset{[+\text{initial}]}{\text{Foot}} \right) \text{Foot}^* \; \text{Foot}$$

re-activ-ation

$$\underset{\langle-\text{initial}}{\text{Foot}} \;\to\; \left\langle \begin{bmatrix} \text{Syllable} \\ +\text{stress} \\ +\text{heavy} \end{bmatrix} \left(\begin{bmatrix} \text{Syllable} \\ -\text{stress} \\ -\text{heavy} \end{bmatrix} \right) \right.$$

⟨∅ -re-, áct-∅, áctive
(∅ denotes absence
of a syllable, and ⟨
denotes codependent
units)

$$\text{Foot} \;\to\; \underset{[+\text{stress}]}{\text{Syllable}} \begin{bmatrix} \text{Syllable} \\ -\text{stress} \\ -\text{heavy} \end{bmatrix} \begin{bmatrix} \text{Syllable} \\ -\text{stress} \\ -\text{heavy} \end{bmatrix}$$

áct-i-on

$$\underset{[+\text{Latinate}]}{\text{Morphology}} \;\to\; \underset{[+\text{Latinate}]}{\text{Prefix}^*} \;\underset{[+\text{Latinate}]}{\text{Stem}} \;\underset{[+\text{Latinate}]}{\text{Suffix}^*}$$

in-ert-ia

$$\underset{[\alpha\text{heavy}]}{\text{Syllable}} \;\to\; (\text{Onset}) \;\underset{[\alpha\text{heavy}]}{\text{Rime}}$$

(p)it

$$\underset{[\alpha\text{voi}]}{\text{Onset}} \;\to\; \underset{[\alpha\text{voi}]}{\text{Affricate}}$$

č

$$\underset{[-\text{voi}]}{\text{Onset}} \;\to\; \text{Aspirate}$$

h

$$\underset{[\alpha\text{voi}]}{\text{Onset}} \;\to\; \left(\underset{[\alpha\text{voi}]}{\text{Closure}} \right) (\text{Glide})$$

((s)p)(r)

$$\underset{[-\text{voi}]}{\text{Closure}} \;\to\; ([\text{s}]), \text{C}$$

(Either　order)
(s)p, p(s)

(Linear precedence constraint: in onsets, [s] < C)

sp

$$\underset{[\alpha\text{heavy}]}{\text{Rime}} \;\to\; \underset{[\alpha\text{heavy}]}{\text{Nucleus}} \left(\underset{[\alpha\text{heavy}]}{\text{Coda}} \right)$$
etc. etc.

eyt, ant

Figure 12: Partial phrase structure grammar of English phonotactic structure

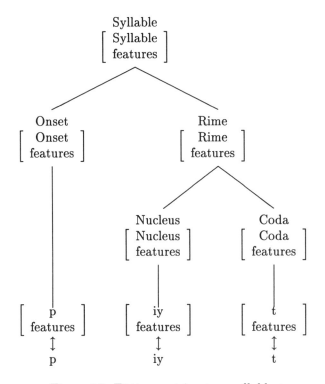

Figure 13: Fitting a string to a syllable-tree

in normalized orthography is *parsed*, using a Unification Grammar of English words. Part of a very simplified version of such a grammar is shown in Figure 12. YorkTalk includes a comprehensive and detailed grammar of English syllables, and a grammar of word-structure and stress. These grammars are used to assign phonological structures such as Figure 13 and Figure 5 to input strings of phoneme-symbols, determining stress, syllabification, rhythm and many other phonological phenomena. Following the construction of such phonological representations, the input string of phoneme-like symbols is discarded.

The parser returns a graph, representing the intended phonological structure. These graphs are very large Prolog terms, which encode a great quantity of phonological information even in the representation of single syllables. For readability, however, the example structures presented here shall only be *partial* representations of the actual YorkTalk graphs.

As well as determining the phonological structure, the parser distinguishes one constituent in each subtree as the *head* of that subtree. In the string /piyt/ (*peat*), /iyt/ (—*eat*) is the head; and in /iyt/ (—*eat*), /iy/ (—*ea*—) is the head. The theoretical relevance of headed structures is discussed in Coleman (1992a), but headedness also has practical importance in declarative speech synthesis from structured phonological representations, because it is used to determine which constituent should be interpreted first in the model of coarticulation described below (see Section 4).

After parsing the input string, the phonological structure is represented using a graph such as Figure 13, but with the information represented in the terminal nodes percolated to nonterminal nodes, and the terminal nodes subsequently discarded.

The structure may now be provided with a phonetic interpretation. This stage involves two interacting tasks: (i) the assignment of temporal "landmarks" to each node in the graph, relative to which the parametric time-functions will be calculated (temporal interpretation); and (ii) the determination of such time functions within specific temporal limits, which typically *differ* from parameter to parameter within the interpretation of a single phonological constituent (parametric interpretation).

Prolog's suitability to solving problems about *relations* enables two important kinds of relational constraints to be specified over structures such as that shown in Figure 13: a) feature-agreement constraints, and b) temporal constraints. Feature-agreement constraints are employed to encode phonotactic constraints, feature-spreading. and so forth, as described above. Temporal constraints are used in the phonetic interpretation component to assign temporal landmarks (*notional* start and end times) to each node in the graph.

The following temporal constraints are self-explanatory: *syllable start time = onset start time*, *syllable end time = rime end time*, and *rime end time = coda end time*. A number of other important temporal constraints concerning constituent overlap are discussed in Coleman (1992a).

After temporal interpretation, the syllable structure can be represented as in Figure 14. In this figure, the temporal intervals in round brackets are not part of the phonological representation, but are part of the phonetic interpretation of the node under which they are written.

Note that as a result of temporal interpretation, the onset co-starts with the nucleus, and the coda co-ends with the nucleus, which implements the "coproduction" model of coarticulation discussed above. (The parametric aspects of coarticulation are discussed below.)

After temporal interpretation, the structure is assigned a parametric interpretation. The parametric phonetic interpretation is simply a *relation* between phonological categories (feature-structures) at temporally-interpreted *places in structure* (i.e., nodes in the syllable-tree) and sets of *parameter sections*. A parameter section is a sequence of ordered pairs,

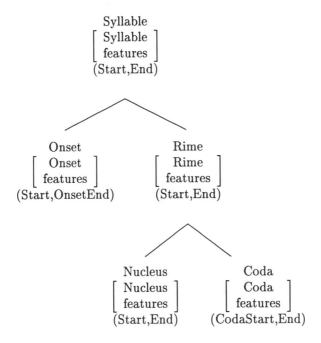

Figure 14: Syllable-tree after constraint satisfaction

each of which represents the value of that parameter at a particular (salient) time. For instance, the parameter section $[(t_1, v_1), (t_2, v_2), (t_3, v_3)]$ denotes value v_1 at time t_1, value v_2 at time t_2 and value v_3 at time t_3 for some parameter. The times may be constants, denoting absolute times in ms, or they may be functions of the start and end times of the constituent being evaluated, denoting relative times. For instance *(Onset End, Value)* might denote the value of some parameter at the notional transition point that marks the boundary between onset and nucleus. Likewise, *(Coda End − 100, Value)*, *(Rime End − 100, Value)* and *(Syllable End − 100, Value)* all denote the same parameter-value at a point in time 100 ms from the end of the syllable, given that the temporal constraints presented above hold. Although they are *extensionally* equivalent, these three pairs are *intensionally* distinct, a circumstance which sometimes demands close attention. For example, if labiality is observed throughout the entire extent of a syllable utterance, it is necessary to determine whether the phonological representation of labiality is located at the syllable-node, or whether, for instance, it is located at a lower node, the phonetic exponents of which happen to be coextensive with the phonetic exponents of the syllable-node. The first analysis takes labiality to be a syllable-level phonological distinction, and its whole-syllable extent follows from the temporal interpretation of the syllable node; the second analysis requires the "excessive" duration of labiality to be explicitly specified in the phonetic interpretation component by temporal constraints. Thus the *phonological* domain of a phonetic phenomenon cannot be determined simply by measurement and comparison of its extent with *phonetic* phenomena of similar extent.

The parametric interpretation relation, which is called *exponency*, is simply a (large) set of ordered pairs of the form ⟨*Category, Parameter Definition* which can also be represented as *Category* $\xrightarrow{e}$ *Parameter Definition*. The parameter definitions may be descriptions of parameter sections, or definitions of particular parameter values, or salient times (e.g., 4, 1, or 5, respectively). These definitions are *not* rewrite-rules; the arrows simply denote a (possibly many-to-many) mapping between two dissimilar domains of description: linguistic feature-structures, representing distinctions and similarities between phonological objects, and phonetic parameters, representing the "controls" for the speech model.

Some example exponency statements used in the interpretation of the word *take* are the following:

$$
(1) \quad \left[N: \left[\begin{array}{ll} long: & + \\ V1: & [\ height: \quad mid\ ] \\ V2: & [\ height: \quad close\ ] \end{array} \right] \right] \xrightarrow{e} F1_{start} = 540\ Hz
$$

$$
(2) \quad \left[N: \left[\begin{array}{ll} long: & + \\ V1: & [\ height: \quad NOT(close)\ ] \\ V2: & [\ height: \quad close\ ] \end{array} \right] \right] \xrightarrow{e} F1_{end} = 380\ Hz
$$

Note that the feature-structure relevant to the determination of $F1_{start}$ is different from that relevant to $F1_{end}$. Constraint 1 applies to all mid-closing diphthongs, such as /ey/ and /ow/, and Constraint 2 applies to all closing diphthongs, including open-closing diphthongs such as /aw/ and /ay/. Both statements are oblivious to whether the diphthongs are front or back. This underspecification ability is a further notable characteristic of Unification-based nonsegmental phonological representation.

The interpretation of the second formant bandwidth B2 in constraint 3 is insensitive to whether the nucleus is a monophthong or diphthong, treating mid-front vowels such as /e/ and diphthongs which begin mid-front, such as /y/, alike. In non-segmental phonetic terminology, it can be said that B2 is monophthongal even in a phonologically diphthongal nucleus.

(3) $\left[\; N: \; \left[\; V1: \; \left[\begin{array}{ll} grv: & - \\ height: & mid \\ rnd: & - \end{array} \right] \; \right] \; \right] \xrightarrow{e} B2=130\ Hz$

Constraint 4 defines a description of the amplitude of voicing, AV, for the nucleus between time-points 200 ms following the start of the nucleus to 200ms before the end of the nucleus. Thus the nucleus is regarded as an interval of voicing (the audible part of the vowel) flanked by 200ms silences within which onset and coda exponents may lie. These periods without voicing are regarded as part of the nucleus exponency, however, because the vocalic place of articulation is maintained throughout the onset and coda in the form of consonantal secondary articulation (see the discussion of coarticulation above). The interpolation $\xrightarrow{i}$ is also shown.

(4) $\quad N \xrightarrow{e}$

$$AV\left[(N_{start}+200,60),(N_{end}-200,60)\right] \xrightarrow{i}$$
$$AV = 60\ dB \left|\begin{array}{l} t=N_{end}-200 \\ t=N_{start}+200 \end{array}\right.$$

The interpretation of the coda depends on the interpretation of the nucleus, because it coarticulates with it. As shown above, the coda is temporally coproduced with the nucleus by equating the end of the coda with the end of the nucleus. The beginning of the coda is therefore the difference between the end of the coda and the duration of the coda. The duration of the coda in its turn depends on its phonological representation. For example, in the YorkTalk system, voiceless codas are regarded as being longer than voiced codas (by Constraint 5). The consequence of this is that voiceless codas start earlier in the rime than voiced codas. The difference between the end of the onset and the beginning of the coda (that is, the audible portion of the nucleus) is thus less for voiceless codas than voiced codas. The distinction in coda duration, then, gives rise to the effect that vowels are shorter before voiceless codas than before voiced codas, a well-known exponent of the coda voiced/voiceless opposition in English. This effect is not achieved by manipulating the duration of the nucleus at all, though. It follows as a consequence of the locally-defined coda duration and its interaction with other independently-motivated temporal exponents of syllable structure.

(5) $\quad [\; Co: \; [\; C: \; [\; voi: \; - \;] \;] \;] \xrightarrow{e} Co_{dur} = 250\ ms$

Dennis Klatt in Allen et al. 1987:113-115, presents a theory of onset
formant-frequency transitions which takes account of the formant-frequency
motions of the nucleus. Klatt's method is as follows, using the second-
formant frequency motion of the monosyllablic word *go* by way of example.
Firstly, the motion for the *isolation form* of the nucleus F2 is determined.
Klatt models this motion as a constant 1100 Hz for the interval from 200
ms to 230 ms, a linear fall from 1100 Hz at 230 ms to 850 Hz at 380 ms,
and a constant 850 Hz from 380 ms to 460 ms. (The absolute values of the
specific times mentioned in this description are arbitrary, and could all be
increased or decreased by an equal amount if required.)

The onset part of the second-formant motion is then evaluated over the
overlapping interval from 200 ms (the time at which the velar closure is
released) to 280 ms (the time at which the underlying formant motion for
the nucleus appears independent of the onset). The value of the second
formant frequency at 200 ms is a function of three variables: a backward-
extrapolated locus L for the F2 value during the closure, the value V of the
second formant at the 280 ms consonant-vowel boundary, and a measure
of coarticulation C between the (extrapolated) consonant locus and the
(observed) vowel value. This function is

(6) $F2_{burst} = L + C(V - L)$

Consequently, in YorkTalk, parametric phonetic interpretation of the
syllable-tree is performed top-down and head-first (i.e., heads are interpreted before non-heads). The motivation for this flow-of-control régime is
so that the parameters of the nucleus (syllable head) are evaluated before
onset and coda (non-heads), both of which are dependent on the nucleus.
Formant transitions are modelled using Klatt's locus theory. The values of
the terms in the locus-theory equation are usually somewhat different for
onsets and codas, even for units that are regarded as "the same unit" in
segmental accounts, for example, onset /t/ and coda /t/. The YorkTalk
notation for Klatt's locus-theory equation, (7), is the same with codas, although the sequence of events in the onset release in Constraint 8 (boundary, closure, transition, and target) is the reverse of the sequence of events
in the coda closure.

(7) $F1_{trans} = F1_{locus} + F1_{coart} * (F1_V - F1_{locus})$

The general shape of the onset F1 transition given by Constraint 8 holds
for all non-nasal closure onsets, with details specific to particular subcases
given by equations like (2) and (7). The interpolation $\xrightarrow{i}$ is also shown for
particular values of $F1_{val}$, $F1_{trans}$ and $F1_V$.

(8)

$$\left[O: \left[C: \left[\begin{array}{c} cnt: \quad - \\ nas: \quad - \end{array} \right] \right] \right] \xrightarrow{e}$$

$$F1 \left[(O_{start} + 180, F1_{val}), (O_{start} + 200, F1_{trans}), @(O_{start} + O_{dur}, F1_V) \right] \xrightarrow[\;t = O_{start} + 180\;]{\;t = O_{start} + 200\;} i$$

$$F1 = 431.7 + 31.7001 \; sin(270 + (\tfrac{90}{20} * (t - (O_{start} + 180)))) \; Hz \; \Big|_{t = O_{start} + 180}^{t = O_{start} + 200}$$

$$F1 = 431.7 + 2.40666(t - (O_{start} + 200)) \; Hz \; \Big|_{t = O_{start} + 200}^{t = O_{start} + O_{dur}}$$

After every applicable parametric interpretation statement has been evaluated, it is possible to determine a unique value for each parameter at every moment in time during the utterance. Parameter-values are calculated at 5 ms intervals. The result of this process is a two-dimensional array of parameter-values and times. Such an array is an appropriate input to the Klatt formant synthesis program.

3.3 Conclusion

YorkTalk began merely as an experimental demonstration of the *possibility* of speech synthesis from nonsegmental phonological representations, but it is now designed to demonstrate the applicability of these methods in a text-to-speech system. It is intended to replace the phoneme-to-allophone rule component of a segmental synthesis-by-rule system, as well as the allophone-to-parameter component and the prosodic component. YorkTalk thus does rather the same sort of task as a synthesis-by-rule system, but it does not use context-sensitive rewrite rules or transformations. Instead, it employs more sophisticated ways of representing phonological information, such as structured phonological categories, together with the declarative constraint-satisfaction mechanism for constructing phonological representations on the basis of a grammar, and providing a phonetic interpretation for those representations.

As well as being computationally "clean," highly constrained, and efficient, this method of synthesis has the additional merit of being genuinely non-segmental in (at least) two respects: there are no segments in the phonological representations, in either the established phonological theoretical sense (i.e., phonemes, allophones) or other kinds of concatenative units such as diphones, Wickelphones or demisyllables, and there is no *cross-parametric* segmentation in the phonetic representations. The resulting speech consequently does not manifest the discontinuities and rapid cross-parametric changes which often cause clicks, pops, and the other disfluencies which typify some synthetic speech. As a result, the speech is fluent, articulate and very human-like. When the model is wrong in some respect, it usually sounds like a speaker of a different language or dialect, or someone with dysfluent speech. For all these reasons, the YorkTalk model is attracting considerable interest in the speech technology industry and research community, a circumstance which I hope will promote a widespread change of approach to speech synthesis in future.

Acknowledgements

I would like to record my special thanks to John Local, Adrian Simpson, and Richard Ogden, who have all contributed extensively to the development of the YorkTalk system. Rob Fletcher of the University of York Computing Service wrote an interactive graphics editor for synthesizer parameter files, described in Fletcher et al. 1990, which was an invaluable and much-used tool. Earlier versions of this paper were presented at the 13th International Conference on Computational Linguistics (COLING-90), Helsinki, and the ESCA Workshop on Speech Synthesis, 1990. The second half of this paper is an abridged version of Coleman (1992b). I am grateful to Ted Briscoe, Nick Campbell, Nick Clements, Henrietta Cedergren, Bob Damper, Lauri Karttunen, and Klaus Köhler for comments arising from those presentations, and Richard Ogden for detailed written comments on this paper. Any faults which may remain I acknowledge as mine.

References

Allen, J., S. Hunnicutt, and D. Klatt. 1987. *From Text to Speech: The MITalk System.* Cambridge: Cambridge University Press.

Anderson, J. and C. Jones. 1974. Three theses concerning phonological representations. *Journal of Linguistics* 10:1–26.

Anderson, S. R. 1976. Nasal consonants and the internal structure of segments. *Language* 52:2.326–344.

Anderson, S. R. 1985. *Phonology in the Twentieth Century.* Chicago: University of Chicago Press.

Bach, E. and D. Wheeler 1981. Montague Phonology: A first approximation. In W. Chao and D. Wheeler (eds.), *University of Massachusetts Occasional Papers in Linguistics VII*, pp. 27–45.

Bachenko, J. and E. Fitzpatrick. 1990. A computational grammar of discourse-neutral prosodic phrasing in English. *Computational Linguistics* 16:3.155–170.

Bear, J. 1990. Backwards Phonology. In Karlgren 1990, vol. 3, pp. 13–20.

Bird, S. 1990. *Constraint-based Phonology.* Ph.D. dissertation, Centre for Cognitive Science, Edinburgh University.

Bird, S. 1991. Feature structures and indices. *Phonology* 8:137–144.

Bird, S. (ed.). 1991. *Declarative perspectives on phonology.* Edinburgh: Centre for Cognitive Science, University of Edinburgh.

Bird, S. and P. Blackburn. 1991. A logical approach to Arabic phonology. In *Proceedings of the 5th Meeting of the Association for Computational Linguistics, European Chapter, Berlin.* Reprinted in Bird 1991.

Bird, S. and E. Klein. 1990. Phonological events. *Journal of Linguistics* 26:33–56.

Booij, G. E. and J. Rubach. 1984. Morphological and prosodic domains in Lexical Phonology. *Phonology Yearbook* 1:1–27.

Broe, M. 1988. A unification-based approach to prosodic analysis. *Work in Progress: Department of Linguistics, University of Edinburgh* 21:63–82. Reprinted in Bird 1991.

Browman, C. P. and L. Goldstein. 1986. Towards an articulatory phonology. *Phonology Yearbook* 3:219–252.

Browman, C. P. and L. Goldstein. 1990. Tiers in articulatory phonology, with some implications for casual speech. In Kingston and Beckman 1990, pp. 341–376.

Browman, C. P. and L. Goldstein. 1992. 'Targetless' schwa: An articulatory analysis. In G. Docherty, and D. R. Ladd (eds.), *Gesture, segment, prosody: Papers in Laboratory Phonology II.* Cambridge: Cambridge University Press.

Cahill, L. 1990. Syllable-based morphology. In Karlgren 1990, vol. 3, pp. 48–53.

Carlson, R. and B. Granström. 1974. A phonetically oriented programming language for rule description of speech. In *Speech Communication Seminar, Stockholm, Aug. 1–3,* vol. 2, pp. 245–253.

Chomsky, N. 1963. Formal properties of grammars. In R. D. Luce, R. R. Bush and E. Galanter (eds.), *Handbook of Mathematical Psychology Vol. II,* pp. 323–418. New York: John Wiley.

Chomsky, N. A. and M. Halle. 1968. *The sound pattern of English.* New York: Harper and Row.

Church, K. 1983. *Phrase structure parsing: A method for taking advantage of allophonic constraints.* Ph.D. dissertation, Massachusetts Institute of Technology.

Church, K. 1985. Stress assignment in letter to sound rules for speech synthesis. In *Proceedings of the 23rd Annual Meeting of the Association for Computational Linguistics,* pp. 246–253.

Cohen, P. S. and R. L. Mercer. 1975. The phonological component of an automatic speech-recognition system. In D. Raj Reddy (ed.), *Speech Recognition: Invited Papers Presented at the 1974 IEEE Symposium.* New York: Academic Press.

Coker, C. H. 1976. A model of articulatory dynamics and control. *Proceedings of the IEEE,* 64:4.452–460.

Coleman, J. S. 1990. Unification phonology: Another look at 'synthesis-by-rule'. In Karlgren 1990, vol. 3, pp. 79–84.

Coleman, J. S. forthcoming. Declarative Lexical Phonology. To appear in J. Durand and F. Katamba (eds.), *Frontiers of Phonology: Primitives, architectures and derivations.* London: Longman.

Coleman, J. S. 1992a. The phonetic interpretation of headed phonological structures containing overlapping constituents. *Phonology* 9:1–44.

Coleman, J. S. 1992b. 'Synthesis-by-rule' without segments or rewrite-rules. In G. Bailly, C. Benoit and T. R Sawallis (eds.), *Talking machines: Theories, models, and applications.* Amsterdam: Elsevier.

Coleman, J. S. and J. K. Local. 1992. Monostratal phonology and speech synthesis. In P. Tench (ed.), *Studies in Systemic Phonology.* London: Francis Pinter.

Dirksen, A. and H. Quené. 1991. Prosodic analysis: The next generation. In V. J. van Heuven and L. Pols (eds.), *Analysis and synthesis of speech.* Dordrecht: Foris.

Dresher, B. E. and J. D. Kaye. 1990. A computational learning model for metrical phonology. *Cognition* 34:137–195.

Dresher, B. E. 1991. YOUPIE: A parameter-based learning model for metrical phonology. In S. Hockey, N. Ide, and I. Lancashire (eds.), *Research in Humanities Computing I: Papers from the 1989 ACH-ALLC Conference.* Oxford: Oxford University Press.

Evans, R. and G. Gazdar (eds.). 1989, 1990. *The DATR Papers.* Computer Science Research Papers, University of Sussex.

Evans, R. and G. Gazdar. 1989a. Inference in DATR. In *Proceedings of the 4th Meeting of the Association for Computational Linguistics, European Chapter, Manchester,* pp. 66–71.

Evans, R. and G. Gazdar. 1989b. The semantics of DATR. In A. G. Cohn (ed.), *Proceedings of the 7th Conference of the AISB,* pp. 79–87. London: Pitman/Morgan Kaufmann.

Fletcher, R. P., J. K. Local, and J. S. Coleman. 1990. Speech synthesis — How to do it, and using graphics to get it right. *Proceedings of the DECUS (UK, Ireland and Middle-East) Conference, Keele University, March 1990.*

Fourakis, M. S. 1980. A phonetic study of sonorant fricative clusters in two dialects of English. *Research in Phonetics* 1. Department of Linguistics, Indiana University.

Fowler, C. A. 1983. Converging sources of evidence on spoken and perceived rhythms of speech: Cyclic production of vowels in monosyllabic stress feet. *Journal of Experimental Psychology: General* 112:386–412.

Gay, T. 1977. Articulatory movements in VCV sequences. *Journal of the Acoustical Society of America* 62:182–193.

Gibbon, D. and S. Reinhart. 1991. Prosodic inheritance and morphological generalisations. In *Proceedings of the 5th Meeting of the Association for Computational Linguistics, European Chapter, Berlin.*

Griffen, T. D. 1985. *Aspects of Dynamic Phonology* (Amsterdam studies in the theory and history of linguistic science. Series 4: Current issues in linguistic theory, vol. 37). Amsterdam: Benjamins.

Halle, M. and K. P. Mohanan. 1985. Segmental Phonology of Modern English. *Linguistic Inquiry* 16:1.57–116.

Halle, M. and J.-R. Vergnaud. 1987. *An essay on stress.* Cambridge, MA: MIT Press.

Hertz, S. R. 1982. From text to speech with SRS. *Journal of the Acoustical Society of America* 72:1155–1170.

Hertz, S. R. 1990. The Delta programming language: An integrated approach to non-linear phonology, phonetics and speech synthesis. In Kingston and Beckman 1990, pp. 215–257.

Holmes, J. N., I. G. Mattingly, and J. N. Shearme. 1964. Speech synthesis by rule. *Language and Speech* 7:127–143.

Horne, M. 1987. *Towards a discourse-based model of English sentence intonation.* Working Papers No. 32. Department of Linguistics and Phonetics, Lund University.

Horne, M. 1988. Towards a quantified, focus-based model for for synthesizing English sentence intonation. *Lingua* 75:25–54.

Inkelas, S. 1989. *Prosodic constituency in the lexicon.* Ph.D. dissertation, Stanford University.

Jespersen, O. 1933. *Essentials of English grammar.* London: George Allen and Unwin.

Karlgren, H. (ed.). 1990. *COLING-90. Papers presented to the 13th International Conference on Computational Linguistics.* International Committee on Computational Linguistics.

Karttunen, L. and M. Kay. 1985. Structure sharing with binary trees. In *Proceedings of the 23rd Annual Meeting of the Association for Computational Linguistics,* pp. 133–136a.

Kay, M. 1987. Nonconcatenative Finite-State Morphology. In *Proceedings of the 3rd European Meeting of the Association for Computational Linguistics,* pp. 2–10.

Kelly, J. L. and L. J. Gerstman. 1961. An artificial talker driven from a phonetic input (abstract). *Journal of the Acoustical Society of America* 33:835.

Kelly, J. and J. K. Local. 1989. *Doing phonology.* Manchester: Manchester University Press.

Kingston, J. and M. Beckman (eds.). 1990. *Papers in Laboratory Phonology I: Between the grammar and physics of speech.* Cambridge: Cambridge University Press.

Klatt, D. 1977. Review of the ARPA Speech Understanding Project. *Journal of the Acoustical Society of America* 62:6, 1345–1366.

Klatt, D. 1980. Scriber and Lafs: Two new approaches to speech analysis. In W. Lea (ed.), *Trends in speech recognition.* Englewood Cliffs, NJ:Prentice-Hall.

Klein, E. 1987. Towards a Declarative Phonology. ms., Centre for Cognitive Science, Edinburgh University.

Klein, E. and J. Calder. 1987. Declarative Phonology. ms., Centre for Cognitive Science, Edinburgh University.

Koskenniemi, K. 1983. *Two-Level Morphology: A general computational model for word-form recognition and production.* Publication 11 of the Department of General Linguistics, University of Helsinki.

Ladd, D. R. 1987. A model of intonational phonology for use in speech synthesis by rule. In J. Laver and M. A. Jack (eds.), *European Conference on Speech Technology, Edinburgh — September 1987,* pp. 21–24. Edinburgh: CEP Consultants Ltd.

Ladefoged, P. 1977. The abyss between phonetics and phonology. In *Proceedings of the 13th Meeting of the Chicago Linguistic Society,* pp. 225–235.

Liberman, M. Y. 1975. *The intonation system of English.* Ph.D. dissertation, Massachusetts Institute of Technology. Published in 1979 by Garland Press, New York.

Local, J. K. 1992. Modelling assimilation in non-segmental rule-free synthesis. In Docherty and Ladd 1992, pp. 190–223.

Mattingly, I. G. 1968. *Synthesis by rule of General American English.* Supplement to: Status Report on Speech Research. April, 1968. Haskins Laboratories.

Mattingly, I. G. 1981. Phonetic representations and speech synthesis by rule. In T. Myers, J. Laver, and J. Anderson (eds.), *The cognitive representation of speech.* Amsterdam: North-Holland.

McCarthy, J. 1979. *Formal problems in Semitic phonology and morphology.* Ph.D. dissertation, Massachusetts Institute of Technology. Published in 1982 by Indiana University Linguistics Club.

Mohanan, K. P. 1986. *The theory of Lexical Phonology.* Dordrecht: D. Reidel.

Nespor, M. and I. Vogel. 1986. *Prosodic phonology.* Dordrecht: Foris.

Öhman, S. E. G. 1966. Coarticulation in VCV utterances: Spectrographic measurements, *Journal of the Acoustical Society of America* 39:151–168.

Oliveira, L. C., M. C. Viana, and I. M. Trancoso. 1991. DIXI — Portuguese text-to-speech system. *Proceedings of Eurospeech 91. (2nd European Conference on Speech Communication and Technology, Genova, Italy, 24–26 September 1991.)* 3:1239–1242.

Pereira, F. C. N. 1985. A structure-sharing representation for unification-based grammar formalisms. In *Proceedings of the 23rd Annual Meeting of the Association for Computational Linguistics*, pp. 137–144.

Perkell, J. S. 1969. *Physiology of speech production: Results and implications of a quantitative cineradiographic study.* Cambridge, MA: MIT Press.

Pierrehumbert, J. 1981. Synthesizing intonation. *Journal of the Acoustical Society of America* 70:4.985–995.

Pierrehumbert, J. and M. Beckman. 1988. *Japanese Tone Structure.* Cambridge, MA: MIT Press.

Pollard, C. and I. A. Sag. 1987. *Information-based syntax and semantics. Vol. 1: Fundamentals.* CSLI Lecture Notes No. 13. Stanford, CA: CSLI.

Randolph, M. A. 1989. *Syllable-based constraints on properties of English sounds.* Ph.D. dissertation, Massachusetts Institute of Technology.

Sag, I. A. 1982. A semantic theory of "NP-movement" dependencies. In P. Jacobson and G. K. Pullum (eds.), *The nature of syntactic representations,* pp. 427-466. Dordrecht: D. Reidel.

Scobbie, J. M. 1991. *Attribute Value Phonology.* Ph.D. dissertation, Centre for Cognitive Science, Edinburgh University.

Selkirk, E. O. 1984. *Phonology and syntax: The relation between sound and structure.* Cambridge, MA: MIT Press.

Shieber, S. M., H. Uszkoreit, F. C. N. Pereira, J. J. Robinson, and M. Tyson. 1983. The formalism and implementation of PATR-II. In *Research on Interactive Acquisition and Use of Knowledge.* Artificial Intelligence Center, SRI International, Menlo Park, CA.

Shieber, S. M. 1985. Criteria for designing computer facilities for linguistic analysis. *Linguistics* 23:2.189–211.

Shieber, S. M. 1986. *An introduction to unification-based approaches to grammar.* CSLI Lecture Notes No. 4. Stanford, CA: CSLI.

Sproat, R., and B. Brunson. 1987. Constituent-based morphological parsing: A new approach to the problem of word-recognition. In *Proceedings of the 25th Annual Meeting of the Association for Computational Linguistics*, pp. 65–72.

Stevens, K. N., A. S. House and A. P. Paul. 1966. Acoustical description of syllabic nuclei: An interpretation in terms of a dynamic model of articulation. *Journal of the Acoustical Society of America* 40:1.123–132.

Touretzky D. S., D. W. Wheeler, and G. Elvgren III. 1990a. Rules and Maps II: Recent progress in Connectionist symbol processing. Report CMU-CS-90-112. Department of Computer Science, Carnegie-Mellon University.

Touretzky D. S., D. W. Wheeler, and G. Elvgren III. 1990b. Rules and Maps III: Further progress in Connectionist phonology. Report CMU-CS-90-138. Department of Computer Science, Carnegie-Mellon University.

Williams, S. 1990. Lexical Phonology: A computational system. Talk presented at the First UK Workshop on Computation and Phonology, University of York, December 7–8.

Woods, W. and V. W. Zue. 1976. Dictionary expansion via phonological rules for a speech understanding system. In *1975 IEEE International Conference on Acoustics, Speech and Signal Processing, Philadelphia, PA*, pp. 561–564.

Youd, N. J. and F. Fallside. 1987. Generating words and prosody for use in speech synthesis. In J. Laver and M. A. Jack (eds.), *European Conference on Speech Technology, Edinburgh — September 1987*, pp. 17-20. Edinburgh: CEP Consultants Ltd.

Eliminating Cyclicity as a Source of Complexity in Phonology

Jennifer S. Cole[1]

University of Illinois at Urbana-Champaign

This paper examines the analysis of cyclicity, a hallmark of the standard derivational theory, in a non-derivational approach to phonology. It is shown that cyclic systems can be given a constraint-based analysis by composing the metrical structures assigned independently, and in parallel, in each cyclic domain. However, this approach leads to a problem of constraint conflict. The proposed analysis resolves constraint conflict through the mechanism of disjunctive constraint ranking: a high-ranking constraint takes precedence over a lower-ranking constraint. Consideration is given to the possibility of an additive effect of constraint violation, in which a disjunctive ranking is reversed in forms where there are multiple violations of the lower-ranking constraints. The analyses of the cyclic stress systems of Chamorro and English are presented in the form of constraint-based unification grammars operating on representations that specify feature structures for syllable and metrical structure.

1 Introduction

Recent years have shown remarkable advances in the implementation of syntactic theories in computer systems that generate and parse natural language. These advances follow directly from the shift away from transformational grammars to grammars based on enriched and highly structured syntactic representations. An attractive feature of many current natural language processing systems is their declarative nature, which makes it theoretically possible to utilize the same expression of the grammar for tasks involving parsing and generation. Parallel to the paradigmatic shift in syntax, phonology has witnessed radical changes in recent years. The result is a theory with richly structured phonological representations, in which constraints on structures involving distinctive features and prosodic categories play a large role in explaining phonological patterns. In modern phonological theory, as in syntactic theory, there is a decreased reliance on transformations and purely structure-changing phonological rules. This trend in phonology has given rise to a number of proposals which highlight the role of the constraint grammar in non-procedural or declarative theories

---

[1] Thanks goes to Steven Abney, John Coleman, Mike Hammond, José Ignacio Hualde, and Charles Kisseberth for useful discussion on topics related to this paper.

of phonology (Scobbie 1991, Bird 1991, Coleman 1991, Prince and Smolensky 1993[2])—work which prepares the way for the computer implementation of phonological grammar (Bird and Ellison 1994, Coleman 1992)

Despite recent advances, there remain certain aspects of phonology that are problematic for constructing a computable model. One such problem arises from cyclic rule application. As shown in Johnson (1972), a standard transformational grammar of phonology with cyclic rule application is an unrestricted rewriting system, with the generative capacity of a Turing machine. Johnson (pp.42-46) shows that if phonological rules are restricted from reapplying to their own output, the resulting phonological grammars would in fact derive only the finite state automaton, or regular, languages.[3] So, it is the iterative, feeding aspect of cyclic rule application alone which relegates phonology to the basement of the Chomsky hierarchy. Although many differences distinguish current phonological theory from the generative transformational theory of SPE, the analysis and role of cyclicity in current theory is little changed from its precursor, and thus Johnson's result continues to obtain for the current phonological theory.[4]

Cyclic phonology is fundamentally at odds with the notion that phonological constraints can be expressed by non-derivational, declarative grammars. In cyclic phonology, rules apply to each cyclic domain in sequence, with the output of a cyclic domain feeding the analysis of the next highest domain. I refer to this conception of rule domains as the "derivational cycle." This paper presents an alternative to the derivational cycle of standard theory through the formulation of a declarative analysis of two classically "cyclic" stress systems, English and Chamorro. I argue that cyclicity re-

---

[2]The present paper was conceived, written and submitted prior to the appearance of Prince and Smolensky 1993, which lays the foundation of Optimality Theory (OT). However, there are close connections between OT and the approach developed in this paper. Specifically, the problem of conflicting constraints is resolved through constraint ranking in both approaches. See discussion in section 3.

[3]This result is confirmed in Kaplan and Kay 1994, where *SPE*-style transformational grammars are characterized as regular relations. They demonstrate that every noncyclical rewriting grammar denotes a regular relation, mapping a regular language onto a regular language, and can be modeled by a finite state transducer. However, a grammar with cyclic rule application cannot be expressed as a regular relation. Kaplan and Kay (p. 365) state that "*in the worst case, in fact, we know that the computations of an arbitrary Turing machine can be simulated by a rewriting grammar with unrestricted rule reapplication.*

[4]In addition to cyclicity, there are other potential sources of complexity in current phonological theory, such as rule ordering, and long-distance or iterative processes. Though not discussed here, both of these issues have been addressed recently in the computational phonology literature (Bird 1991, Coleman 1991, Scobbie 1991). Rule ordering, in particular, has been given an non-procedural treatment in a variety of frameworks, including the finite-state transducer model of Kaplan and Kay 1994, the related three-level network-based model of Touretzky and Wheeler 1990, 1991, and the constraint-based model of Prince and Smolensky 1993.

quires no more than the postulation of intra-word domains within which metrical feet pick out prominent syllables. Cyclic domains are constructed on the basis of the internal morphological structure of a word, and cyclic rules are simply those which apply within the cyclic domains.[5] Further, the declarative analysis of cyclic stress allows each cyclic domain to be analyzed at the same time, thus eliminating the iterative, feeding application of cyclic rules allowed under the standard derivational analysis of cyclicity. This interpretation of cyclicity resolves the complexity of the standard analysis demonstrated by Johnson, and brings phonology back into the class of tractable grammars.

2   Cyclic Rule Application

2.1   The Derivational Cycle

In the phonological literature over the past twenty years, various proposals have been made that phonological rules may apply cyclically. The cyclic domains are defined by morphological constituent structure, with cyclic rules applying to the most deeply embedded constituent first and reapplying to each successively larger constituent. For example, in a morphological structure [[[A] B] C], the cyclic rules will first apply to the string [A], then apply to [A B], and finally to the entire string [A B C]. Within a cycle, the entire set of cyclic rules may apply, possibly in an ordered fashion, if there exist extrinsic ordering statements. Thus, the number of steps in the derivation of a word is bounded for a particular language by the number of distinct phonological rules in the grammar and by the maximum number of cycles, defined by the morphology in terms of the maximum number of affixes that can attach to a base. Curiously, no reported phonological system has even approached the level of derivational complexity afforded by the cyclic theory, an observation which forces us to question whether cyclic rule application provides phonological theory with excessive power.

The strongest evidence for cyclic rule application derives from those systems where the effects of rule application on an inner cycle are present in the "surface" phonetic representation—effects which could not be derived from assuming the non-cyclic application of the rule on the entire string. For example, in English, secondary stress in poly-morphemic words corresponds to primary stress on an inner cycle (Chomsky and Halle 1968, Hammond 1989, Halle and Kenstowicz 1991). Contrast the location of secondary stress in the words *originálity* and *clàssificátion* (examples due to Hammond 1989). Both words have a sequence of three light syllables

---

[5]This leads to the conclusion that the requirements of "cyclic" phonology in a declarative approach are not consistent with theories like Lexical Phonology, which place strict limits on access to morphological structure in the phonology.

preceding the main stress, yet secondary stress shows up on the second syllable in one word and on the first syllable in the other. There is no syllable-counting algorithm which could correctly predict the location of secondary stress in words like these, based only on the surface string of syllables. Rather, the stress assigning algorithm must know that the stems from which the words are formed are *original* and *clássify*, with primary stress on the same syllable which receives secondary stress in the derived form. Thus, it would appear that the stress assigning algorithm makes two passes, or cycles, in the derivation of the suffixed forms. To account for these facts, the standard cyclic analysis allows the stress rules (along with other rules of English phonology) to apply first to the innermost cycle, with the input to each successive cycle preserving a record of stress placement on the immediately preceding cycle.[6]

2.2   The Non-derivational Cycle

In the analysis of cyclic stress which relies on a derivational cycle, the output of cycle i serves as the input to cycle $i+1$, allowing for intricate feeding relationships between each cycle of stress assignment. A more constrained alternative to this approach is to allow stress to be assigned *simultaneously* to each cyclic domain. The non-derivational cycles can be analyzed at the word level, when the input consists of a string of morphemes which constitute a morphological word, or possibly even at a higher level of structure, including clitic groups or perhaps even phrases (though in this paper we restrict our attention to the analysis of the word level). This alternative interpretation of cyclicity has the effect of generating a stress for each cyclic domain, but removes the possibility, inherent in the derivational cyclic analysis, that stress assignment on cycle n could have an effect on stress assignment, or any other phonological operation applying on cycle $n+1$. I use the term "non-derivational cycle" to refer to the cyclic domains which are subject to simultaneous analysis in the declarative approach.

Consider the declarative treatment of stress assignment in the English words *originá, lity* and *clàssificátion*. Each word has two cyclic domains. Below we see the assignment of stress on the inner cyclic domain (1a), the outer cyclic domain (1b), and putting the two together, stress as it is simultaneously assigned to both domains (1c):[7]

---

[6]There have been various proposals on how best to implement the "memory" of inner-cycle stress; see, for example, Halle and Vergnaud (1987) and Hammond (1989). The details of such arguments are not of concern here, because in the analysis proposed below, all stresses are simultaneously assigned.

[7]I assume *original* rather than *origin* as the base of *originality*, based on the rather opaque semantic correspondence between the first two forms. Note that the rules of English stress are considerably more complex than this simple example suggests. As discussed in Section 3, the process of secondary stress assignment may involve a left-to-

(1) a.   [clássify]   [oríginal]

　　b.   [classificátion]   [originálity]

　　c.   [[clássifi] cátion]   [[oríginál] ity]

The result of this analysis is a surface string with two stressed syllables in each word. Additional principles are required to specify that the stress generated in the outer cyclic domain is the main stress, and inner cycle stresses are secondary. In the following sections, we consider in detail the principles of stress assignment in a declarative, non-derivational treatment of Chamorro and English stress.

3   Chamorro Stress

3.1   The Data

Chamorro is a classic example of a language with a cyclic stress system. The cyclic analysis of stress assignment in Chamorro is presented by Chung (1983), drawing on her own fieldwork and on the grammar by Topping and Dungca (1973). The basic stress pattern in Chamorro places stress on either the penult or the antepenult in unsuffixed words, the choice determined by the lexical item, as in (2a,b). Suffixed words are all stressed on the penult, as in (2c).

(2) a.   **Stress on antepenult:**

mámati	'reef'	dáŋkulu	'big'
píkaru	'sly'	éntalu?	'middle'
kúnanaf	'to crawl'	éŋŋulu?	'to peep'

　　b.   **Stress on penult:**

kítan	'cross-eyed'	aságwa	'spouse'
púgwa?	'betel nut'	inéksa?	'cooked rice'
lémmay	'breadfruit'	paníti	'to strike'

　　c.   **Suffixed words stressed on penult:**

nána	'mother'	nanáhu	'my mother'
gúma?	'house'	gumá?mu	'your(sg.)house'
dáŋkulu	'big'	dàŋkulónña[8]	'bigger'

---

right parse, which is independent of the right-edge parse that places main stress on each cyclic domain. See for example the discussion in Halle and Kenstowicz (1991).

[8]The secondary stress that surfaces on this form, and some other suffixed forms, is

These data are analyzed by assigning a single left-headed, binary foot at the right edge of the word, which will place stress on the penultimate syllable. In words with antepenult stress, the final syllable is lexically specified as extrametrical. This syllable loses its extrametricality when it is followed by a suffix, as shown by the stress of *dàŋkulú-ña* 'bigger' (2c) (compare *dáŋkulu* (2a)).

The straightforward stress pattern illustrated in (2) is complicated by the presence of a class of accented prefixes, which surface with primary stress in the forms in (3).

(3) **Lexically stressed prefixes attract stress:**

mantíka	'fat'	mímantìka	'abounding in fat'
díŋu	'to leave'	ắdìŋu	'to leave one another'
paníti	'to strike'	ắpanìti	'to strike one another'
púgas	'uncooked rice'	mípùgas	'abounding in uncooked rice'

The accentual property of prefixes is not predictable, and must therefore be specified in underlying representation. For the present analysis, we can say that the accented prefixes have lexically specified metrical structure (or equivalently, lexically specified grid marks).[9] The forms in (3) show a secondary stress on the penult syllable, which can be derived through assignment of the trochaic foot at the right edge of the word. A simple strategy to realize the prefix stress as primary, rather than the stress generated by the foot parsed at the right edge, is to build another layer of foot structure on top of both stresses, marking the leftmost stress as the head.[10] The two layers of metrical structure are illustrated in (4), adopting the bracketed grid formalism of Halle and Vergnaud 1987.

(4)
```
             mí-    man    tì    ka
line 0:    ( * )     *    ( *    * )
line 1:    ( *             * )
line 2:      *
```

Up to this point, we treat the entire word as a single stress domain, with a single (two-layer) metrical structure generating primary and sec-

---

discussed immediately below.

[9]Prefixes which are not accented have no effect on the surface stress pattern, e.g., *man-géftaw* 'generous (pl.)'.

[10]The directionality of this analysis could be avoided if there were an explicit principle which favored lexically specified metrical structure over the regular edge-oriented metrical structure. In an Optimality Theoretic analysis, such a principle is available in the form of the Faithfulness constraints.

ondary stresses, as in (5). Yet there is another source for secondary stresses, demonstrated by the following examples.

(5) a. swéddu   'salary'   b. swèddunmámi   'our (excl.) salary'
        inéŋŋuluʔ   'peeping'   inèŋŋuluʔníha 'his peeping'

These words show that the primary stress shifts rightward when a suffix is added to the base, and in addition, a secondary stress appears on the syllable which would receive stress on the inner cycle. There is no general algorithm for assignment of secondary stress, operating in the domain of the entire word, that could correctly stress both of the suffixed words in (5). Comparing the two suffixed forms, the secondary stress appears two syllables before the primary stress, on the initial syllable in *swèddunmámi*, whereas in *inèŋŋuluʔníha* secondary stress appears three syllables before the primary stress, on the second syllable. Yet cyclic stress assignment generates both stresses. Applying the regular stress rule in each domain picks out the penultimate syllable of each domain (excluding extrametrical syllables) as the head of a stress foot.

(6) a. [[sweddun] mami]   b. [[ineŋŋu   luʔ]   niha]
        (*   *)   (* *)   *(* *)   <*>   (* *)
           *   *   *   *

Unlike the examples above with stressed prefixes, in the suffixed words in (5) it is the rightmost of the two stressed syllables that receives primary stress. Further, the primary stress can shift rightward under suffixation even when the stem contains an accented prefix, as seen in (7).

(7) a. [[mi [mantika]] na]   mìmantikáña   'abounding in fat'

Applying the stress rule in each cyclic domain of *mìmantikáña* gives the following representation:

(8) [mí   [[mantíká]   na]]
      *   * **   *
      *   * *

The first syllable is lexically marked for stress. The third syllable is the penult in both the stem cycle and the prefix cycle. The fourth syllable is the penult of the suffix cycle, the highest cycle, and surfaces with primary stress, in accordance with the generalization that the highest cyclic stress is dominant. Note that the stress on the syllable *ti* is not realized at all in the surface form. This follows from another generalization about Chamorro stress, namely that the syllable immediately preceding the primary stressed syllable is never stressed. This point is addressed further below.

3.2   Cyclicity as Domain Ranking

A cyclic principle is obviously at work in Chamorro—it is the stress associated with the highest morphological domain which is primary. The stem stress subordinates to both the prefix and the suffix domain stress, and the prefix stress subordinates to stress assigned on an external suffix domain. How can this principle of cyclic dominance be encoded in a non-derivational analysis? One possibility is to impose a ranking of cyclic domains which reflects the morphological constituent structure: Stem < Prefix < Suffix. The cyclic suffixes belong to the "strongest" domain. The stress assigning principles can be formulated with reference to the domain ranking, so that the stressed syllable in the "strongest" domain is realized as primary stress.[11] The hypothesis of declarative phonology, as with declarative syntax, is that all grammatical constraints are applied simultaneously to the entire string, yielding a single structure—the surface representation. Thus, in order to express the principle of cyclic stress assignment in Chamorro, stated in terms of domain ranking, it is necessary that the internal morphological structure of the word be visible in evaluating the stress-licensing principles. In terms of the representations in (6), the stress generated on the suffix domain (the rightmost stress) will be realized as primary, since it is the most highly ranked domain in those forms.

Domain ranking is a brute force way of encoding the principle of cyclic dominance. The fact that the outermost cyclic domain realizes primary stress does not follow in any way from the algorithm that assigns stress or from any other aspect of the declarative analysis. Yet, the declarative analysis is certainly no worse off than a derivational cyclic analysis of these data. In a metrical theory like that of Halle and Vergnaud (1987), the distinction between primary and secondary stress is made by constructing feet on the metrical grid on lines 0 and 1, as in (3), above. Analyzed in that fashion, the primary stress must appear uniformly as the rightmost or leftmost of all stressed syllables, in every word. As we have observed, such an analysis will not work for Chamorro. Applying metrical stress rules cyclically still does not yield the correct results for Chamorro, since on the prefix cycle, main stress will be leftmost, while it is rightmost on the suffix cycle. The only solution is to allow different rules to operate on prefix

---

[11]The domain-ranking solution proposed here was developed independently of Optimality Theory (OT), although it shares some of its essential properties. In both cases ranking is used to eliminate properties of sequential derivation—rule ordering of OT, and cyclicity in this proposal. The possibility exists of integrating the domain-ranking analysis with constraint-based OT grammars, but a detailed exploration of such an approach goes beyond the scope of the present paper.

and suffix cycles. The prefix rule would build a left-headed foot over the asterisks on line 1 of the grid, while the suffix rule would build a right-headed line 1 foot. The effect of allowing two distinct rules for parsing line 1 on prefix and suffix cycles is that the new stress introduced on each cycle will always be designated primary. In effect, the headedness parameter is encoding the principle of cyclic dominance. Yet the headedness parameter itself is an arbitrary setting; the fact that on the prefix cycle the line 1 foot is left-headed is not in any way related to the fact that the stress which is newly introduced on that cycle appears as the *leftmost* prominent syllable in the string. So, the principle of cyclic dominance is really no less a stipulation under a derivational cyclic analysis than under the declarative analysis with overtly ranked cyclic domains.[12]

Both the derivational and non-derivational approaches to cyclicity allow phonological rules to apply to each individual cyclic domain in the word. And, as argued above, both approaches require a stipulation to the effect that in Chamorro, the stress assigned in the outermost cycle is primary—the principle of cyclic dominance. But the theory with derivational cyclicity is more powerful, since it allows the analysis of an inner cycle to feed the analysis of an outer cycle. It is of interest to note that no cyclic feeding is observed in the stress system of Chamorro, and the non-derivational notion of cyclicity is sufficient for the analysis of these data.

The following points summarize the main results of this section.

1. In Chamorro, inner cycle stresses are preserved as secondary stress in the surface string, requiring stress assignment in each cyclic domain.

2. The internal morphological structure of a word must be visible in order to assign stress to each cyclic domain, in a non-derivational analysis.

3. Cyclicity can be encoded as domain ranking.

4. Cyclic feeding is not observed in the Chamorro stress system.

---

[12] Halle and Vergnaud (1987) present a cyclic analysis of Chamorro stress that resembles the one sketched here. They allow only a single set of rules to assign stress on every cycle, but do not carry over an inner cycle stress onto an outer cycle. Stress is assigned on each cyclic domain, but only the last cyclic stress is preserved, as main stress. Stresses assigned on non-final cycles are stored away (requiring a special representation to serve as a "memory" cell) and reintroduced by a post-cyclic rule generating secondary stresses. The addition of a special "memory" to metrical theory provides the theory with excessive power, and is required by the Halle and Vergnaud theory only to overcome the effects of cyclic stress deletion in languages like Chamorro and English, that preserve cyclic stresses.

3.3 Stress licensing Conflicts

In this section, I consider further the details of Chamorro stress, focusing on the "destressing" that results from stress clash. The analysis of cyclic stress assignment described in the last section operates with the following two principles.[13]

(9) **Cyclic Stress Principles**

Parse: parse the penult as the head of a foot, in each cyclic domain.

$$\sigma \quad \sigma \ ]_n \quad \longrightarrow \quad \sigma \qquad\qquad \sigma$$
$$[\text{FOOT}_n : \text{head}] \quad [\text{FOOT}_n : \text{nonhead}]$$

Assign Prominence: Assign stress prominence to the head of the leftmost foot, in each cyclic domain.[14]

$$\sigma^* \qquad \sigma \qquad \longrightarrow \qquad \sigma$$
$$[\text{FOOT:head}] \qquad\qquad [\text{STRESS:stressed}]$$

(10) **Word-level Stress Principle**

Primary: Assign extra stress prominence (ie., primary stress) to the prominent syllable in the highest ranking cyclic domain.

$$\begin{bmatrix} \sigma \\ \text{DOMAIN:}n \\ \text{STRESS:stressed} \end{bmatrix} \quad \longrightarrow \quad \begin{matrix} \sigma \\ \ \\ \ \end{matrix} \quad [\text{STRESS:primary}] \quad \text{Where } n \text{ is the highest domain.}$$

---

[13]Each constraint is stated first in prose, followed by a formalization of the constraint as a context-sensitive grammar rule. The formalization is modeled after the unification constraint-based grammar formalism presented in Scobbie (1991). Each constraint is stated as a conditional. If the antecedent of the constraint subsumes some feature structure S, then the consequent of the constraint must unify with S. If the antecedent does not subsume S, there is no effect on S. The formal status of such constraints is not the primary concern here; rather, the formalization is offered as a way of indicating the overall form of a grammar which expresses the analysis proposed here.

[14]The syllable that is assigned stress prominence may be preceded by any number of unfooted syllables. This can be encoded in the constraint by introducing the value 'unfooted' for the feature FOOT, and requiring that every syllable which precedes the syllable marked as FOOT:head must have the specification FOOT:unfooted. 'Unfooted' is being used here in place of a null feature value, although neither of these feature structures would actually be required in the expression of this constraint in metrical theory. In phonological theory it is often argued that constraints should not be able to refer to the absence of structure, or equivalently, null feature values.

3.3.1   Overgeneration of Stress

The data in (11) demonstrate that a stress assigned by the cyclic Assign Prominence principle is not realized when it immediately precedes a stressed syllable in a higher ranked domain.

(11)	a.	[[kwéntú] si]	kwentúsi	'to speak to'
	b.	[[mÁypén] ña]	maypénña	'hotter'
	c.	[[mantíká] ña]	mantikáña	'fatter'
	d.	[[mí [mantíká] ña]]	mìmantikáña	'more abounding in fat'
	e.	[mí [bátku]]	míbàtku	'abounding in ships'
	f.	[mí [bátkón] ña]	mìbatkónña	'more abounding in ships'
	g.	[mí [bóti]]	míbòti	'abounding in boats'
	h.	[mí [bótín] ña]	mìbotínña	'more abounding in boats'

Since cyclic Assign Prominence overgenerates stresses, an additional constraint is required. One might try to revise Assign Prominence itself, so that a stress is licensed in a cyclic domain *only if* it does not precede a stressed syllable in a higher ranking domain. The problem with this solution is that it is not strictly non-derivational. In order for the revised principle to work, the stress on the outer cyclic domain must be present in order to determine whether stress will be licensed on the inner cyclic domain. The declarative analysis adopts the hypothesis that all domains are analyzed simultaneously, which means that there is only a single string which is the input to phonological analysis. The revised Assign Prominence principle requires in essence that there be an intermediate representation, which follows the assignment of stress on the outer cycle, and which serves as the input to stress assignment on the inner cycle. In fact, there will be *n* such intermediate representations for a word with *n+1* cyclic domains.

Alternatively, one can view the destressing illustrated in (11) as a function of stress assignment. Cyclic Assign Prominence designates a syllable as a stress peak, and immediately preceding the peak there must typically be a stress trough. This phenomenon is common to the stress systems of many languages and reflects the rhythmic nature of stress. In the Chamorro data, the only time the trough-peak pattern is not observed is when the syllable preceding a stress peak bears a lexical stress, as in the case of stressed prefixes. The construction of a stress trough can be achieved by an additional principle.[15]

---

[15]As stated here, Trough must be evaluated after cyclic stress parsing, since it refers to the presence of a stressed syllable. This type of dependency between phonological principles must be accommodated in the declarative analysis, and arises in many other situations. For example, stress is assigned to syllables, and therefore the stress assigning principles must apply after the principles which parse a string into syllables. We assume

(12)   **Trough:**   The syllable preceding a stressed syllable
                     is a stress trough (unstressed).

σ   σ   ⟶   σ   σ
[STRESS:stressed]   [STRESS:unstressed]   [STRESS:stressed]

Applying Trough and cyclic Assign Prominence to each cyclic domain
leads to an immediate problem. In forms like *mantiká-ña*, Assign Prominence tries to stress the syllable *ti*, which Trough designates as unstressed.
As shown in (13), the conflict arises between Assign Prominence applying
in the inner cyclic domain, and Trough applying in the outer cyclic domain,
and it is Trough which wins. (In (13) and subsequent examples, a stress
trough is marked over a vowel as: *v̆.*)

(13)   inner-cycle   [măntíka]
       outer-cycle   [mantĭkáña]
       surface   ?? măntĭkáña, măntíkáña

Another conflict arises in words with lexically stressed prefixes, such
as *mí-bàtku*. Trough tries to make the prefix syllable unstressed, since it
precedes the stressed syllable from the inner cycle; yet the prefix syllable
bears the primary stress, as determined by Primary as it applies to the
prefixed word. In this case, Primary wins over Trough, and the prefix
surfaces with primary stress.

The conflict between independent stress principles observed here is a
direct consequence of the non-derivational analysis, and does not arise in a
standard derivational analysis of Chamorro. In a derivational analysis, it is
a simple task to assign each cyclic stress, promote the highest cyclic stress
to main stress, and then destress other syllables in trough positions. In
contrast, in a non-derivational account, if a syllable surfaces without stress,
it is because stress is simply never licensed on that syllable.[16] Thus, the
challenge is to come up with a non-derivational analysis that never assigns
stress to the "destressed" syllables illustrated by the examples in (11).

One solution to the problem of the conflicting stress principles is to allow
the cyclic Assign Prominence, Primary and Trough principles to operate

---

here that if a phonological principle makes reference to some type of structure, that
structure must be built before the principle can apply. A very similar proposal has
been made for the ordering of default rules in Underspecification phonology (cf. the
Redundancy Rule Ordering Constraint in Archangeli 1984).

[16]Monotonicity is considered an important feature of the declarative framework, and
prevents any destructive phonological operations. It is closely related to the claim that
there are no intermediate levels in phonological derivation.

independently, and specify the result of conflict when it arises. Thus, it is always the case that when Assign Prominence conflicts with Trough, as in the analysis of *mantiká-ña* in (13), it is Trough which wins. By imposing a disjunctive ranking on the independent principles, we can establish that, for example, Trough will apply to the exclusion of cyclic Assign Prominence, if the two principles yield different and incompatible values for some portion of the phonological string.

3.3.2   Non-cyclic secondary stress

The strategy of establishing a ranking for the stress principles which come into conflict resolves another problem in the analysis of Chamorro. Chung states that the initial syllable of a word receives a secondary stress when it precedes a stressless syllable. Some examples appear in (14).

(14)   pùtamunéda   'wallet'
       èspiyósña   'his mirror'
       àtmaygósu   'vegetable sp.'
       kìmasón   'to burn'

The secondary stresses in (14) do not derive from a primary stress on an inner cycle. These secondary stresses can be generated by a constraint which directly places stress prominence on the initial syllable of the word domain, as in (15). [17]

(15)   **Secondary:**   Stress the initial syllable of a word.

$$[_{\text{Word}}\sigma \quad \longrightarrow \quad \sigma$$
$$[\text{STRESS:stressed}]$$

The Secondary principle comes into immediate conflict with Trough, when the second syllable in a word is assigned stress. For example, in the analysis of *măntíka*, Cyclic Assign Prominence assigns stress to the penult syllable in the stem cycle domain. On the basis of the penult stress, Trough requires the initial syllable to be stressless. Yet, Secondary assigns a stress to the initial syllable. The surface form shows that once again Trough wins, suggesting that Trough is ranked above both the Assign Prominence and Secondary stress principles. The word *ĭnnèŋuluʔ-níha* (5b) provides

---

[17]Halle and Vergnaud (1987) account for the secondary stresses in (14) by the left-to-right construction of left-headed binary feet. They predict that in words where more than three unstressed syllables precede the main stress, every odd-numbered syllable will receive a secondary stress. Unfortunately, none of the words cited by Chung (1983) are long enough to test this prediction. The analysis proposed here does not posit metrical structure to place secondary stress, but it is consistent with an alternative analysis in which a left-headed metrical foot is positioned at the left edge of a word.

another example where Secondary fails to stress an initial syllable in the presence of a stress on the second syllable. Moreover, in this example, the stress on the second syllable is not the primary stress, showing that Trough must be stated generally—to realize a syllable as stressless if it precedes *any* stressed syllable.[18]

3.4 Gemination

The analysis of Chamorro presented above is complicated by some additional facts concerning stress, "destressing," and gemination. The interaction of these processes seems to require extrinsic rule or principle ordering. In this section we demonstrate that extrinsic ordering can be avoided by distinguishing between metrical structure, stress, and syllable structure in the phonological representation, and making all structure internal to a word visible to the phonological system.

The data in (16) illustrate a process of gemination wherein a syllable with main stress is geminated if it follows a heavy stressed syllable. The words in (16a,b) show gemination of the initial consonant of the suffixes *-mu* '2 possessive' and *-ña* 'more', while the form in (16c), with no heavy syllable, shows no gemination of the suffix initial consonant. (The geminated consonant is in boldface.)

(16)a. déddigu   'heel'
         dèddigómmu   'your heel'

   b. dáŋkulu   'big'
        dàŋkulónña   'bigger'

   c. hígadu   'liver'
        hìgadúña   'his liver'

Gemination ensures a kind of metrical parallelism. If a metrically prominent, stressed syllable in a word is heavy, then a following stressed syllable will also be heavy, with Gemination acting as the mechanism Chamorro uses to create a heavy syllable. Note that Gemination operates strictly left-to-right, and not cyclically, since a heavy stressed syllable in the stem does not trigger Gemination of a prefix stressed syllable in a word like *mí-bàtku* 'abounding in ships'.[19] These data require adding to the grammar a

---

[18]Recall from the discussion above that Trough will not apply to an initial syllable that is an accented prefix. The accented prefixes have inherent prominence, represented here with lexically specified metrical structure. The stress assigning principles observe monotonicity in only being able to add structure, not delete it.

[19]There are apparently no lexically stressed prefixes that consist of a closed syllable, so we cannot determine the effect a heavy stressed prefix would have on the weight of a stressed stem syllable.

Gemination principle, formulated below.[20]

(17) **Gemination:** (preliminary) A syllable with primary stress is
is strengthened (by gemination) if it follows
a heavy stressed syllable.

$$
\left[
\begin{array}{c}
\sigma_i \\
\text{SYLL:}\mu\mu \\
\text{STRESS:stressed}
\end{array}
\right]
\qquad
\begin{array}{c}
\sigma_j \\
\text{[STRESS:primary]}
\end{array}
\qquad \longrightarrow \qquad
\begin{array}{cc}
\sigma_i & \sigma_j \\
& \text{[SYLL:}\mu\mu]
\end{array}
$$

Cond: $i <^* j$

Gemination can account for the data in (16), but fails in forms like *mìbatkónña*, where Gemination applies even though the heavy syllable that triggers Gemination surfaces with no stress, by Trough. The structure of this word is repeated here from (11f), with all the stresses licensed by cyclic Assign Prominence indicated:

(18) [mí [bátkón] ña]   mìbatkónña   'more abounding in ships'

As discussed above, cyclic Assign Prominence overgenerates stress, but is constrained by Trough, which prevents stress from being assigned to the syllable preceding the primary stress in (18). Since the suffix initial consonant is geminated in the surface form, the syllable *bat* must be functioning as a gemination trigger, and therefore must in some way count as stressed.[21] Yet by the monotonicity of the non-derivational analysis, *bat* must *not* be stressed since it does not bear stress on the surface. Unlike the problems considered in the previous section, the problem here cannot be solved by appealing to a ranking of the relevant principles. In particular, a disjunctive ranking where Gemination wins over Trough will not give the correct surface form, since Trough obviously does apply.

In a derivational analysis which generates cyclic stresses, we might say that Gemination is ordered before Destressing. In terms of the present analysis, that solution would imply ordering the Gemination and Trough principles, and therefore is not available. However, there is an alternative solution consistent with the non-derivational hypothesis that all principles

---

[20]More technically, the gemination procedure makes the stressed syllable heavy by the addition of an extra mora to that syllable. The mora is then filled by spreading from the following consonant, accomplished by an independent principle of bare mora realization. Note that $<$ is the symbol used for the immediate precedence relation, and $<^*$ is the transitive closure of that relation, or simply precedence.

[21]The form *sitbesá-ña* 'beer' shows that not every heavy syllable triggers gemination. The heavy syllable must be stressed on an inner cycle.

of the phonology apply simultaneously. The key to the solution lies in recognizing the distinction between the metrical structure that identifies certain syllables as prominent (in this case the penultimate syllable in each domain), and the principles which assign stress to prominent syllables. Although Trough fails to license a stress on the syllable *bat* in *mibatkónña*, it is nonetheless true that *bat* is picked out as a prominent syllable by the cyclic Parse principle. This suggests that Gemination is sensitive not to the presence of stress on a heavy syllable, but rather to the metrical prominence of a heavy syllable, reflected in the foot structure. Although the same property of metrical prominence causes cyclic Assign Prominence to license a stress on the syllable *bat*, that stress is not realized due to the effects of the more highly ranked Trough. As long as we distinguish between the presence of a stress feature and the metrical structure which, in part, licenses that structure, the problem of the stressless gemination trigger in Chamorro can be resolved. The revised Gemination principle is given in (19).

(19)   **Gemination:**   (revised) A syllable with primary stress is
                            strengthened (by gemination) if it follows
                            a heavy syllable that is metrically
                            prominent (the head of a foot).

$$
\begin{bmatrix} \sigma_i \\ \text{SYLL:}\mu\mu \\ \text{FOOT:head} \end{bmatrix} \quad \begin{matrix} \sigma_j \\ [\text{STRESS:primary}] \end{matrix} \quad \longrightarrow \quad \sigma_i \quad \begin{matrix} \sigma_j \\ [\text{SYLL:}\mu\mu] \end{matrix}
$$

Cond: $i <^* j$

This solution extends nicely to account for yet another wrinkle in the facts concerning Gemination. As illustrated by the forms in (20), another constraint of Chamorro causes an underlying geminate consonant to surface with no gemination if it precedes the syllable with primary stress.

(20) a.   [[lébblú] ña]   leblónña   'his book'
     b.   [[maléffá] mu]   málefámmu   'your forgetting'

Notably, the "degeminated" consonants in the stem contribute weight to the preceding stem syllable, qualifying it as a trigger for gemination of the suffix-initial consonant. It looks as though the degemination observed in (20) must apply after evaluation of Gemination, in counter-bleeding order. However, the ordering problem does not arise as long as we view Degemination as a licensing principle affecting moraic structure, and not as a rule of consonant deletion.[22] Following Hayes (1989), we may analyze a geminate consonant as being underlyingly moraic. The sequence /alla/ is derived by the obligatory formation of an onset by feature-sharing with the moraic /l/.

(21)

In this approach, degemination involves the loss of a mora. The proposal for Chamorro is that degemination involves a licensing condition which prevents the second mora of a heavy syllable from being realized, although it is present in the phonological representation. The result relies crucially on the distinction between the *phonological representation*, in which the geminate in the stem contributes weight to the stem stressed syllable, and the *phonetic interpretation* of that syllable as light, taking into account the representation together with the licensing conditions.[23] The constraint in (22) defines the licensing condition for heavy syllables which results in degemination.

(22) **Degemination:**   A syllable immediately preceding the syllable with primary stress licenses only one mora.

$$\sigma_i \qquad \sigma_j \qquad \longrightarrow \qquad \sigma_i \qquad \sigma_j$$
$$\text{[SYLL:}\mu\mu] \quad \text{[STRESS:primary]} \qquad \text{[STRESS:}(\mu)\mu]$$

Cond: $i < j$

In the examples in (20), Degemination prevents the underlying geminate from being realized, since its mora is not licensed. Thus, Degemination overrides the lexical representation of the root, which specifies the stem consonant as moraic. Treating Degemination as a licensing principle allows us to leave unaltered the statement of Gemination in (19). Degemination does not delete the mora which defines the heavy syllable in the stem, and so that syllable can still be identified as heavy for Gemination. The representation of *malefámmu* in (23) shows the effects of Gemination and Degemination

---

[22]It is possible that Degemination is not in fact an independent principle, but is a component of Trough. Both require that the syllable preceding a stressed syllable be metrically weak: stressless, and in the case of geminates, light.
[23]Coleman (1991) proposes a model-theoretic declarative phonology based on this distinction.

on the lexical representation, shown on the left with the two cyclic stress feet indicated. (Inserted structure is indicated in boldface, and the mora which fails to be licensed is enclosed in parentheses.)

(23)

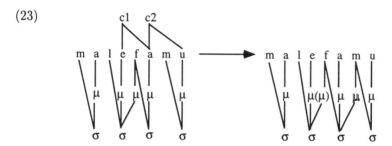

Degemination predicts that all CVC syllables preceding primary stress will undergo mora loss, and surface as light. Yet, there is no discernible effect from this principle on words like *mibatkónña*. The stem syllable *bat* must be recognized as heavy, since it triggers gemination of the consonant in the suffix *ña*. What happens to the final consonant in *bat* when it loses a mora? One solution would be to revise Degemination so that it blocks the licensing of a moraic consonant preceding primary stress **only** when the consonant is a geminate, that is, when it is multiply linked to the onset of the stressed syllable. This analysis would leave the bimoraic syllable *bat* intact. Another solution would be to reduce *bat* to a monomoraic syllable, but allow the final consonant to associate to the mora of the vowel, as in (24). Either approach is consistent with the data, and there is no additional evidence to bear on the real surface weight of the syllable preceding primary stress.

(24)

$$
\begin{array}{c}
\text{b} \quad \text{a} \quad \text{t} \\
\diagdown\;\diagdown\!\diagup \\
\mid \quad \mu \\
\mid \\
\sigma
\end{array}
$$

3.5 Summary

Restated here are the six principles involved in the analysis of Chamorro stress presented above, and the disjunctive ranking necessary to resolve conflicts.

Parse: Parse the penult as the head of a foot, in each cyclic domain.

Assign Prominence: Assign stress prominence to the head of the leftmost foot, in each cyclic domain.

Primary: Mark the stress in the highest cycle as primary.

Trough: Mark as stressless a syllable preceding stress.

Secondary: Assign stress to the initial syllable in the word.

Gemination: Geminate a consonant following a primary stress to make a primary stressed syllable heavy.

Degemination: Weaken a syllable preceding primary stress, by degemination (via licensing condition).

Ranking: Primary > Trough, Trough > Assign Prominence, Trough > Secondary

4 English Stress

English stress has certain similarities to the Chamorro stress system, and, like Chamorro, is amenable to a non-derivational analysis based on independently applied principles of stress assignment. As in Chamorro, the declarative analysis gives rise to conflicts when two principles try to assign different values to a single feature in the phonological representation. Our analysis of English stress is in essence a declarative interpretation of the analysis proposed by Halle and Kenstowicz (1991), influenced by the findings of Hammond (1989). Most of the data presented below is drawn from those sources.[24]

The main features of English stress can be summarized as follows:

- Stress is assigned to the penult in each cyclic domain (reflecting a binary, left-headed foot parsed at the right edge).[25]

- Secondary stress is licensed on every odd syllable from the left (reflecting a binary, left-headed foot parsed at left edge).

- The outermost cyclic domain licenses primary stress.

- A syllable preceding a stressed syllable is stressless.

---

[24]See also the lengthy treatment of English stress in Halle and Vergnaud (1987).

[25]Stress is licensed on the antepenult when the domain final syllable is lexically specified as extrametrical, as in nouns and suffixed adjectives.

These features can be analyzed by adopting in large part the principles from the analysis of Chamorro: Parse, Assign Prominence, Primary, and Trough. The secondary stress principle will have to be a little different for English, since secondary stress appears on alternating syllables from the left edge of the word, and not just on the initial syllable. To correctly place secondary stress in English requires an independent Parse principle that will parse an initial string of syllables into left-headed binary feet, up until the primary stress foot. There is yet another, more significant difference between Chamorro and English: stress in English is quantity sensitive. Thus, primary stress on nouns falls on the antepenult only when the penult is light, as in *Cánada, alúminum*, and otherwise falls on the heavy penult, as in *agénda, cerébrum*. Furthermore, as demonstrated by Hammond (1989), secondary stress is also quantity sensitive, as seen in the mono-morphemic words in (25). In a sequence of three light pre-tonic syllables LLL, the first receives secondary stress, whereas in a pre-tonic sequence of LHL or HHL, secondary stress is assigned to the heavy syllable(s).[26] In light of these data, the parsed feet that are assigned stress by Assign Prominence and Secondary must be quantity-sensitive.

(25)   LLL: Tàtamagoúchi   LLL: Wìnnepesáukee
        LHL: Monòngehéla   HHL: Tìcònderóga

The Secondary stress and Trough principles conflict in words with an odd number of light pretonic syllables. Trough prevails in this case, as the light syllable preceding primary stress always surfaces as stressless, as in *Tatamăgóuchi*. Imposing a ranking of Trough > Secondary captures this fact, but in this case an alternative analysis is possible. In a word with three pretonic syllables, the third syllable forms a degenerate foot, and the Secondary stress principle can be formulated so as not to stress a degenerate foot.[27]

In contrast to the pattern in (25), the rightmost pretonic syllable can optionally bear a non-primary stress if it is heavy, as in *sèrèndípity, Trànsỳl vánia*, and *pàraphèrnália*.[28] The quantity-sensitive nature of primary and secondary stress can be captured by adding a principle of Heavy Syllable

---

[26]Halle and Kenstowicz note that on the pretonic HHL sequence in *Ticonderoga*, one of the two non-primary stresses may be stronger, introducing a three-way contrast in surface stress. They account for this by parsing the non-primary stresses into a foot which freely alternates as right- or left-headed.

[27]Alternately, following Hayes (1991), we might disallow the construction of degenerate feet altogether (but cf. Kenstowicz (1994) for arguments challenging that position).

[28]In the midwestern American dialect of the author, the pretonic syllable may contain an unreduced vowel, in which case it is realized with tertiary stress. The alternate pronunciation, with a reduced and stressless pretonic vowel is also possible.

stress, as in (26), and reformulating Secondary so that foot construction respects (26). The optional stress on heavy syllables before primary stress is accounted for by disjunctive ranking of Trough and Heavy Syllable, vacillating between Trough > Heavy Syllable and Heavy Syllable > Trough, according to dialect.

(26) **Heavy Syllable:**   A heavy syllable must be the head of a stress foot.

$$\sigma \quad \longrightarrow \quad \sigma$$
$$[\text{SYLL}:\mu\mu] \qquad\qquad [\text{FOOT:head}]$$

The analysis of derived words follows the same set of principles used for monomorphemic words (Parse, Assign Prominence, Primary, Secondary, Trough, and Heavy Syllable), but in derived words the cyclic Assign Prominence licenses a stress in each cyclic domain. An inner cycle stress may surface as secondary stress, as in the following examples:

(27) clássify   clàssificátion
      oríginal   orìginálity
      sensátional   sensàtionálity
      arístocrat   arìstocrátic
      accéssible   accèssibílity
      syllábify   syllàbificátion
      mánifest   mànifestátion

The inner cycle stress is not realized if it is assigned to a light syllable preceding the primary stress, as shown in (28a), and is optionally realized if it is assigned to a heavy syllable preceding primary stress, as in (28b).

(28)a.   cívil   cĭvílity
         cólumn   cŏlúmnal
         átom   ătómic

    b.   phóneme   phònémic / phŏnémic
         tótal   tòtálity / tŏtálity
         recomménd   rècommèndátion / rècommĕndátion
         gráde   gràdátion / grădátion
         móral   mòrálity / mŏrálity

The suffixed forms in (28a) show that Trough prevails over both Assign Prominence and Secondary. Trough requires a stressless initial syllable preceding primary stress, while Assign Prominence and Secondary license a non-primary stress on the initial syllable. Although the conflict between Trough and Secondary may be implicitly resolved (as suggested above), an explicit ranking is required to suppress the licensing of the inner cyclic stress, thus Trough > Assign Prominence, as in Chamorro. In contrast, the suffixed forms in (28b) show that Trough does not necessarily prevail when Assign Prominence, Secondary, and Heavy Syllable all license stress on the pretonic syllable. Thus, as in mono-morphemic words like *serendipity*, a heavy syllable preceding primary stress may optionally bear a non-primary stress. The disjunctive ranking of Trough > Heavy Syllable freely alternating with Heavy Syllable > Trough achieves the correct results.

4.1 Additive Effects of Stress Licensing Conflicts

There is an interesting distinction in the realization of non-primary stress on heavy syllables in the midwestern American dialect taken as the source for the data in (28). For the words in (28b), the normal citation form is the one where the initial heavy syllable is realized with a non-reduced vowel bearing secondary stress. The initial syllable is stressless as an option only in fast speech. However, the situation seems to be different in words in which the syllable preceding primary stress is heavy, but not initial, as in the following examples.

(29)   restóre   rèstŏrátion
       condénse   cònděnsátion
       molést   mòlěstátion
       dispóse   dìspŏsítion

In these words, the normal citation form has a reduced and stressless vowel (marked in boldface) preceding the primary stressed syllable, even though the reduced vowel is in a heavy syllable. The difference between (29) and (28b) seems to be in the position of the pretonic syllable. In (28b), the pretonic syllable is initial, a position which is always targeted for secondary stress, whereas in (29), the pretonic syllable is second from the left, a position which receives secondary stress only if it is a heavy syllable.[29] The contrast between these examples may reflect an additive effect of the principles that license stress. Thus, in (28b), Secondary, Assign Prominence, and Heavy Syllable all license stress on the pretonic initial syllable, whereas in (29) only Heavy Syllable and Assign Prominence license stress on the pretonic second syllable. Trough is able to overcome the Heavy Syllable and cyclic Assign Prominence principles licensing stress in (29), providing the

---

[29]Halle and Kenstowicz (1991) note that for the parametric algorithm for learning stress proposed by Dresher and Kaye (1990), the presence of a secondary stress on the initial syllable provides an essential cue for a left-to-right parse.

preferred citation form, but perhaps cannot so easily overcome the additive effects of Heavy Syllable, Assign Prominence, *and* Secondary in (28b). In order to account for the additive effect noted here, it is important to state the ranking of the principles in such a way that the ranking $P_i > P_j$ and $P_i > P_k$ does not imply that $P_i > (P_j \ and \ P_k)$.

5 Conclusion

The preceding sections demonstrate that the distribution of surface stresses in Chamorro and English can be accounted for within a non-derivational, constraint-based approach to phonology. The cyclicity of these stress systems results from (i) the presence of intra-word cyclic domains for the construction of the metrical feet used to identify stressed syllables, and (ii) a ranking of cyclic domains that assigns the primary stress to the highest ranking domain. The non-derivational account of cyclicity provides a more constrained grammar, since there is no possibility of feeding or bleeding interaction between the analyses of cyclic domains.

The simultaneous analysis of cyclic domains is seen to overgenerate stresses and it incorrectly predicts stress clash when the stressed syllables in adjacent cyclic domains are string adjacent. To prevent this overgeneration, the present analysis proposes imposing a disjunctive ranking on stress licensing principles to the effect that a syllable is required to be stressless if it precedes a stressed syllable, even if the first syllable is predicted to bear stress on a lower cycle. The disjunctive ranking has the effect that a lower-ranking constraint can be violated in favor of the satisfaction of a higher ranking constraint. The English data suggest that the phonology may in fact be sensitive to the number of constraints that are violated due to disjunctive ranking—one violation is tolerated, but two are less so—reflected in the optional realization of tertiary stress on a syllable preceding primary stress.

Structured phonological representations play a crucial role in the analysis of the English and Chamorro data seen here. Equally important is the distinction between the phonological representation and its phonetic interpretation. Thus, in Chamorro a syllable containing two moras may be identified as heavy in phonological representation, even though it is realized as light (via "degemination") due to a licensing condition which allows only one mora to be realized. The proposed analysis departs from other frameworks for declarative phonology by allowing licensing conditions to account for a limited degree of apparent deletion.

It is argued above that the principle of cyclic dominance, which allows the outermost cycle to license the strongest stress, derives from a stipulative ranking of cyclic domains. This analysis predicts that other languages may pose alternative rankings which give prominence to a non-final morphological cycle. Preliminary investigation suggests that this flexibility is required. Cole and Coleman (1992) present data from several unrelated languages that challenge the standard derivational view of cyclic phonology. These languages require the presence of intra-word domains for the application of stress and harmony rules, where the domains do not correspond to morphological constituents, although they are defined by morpheme boundaries— similar to the well-known cases of bracketing paradoxes. It is argued that the domain-based approach to cyclicity, as exemplified here, extends naturally to account for such cases with no extra machinery. When the so-called cyclic domains of phonology no longer correspond to the morphological cycles, then cyclic dominance cannot be said to follow from the morphological structure, and must simply be stipulated. And in fact a variety of patterns emerge in the languages discussed by Cole and Coleman. It remains for future research to identify principles that may govern the construction of morphologically based phonological domains, and in particular to determine whether the unmarked case is to preserve isomorphism between the morphological and phonological domains, as in English and Chamorro.

References

Archangeli, D. 1984. *Underspecification in Yawelmani phonology.* Ph.D. dissertation, Massachusetts Institute of Technology.

Bird, S. 1991. *Constraint-based phonology.* Ph.D. dissertation, Edinburgh University.

Chomsky, N. and M. Halle. 1968. *Sound pattern of English.* New York: Academic Press.

Chung, S. 1983. Trans-derivational constraints in Chamorro phonology. *Language* 59:1.35–66.

Cole, J. S. 1990. Arguing for the cycle: A critical review. *Proceedings of the Formal Linguistics Society of Mid-America.* 1:55–81.

Cole, J. S. and J. S. Coleman. 1992. No need for cyclicity in generative phonology. *Proceedings of the Chicago Linguistic Society* 28.

Coleman, J. S. 1991. *Phonological representations — their names, forms and powers.* D.Phil. thesis, Department of Language and Linguistic Science, University of York.

Dresher, E. and J. Kaye. 1990. A computational learning model for metrical phonology. *Cognition* 34:2.137–195.

Halle, M. and M. Kenstowicz. 1991. The free element condition and cyclic versus non-cyclic stress. *Linguistic Inquiry* 22:3.477–502.

Halle, M. and J.-R. Vergnaud. 1987. *An essay on stress.* Cambridge, MA: MIT Press.

Hammond, M. 1989. Cyclic secondary stress and accent in English. *Proceedings of the West Coast Conference on Formal Linguistics* 8:139–153.

Hayes, B. 1989. Compensatory lengthening in moraic phonology. *Linguistic Inquiry* 20:253–307.

Hayes, B. 1994. *Metrical stress theory: Principles and case studies.* Chicago: University of Chicago Press.

Johnson, C. D. 1972. *Formal aspects of phonological description.* The Hague: Mouton.

Kenstowicz, M. 1994. On metrical constituents: Unbalanced trochees and degenerate feet. In J. Cole and C. Kisseberth (eds.), *Perspectives in Phonology,* pp. 113-132. Stanford: CSLI

Kenstowicz, M. and C. Kisseberth. 1979. *Generative phonology.* New York: Academic Press.

Prince, A. and P. Smolensky. 1993. *Optimality Theory.* Manuscript, Rutgers University and University of Colorado.

Scobbie, J. 1991. *Attribute Value Phonology.* Ph.D. dissertation, Edinburgh University.

Topping, D. and B. Dungca. 1973. *Chamorro reference Grammar.* Honolulu: University of Hawaii Press.

Touretzky, D. and D. Wheeler. 1990. A computational basis for phonology. In D. S. Touretzky (ed.), *Advances in neural information processing systems 2.* San Mateo, CA: Morgan Kaufmann.

Wheeler, D. and D. Touretzky. 1991. From syllables to stress: A cognitively plausible model. In K. Deaton, M. Noske, and M. Aiolkowski (eds.), *Chicago Linguistics Society 26-II: Papers from the parasession on the syllable in phonetics and phonology.* Chicago: Chicago Linguistic Society.

Pitch Accent Prediction from Text Analysis

Julia Hirschberg and Richard Sproat

AT&T Bell Laboratories

1 Introduction

How speakers decide what to emphasize and de-emphasize in natural speech, has long been the subject of scholarly debate. In natural speech, words that appear more intonationally prominent than others are said to bear *pitch accents*. While, in English, each word has a characteristic (lexical) stress pattern, not every word is accented. Although pitch accent is a perceptual phenomenon, words which hearers typically identify as accented tend to differ from their *deaccented* versions (those not bearing pitch accents) in pitch, duration, amplitude, and spectral characteristics. Accented words are usually identifiable in the *fundamental frequency contour* (f0) as local maxima or minima, aligned with the word's stressed syllable; their duration and amplitude tend to be greater than their deaccented counterparts. The vowel in the stressed syllable of a deaccented word is often reduced from the full vowel of the accented version. Words that are deaccented may or may not be *cliticized*. That is, they may lack adjacent word boundaries as well as exhibiting vowel reduction.

While formerly it was believed that syntactic information determines speakers' accent decisions, it is now recognized that many kinds of information contribute (Bolinger 1972). Experimental studies – for example, Brown 1983, Terken and Nooteboom 1987 – have shown that speakers associate accent with a word's *given/new status*, that is, whether the item represents 'old' information, which a speaker is entitled to believe is shared with a hearer, or 'new' information in a discourse (Prince 1981). And analyses of large corpora of recorded speech – for example, Altenberg 1987 – provide evidence that part-of-speech information or constituent structure alone are insufficient for modeling pitch accent assignment in natural speech. However, such findings have yet to be reflected in algorithms for accent assignment in speech synthesis. Commonly, speech synthesizers use only a simple distinction between function words (for example, prepositions, pronouns) and content words (for example, nouns, verbs) – possibly with minimal information about surface position – to assign pitch accent. Such approaches tend to accent too many words in synthesis of longer stretches of text; in isolated sentences, they predict only about 75-80% 'acceptable' accent assignment. More successful accent assignment is possible in 'message-to-speech' systems, which synthesize speech from an abstract representation of the message to be conveyed (Young and Fallside 1979, Danlos et al. 1986,

Davis and Hirschberg 1988). But the problem of improving accent assignment, together with other prosodic features, for unrestricted text, remains to be resolved for most text-to-speech applications.

This paper presents work incorporating various types of *information status*, including a given/new distinction, limited information on *focus*, *topic*, and *contrast*, more sophisticated part-of-speech distinctions, and prediction of citation-form stress assignment in premodified nominals, to assign pitch accent for unrestricted text. The algorithm described has been trained on prosodically labeled corpora of read speech. This algorithm is currently implemented in the Bell Laboratories Text-to-Speech System (*TTS*) (Olive and Liberman 1985, Sproat et al. 1992). It is also being used to hypothesize accentuation information for large corpora of prosodically unlabeled speech so that accent can be used as a variable in statistical analysis, and to provide a prosodic hypothesis used to speed prosodic labeling of other speech corpora.

2   Testing and Training Corpus

The corpus originally used for training and testing the procedures that will be described below was a portion of the FM Radio Newscasting Database, a series of multi-speaker studio recordings of newscasts and other material provided by National Public Radio Station WBUR in association with Boston University, which is currently being collected by SRI International (Patti Price), Boston University (Mari Ostendorf), and MIT (Stefanie Shattuck-Hufnagel). (The database itself is eventually intended to comprise several hours of prosodically labeled speech.) The prosodic labeling used for the current analysis was done at Bell Laboratories. Three news stories were used in this sample, representing approximately 15 minutes of speech, produced by a total of thirteen speakers. An orthographic transcription of a sample paragraph is presented below (where '(.hhh)' indicates 'audible breath'.)

> Wanted. Chief Justice of the Massachusetts Supreme Court. In April the SJC's current leader Edward Hennessy (.hhh) reaches the mandatory retirement age of seventy and a successor is expected to be named in March. (.hhh) It may be the most important appointment Governor Michael Dukakis makes during the remainder of his administration and one of the toughest. (.hhh)....

While, again, these stories appear typical of radio speech, the inclusion of 'sound bites' from interviewed speakers makes them somewhat less useful as exemplars of coherent read text. There are some disfluencies in the recordings.

Each story was labeled by hand for presence or absence of pitch accent and, if present, type of pitch accent—see Pierrehumbert 1980; deaccented items were marked as cliticized or not. In addition, intonational phrasing was annotated, although this information was not used in the current study. Labeling was done using *WAVES* speech analysis software (Talkin 1989), from waveforms and f0 contours.

3   Accent Assignment from Text Analysis

TTS accent assignments are based upon more sophisticated use of syntactic information as well as higher-level discourse information. TTS's text analysis component uses part-of-speech information from the stochastic part-of-speech tagger described in Church 1988. Some errors in accent prediction occur because an item's part-of-speech assignment is ambiguous between function and content word, such as preposition vs. verbal preposition/particle (for example, *John left IN the limo* vs. *John left IN the typo*) or conjunction vs. discourse marker (for example, *They left after lunch AND landed in France in time for dinner.* vs. *They left after lunch. AND, they landed in France in time for dinner.*) However, not all function words that are correctly classified are in fact deaccented, as illustrated by a sample paragraph from the FM Radio Newscasting Database (where accented words are represented in upper-case and deaccented in lower-case).

(1)   a.   In NINETEEN SEVENTY-SIX, DEMOCRATIC GOVERNOR
            MICHAEL DUKAKIS FULFILLED a CAMPAIGN promise to
            DE-POLITICIZE JUDICIAL APPOINTMENTS.

      b.   He NAMED REPUBLICAN Edward HENNESSY, to HEAD
            the STATE SUPREME JUDICIAL COURT.

      c.   For HENNESSY, it was ANOTHER STEP along a
            DISTINGUISHED CAREER THAT BEGAN as a TRIAL
            LAWYER, and LED to an APPOINTMENT AS ASSOCIATE
            Supreme Court Justice in nineteen seventy-ONE.

      d.   THAT YEAR THOMAS MAFFY, NOW PRESIDENT of the
            MASSACHUSETTS BAR Association, was HENNESSY'S
            LAW clerk.

The relative pronoun *THAT* in (1c), the determiner *THAT* (1d), and the preposition *AS* (1c) are all accented. A function-content distinction operating even on correctly tagged data will successfully predict 85% of pitch accents in the FM Radio sample presented above. This relatively high success rate results in part from the tendency of news readers to accent content words at the end of phrases, even where other speakers normally would not (Bolinger 1989), as exemplified in (1c) above, where *LAWYER* is accented, despite its presence in the standardly left-stressed compound *trial lawyer*. And overall, the function-content distinction predicts 80% of accent decisions correctly in the 5-minute text from which this sample was taken.

If function words are not always deaccented, content words are not always accented. Consider, for example, *CAMPAIGN promise* in (1a), and *MASSACHUSETTS BAR Association* and *LAW clerk* in (1d). These *complex nominals* are sequences of nouns whose semantico-syntactic structure maps to differences in stress assignment. Some, like *CAMPAIGN promise* are stressed on the left, with consequent deaccenting of the right member of the nominal. Others, like *NINETEEN SEVENTY-SIX* and *STATE SUPREME JUDICIAL COURT* (1a), are stressed on the right. Still others, like *judicial appointments* (1a), may be stressed either on the right or left. TTS gets citation-form stress assignment for complex and other *premodified nominals* from the NP parser described in some detail in the next section (and see also, Sproat 1990, Sproat 1994).

However, while there are regularities in the citation form of stress assignment for such phrases, these explain only part of the accenting of premodified nominals. Note, for example, that while *NINETEEN SEVENTY-SIX* (1a) is entirely accented, the subsequent *nineteen seventy-ONE* in (1c) exhibits a different pattern; and only *ASSOCIATE* is accented in the nominal *ASSOCIATE Supreme Court Justice* in (1c), although in citation form, all components would be accented. We can explain this behavior in terms of the sensitivity of accent decisions to context. In simple terms, *nineteen seventy* and *Supreme Court Justice* are deaccented in (1c) because they represent *given* information in their context of utterance.

4   Accenting Premodified Nominals

Since the assignment of the citation form of stress assignment for premodified nominals is a fairly intricate process, we describe the methods for doing this assignment in some detail in this section. More recent work (reported in Sproat 1994) incorporates statistical methods for accent prediction in addition to the rule-based methods reported here. Let us start by defining the scope of the term *premodified nominal* for the purposes of this discussion. We shall include under this rubric, sequences of one or more adjectives (or adjective phrases) modifying a noun as in (2a) below; a head noun is preceded by some number of other nouns (2b); complex proper name (2c); constructions which involve some combination of the above, as in (2d) where the noun-noun sequence *Attorney General* is modified by the adjective *former* and the resulting construction modifies the complex proper name *Edwin Meese III*.

(2)   a.   several very large ornamental ducks
      b.   computer communications network performance analysis primer
      c.   *New York Avenue*
      d.   former Attorney General Edwin Meese III

Note that a few such constructions – for example (2b) above or certain adjective noun sequences such as *electrical engineer* – fall into the category of *complex nominals* as discussed in Levi 1978.

     Traditional linguistic description (Chomsky and Halle 1968—see also Liberman and Sproat 1991) argues that one needs to know two things in order to algorithmically assign appropriate citation-form stress to a pre-modified nominal. First, one must know the structure of the nominal in terms of a (binary branching) tree. Secondly, one must know the node labels of the tree; it is commonly assumed that compound *words* are stressed on the left, whereas *phrases* are stressed on the right.

Type	Syntactic Node Label	Stress Pattern	Example
Nominal compound	N^0	LEFT	*DOG house*
Nominal phrase	$\bar{N}$	RIGHT	*nice HOUSE*

However, both stress and structure are hard to compute in general, since the decision is often not constrained by syntactic considerations. So, knowing the parts of speech for the words in a nominal is only a partial predictor of the stress pattern; for example, N-N sequences are stressed on the left between 75% and 95% of the time depending upon the type of text (Liberman and Sproat 1991), but there are many (systematic) exceptions (*lobster RAGOUT*). And part-of-speech information can be useless in computing the structure of very long nominals; for (2b), the most plausible structure seems to be as in (3).

(3)   [[*computer* [*communications network*]] [[*performance analysis*] *primer*]]
Yet part-of-speech information only tells us that we have a sequence of nouns, which does not constrain the possible structures. Often the best structure in such cases must be picked on the basis of semantic plausibility. Since such semantic analysis is difficult, most nominal analyzers have been designed for a restricted domain, and have been built on top of a fairly complete knowledge representation for that domain (Finin 1980). Yet such nominals are common in English text—over 70,000 tokens per million words of text as estimated from the Brown Corpus (Francis and Kucera 1982),

and since in the TTS domain one cannot typically restrict the input, one would like to provide a treatment of premodified nominals which is both general and accurate.

While we cannot as yet hope to do thorough semantic and structural analyses for premodified nominals in unrestricted English text, one can usefully do fairly substantial analyses using simple and easily obtained lexical and statistical information.

4.1   A Description of NP

For each noun phrase, NP uses a CKY (context-free) recognition algorithm (see Harrison 1978, Section 12.4) to build a chart of possible constituents. The recognizer uses the following kinds of context-free rules.

- Phrase structure rules—for example, $NP \rightarrow DET + \bar{N}$. There are currently about 40 such rules.

- Context-free semantic/lexical schemata which predict the category label of the mother node. For example:

  - General schemata: a term for FURNITURE combines with a term for ROOM to form an $\bar{N}$ (that is, righthand stress—*kitchen TA-BLE*).

  - Schemata with particular head nouns: street names ending in the word *Street* are N^0 (that is, lefthand stress—*PARK Street*). Currently there are about 600 of these first two kinds of rules, with about 95% of those being specific to food terms.

  - Lists of particular nominals with information about their phrasal status—for example, *WHITE House* is an N^0 (taking lefthand stress). There are currently about 6500 entries of this kind.

In constructing the semantic rules, on-line thesauruses have proved useful.

Having built the chart, NP picks one of the set of trees defined therein by doing a top-down walk and applying the following heuristics at each node.

- Given a choice of n possible expansions of a node, prefer the expansion which is derived by semantic schemata over the expansion which is derived purely by syntactic schemata.

- *Ceteris paribus*, given a choice of n expansions of a node, pick the higher bar-level expansion (for example, pick $\bar{N}$ over N^0).

- *Ceteris paribus*, given a choice of n expansions of a node, pick the expansion which has the more right branching structure. (In English, a right branching – or flat – structure has stress close to the right edge of the phrase, and if there is little evidence, it is better to err in the direction of putting stress too far to the right than to err in the opposite direction.)

Once a tree has been built over as much of the nominal as is feasible, NP passes the tree to the phonology, where the position of the primary stress is determined, and the rhythm rule is applied. Additionally, in nominals with sufficiently long subconstituents, minor intonational phrase boundaries are inserted.

As an example of the parsing algorithm, consider the sentence *I put it on the living room table*. The part-of-speech algorithm assigns part-of-speech labels to the words in the sentence and brackets the nominal *the living room table*. NP then applies syntactic and semantic rules to the nominal. For example, NP knows that *living room* is a ROOM (and also that it is an N^0), so it places a node [N^0,ROOM] in the chart, spanning *living room*. It also knows that *table* is a kind of FURNITURE, and that a ROOM term and FURNITURE term can combine into an $\bar{N}$, so it places the node [$\bar{N}$,ROOM&FURNITURE] in the chart, spanning the string *living room table*. Finally, the determiner *the* can combine with an $\bar{N}$ to make an NP. Having put these (and other) nodes into the chart, the algorithm starts at the top of the chart, first expanding the NP node spanning the string *the living room table* (because that is the only node at that level) and then expanding the node [$\bar{N}$,ROOM&FURNITURE] (spanning *living room table*), which wins over other candidates because it is of a high bar level ($\bar{N}$ rather than N^0 – cf., the second heuristic above) and because it has a semantic annotation – cf., the first heuristic above. We therefore arrive at the correct structure, given in (4a). Phonological rules are then applied to yield the correct citation-form stress assignment, given in (4b).

(4)   a.   [$_{NP}$ *the* [[$_{\bar{N}}$ N^0 *living room*] *table*]].

       b.   *the LIVING room TABLE.*

4.2   Evaluation of NP

The most tangible improvement which NP affords in premodified nominals over the citation-form stress assignment produced by default in the TTS system is in the placement of primary stress. Other improvements, such as the correct placement of accents within the long nominal prior to the primary stress are noticeable, but are not as striking. In this discussion, therefore, we concentrate on the evaluation of the current performance of NP at predicting primary stress placement.

Five hundred nominals containing two or more words (not counting determiners and pronominal possessives) were chosen at random from a day's worth of the Associated Press Newswire, and primary stress was predicted for those nominals using NP. An independent judge listened to the output and was asked to evaluate it as a discourse neutral way of saying the nominal, using a three-point scale: GOOD (= "that's how I would say it"); MAYBE (= "not how I would say it, but it is still acceptable"); BAD (= "I couldn't imagine it being said that way"). The totals for each judgment were as follows.

- GOOD: 455 (91%)
- MAYBE: 27 (5.4%)
- BAD: 18 (3.6%)

So, NP gets primary stress acceptably in 96.4% (= 91+5.4) of the cases. To put this in proper perspective, one needs to compare NP's performance at stress placement with two simpler algorithms: *Method A* always places stress on the last word of the nominal (what our TTS system traditionally has done); *Method B* places stress on the penultimate word of the nominal if and only if the nominal ends in two nouns. The following table shows the performance of these methods (in percentage correct) on the 500 nominal sample.

Method A	Method B	NP
77%	93.8%	96.4%

Clearly Method B works much better than Method A, meaning that – on this particular corpus – a fair amount can be achieved by just having part of speech information. However, the performance of NP shows that we can do better still. Furthermore, while purely syntactic algorithms like Method B can never achieve full coverage for reasons already discussed, it is possible to extend NP's coverage. For example, one of the errors made by NP on the test corpus involved failing to place final stress on *red snapper RAGOUT*. Although NP knows that FISH and STEW terms can combine to form N̄s, it does not know that *red snapper* is a kind of fish; such information is easily added to NP's database however.

Of course, there are additional advantages of an approach like NP's over a simple stress assignment algorithm like that of Method B: NP can also assign structure to a nominal, which is useful for assigning appropriate nominal-internal intonational boundaries, as mentioned above.

5 Implementing Accent Assignment More Generally

We return, now to accent prediction in the TTS system as a whole. In this system, the ultimate accentual fate of content words in general – and pre-modified nominals in particular – is mediated by the inference of discourse-level information on the information status of mentioned entities. Drawing upon work in artificial intelligence, the current study makes use of Grosz and Sidner's (1986) notion of a discourse's *attentional structure* to distinguish between 'given' and 'new' information in a text. In this model of discourse, discourse structure itself comprises three structures: a *linguistic structure*, which is the text/speech itself; an *attentional structure*, which includes information about the relative salience of objects, properties, relations, and intentions at any point in the discourse; and an *intentional structure*, which relates the intentions underlying the production of speech segments to one another. The attentional structure is represented as a stack of *focus spaces*, which is updated by pushing items onto or popping them from the stack. (Note that no attempt has been made at this stage to model Grosz and Sidner's attentional structure entirely. In particular, no aspect of intentional structure is included, and objects, properties and relations are represented here by their roots rather than by some more abstract conceptual representation.) At any point in the discourse, the current focus space should contain, *inter alia*, some representation of items that are most salient in the discourse (in *local focus* (Brennan et al. 1987, Grosz et al. 1983, Sidner 1983)) perhaps with some ordering placed on them. The relationship between items in a particular focus space – as well as the relationship between items in different focus spaces – are not well understood. However, some hierarchical relationship between focus spaces is usually assumed in the literature. Specifically, items in a focus space that is associated with a portion of the discourse that is understood as superordinate to another portion (for example, a supertopic perhaps), are generally assumed to be available during the processing of the subtopic. TTS infers hierarchical structure of a text from certain lexical and orthographic features, including paragraphing and punctuation as well as *discourse markers*, words such as *now* and *well,* which convey explicit information about discourse structure. These indicators are used to build up a model of the text's *attentional structure*, a hierarchical structuring of concepts mentioned or evoked in the discourse, which can be taken to represent information that is 'given' in the text. This structure is implemented as a stack of *focus spaces*, each being a set of roots of open-class items mentioned within a portion of the discourse. Focus spaces are updated depending upon the topic structure inferred from the text. Side by side with this notion of local focus is a notion of *global focus*, by which concepts central to the main purpose of the discourse remain salient throughout the discourse. The first local focus space collected is hypothesized to represent the *global focus* for the text, intuitively, the set of general concepts characterizing the text. While the set of items in local focus is constantly subject to change, items in global focus remain so throughout the discourse. These focus spaces can be understood as similar to the nested contexts of a block-structured programming language.

In an earlier implementation of the accent assignment algorithm, items in either global or local focus were treated as given information. Subsequent mention of given items was deaccented, in line with empirical results (Brown 1983) suggesting that listeners associate accented items with new information and deaccented items with old information. While questions such as the domain over which items remain given – and the process by which they lose their givenness – are open research questions, it is also clear that not every item which is given – under any reasonable definition – will be deaccented. Consider, for example, the accenting of the clearly 'given' *HENNESSY* in (1b)-(1d) above. To address this phenomenon, TTS does limited inference of additional discourse characteristics, such as topic and focus, which also influence human accent assignment. For example, the accenting of *HENNESSY* discussed above can be explained in terms of change in topic, from Dukakis to Hennessy to Maffy and then back to Hennessy. Accent here is used to indicate these shifts. To infer likely topic and focus behavior, TTS currently uses surface order and part-of-speech together with local and global focus information. This represents only a start, however, on the approximation of these discourse features.

6   The Accent Assignment Algorithm

Thus far, results from testing variations of TTS's algorithm on samples of recorded (read) speech suggest certain preliminary conclusions. (It should be stressed that analysis of a much larger amount of labeled speech will be necessary to demonstrate their usefulness—and will also permit the analysis of interactions among the structural and discourse features described below.) Clearly, the simple association of function word with deaccenting employed in most text-to-speech systems must be modified. In TTS's current accent assignment algorithm, closed-class items are divided into three categories. The first consists of those closed-class items which are commonly deaccented. This group includes possessive pronouns (including *wh*-pronouns), definite and indefinite articles, copulas, coordinating and subordinating conjunctions, existential *there*, *have*, accusative pronouns and *wh*-adverbials, most prepositions, positive modals, positive *do*, as well as some particular adverbials like *ago*, nominative and accusative *it* and nominative *they*, and some nominal pronouns (for example, *something*). A subgroup of this group of closed-deaccented items is the closed-cliticized group:

those items which are commonly *cliticized* (adjacent word boundaries are removed and the vowel of the stressable syllable is reduced). Finally, closed-accented items include those closed-class items which, in the data examined, were commonly accented, including the negative article, negative modals, negative *do*, most nominal pronouns, most nominative and all reflexive pronouns, pre- and post-qualifiers (for example, *quite*), pre-quantifiers (for example, *all*), post-determiners (for example, *next*), nominal adverbials (for example, *here*), interjections, particles, most *wh*-words, plus some prepositions (for example, *despite, unlike*). Other word classes (adjectives, adverbials,common and proper nouns, verbs) are termed open-class items. For purposes of acquiring given/new information, only open-class items are considered, although how much of this category to consider is also subject to variation.

The collection and manipulation of the attentional state representation has been varied experimentally in the following ways: Both global and local focus representations have been manipulated independently such that the global focus space may be set, and the local focus spaces updated, by the orthographic phrase, the sentence, or the paragraph. So, for example, the global space may be set after the first phrase, sentence or paragraph of a text. The local stack can be updated independently at the end of each phrase, sentence or paragraph—although discourse markers will push or pop the stack as well. For the current experiments, the best results to date have come when the global space is defined to be the first full sentence of the text and the local attentional stack is updated by paragraph. The content of both global and local focus spaces have also been varied systematically by word class, so that all open-class words, nouns only, or nouns plus some combination of verbs and modifiers are allowed to affect – and be affected by – the attentional state representation. Preliminary results, which again should be taken as suggestive only, indicate that focal spaces defined in terms of roots of all content words, rather than nominals only, or even all nonverb roots, provide the best accent prediction.

Finally, some experimentation has been done to relate the accenting of items currently in local focus with structural and discourse-based indicators of contrastiveness. For example, the referential strategy of *proper-naming* (Sanford et al. 1985), in which the use of proper names was found to focus attention, helps to explain behavior such as the accenting of *HEN-NESSY*, described above. It is conjectured that such referential behavior might indicate the speaker's attempt to focus attention upon persons recently mentioned, when other focii have intervened since their introduction. This strategy, together with others which can be inferred from surface and syntactic features of the text, such as the preposing of adverbials and of prepositional phrases (for example, *THAT YEAR* in (1d)) and the reintroduction of items in global but not in local focus, have been tested as predictors of accent with some success.

The improved algorithm developed from these experiments and currently implemented in TTS operates on text in which standard orthographic indicators of paragraph and sentence boundaries are preserved. Tables are maintained of word classes and individual items divided into four broad classes – closed-cliticized, closed-deaccented, closed-accented, and open – where distinctions among the closed class are based upon frequency distributions in the training data. As processing of the labeled text proceeds from left to right, the following information is added to a record maintained for each item: (1) Preposed adverbials are identified from surface position and part-of-speech, as are fronted *PPs*, and labeled as *preposed*. (2) Cue phrases are identified from surface position and part-of-speech as well, and their accent status is predicted following work of Litman and Hirschberg (Litman and Hirschberg 1990, Hirschberg and Litman 1987). (3) Verb-particle constructions are identified from table look-up currently. (4) Local focus is implemented in the form of a stack of roots of all nouns, verbs, and modifiers in the previous text. New items are pushed on the stack as each phrase is read. Individual cue phrases trigger either push or pop operations, roughly as identified in Grosz and Sidner 1986. Paragraph boundaries cause the entire stack to be popped. As new items are read, those whose roots appear in local focus are marked as 'given', while others are labeled 'new'. Additionally, items with prefixes such as *un, il*, and so on whose roots appear in local focus are marked as 'prefixed'. (5) Global focus is defined as simply the set of all content words in the first sentence of the first paragraph of the text. Nouns, verbs and modifiers whose roots appear in global focus are so marked. (6) Long nominals are shipped to NP and analyzed as described in Section 4; their stress pattern in citation form is stored with the nominal for subsequent processing. Other information collected for these nominals for subsequent evaluation includes whether or not they are inferred to be proper names (for example, street names, personal names that include titles, acronyms, and so on). (7) Finally, possible contrastiveness within a premodified nominal is inferred by comparing the presence of roots of elements of the nominal in local focus; roughly, if some items are 'given' and others 'new', the new items are marked as potentially contrastive.

When each record is complete, a simple decision tree determines whether the item will be cliticized, deaccented (but not cliticized), or accented. The final accent assignment algorithm is presented below.

For each item w_i labeled with part-of-speech p_i:

If w_i is a phrasal verb, deaccent;
Else if p_i is classified 'closed-cliticized', cliticize;
Else if p_i is classified 'closed-deaccented', deaccent;
Else if w_i is marked 'contrastive', 'prefixed', or 'preposed', assign it emphatic accent;
Else if w_i is part of a proper nominal
    If w_i's status is 'given', assign emphatic accent,
    else assign a simple pitch accent;
Else if w_i is in global focus but not in local focus ('given'), assign emphatic accent;
Else if w_i is classified 'closed-accented', accent;
Else if w_i is in local focus ('given'), deaccent;
Else if w_i is part of a (common) premodified nominal
    If w_i is predicted to be accented in citation form, accent
    Else deaccent;
Else accent w_i.

7 Discussion

This paper has described the pitch accent assignment strategy employed in the Bell Labs Text-to-Speech System, which employs a hierarchical representation of the attentional structure of the discourse, together with more traditional syntactic information, to assign intonational features in the synthesis of unrestricted text. It has also sketched experiments currently being performed to refine that algorithm, by modifying traditional uses of word class, key word, and surface position information, and by varying the construction of and interaction between the components of a model of attentional state. The testing of various discourse models against pitch accent placement in actual speech should also add to our set of evaluation criteria for such models.

From a theoretical point of view, such analysis should bring us closer to understanding how to model pitch accent in human speech. However, real progress will depend upon the availability of large amounts of prosodically labeled data. An immediate application for TTS's accent assignment algorithm is to provide prosodic labeling hypotheses to speed the subsequent hand labeling of prosodic features for large corpora; the post-editing of prosodic labels appears to be considerably faster and the labeled speech can then be used in further training of the algorithm. Lacking such labeled corpora, the algorithm can be used as a rough substitute for accent information. Currently, it is being used to predict accent assignment for a large corpus of read sentences being analyzed for durational characteristics, with remarkable accuracy. Checking 300 sentences from a corpus of 2775 uncovered only thirty (word) errors in accent assignment (accented, deaccented, cliticized).

While the use of higher level discourse information to inform algorithms for pitch accent assignment appears to be a useful strategy for modeling accent assignment in natural speech, it may indeed turn out not to be desirable to emulate natural speech in synthetic speech. However, clearly, whatever variation eventually emerges as desirable between synthetic speech and human speech should clearly be intentional rather than chance. Demonstrating that one speech synthesizer is preferable to another, or that one prosodic strategy is to be favored over another, in terms of simple human preference, is notoriously difficult to accomplish. Comparison of the output of algorithms used to assign intonational features in synthetic speech with prosodic features in natural speech would thus appear a useful alternative.

Acknowledgments

We wish to thank Jill Burstein for her role as the independent judge in the evaluation of NP. We also wish to thank Ken Church, Richard Omanson, and David Talkin for helpful comments and discussion.

References

Altenberg, B. 1987. *Prosodic patterns in spoken English: Studies in the correlation between prosody and grammar for text-to-speech conversion.* Lund: Lund University Press.

Bolinger, D. 1972. Accent is predictable (if you're a mind reader). *Language* 48:633–644.

Bolinger, D. 1989. *Intonation and its uses: Melody in grammar and discourse.* London: Edward Arnold.

Brennan, S., M. Friedman, and C. Pollard. 1987. A centering approach to pronouns. In *Proceedings of the 25th Annual Meeting of the Association for Computational Linguistics,* pp. 155–162.

Brown, G. 1983. Prosodic structure and the given/new distinction. In D. R. Ladd and A. Cutler (eds.), *Prosody: Models and measurements,* pp. 67–78. Berlin: Springer Verlag.

Chomsky, N. and M. Halle. 1968. *The sound pattern of English.* New York: Harper and Row.

Church, K. 1988. A stochastic parts program and noun phrase parser for unrestricted text. In *Proceedings of the Second Conference on Applied Natural Language Processing*, pp. 136–143. Association for Computational Linguistics.

Danlos, L., E. LaPorte, and F. Emerard. 1986. Synthesis of spoken messages from semantic representations. In *Proceedings of the 11th International Conference on Computational Linguistics*, pp. 599–604.

Davis, J. and J. Hirschberg. 1988. Assigning tonal features in synthesized spoken directions. In *Proceedings of the 26th Annual Meeting of the Association for Computational Linguistics*, pp. 187–193.

Finin, T. 1980. *The semantic interpretation of compound nominals.* Ph.D. dissertation, University of Illinois at Urbana-Champaign.

Francis, W. N. and H. Kucera. 1982. *Frequency analysis of English usage.* Boston: Houghton Mifflin.

Grosz, B., A. Joshi, and S. Weinstein. 1983. Providing a unified account of definite noun phrases in discourse. In *Proceedings of the 21st Annual Meeting of the Association for Computational Linguistics*, pp. 44–50.

Grosz, B. and C. Sidner. 1986. Attention, intentions, and the structure of discourse. *Computational Linguistics* 12:3.175–204.

Harrison, M. 1978. *Introduction to formal language theory.* Reading, MA: Addison Wesley.

Hirschberg, J. (1993). Pitch accent in context: Predicting intonational prominence from text. *Artificial Intelligence*, 63.

Hirschberg, J. and D. Litman. 1987. Now let's talk about *now*: Identifying cue phrases intonationally. In *Proceedings of the 25th Annual Meeting of the Association for Computational Linguistics*, pp. 163–171.

Levi, J. 1978. *The syntax and semantics of complex nominals.* New York: Academic Press.

Liberman, M. and R. Sproat. 1991. The stress and structure of modified noun phrases in English. In I. Sag (ed.), *Lexical Matters.* Chicago: University of Chicago Press.

Litman, J. and J. Hirschberg. 1990. Disambiguating cue phrases in text and speech. In *Papers Presented to the 13th International Conference on Computational Linguistics*, pp. 251–256.

Olive, J. and M. Liberman. 1985. Text-to-speech—an overview. *Journal of the Acoustic Society of America, Suppl. 1*, 78:6.

Pierrehumbert, J. 1980. *The phonology and phonetics of English intonation*. Ph.D. dissertation, Massachusetts Institute of Technology. Distributed by the Indiana University Linguistics Club.

Prince, E. 1981. Toward a taxonomy of given-new information. In P. Cole (ed.), *Radical Pragmatics*, pp. 223–255. New York: Academic Press.

Sanford, A. 1985. Aspects of pronoun interpretation: Evaluation of search formulations of inference. In G. Rickheit and H. Strohner (eds.), *Inferences in text processing*, pp. 183–204. Amsterdam: North Holland.

Sanford, A., S. Garrod, K. Moar, and H. Al-Ahmar. 1985. Naming, role-descriptions, and main and secondary characters in discourse comprehension. Reported in Sanford (1985).

Sidner, C. 1983. Focusing in the comprehension of definite anaphora. In M. Brady (ed.), *Computational models of discourse*, pp. 267–330. Cambridge, MA: MIT Press.

Sproat, R. 1990. Stress assignment in complex nominals for English text-to-speech. In *Proceedings of the Tutorial and Research Workshop on Speech Synthesis*, pp. 129–132. European Speech Communication Association.

Sproat, R. (1994). English noun-phrase accent prediction for text-to-speech. *Computer Speech and Language*, 8:79–94.

Sproat, R., Hirschberg, J., and Yarowsky, D. (1992). A corpus-based synthesizer. In *Proceedings of the International Conference on Spoken Language Processing*, Banff. ICSLP.

Talkin, D. 1989. Looking at speech. *Speech Technology* 4:74–77.

Terken, J. and S. Nooteboom. 1987. Opposite effects of accentuation and deaccentuation on verification latencies for given and new information. *Language and Cognitive Processes* 2:3/4.145–163.

Young, S. and F. Fallside. 1979. Speech synthesis from concept: A method for speech output from information systems. *Journal of the Acoustic Society of America* 66:3.685–695.

CSLI Publications

Lecture Notes

A Manual of Intensional Logic. van Benthem, 2nd edition. No. 1. 0-937073-29-6 (paper), 0-937073-30-X

Emotion and Focus. Nissenbaum. No. 2. 0-937073-20-2 (paper)

Lectures on Contemporary Syntactic Theories. Sells. No. 3. 0-937073-14-8 (paper), 0-937073-13-X

The Semantics of Destructive Lisp. Mason. No. 5. 0-937073-06-7 (paper), 0-937073-05-9

An Essay on Facts. Olson. No. 6. 0-937073-08-3 (paper), 0-937073-05-9

Logics of Time and Computation. Goldblatt, 2nd edition. No. 7. 0-937073-94-6 (paper), 0-937073-93-8

Word Order and Constituent Structure in German. Uszkoreit. No. 8. 0-937073-10-5 (paper), 0-937073-09-1

Color and Color Perception: A Study in Anthropocentric Realism. Hilbert. No. 9. 0-937073-16-4 (paper), 0-937073-15-6

Prolog and Natural-Language Analysis. Pereira and Shieber. No. 10. 0-937073-18-0 (paper), 0-937073-17-2

Working Papers in Grammatical Theory and Discourse Structure: Interactions of Morphology, Syntax, and Discourse. Iida, Wechsler, and Zec (Eds.). No. 11. 0-937073-04-0 (paper), 0-937073-25-3

Natural Language Processing in the 1980s: A Bibliography. Gazdar, Franz, Osborne, and Evans. No. 12. 0-937073-28-8 (paper), 0-937073-26-1

Information-Based Syntax and Semantics. Pollard and Sag. No. 13. 0-937073-24-5 (paper), 0-937073-23-7

Non-Well-Founded Sets. Aczel. No. 14. 0-937073-22-9 (paper), 0-937073-21-0

Partiality, Truth and Persistence. Langholm. No. 15. 0-937073-34-2 (paper), 0-937073-35-0

Attribute-Value Logic and the Theory of Grammar. Johnson. No. 16. 0-937073-36-9 (paper), 0-937073-37-7

The Situation in Logic. Barwise. No. 17. 0-937073-32-6 (paper), 0-937073-33-4

The Linguistics of Punctuation. Nunberg. No. 18. 0-937073-46-6 (paper), 0-937073-47-4

Anaphora and Quantification in Situation Semantics. Gawron and Peters. No. 19. 0-937073-48-4 (paper), 0-937073-49-0

Propositional Attitudes: The Role of Content in Logic, Language, and Mind. Anderson and Owens. No. 20. 0-937073-50-4 (paper), 0-937073-51-2

Literature and Cognition. Hobbs. No. 21. 0-937073-52-0 (paper), 0-937073-53-9

Situation Theory and Its Applications, Vol. 1. Cooper, Mukai, and Perry (Eds.). No. 22. 0-937073-54-7 (paper), 0-937073-55-5

The Language of First-Order Logic (including the Macintosh program, Tarski's World 4.0). Barwise and Etchemendy, 3rd Edition. No. 23. 0-937073-99-7 (paper)

Lexical Matters. Sag and Szabolcsi (Eds.). No. 24. 0-937073-66-0 (paper), 0-937073-65-2

Tarski's World: Macintosh Version 4.0. Barwise and Etchemendy. No. 25. 1-881526-27-5 (paper)

Situation Theory and Its Applications, Vol. 2. Barwise, Gawron, Plotkin, and Tutiya (Eds.). No. 26. 0-937073-70-9 (paper), 0-937073-71-7

Literate Programming. Knuth. No. 27. 0-937073-80-6 (paper), 0-937073-81-4

Normalization, Cut-Elimination and the Theory of Proofs. Ungar. No. 28. 0-937073-82-2 (paper), 0-937073-83-0

Lectures on Linear Logic. Troelstra. No. 29. 0-937073-77-6 (paper), 0-937073-78-4

A Short Introduction to Modal Logic. Mints. No. 30. 0-937073-75-X (paper), 0-937073-76-8

Linguistic Individuals. Ojeda. No. 31. 0-937073-84-9 (paper), 0-937073-85-7

Computational Models of American Speech. Withgott and Chen. No. 32. 0-937073-98-9 (paper), 0-937073-97-0

Verbmobil: A Translation System for Face-to-Face Dialog. Kay, Gawron, and Norvig. No. 33. 0-937073-95-4 (paper), 0-937073-96-2

The Language of First-Order Logic (including the Windows program, Tarski's World 4.0). Barwise and Etchemendy, 3rd edition. No. 34. 0-937073-90-3 (paper)

Turing's World. Barwise and Etchemendy. No. 35. 1-881526-10-0 (paper)

The Syntax of Anaphoric Binding. Dalrymple. No. 36. 1-881526-06-2 (paper), 1-881526-07-0

Situation Theory and Its Applications, Vol. 3. Aczel, Israel, Katagiri, and Peters (Eds.). No. 37. 1-881526-08-9 (paper), 1-881526-09-7

Theoretical Aspects of Bantu Grammar. Mchombo (Ed.). No. 38. 0-937073-72-5 (paper), 0-937073-73-3

Logic and Representation. Moore. No. 39. 1-881526-15-1 (paper), 1-881526-16-X

Meanings of Words and Contextual Determination of Interpretation. Kay. No. 40. 1-881526-17-8 (paper), 1-881526-18-6

Language and Learning for Robots. Crangle and Suppes. No. 41. 1-881526-19-4 (paper), 1-881526-20-8

Hyperproof. Barwise and Etchemendy. No. 42. 1-881526-11-9 (paper)

Mathematics of Modality. Goldblatt. No. 43. 1-881526-23-2 (paper), 1-881526-24-0

Feature Logics, Infinitary Descriptions, and Grammar. Keller. No. 44. 1-881526-25-9 (paper), 1-881526-26-7

Tarski's World: Windows Version 4.0. Barwise and Etchemendy. No. 45. 1-881526-28-3 (paper)

German in Head-Driven Phrase Structure Grammar. Pollard, Nerbonne, and Netter. No. 46. 1-881526-29-1 (paper), 1-881526-30-5

Formal Issues in Lexical-Functional Grammar. Dalrymple and Zaenen. No. 47. 1-881526-36-4 (paper), 1-881526-37-2

Dynamics, Polarity, and Quantification. Kanazawa and Piñón. No. 48. 1-881526-41-0 (paper), 1-881526-42-9

Theoretical Perspectives on Word Order in South Asian Languages. Butt, King, and Ramchand. No. 50. 1-881526-49-6 (paper), 1-881526-50-X

Perspectives in Phonology. Cole and Kisseberth. No. 51. 1-881526-54-2 (paper)

Linguistics and Computation. Cole, Green, and Morgan. No. 52. 1-881526-81-X (paper)

Dissertations in Linguistics Series

Phrase Structure and Grammatical Relations in Tagalog. Kroeger. 0-937073-86-5 (paper), 0-937073-87-3

Theoretical Aspects of Kashaya Phonology and Morphology. Buckley. 1-881526-02-X (paper), 1-881526-03-8

Argument Structure in Hindi. Mohanan. 1-881526-43-7 (paper), 1-881526-44-5

The Syntax of Subjects. Tateishi. 1-881526-45-3 (paper), 1-881526-46-1

Theory of Projection in Syntax. Fukui. 1-881526-35-6 (paper), 1-881526-34-8

On the Placement and Morphology of Clitics. Halpern. 1-881526-60-7 (paper), 1-881526-61-5

The Structure of Complex Predicates in Urdu. Butt. 1-881526-59-3 (paper), 1-881562-58-5

Configuring Topic and Focus in Russia. King. 1-881526-63-1 (paper), 1-881562-62-3

The Semantic Basis of Argument Structure. Wechsler. 1-881526-68-2 (paper), 1-881562-69-0

Other CSLI Titles Distributed by Cambridge University Press

The Proceedings of the Twenty-Fourth Annual Child Language Research Forum. Clark (Ed.). 1-881526-05-4 (paper), 1-881526-04-6

The Proceedings of the Twenty-Fifth Annual Child Language Research Forum. Clark (Ed.). 1-881526-31-3 (paper), 1-881526-33-X

The Proceedings of the Twenty-Sixth Annual Child Language Research Forum. Clark (Ed.). 1-881526-31-3 (paper), 1-881526-33-X

Japanese/Korean Linguistics. Hoji (Ed.). 0-937073-57-1 (paper), 0-937073-56-3

Japanese/Korean Linguistics, Vol. 2. Clancy (Ed.). 1-881526-13-5 (paper), 1-881526-14-3

Japanese/Korean Linguistics, Vol. 3. Choi (Ed.). 1-881526-21-6 (paper), 1-881526-22-4

Japanese/Korean Linguistics, Vol. 4. Akatsuka (Ed.). 1-881526-64-X (paper), 1-881526-65-8

The Proceedings of the Fourth West Coast Conference on Formal Linguistics (WCCFL 4). 0-937073-43-1 (paper)

The Proceedings of the Fifth West Coast Conference on Formal Linguistics (WCCFL 5). 0-937073-42-3 (paper)

The Proceedings of the Sixth West Coast Conference on Formal Linguistics (WCCFL 6). 0-937073-31-8 (paper)

The Proceedings of the Seventh West Coast Conference on Formal Linguistics (WCCFL 7). 0-937073-40-7 (paper)

The Proceedings of the Eighth West Coast Conference on Formal Linguistics (WCCFL 8). 0-937073-45-8 (paper)

The Proceedings of the Ninth West Coast Conference on Formal Linguistics (WCCFL 9). 0-937073-64-4 (paper)

The Proceedings of the Tenth West Coast Conference on Formal Linguistics (WCCFL 10). 0-937073-79-2 (paper)

The Proceedings of the Eleventh West Coast Conference on Formal Linguistics (WCCFL 11). Mead (Ed.). 1-881526-12-7 (paper),

The Proceedings of the Twelth West Coast Conference on Formal Linguistics (WCCFL 12). Duncan, Farkas, Spaelti (Eds.). 1-881526-33-X (paper),

The Proceedings of the Thirteenth West Coast Conference on Formal Linguistics (WCCFL 13). Aranovich, Byrne, Preuss, Senturia (Eds.). 1-881526-76-3 (paper),

European Review of Philosophy: Philosophy of Mind. Soldati (Ed.). 1-881526-38-0 (paper), 1-881526-53-4

Experiencer Subjects in South Asian Languages. Verma and Mohanan (Eds.). 0-937073-60-1 (paper), 0-937073-61-X

Grammatical Relations: A Cross-Theoretical Perspective. Dziwirek, Farrell, Bikandi (Eds.). 0-937073-63-6 (paper), 0-937073-62-8

Theoretical Issues in Korean Linguistics. Kim-Renaud (Ed.). 1-881526-51-8 (paper), 1-881526-52-6

Agreement in Natural Language: Approaches, Theories, Descriptions. Barlow and Ferguson (Eds.). 0-937073-02-4

Papers from the Second International Workshop on Japanese Syntax. Poser (Ed.). 0-937073-38-5 (paper), 0-937073-39-3

Ordering Titles from Cambridge University Press

Titles distributed by Cambridge University Press may be ordered directly from the distributor at 110 Midland Avenue, Port Chester, NY 10573-4930 (USA), or by phone: 914-937-9600, 1-800-872-7423 (US and Canada), 95-800-010-0200 (Mexico). You may also order by fax at 914-937-4712.

Overseas Orders

Cambridge University Press has offices worldwide which serve the international community.

Australia: Cambridge University Press, 120 Stamford Road, Oakleigh, Victoria 31266, Australia. phone: (613) 563-1517. fax: 613 563 1517.

UK, Europe, Asia, Africa, South America: Cambridge University Press, Publishing Division, The Edinburgh Building, Shaftesbury Road, Cambridge CB2 2RU, UK.
Inquiries: (phone) 44 1223 312393 (fax) 44 1223 315052
Orders: (phone) 44 1223 325970 (fax) 44 1223 325959

CSLI Titles Distributed by University of Chicago Press

The Phonology-Syntax Connection.
Inkelas and Zec. 0-226-38100-5
(paper), 0-226-38101-3

On What We Know We Don't Know.
Bromberger. 0-226-07540-0 (paper),
0-226-07539-7

Arenas of Language Use. Clark.
0-226-10782-5 (paper), 0-226-10781-7

Head-Driven Phrase Structure Grammar.
Pollard and Sag. 0-226-67447-9 (paper)

Titles distributed by The University of
Chicago Press may be ordered directly
from UCP. Phone 1-800-621-2736. Fax
(800) 621-8471.

CSLI Titles Distributed by CSLI Publications

*Hausar Yau Da Kullum: Intermediate and
Advanced Lessons in Hausa Language
and Culture.* Leben, Zaria, Maikafi,
and Yalwa. 0-937073-68-7 (paper)

Hausar Yau Da Kullum Workbook.
Leben, Zaria, Maikafi, and Yalwa.
0-93703-69-5 (paper)

Ordering Titles Distributed by CSLI

Titles distributed by CSLI may be ordered
directly from CSLI Publications, Ventura
Hall, Stanford, CA 94305-4115. Orders
can also be placed by FAX (415)723-0758
or e-mail (pubs@csli.stanford.edu).

All orders must be prepaid by check or
Visa or MasterCard (include card name,
number, and expiration date). California
residents add 8.25% sales tax. For
shipping and handling, add $2.50 for first
book and $0.75 for each additional book;
$1.75 for first report and $0.25 for each
additional report.

For overseas shipping, add $4.50 for first
book and $2.25 for each additional book;
$2.25 for first report and $0.75 for each
additional report. All payments must be
made in U.S. currency.